CHILLIN...
..2006..
2012
SÃO PAULO
'02 3 25

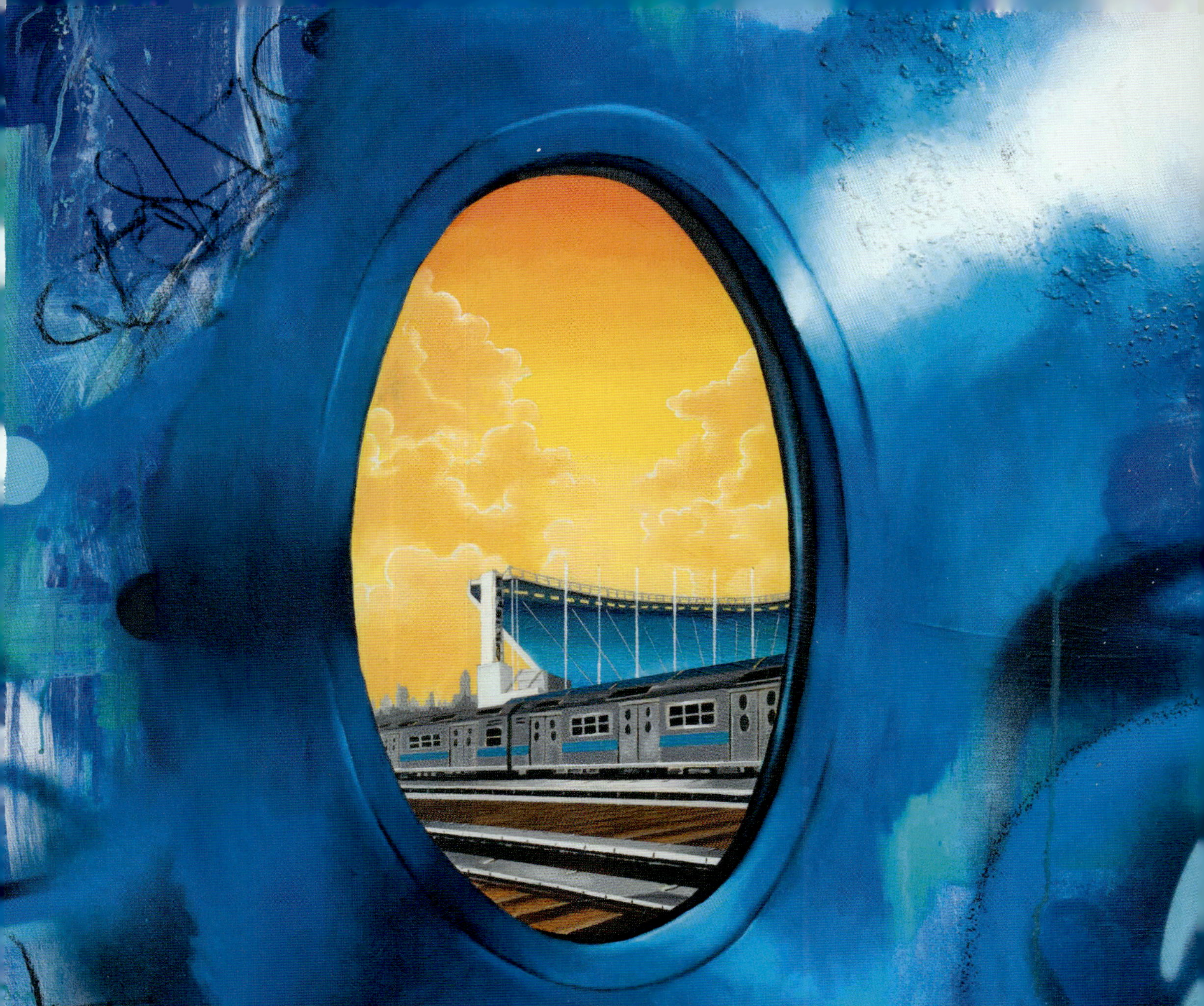

DAZEWORLD

THE ARTWORK OF **CHRIS DAZE ELLIS**

Schiffer Publishing Ltd

4880 Lower Valley Road • Atglen, PA 19310

Library of Congress Control Number: 2016933146

Designed by Molly Shields
Cover design by Justin Watkinson

Front cover: *The Golden Years*, 2009. Spray paint, charcoal, and acrylic on canvas, 46" × 40". Photo © Adam Reich

Back cover: From Across The Room, 2015. Oil, spray paint, and acrylic on canvas, 24" × 24". Photo © Adam Reich
Type set in Univers LT Std/Humanst521 BT
ISBN: 978-0-7643-5105-1
Printed in China

Published by Schiffer Publishing, Ltd.
4880 Lower Valley Road
Atglen, PA 19310
Phone: (610) 593-1777; Fax: (610) 593-2002
E-mail: Info@schifferbooks.com
Web: www.schifferbooks.com

For our complete selection of fine books on this and related subjects, please visit our website at www.schifferbooks.com. You may also write for a free catalog.

Schiffer Publishing's titles are available at special discounts for bulk purchases for sales promotions or premiums. Special editions, including personalized covers, corporate imprints, and excerpts, can be created in large quantities for special needs. For more information, contact the publisher.

We are always looking for people to write books on new and related subjects. If you have an idea for a book, please contact us at proposals@schifferbooks.com.

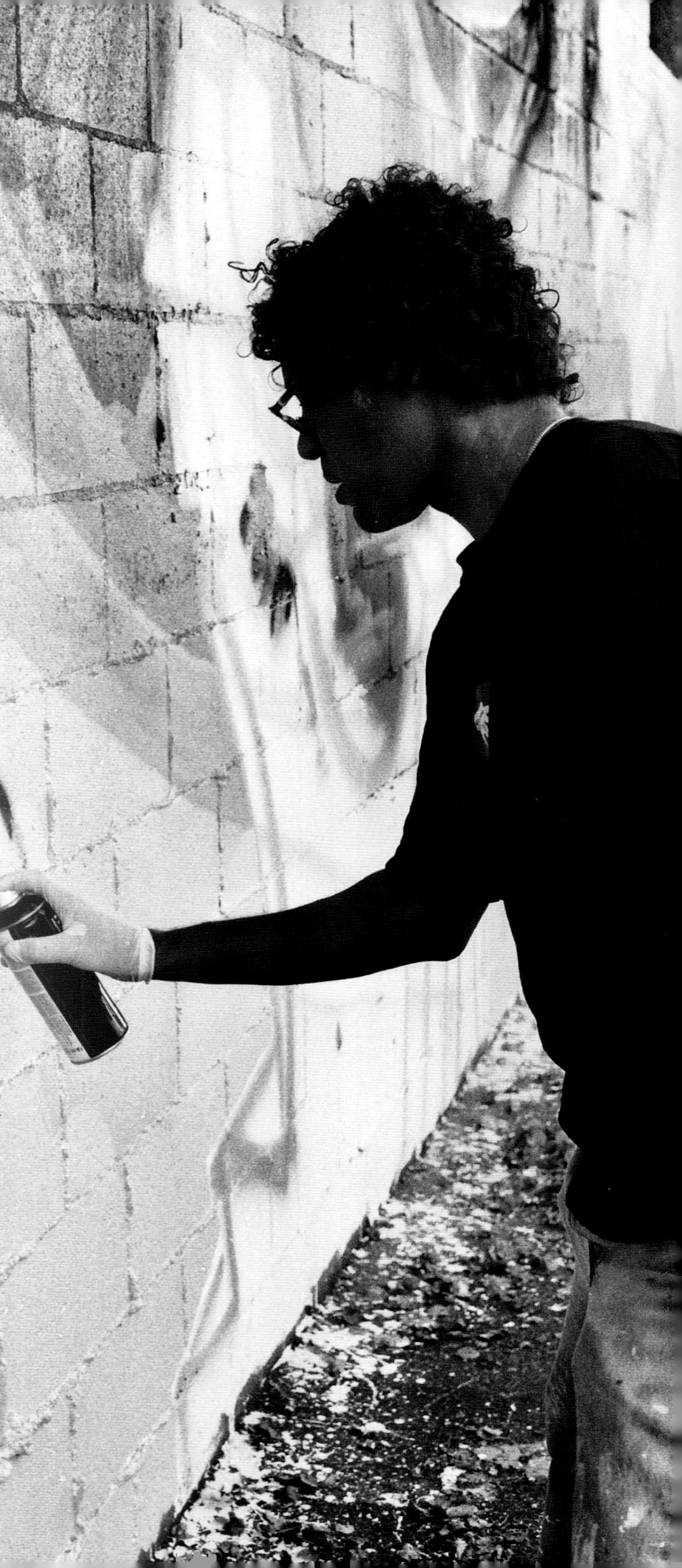

CONTENTS

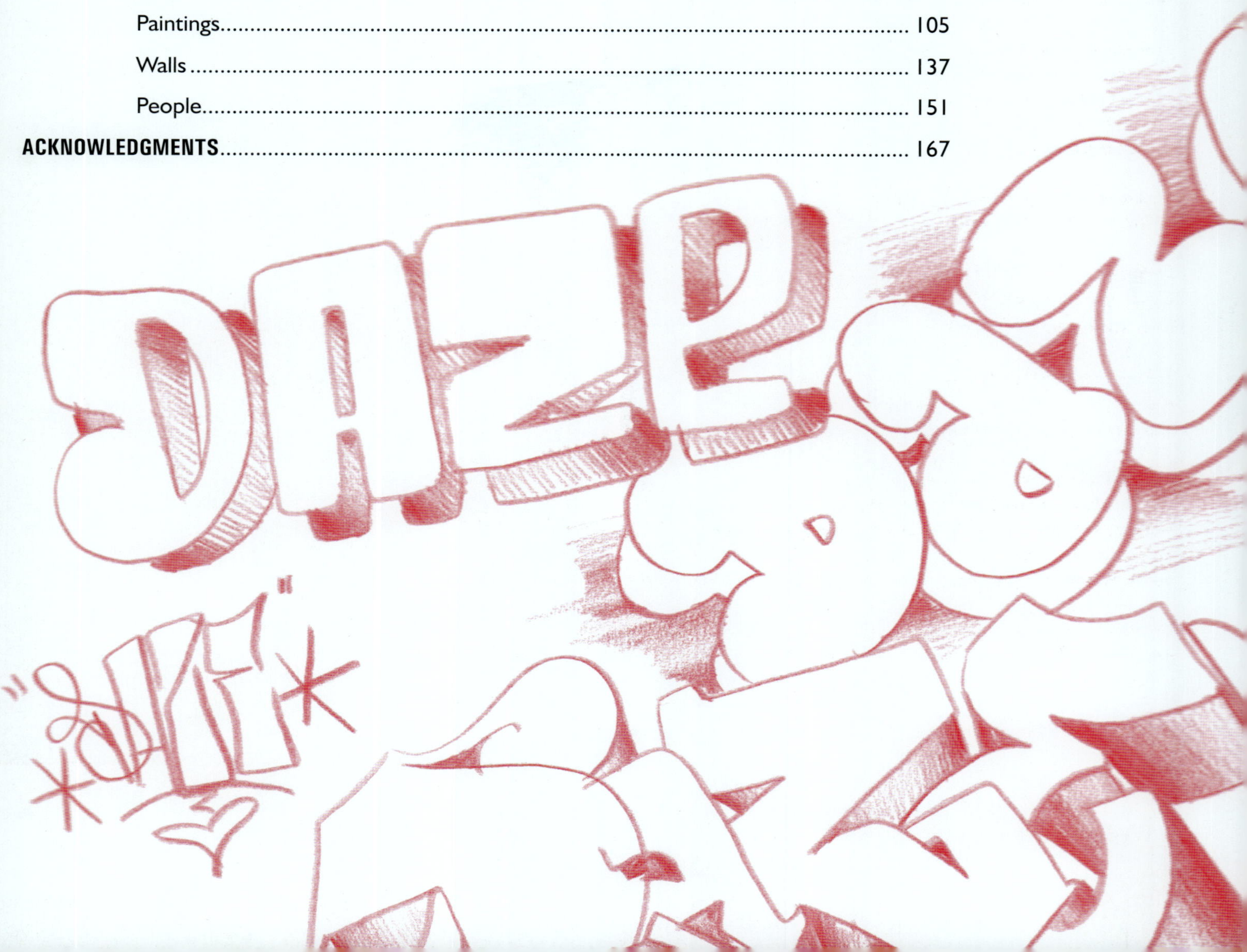

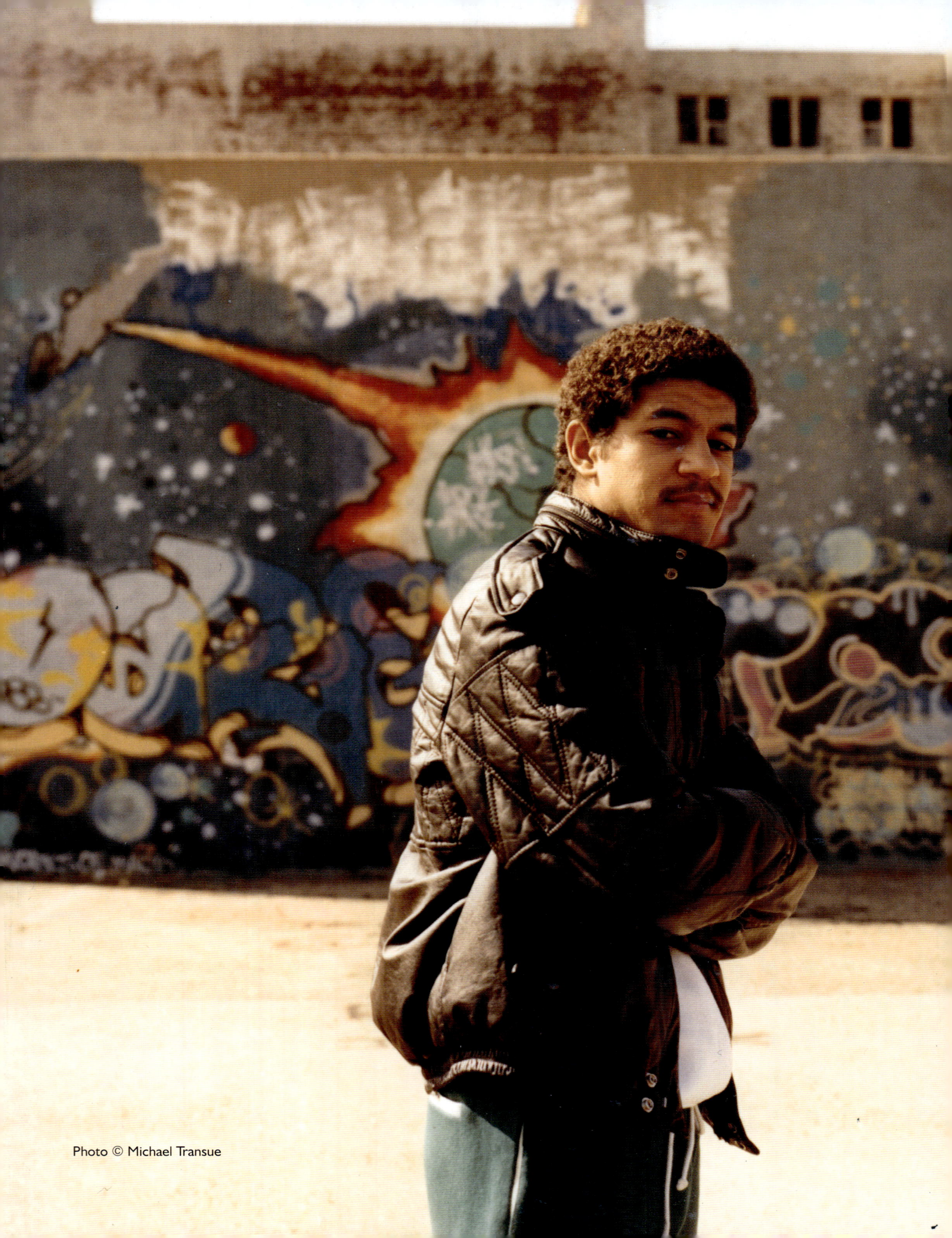

Photo © Michael Transue

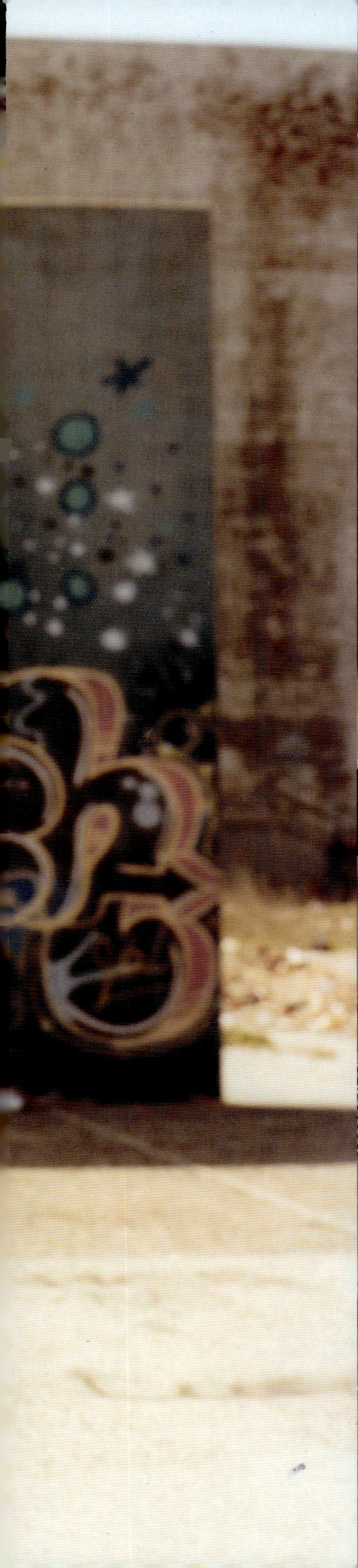

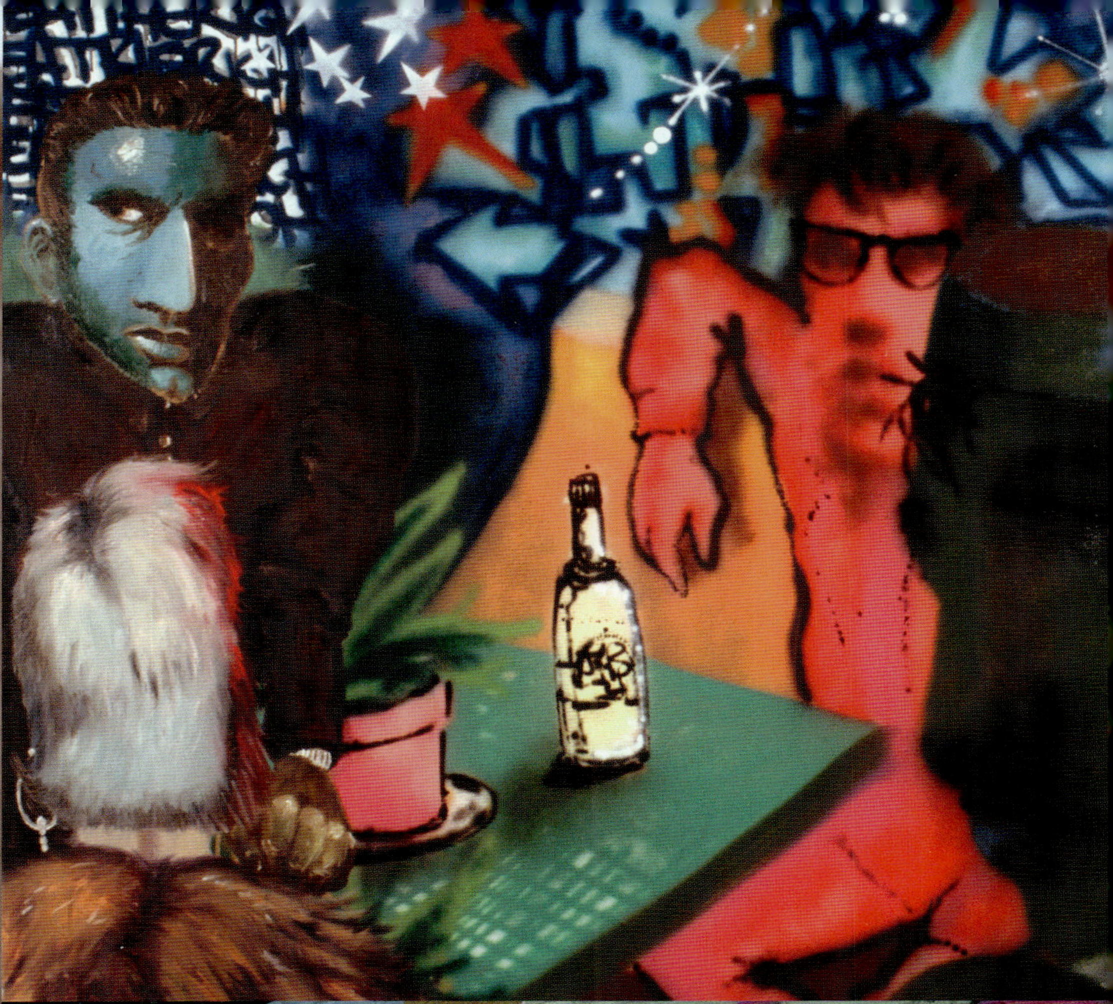

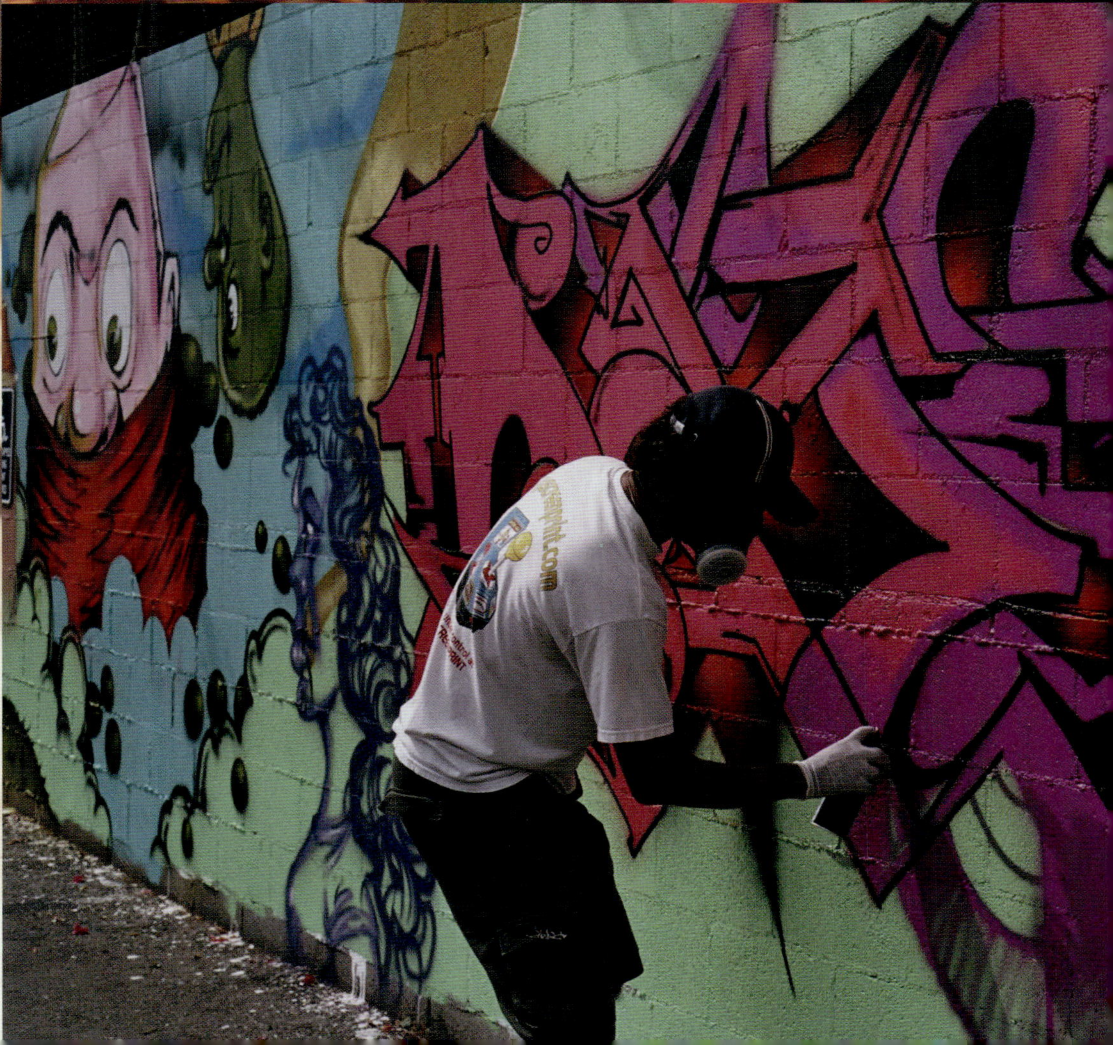

FOREWORD
THE CAREFREE DAZE

BY SACHA JENKINS SHR

Chris "Daze" Ellis is a diplomat who not only has a way with words, but also animates them.

New York City offered a lot of distractions back in the 1970s. These distractions were in real time, and not of the cyber variety. Kids back then didn't really have joysticks in their hands. They instead gripped baseball bats and footballs and 007 knives and cans of Red Devil spray paint. These kids swam in the East River alongside horseshoe crabs and water rats. They played handball and sold fireworks on Canal Street in the weeks leading up to the Fourth of July. They rode brown Ross Apollo three-speed bikes with black, square banana seats that made your ass angry; vertically sliced straws would be fastened around the spokes of their wheels, which made for a gentle pitter-patter as their tires rolled over hot tar that chewed discarded pieces of Wrigley's.

This is the New York that made young Chris want to explore. While most kids were happy running around the city blocks they lived in, Chris considered the five boroughs his swimming pool, and he dove right in, eyes wild and wide, like the baby on the cover of Nirvana's *Nevermind*. Graffiti was happening back then. You could

Kids at play
Photo © Martha Cooper

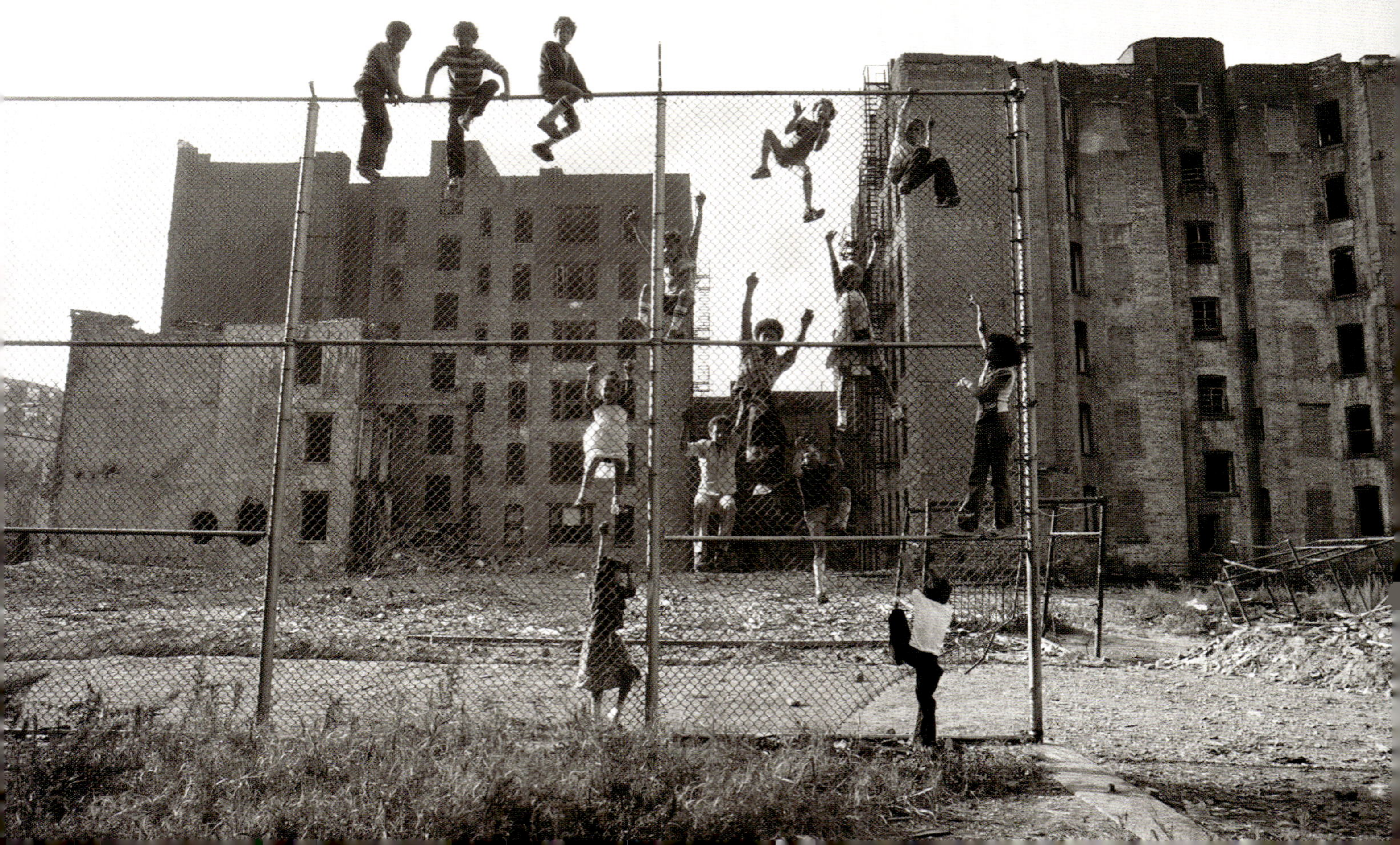

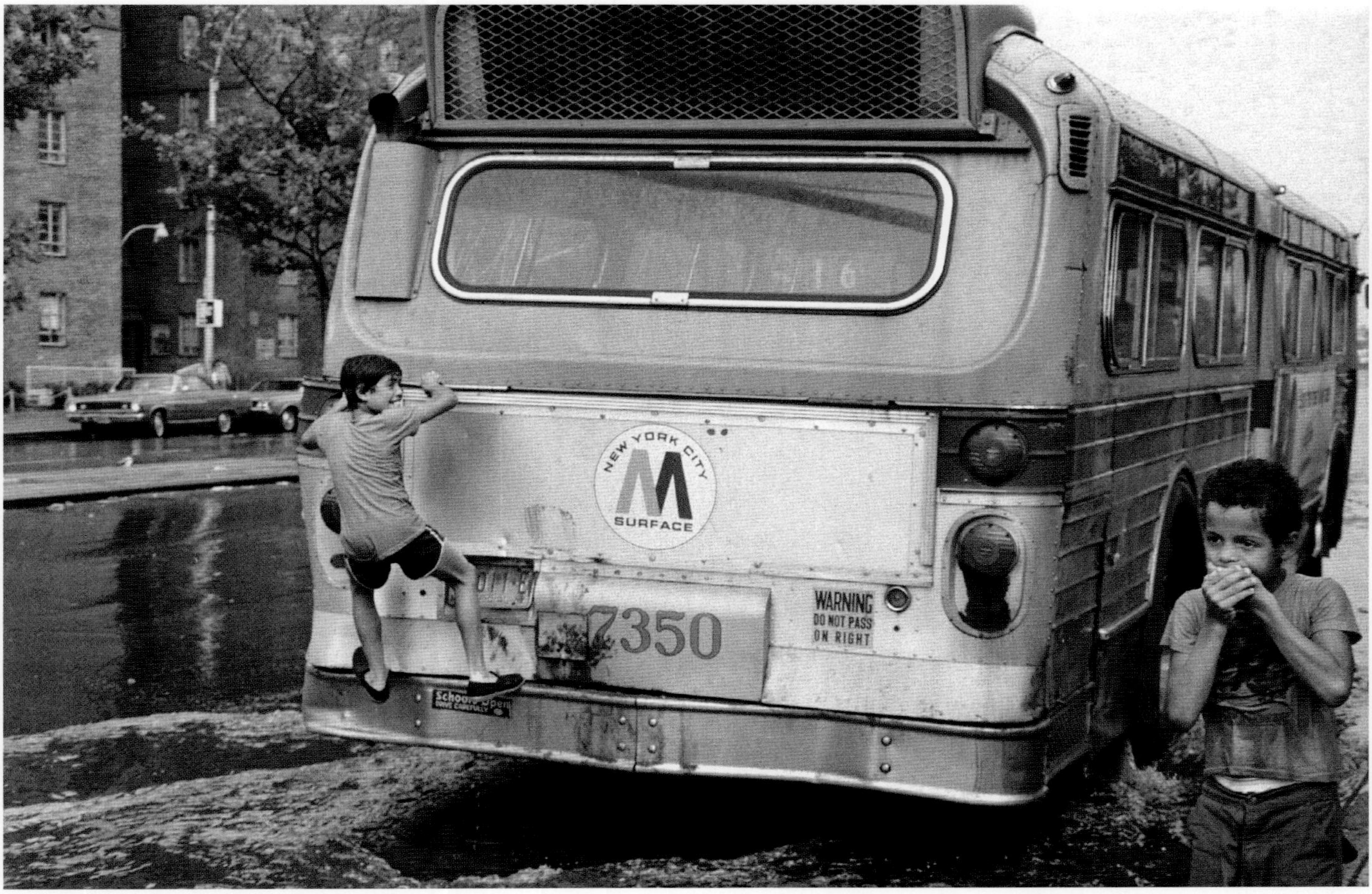

Kids at play
Photo © Martha Cooper

taste the sweet smell of spray paint dancing in the air, sashaying alongside clouds of reefer and cheap perfume. Every kid had an alias. Every kid wanted to become Batman or Spider Man or Wonder Woman, and graffiti gave them the ability to do so. But not all superheroes are created equal, and it just so happened that Chris—now calling himself Daze—had the ability to draw cartoons better than most, which made him the master of his reality: It was his own puppet hand that would draw the rich lines that outlined his destiny, while his other hand manipulating the strings.

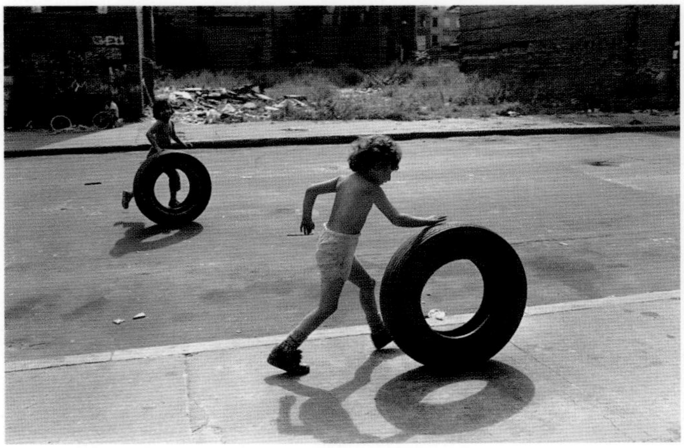

Kids at play
Photo © Martha Cooper

"You start out with a name, try to choose a good one, one that isn't taken," says Daze. "That's an aspect of it people today seem to have forgotten. You try to choose something that's original. And you start out with a signature that you feel is acceptable. Doing tags to me was interesting because it was a way to use up half-full cans of paint you had lying around or whatever—but I

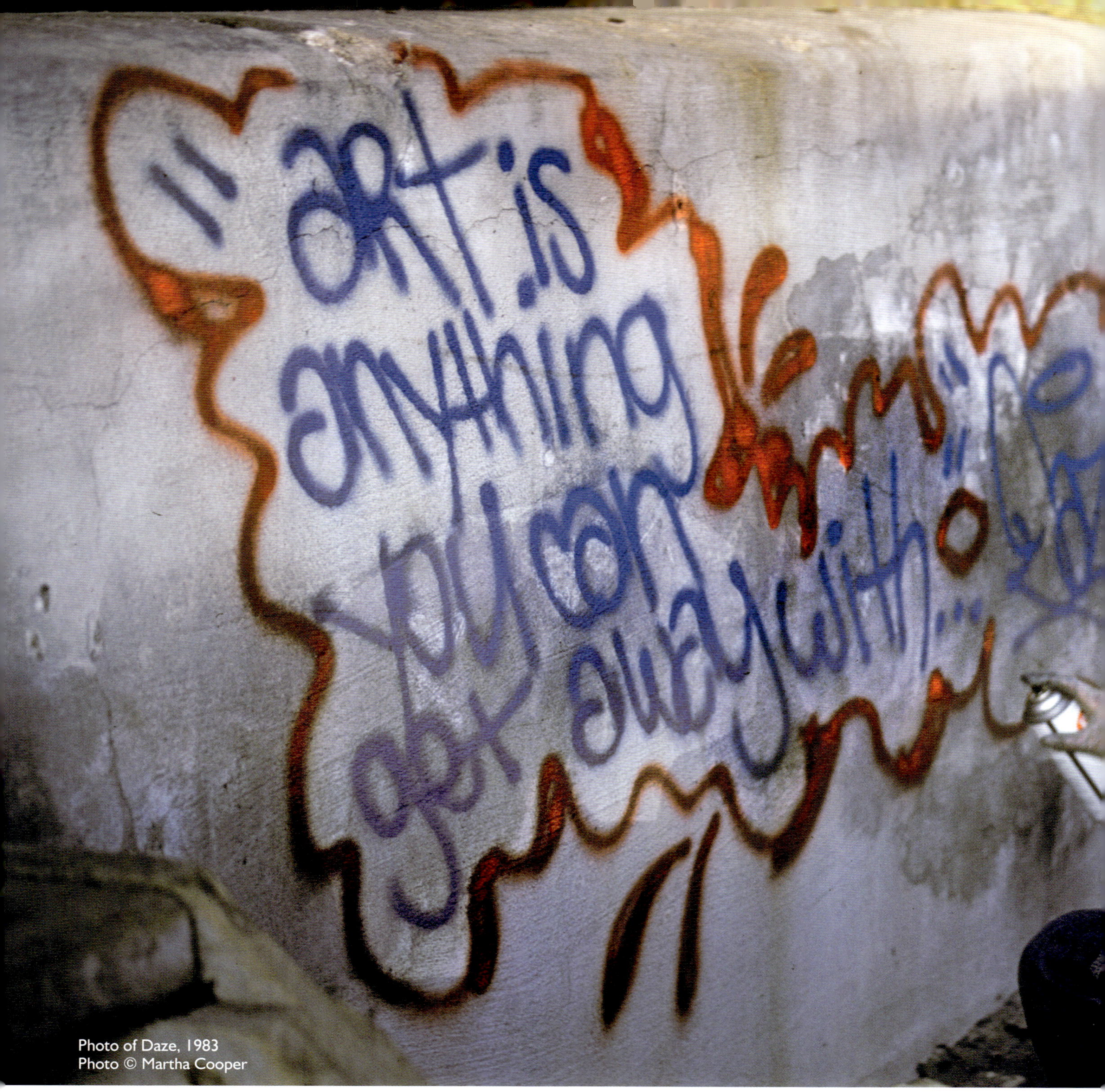

Photo of Daze, 1983
Photo © Martha Cooper

didn't really concentrate on that. I wanted to concentrate on doing pieces more."

He ran through the rail yards and tunnels that still play host to those magnificent giant beasts. He painted them as they slept, as transit workers and police officers smoked cigarettes and ate doughnuts. Graffiti gave Daze and many other youths a sense of pride and a blueprint that would lead them to a brighter world above ground. They emerged as the superheroes they always wanted to be. Only, it often takes superheroes a few years to be fully appreciated. On the subway lines, Daze was one of the greatest. He'd earned his stripes over the many years he risked his freedom to spray where he wasn't supposed

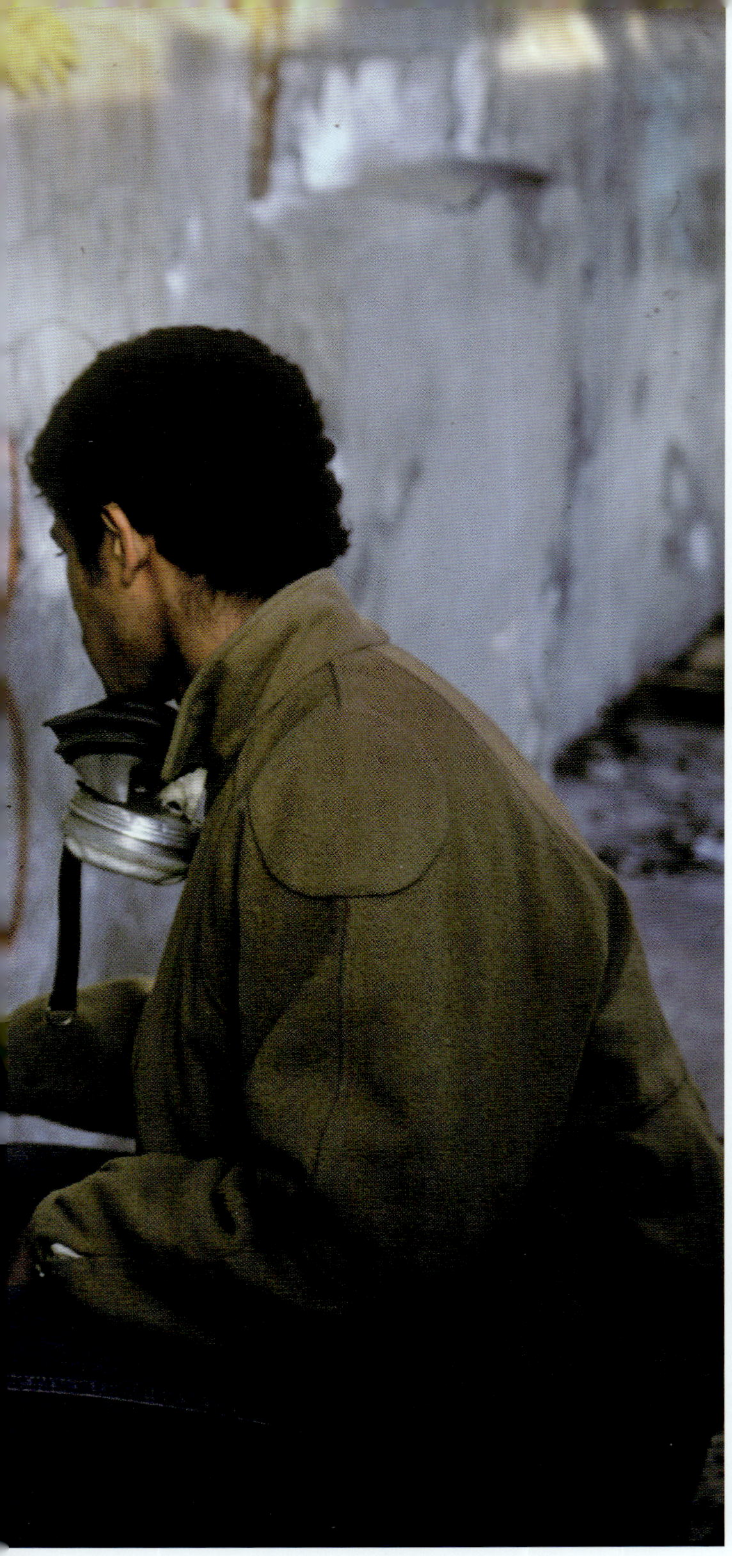

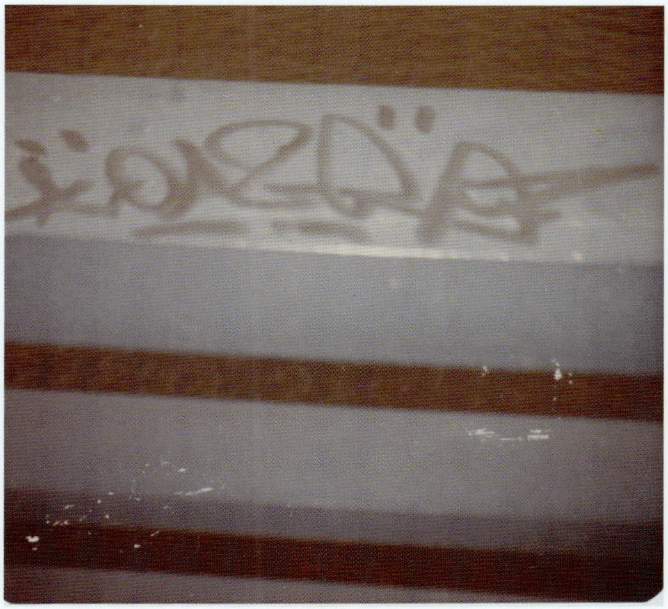

Early tag, 1977
Photo courtesy of the artist

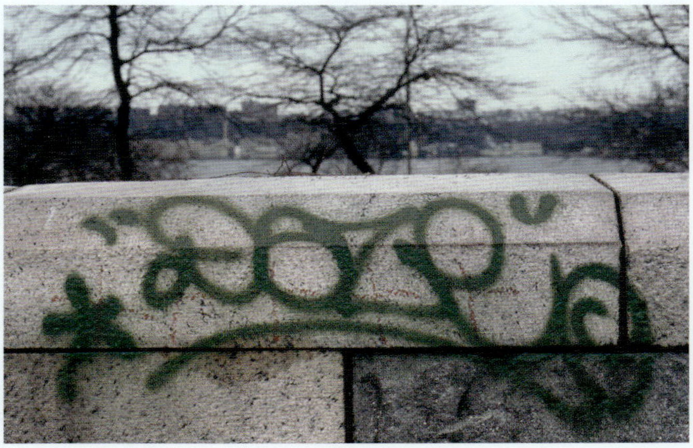

Tag, early '80s
Photo © Martha Cooper

to; too many trains to remember were painted, and painted magnificently. There is photographic proof of this.

"I don't come from a family that has a lot of money at all," Daze recalls. "Buying paint? Nobody did that. It didn't matter what social background you were from. To understand the whole culture of subway writing in the '70s, you really have to understand where New York was. Things like graf were really lightweight compared to the other problems and the other things that were going on in New York City."

Fame didn't come cheap in the Rotten Apple back then, either. For every kid out there stealing spray paint there were two others out there looking to steal their paint. Daze was able to dance atop the flames that broiled the beef in the streets because he knew how to adapt and relate to a diverse range of people. New York City was crazy, but Daze was a diplomat who had a card that could get him into any train yard or tunnel or nightclub, for that matter. Sure, he grew up with the proto hip-hop that was happening in the parks, but he also dug Black Sabbath and Jimi Hendrix. He painted with everyone: white kids from suburban Bronx neighborhoods, Puerto Rican kids from Queens—you name it. Back then, if you weren't on a sports team, you didn't really know anyone who didn't look like you. Daze's vast range of pop cultural reference points made him fluent in many desirable languages. His nuanced perspective shined within his painting. Other writers knew that he was dedicated to the craft and the experience and that he wanted to soak up as much as he could from as many people as possible. Daze went about his business with his wits about him. He was both student and master.

Says Daze: "I don't really look at beef as a development, I look at it as a symptom. And I think that in the '70s there were pretty tough guys in graf—guys you wouldn't want to run into. Guys that were almost like predators that would try to take your paint, rip you off. In the '80s there was more beef because there was more competition for space, too." By the early '80s, Daze was a seasoned veteran of the graffiti war waged by graffiti writers against the

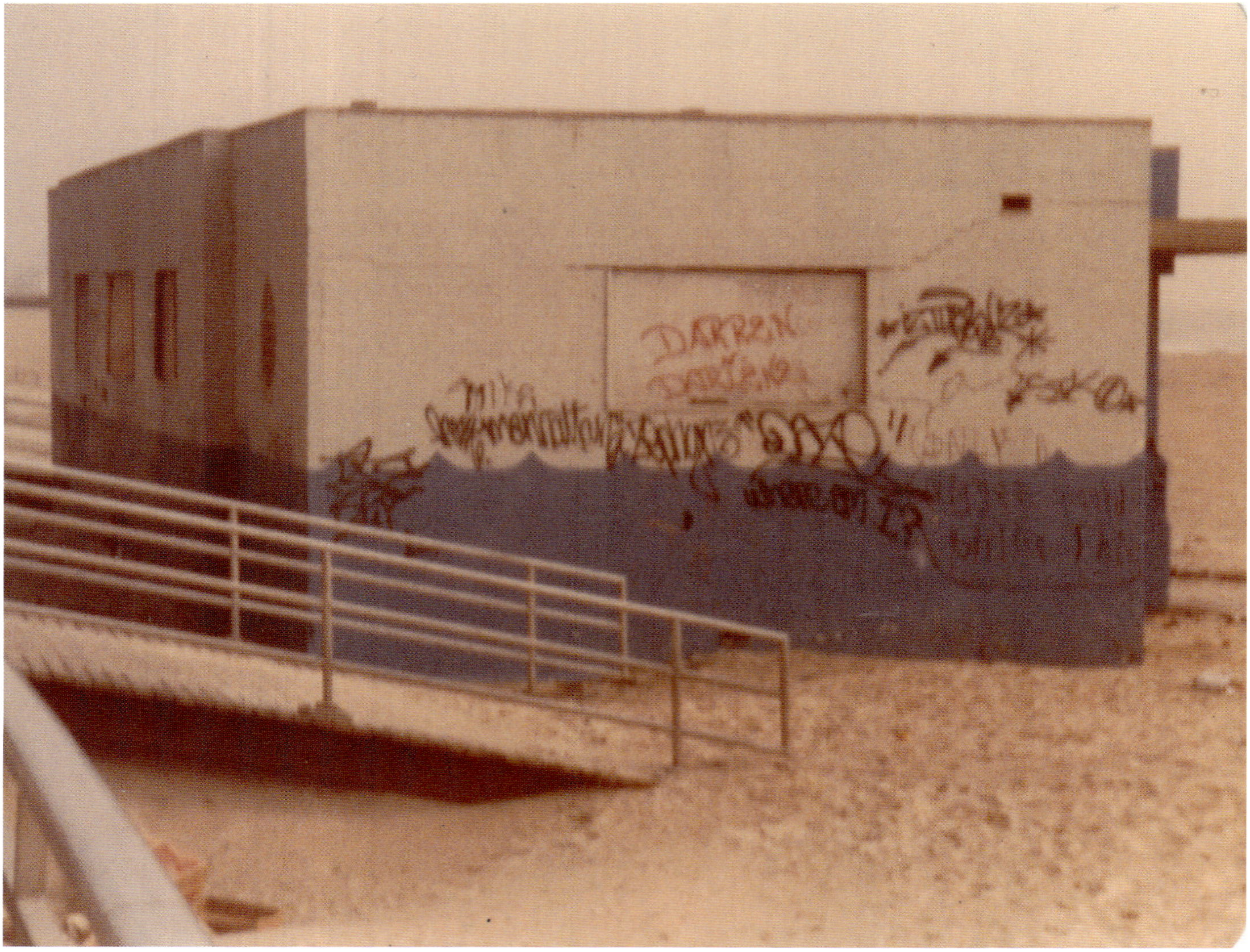

Tag, early '80s
Photo courtesy of Iz the Wiz

Metropolitan Transit Authority. The MTA found new ways to fight back, however. They were putting up deadly razor wire–festooned fences, bringing in German shepherds to patrol the perimeter. They were painting trains white and then burgundy and doing a better and better job of keeping them free of tags and pieces. Writers believed that penalties were becoming stiffer. There was less space to be had on the sides of the giant metal beasts. Plus, cats were getting older. Real life was knocking. You can't scurry like a rat on tracks forever. Daze wanted to continue his evolution as artist.

"I started to slow down in '83," Daze says. "I remember the white trains were coming out, and dudes were busting tags with flooded markers on the outside of trains. And then I thought 'This is where it started—why are dudes doing that now?' In the back of my mind I thought, 'Wow, this is really regressing.' But more importantly, I felt that I made all the statements that I wanted to make. I had painted with all the people I wanted to paint with, and, you know, life was changing for me."

Jean-Michel Basquiat and hip-hop and Blondie's Deborah Harry rapping and clubs and break dancing and all this interest in the culture that came from the streets became super strong. Daze was at the right place at the right time with a good amount of talent and a suitcase full of credibility and respect in his right hand. He swapped painting cars with painting canvases. "In the beginning, I wasn't sure of the potential of making paintings or showing in galleries," Daze remembers, "but at some point I knew it could lead to something and that I should take it seriously. During this period, I was still painting on trains. I never completely stopped painting on trains. . . . I had my foot in both worlds. I just realized that I should just take the painting painting more seriously and pursue it."

Daze's first real taste of the gallery game came by way of his showings at the South Bronx–based Fashion Moda gallery. "I think my involvement with Fashion Moda was a real pivotal point for me because Fashion Moda wasn't really a commercial gallery. It was more of an artist-run alternative art space that was project based. There wasn't a commercial pressure to sell, sell, sell because they were getting funding. And it was really the first space I showed at where the artists were just left to being artists, left to do their own thing."

From Fashion Moda to the world, Daze has shown his work in nearly every corner of the globe. The same dedication and attention to detail that he applied to his subway paintings has been applied to his fine art works. Letters and words are the backbone of the graffiti vernacular but Daze's letters always came alive—so one four-letter word, as distilled by Daze, can feature four individual characters that together speak volumes. His letter A might be the profile of a fish with a soul brother's face; the fish's tail cuts through the letter Z and pops out of the letter E, all the while his letter A is smiling and winking at letter D. That's a classic Daze piece for you. You can pay attention to the words or you can get lost in the souls of the figures that dare you to address them.

Many so-called graffiti writers have tried to transition into the galleries and the so-called legitimate art world. Graffiti is the foundation from which they'd like to leap into the mix, but something gets lost in translation. Letters on canvas—to the uninitiated—feel juvenile. It's a language you have to be schooled in to be able to digest the power of the act itself. For those in the know, these "graffiti" paintings come off like a pride of neutered tigers—tame and living in a cage. Daze is one of the few artists to have emerged from the subway-writing culture who has been able to hold on to his edge. When you look at his work you can see the danger that informed him—and feel the joy and splendor that came with making it back to your bedroom without your parents or the police knowing the damn difference.

Sacha Jenkins SHR is a writer, musician, and filmmaker based in New York City. More importantly, he's a dad.

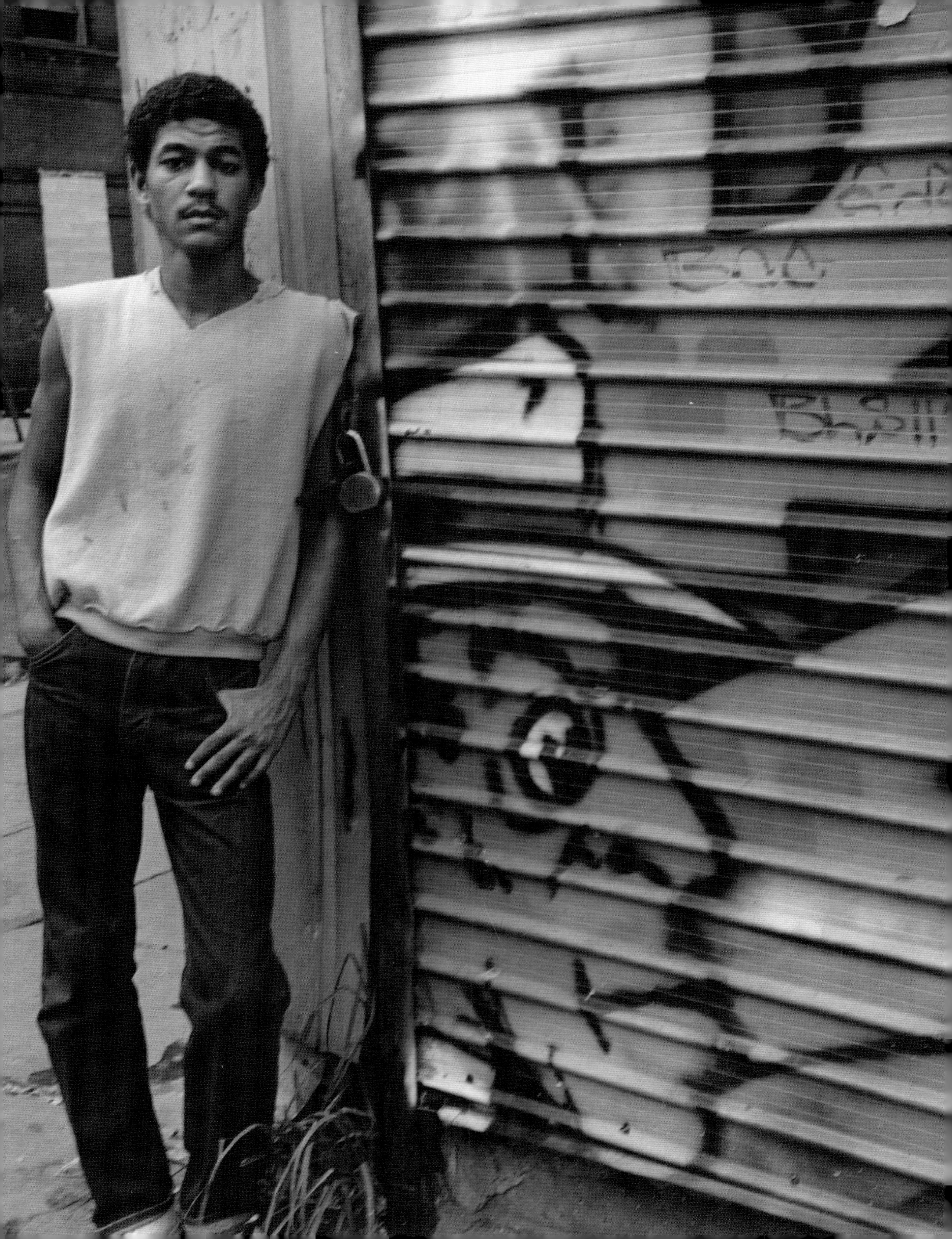

INTRODUCTION

Many people have been quoted saying "there are eight million stories in New York City." I think it's safe to say that number has increased dramatically since that phrase was first coined. In putting this book together I often thought about my own story and how I would present it to the masses. This is not an autobiography in the practical sense. I didn't cover the day-to-day minutia of my childhood or formative teenage years all the way to the present. Rather, I have chosen to take the reader on a journey that covers some of the seminal moments in my life. Those moments shaped my art and allowed me to continue to evolve as an artist.

I focused on events and influences in my early life and how those things inspired me. The most obvious is to discuss my unsanctioned creative activities in the New York Metropolitan Transit System. Everyone wants to hear those stories. The most important thing is that my story doesn't end there. Of equal importance is my transition into exhibiting in galleries and museums in the early 1980s. That was a very exciting period to be a part of and I tried to paint a picture, in vivid spray strokes, of what it was like then.

I've also covered some of the obstacles I had to overcome and how I dealt with them. I've definitely met a lot of colorful characters in my time, but that would be another book in itself. I created this book the same way I would approach a painting: first collecting source material, then sketches, adding and subtracting elements based on their importance, and finally coming up with a proper composition. It is a kind of "greatest hits" book. It covers all of the key elements of my world both new and old and finally points to the future.

Congratulations! Here is your passport to Dazeworld.

Daze, 1982
Photo © Peter Bellamy

CHAPTER 1
THE 1970S

Popular culture came alive for me in the 1970s. Though born in the '60s, I was too young for that era to resonate with me. I mostly remember two things about the 1960s: Vietnam, through reports on the six o'clock news, and Neil Armstrong's first step on the moon in 1968. Flower power? Hippies? The summer of love? That stuff was alien to us in New York. I think you would've gotten a swift, critical beat down if you walked through Times Square with flowers in your hair. The beginning of the '70s signaled the time I became aware of the influence of popular culture en masse. I had no idea, however, that I would carry those influences with me for the rest of my life.

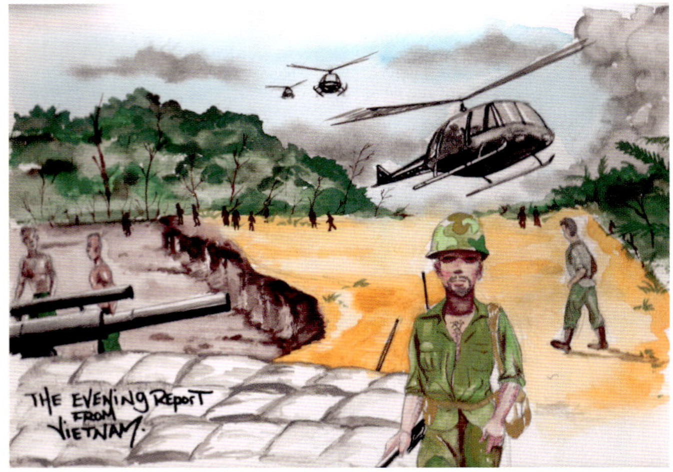

Vietnam War
Illustration © Chris Daze Ellis

Moon Landing
Illustration © Chris Daze Ellis

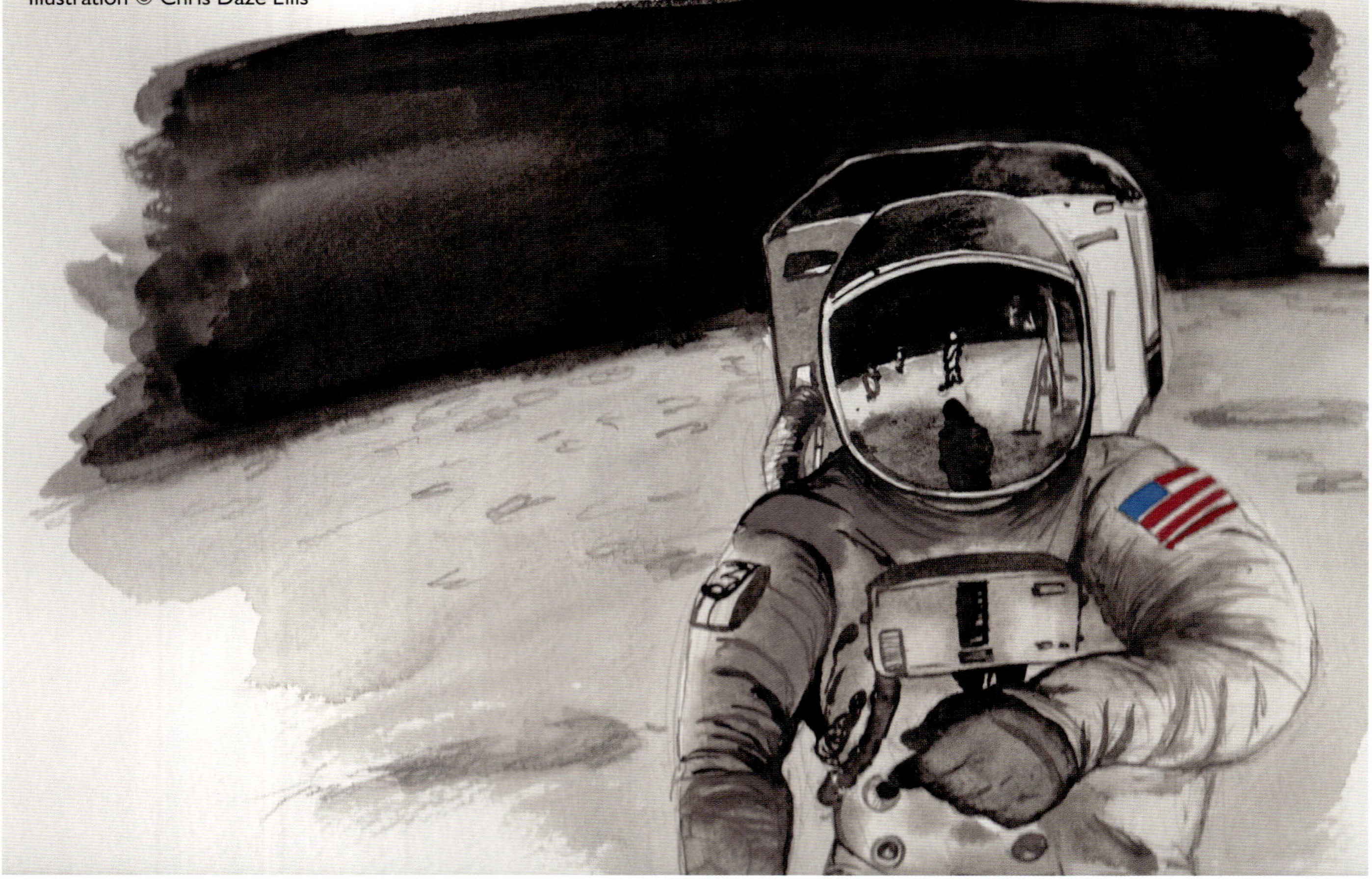

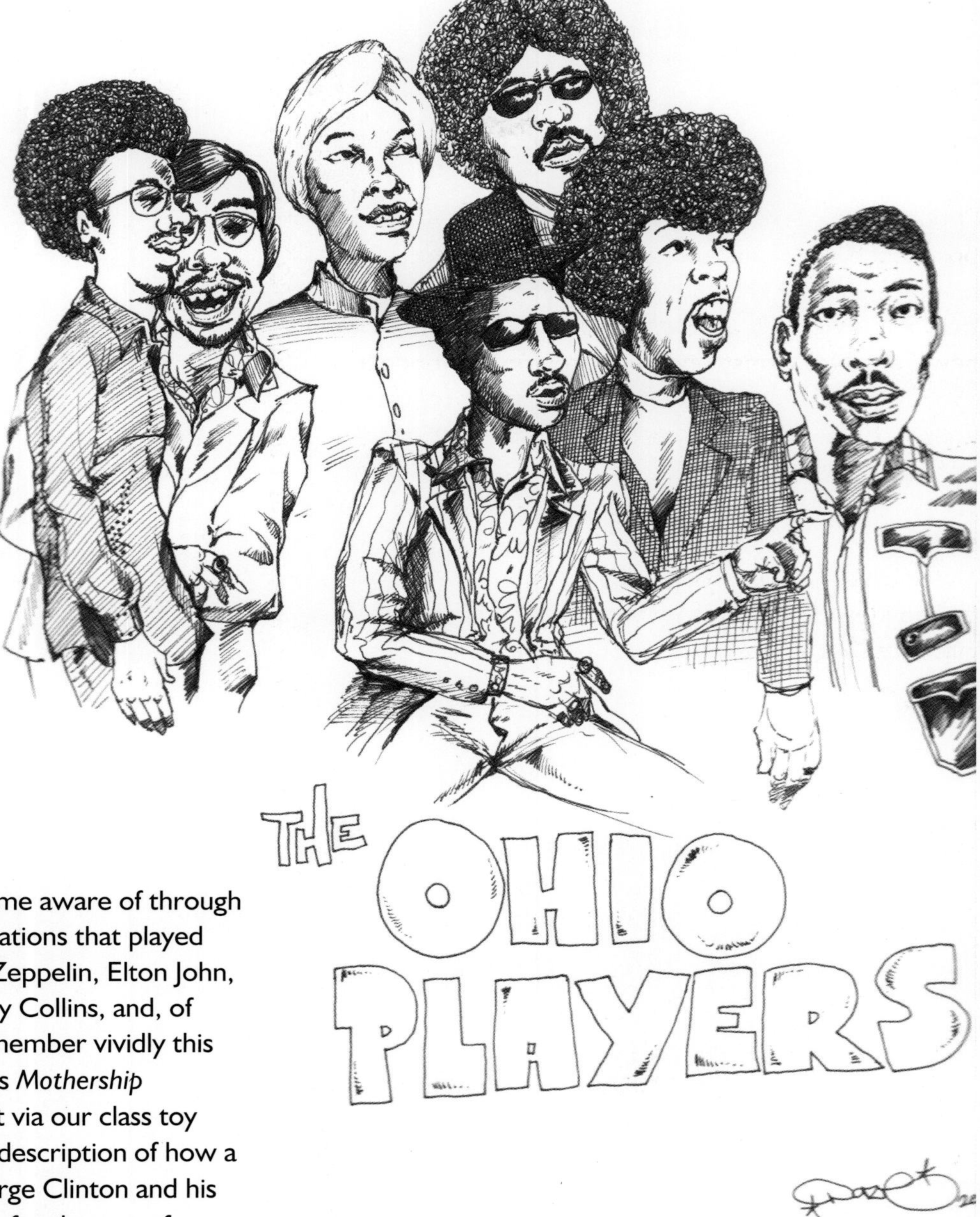

The Ohio Players
Illustration © Chris Daze Ellis

Music was the first thing that I became aware of through radio. As a kid I flickered through stations that played James Brown, Stevie Wonder, Led Zeppelin, Elton John, Aerosmith, the Ohio Players, Bootsy Collins, and, of course, Parliament Funkadelic. I remember vividly this kid bringing in a copy of Parliament's *Mothership Connection* and turning us all on to it via our class toy phonograph. I recall that kid's vivid description of how a UFO would land on stage, and George Clinton and his crew would climb out playing music for throngs of bell-bottomed masses. I was forever feeling the funk after that and ready and willing to be abducted by the mothership at any given moment. It was through Parliament that I discovered Bootsy Collins, then the Ohio Players, who always had a foxy cover, the B.T. Express, the Fatback band, Brass Construction, and many others. This was before the disco era had fully hit, and I had neither the money nor the ability to go see these groups live. Instead I had to settle for catching their shows on the Saturday morning *Soul Train* line-up or *Don Kirshner's Rock Concert*. At the same time, groups like Led Zeppelin, David Bowie, the Beatles, and the Eagles rocked the airwaves .You could enjoy the many variations of rock music from soft to hard, country to folk, and, of course, punk and shock rock. It's funny to think of this now but right around the same time that kid brought the Parliament record to school, one of the only white kids in my school brought in a copy of a Kiss album. Kiss musically did not have a big influence on me. However, I thought that their image was the shit! I couldn't believe how Gene Simmons could spit blood and breathe fire! For both Parliament and Kiss their image was just as important as their music. I could identify with the image because I was already a fan of Marvel Comics superheroes, so for me, these guys were Technicolor superheroes come to life.

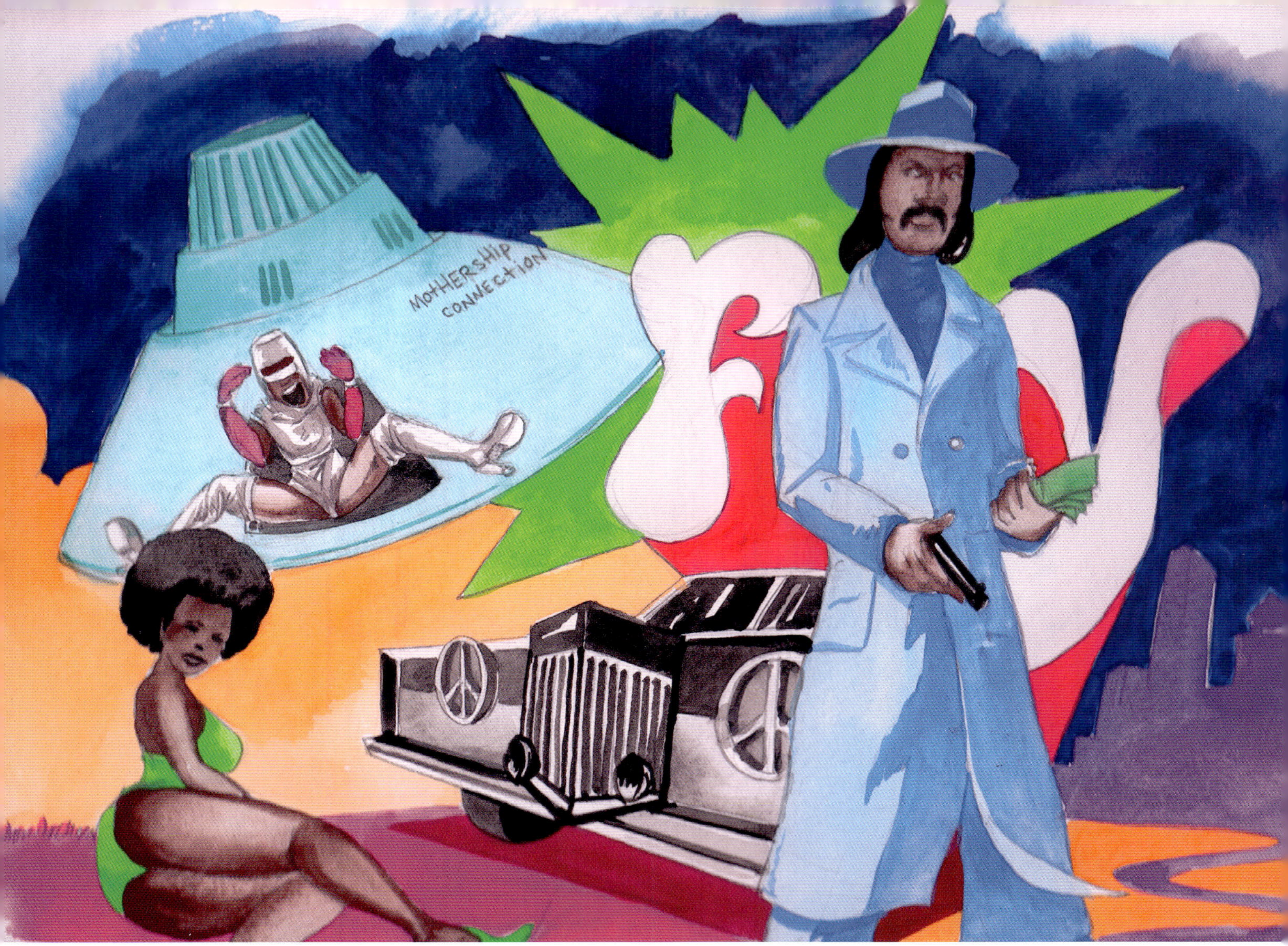

Exploitation Movies
Illustration © Chris Daze Ellis

At the same time I discovered and developed my taste in music, I also discovered movies. I don't care what anyone says, at that time black exploitation films ruled!! What little money I could save, I found myself spending in the movie theater on Hoyt street in Brooklyn watching a triple feature— usually two horror movies and then finally the main event, *Shaft*! I can't even begin to tell you how much of an impact this film had on my friends and me. This was before VHS, Beta, or DVDs, but films were cheap enough then, and you could actually see a film more than once either by remaining in the theater or, as was more the case, sneaking in. Thankfully, soon after *Shaft* came *Super Fly*, *Cleopatra Jones*, *Slaughter*, *Coffy*, *The Mack*, *Willie Dynamite*, and many others. I still secretly bug out whenever I see a copy of that poster of Pam Grier holding a sawed-off shotgun. Wow! The only other genre that we were more excited about was kung fu films. Somehow these genres went hand in hand. Bruce Lee's *Fists of Fury* came first, then *The Chinese Connection*, and finally *Enter the Dragon*. After that kung fu films exploded onto movie marquees in cities nationwide. The pinnacle came for me a couple of years later when you could go to The Deuce (42nd Street), buy one ticket and see, for example, *Slaughter's Big Rip-Off*, *Triple Irons*, or possibly *Carnival of Souls* all in one shot.

Television came of age in the '70s as satirical shows such as *All in the Family*, *Sanford and Son*, *Chico and the Man*, and *Saturday Night Live* covered controversial subjects such as abortion, race, homosexuality, and politics. I remember watching an overabundance of cop shows like *Mannix*, *The Rookies*, *S.W.A.T.*, *Hawaii Five-O*, and *The Mod Squad*. Dudes rocked bell-bottoms, leisure suits, side burns, and jumpsuits while chicks rocked hip-huggers, hot pants, platform shoes, mood rings, and t-shirts.

In 1976 I entered the High School of Art and Design. Up until this time I lived in Brooklyn, and my world was small. I was the class "artist" and coming into Manhattan was like going to a foreign country. One of the great things about that school was that it brought together kids from all over New York. I met kids there from Bayridge, Queensbridge, Harlem, and the Bronx. They brought all the things that influenced them, be it rock, funk, comic books, or fashion. I was suddenly being brewed within a melting pot of disparate cultural ingredients. One of the most important things was graffiti.

Though I was keenly aware of subway writing before 1976 I didn't actually meet anyone who did that until I began school at Art and Design. Prior to that it was an enigma to me. I was like anyone else who wondered where it came from and who did it. Meeting actual writers changed my life completely as all those artistic elements I had been exposed to came together. Writing then was like being a member of a secret society. There were no videos, books, magazines, websites, or social media to go to. No ambition whatsoever except to get your name up. Of all the different elements of the '70s I was exposed, graffiti was the biggest by far. Graffiti culture brought together everything I had been previously exposed to. My entrance into Art and Design brought me into contact with people who were actually painting. Having a dialogue with those artists was one of the greatest things to happen to me during my time there. It was my entire life as it encompassed painting, acquiring paint, drawing, and finally documenting the work.

Though the disco era was in full rage towards the end of the '70s, I had little time for that. I immersed myself in the aerosol haze of tunnels, yards, and lay-ups. Seeing my name go by was all I cared about and hanging with writers is all I did. People don't realize that to be a dedicated writer you gave up certain aspects of your personal life that others enjoy. Oftentimes when others are coming home from a party, dressed up, gassed up, you're sitting across from them on the train ride home, tired, dirty, and ink stained. Nevertheless it was these experiences that would open my eyes to the decade that followed, but that's another story.

Train
Illustration © Chris Daze Ellis

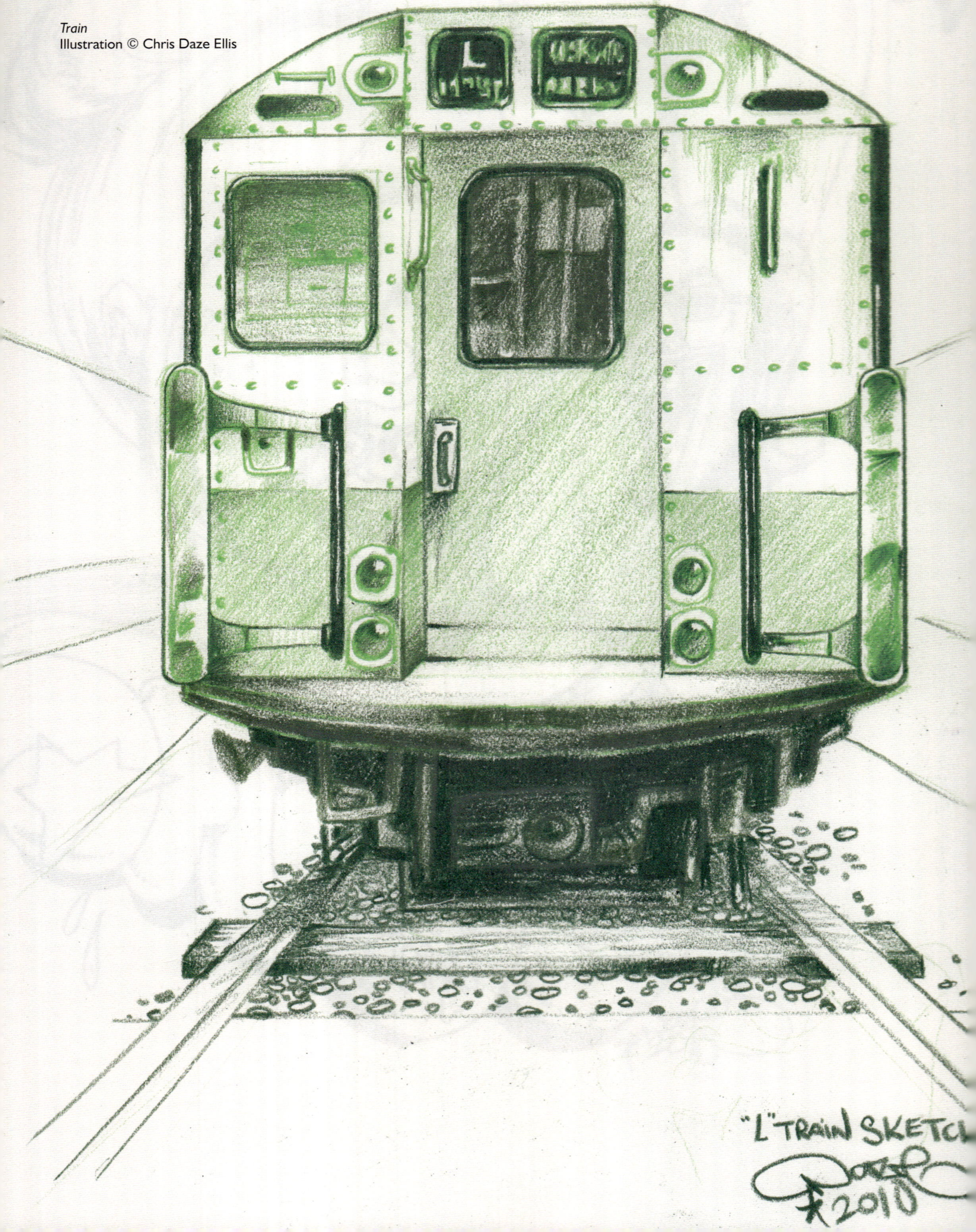

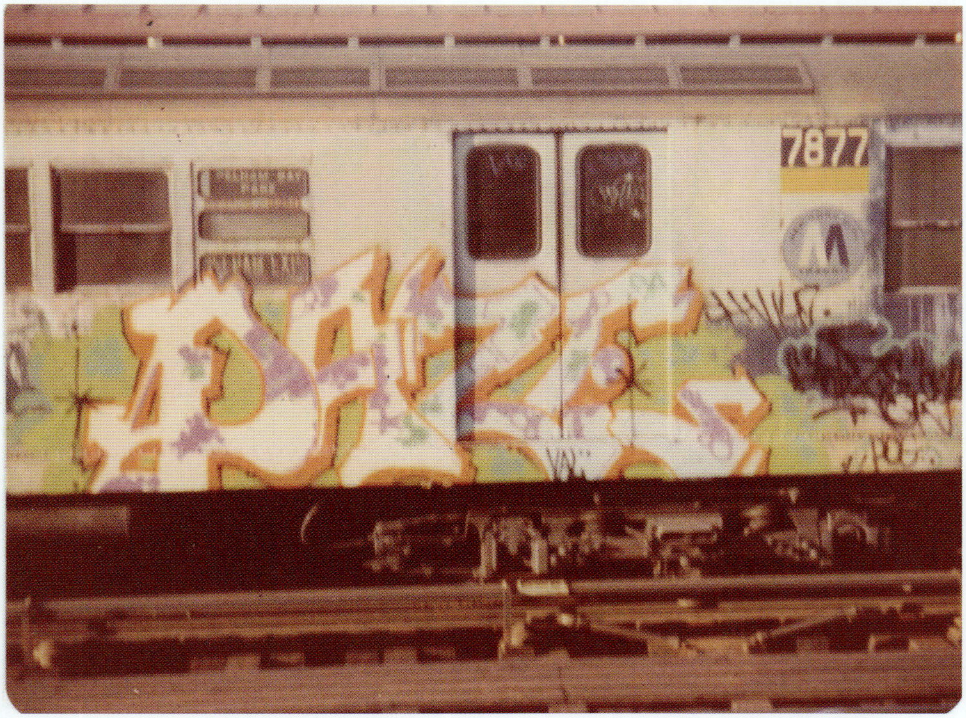

Daze, time to shine on the 6 line
Photo courtesy of the artist

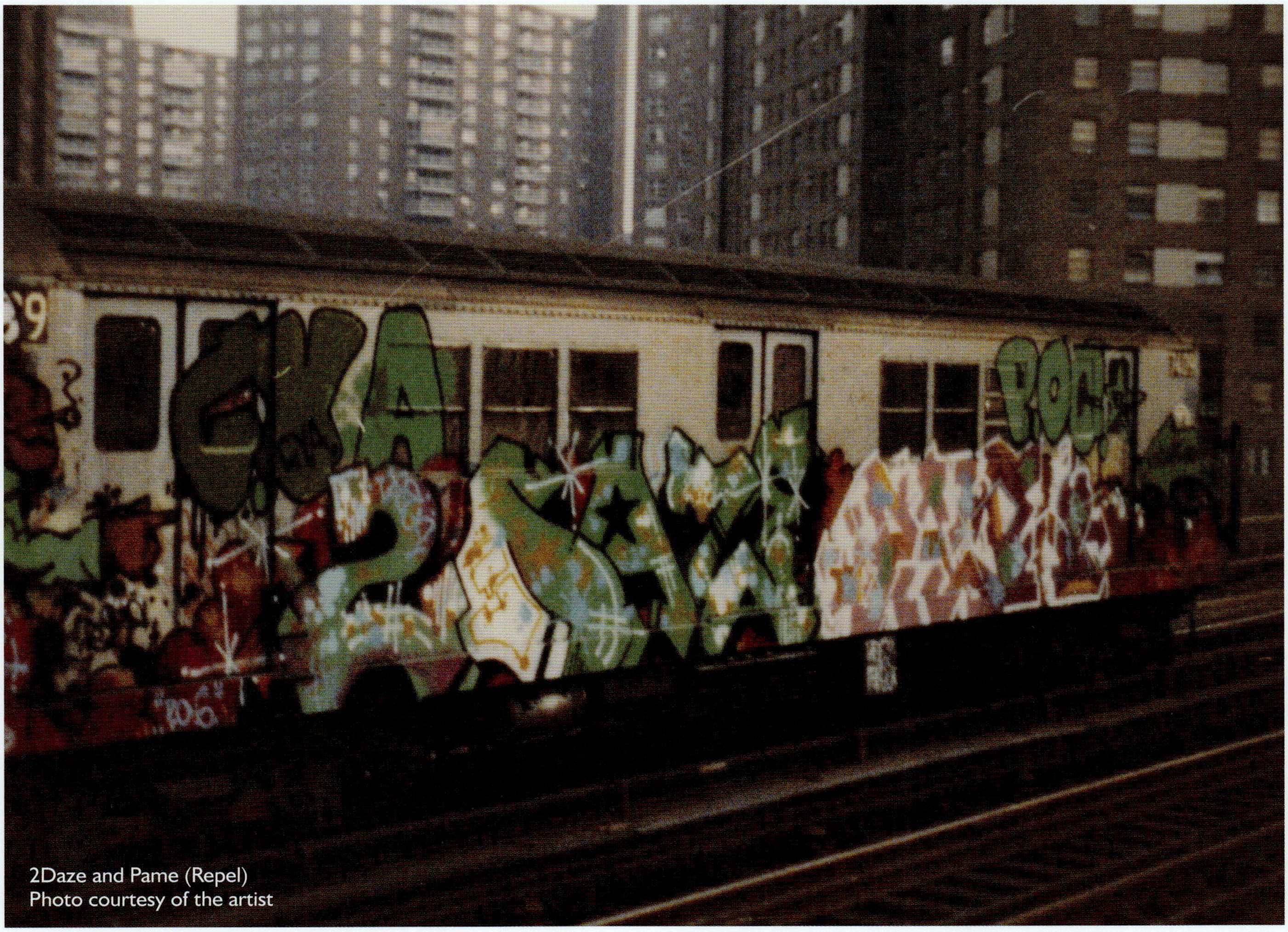

2Daze and Pame (Repel)
Photo courtesy of the artist

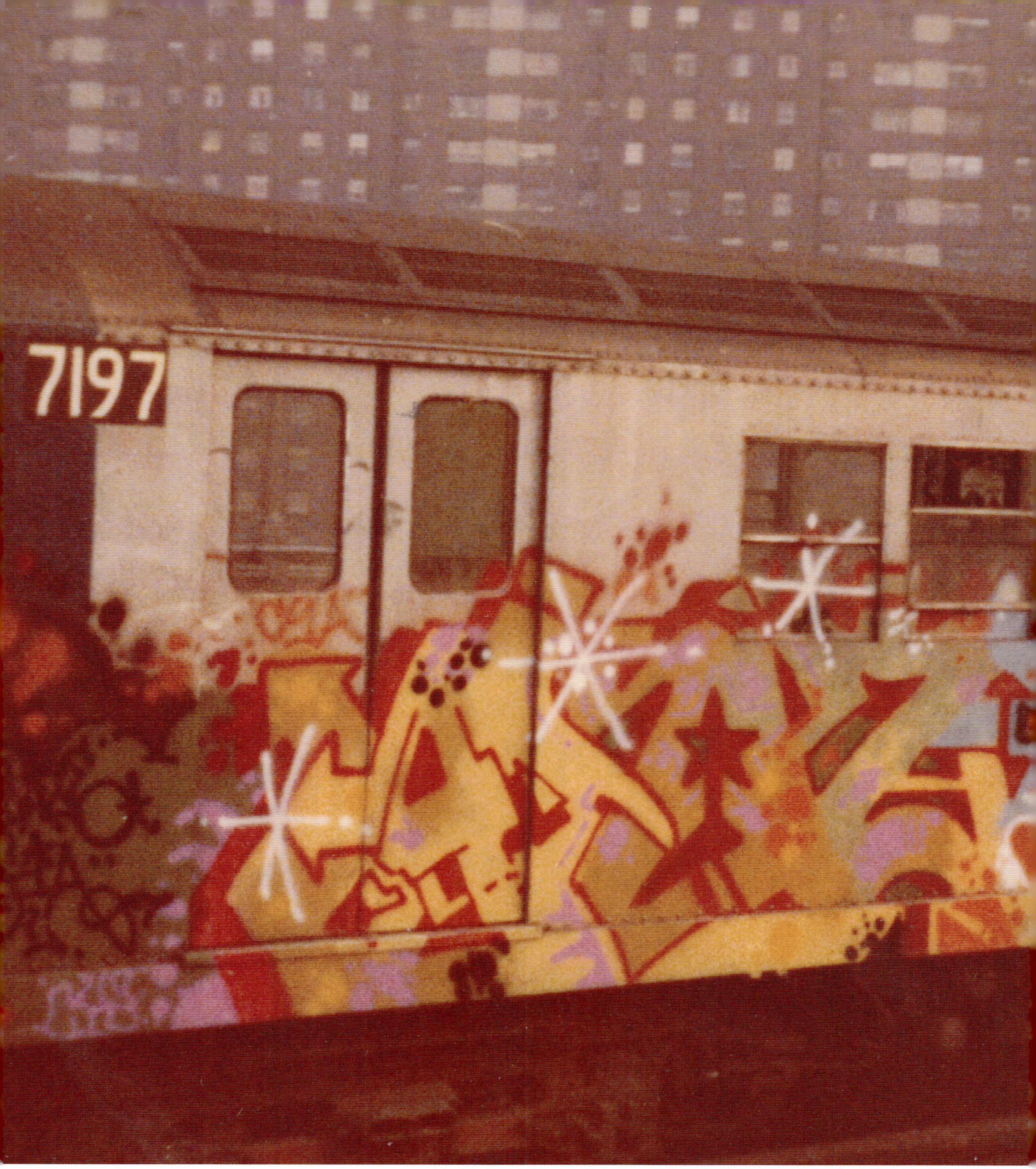

On Broadway
Photo courtesy of the artist

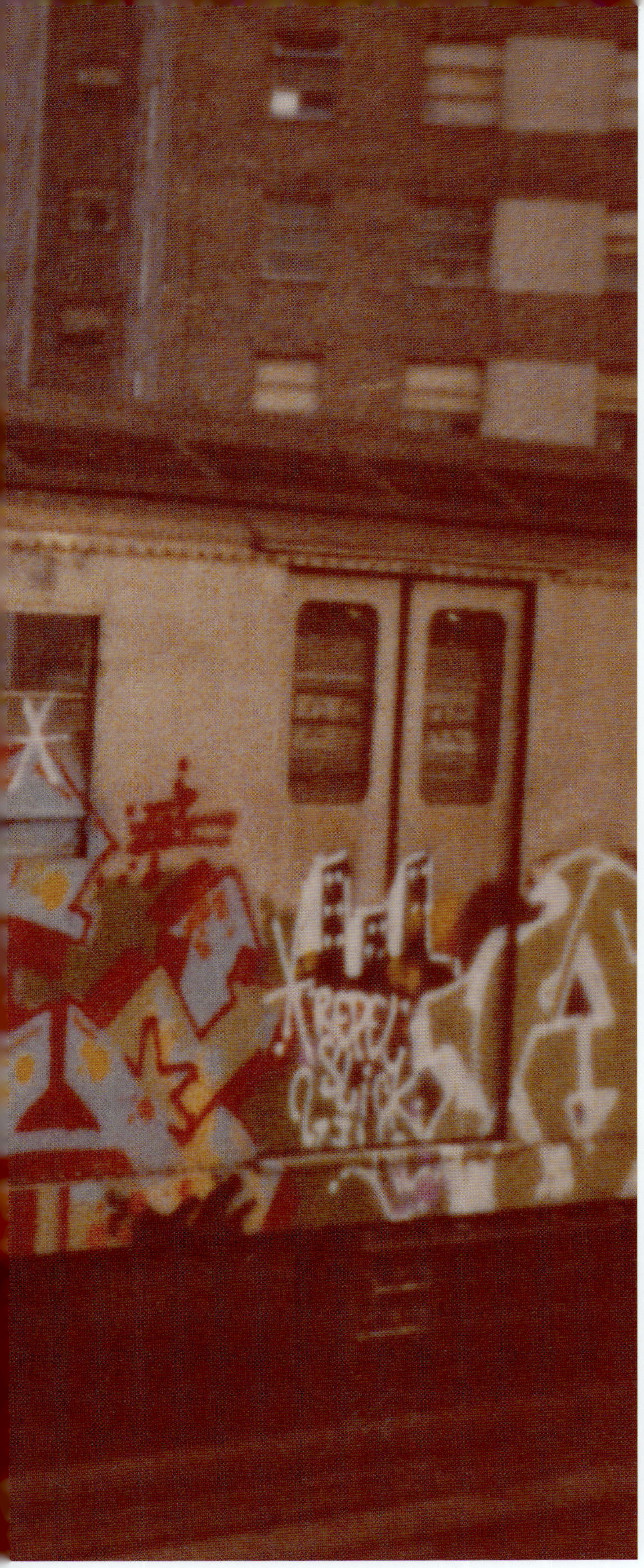

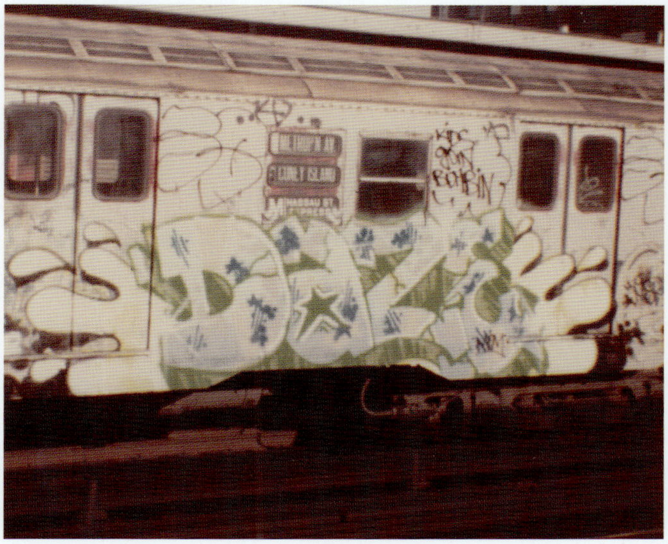

M Line
Photo courtesy of the artist

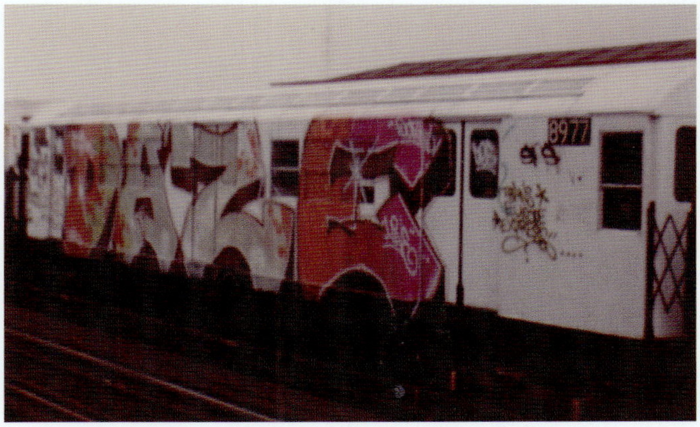

Photo courtesy of the artist

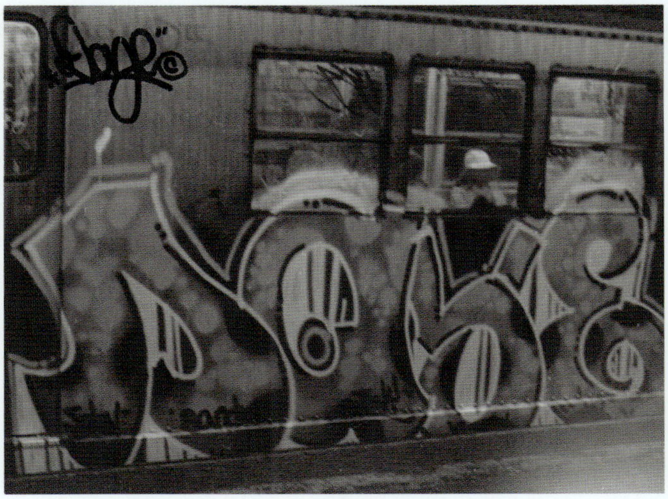

Broadway local, 1982
Photo courtesy of the artist

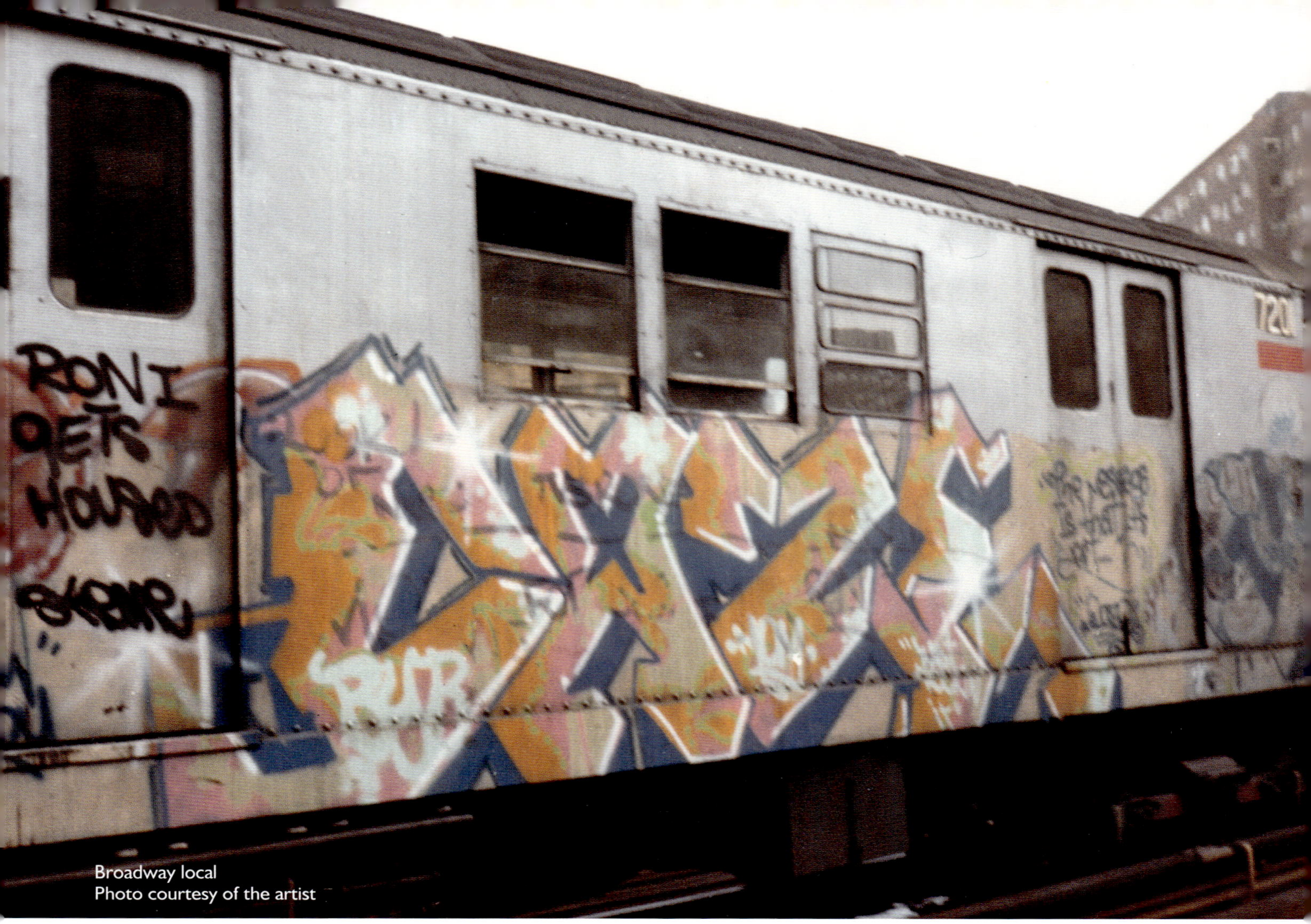

Broadway local
Photo courtesy of the artist

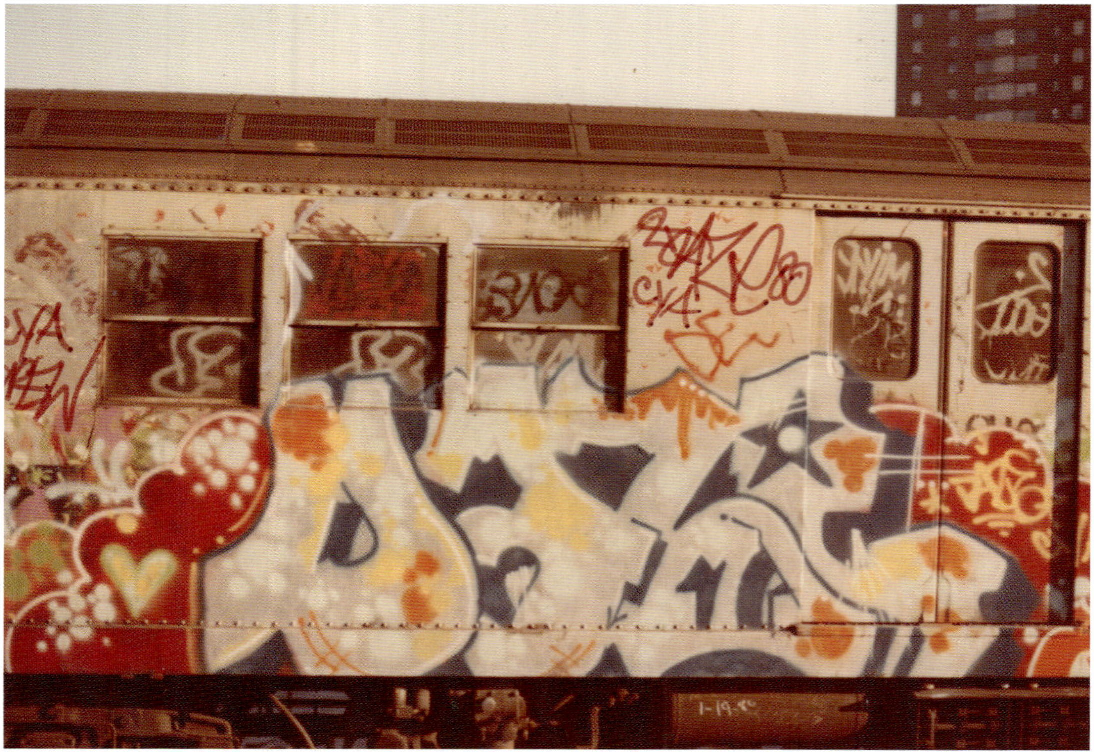

Photo courtesy of the artist

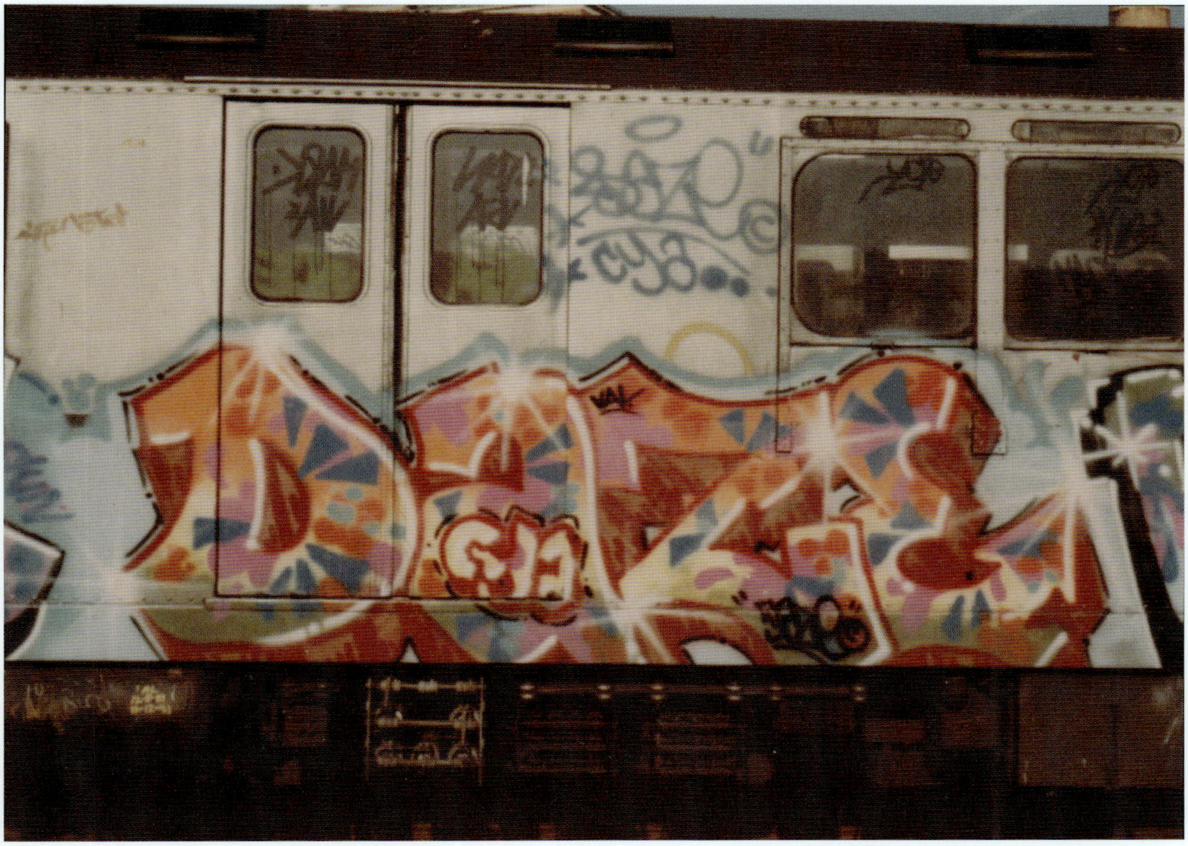

Photo courtesy of the artist

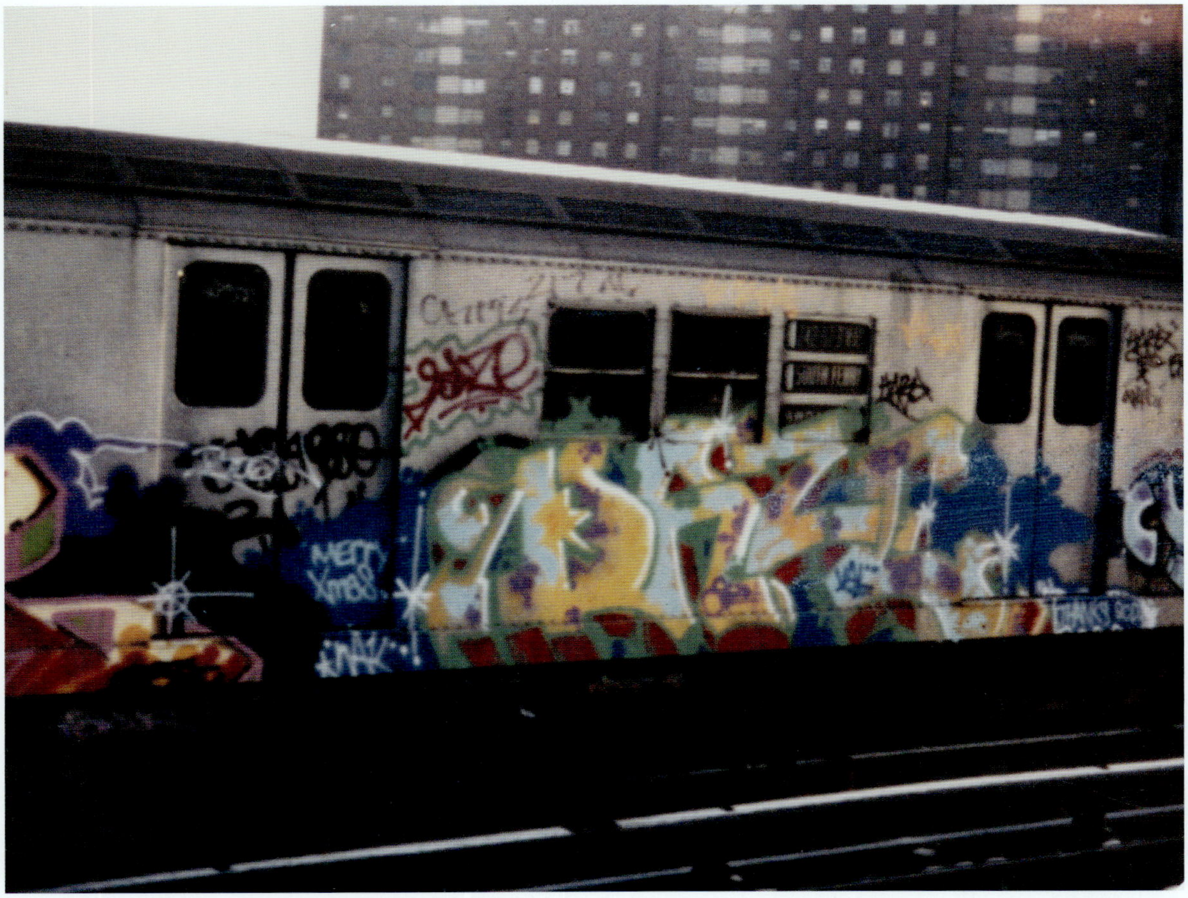

With Kos207, Christmastime Photo courtesy of the artist

CHAPTER 2
THE BENCH AND BEYOND

I came to what was known as the writers' bench at 149th street and Grand Concourse in 1977. At that point it was still being referred to as "the corner." During my time at the High School of Art and Design, writers would often congregate at tables in the lunchroom to exchange information, practice sketches and styles, and make plans to paint. It was a kind of unofficial "graffiti salon" where these types of exchanges would happen daily. It was in this informal setting that I first began to hear about "the bench." When conversations shifted towards talk of the bench, I was in awe. It was described to me as the ultimate place to watch trains and meet legends. It should be noted that most of the legendary writers I really wanted to meet didn't hang out there. Occasionally one or two of them would drop by once a week. Most of the real legends stayed away.

The writers' bench was a place where you could go to critique others' work, meet writers from other boroughs, and compare notes. The uptown and downtown sides were connected by a bridge, which enabled one to view both sides of the train easily. That made it an optimal location for viewing trains.

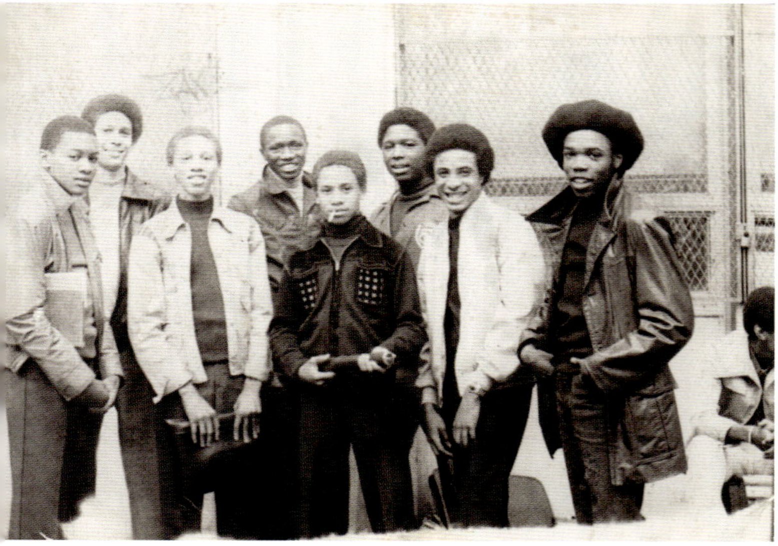

Some of my classmates at the High School of Art and Design, circa 1977

The first afternoon I arrived there after school I was crazily excited. My adrenaline was pumping furiously as I eagerly awaited the 3:00 final school bell. Once it rang, I hurriedly made my way to the train station and found the uptown line. The bench was swarmed with writers in the afternoons. On any given day guys like KC3, KC5, EC3, Pacer1, Cue, Phade, LC, Mr. Mean, Kid56, Ban2, Haro, Polo, Crash, Kel, Mare139, 2Mad, Beo, Blake170, BS119, and Smiley149 would be there. Occasionally older generations would stop by such as Kase2, Bear167, Chain3, or even Comet. Those were days that you didn't want to miss.

Eventually, as I did more pieces on the trains, I began to tire of it. I was active and I no longer saw the need to be there. As great as the 149th Street station was for viewing trains and networking, it was a bad place to try to take photographs. It was indoors, which meant you needed a pretty strong flash to get anything. I began to spend more time on outdoor platforms where I could photograph trains in a better setting. I ultimately realized that hanging at the bench was a great place to network in the beginning but that was it. Eventually you graduate and move up the next rung in the ladder. I was slowly beginning to understand the unspoken hierarchy that existed in subway writing.

The Broadway local line was known to writers simply as "the 1s." I began to be curious about that line as I rarely had time to venture over to the west side. Ultimately what I saw being done on "the 1s" would have a great impact on me. "The 1s" were a kind of underground Valhalla where names lived on simply because the trains were not buffed as often as trains on other lines. It was for this reason that the insides were layered with names of older generations of writers. In 1976 you could still see names like Team, Aztec, Jester, Wasp1, Dean, Karado135, Trex, Fuzz1, and many more competing for space on the insides. The outsides were covered by people like Part, Kool131, Noc167, Chain3, Panic, Kase2, Max, Fuse, Paid3, Dean, Peso131, Scorch170, and others too numerous to mention. I came back from that

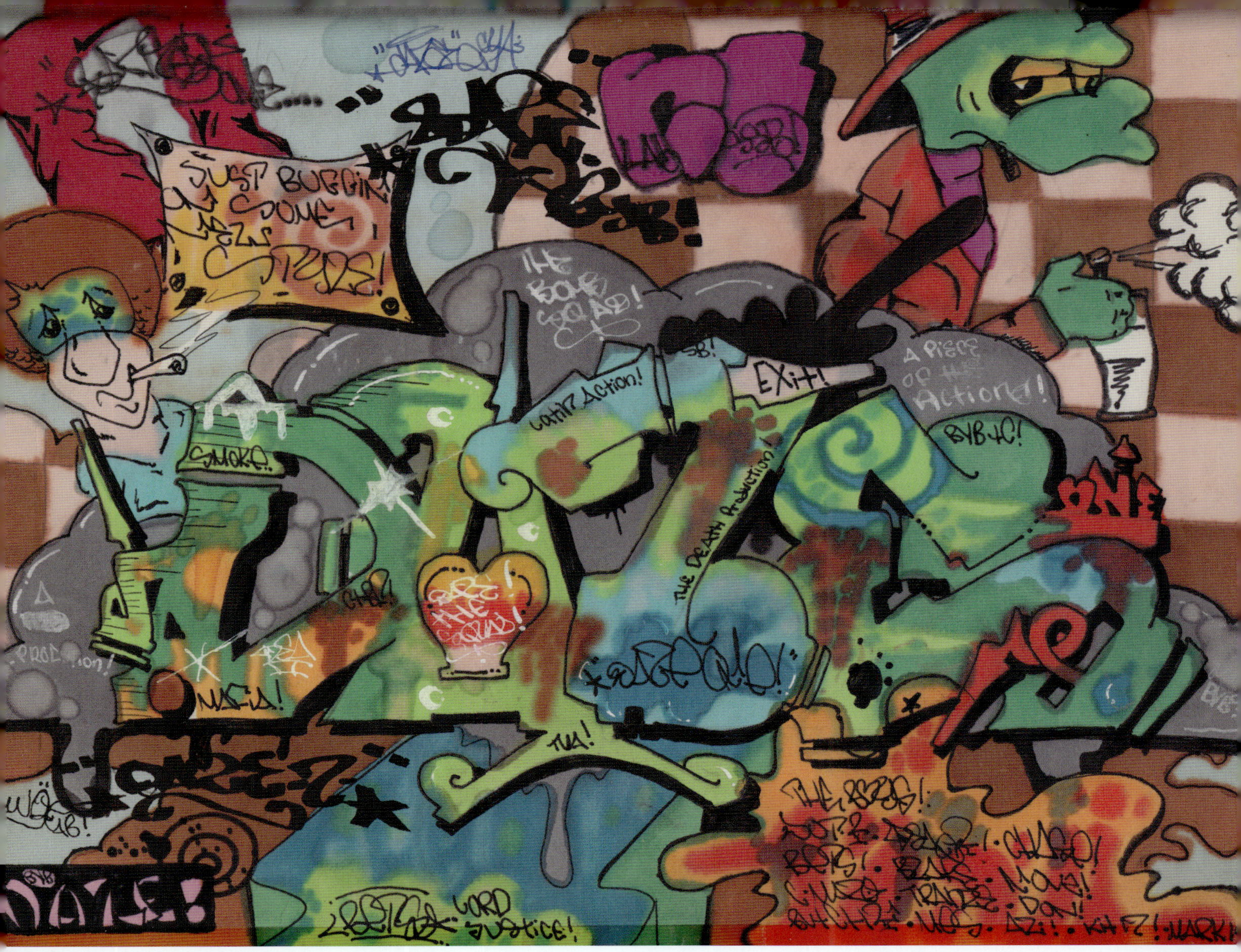

Black book page from 1978

experience dizzied by all that I saw. From that first visit I knew that I'd be back.

The trains at that time had more of an influence on me than anything that was being prescribed in the classrooms at Art and Design. In truth I was a little disappointed in the school itself. Classes such as cartooning and animation were reduced due to budget cuts. The teachers themselves also disappointed me. Many of them were no longer working in the field and what they were teaching, with few exceptions, seemed irrelevant. Armed with these two realizations, it was pretty easy for me to justify spending more time in the lunchroom locked in artistic exchange with my fellow students. In retrospect that was the most important thing I got out of the school—the ever-evolving artistic dialogue among my fellow students. It completely fed my imagination as each day I spent hours honing my style in sketchbooks.

My partner at the time was a guy who wrote as 2Mad. We both seemed to start writing at the same time and seemed to be on a similar track artistically. As an artist he spent a lot of time studying style and constantly drawing. It was amazing to watch his work evolve on a daily basis. He and I would spend several periods drawing in our black books, developing letters, and generally talking shit. After what seemed like months and months of this, we finally made a plan. We were going to hit the number one line. The place to do it: the

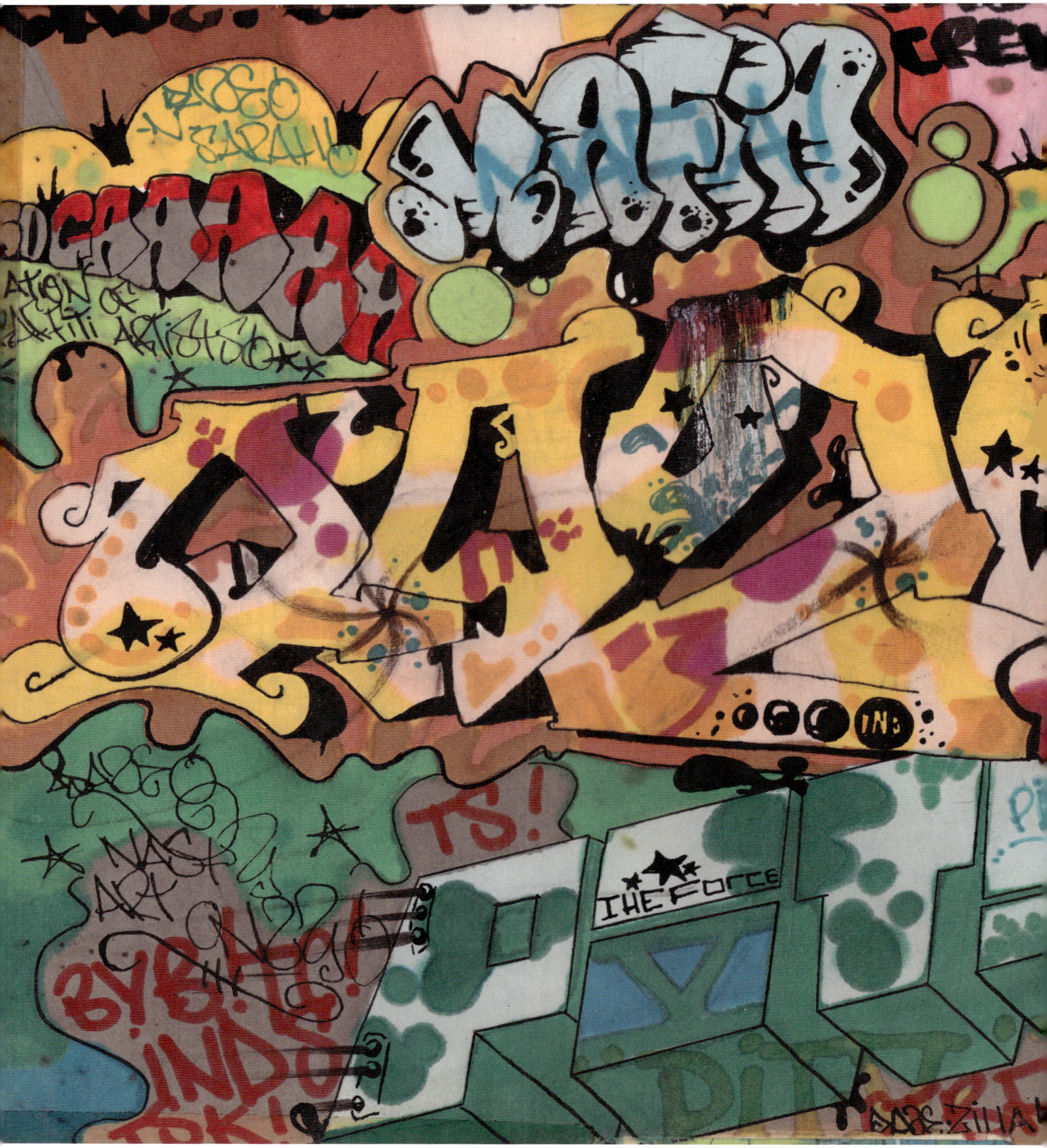

Black book page from 1978

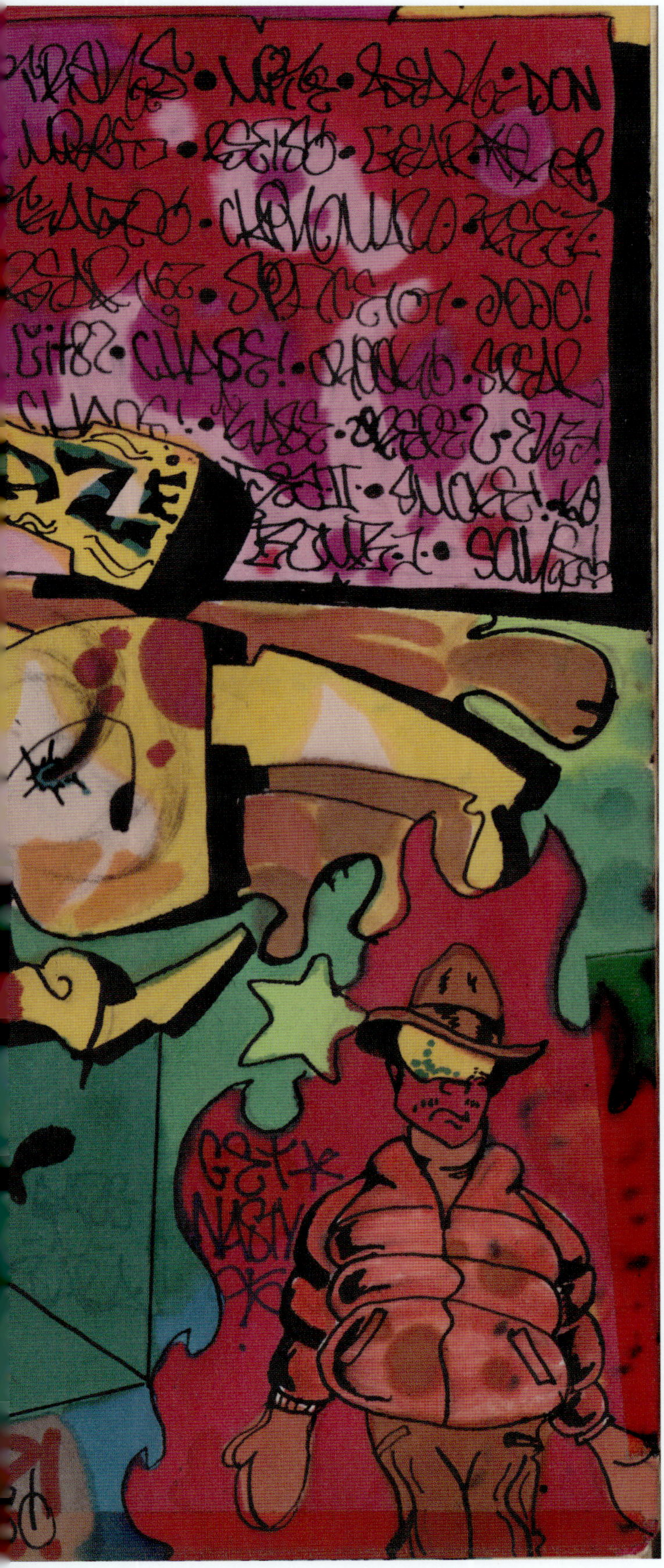

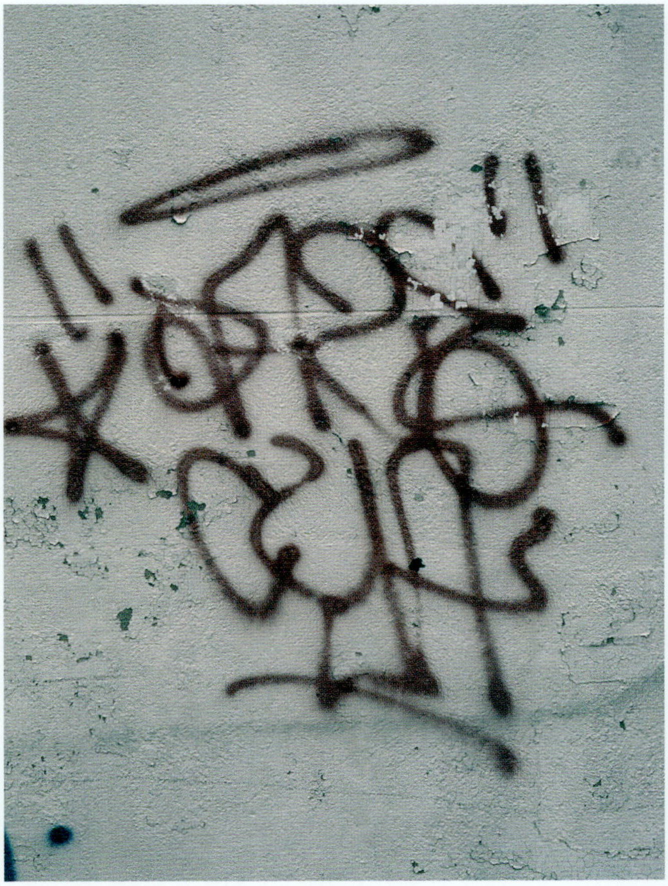

Tag 1979
Photo © Martha Cooper

145th Street tunnel. It's important to note that even until the very end of its era, the 145th Street tunnel always had a mythic reputation that preceded itself. When things were great there you could spend an entire weekend painting uninterrupted. You could even take breaks to go to the McDonald's upstairs and return to continue painting. When things were bad, however, the police would come at you from every entrance, pulling in raid trains, turning on lights, and searching relentlessly for writers who in most cases were long gone. Those who stayed knew exactly where to hide. After such raids would occur, word got out and people generally stayed away. The tunnel was "burnt" and other locations had to be found.

2Mad and I decided the best time to go would be on a cold Sunday morning in January. It was one of those typical New York winters that I came to know only too well. All the snow had fallen three days before and had now turned to sheets of ice as the temperature dropped. This meant all the tunnels would be packed with trains underground to escape the freezing temperatures. To a dedicated writer this was heaven! We were going there not just to paint, but also to do reconnaissance on the tunnel itself for future missions.

The 145th Street tunnel was divided into two sides: an uptown side with a single row of parked trains and an active track, and a downtown side with two lanes of parked trains and one active track. I remember years later on subsequent trips how a passing train would flush the acrid smell of aerosol paint onto the platform. This meant people were busy inside. We decided to go for the downtown side, as there would be more cars to choose from. The tunnel itself had an eerie feel to it. There was the whirring sound of compressors going on and off periodically. It felt as if the tunnel was breathing, waiting for us to venture inside and investigate. We walked off the platform and climbed down a few steps. At once we were inside the belly of the beast. Wading through piles of garbage, we found a car that had a decent amount of light and proceeded to get to work. We painted undisturbed for what seemed like hours to me. Besides the constant shaking of cans, the only other sounds were the clicking of tracks, and trains going by every fifteen or twenty minutes. It was freezing outside but the tunnel and the flow of our adrenaline kept us warm. The car that 2mad and I did that day said: "CYA, Daze." 2Mad chose to do a CYA piece to announce the presence of our new group Crazy Young Artists. I did a Daze piece that had a cartoon character's face in place of the "A." Even though I had already done a few pieces I was quite proud of this technically. In spite of the freezing cold we had no problems. We left early that afternoon, filled with excitement, promising to return. As luck would have it, that particular train was a number 2 train, which meant that it would be switched back to its original line. First it was seen on the Broadway line, then all over the Bronx. We got a lot of mileage out of that one.

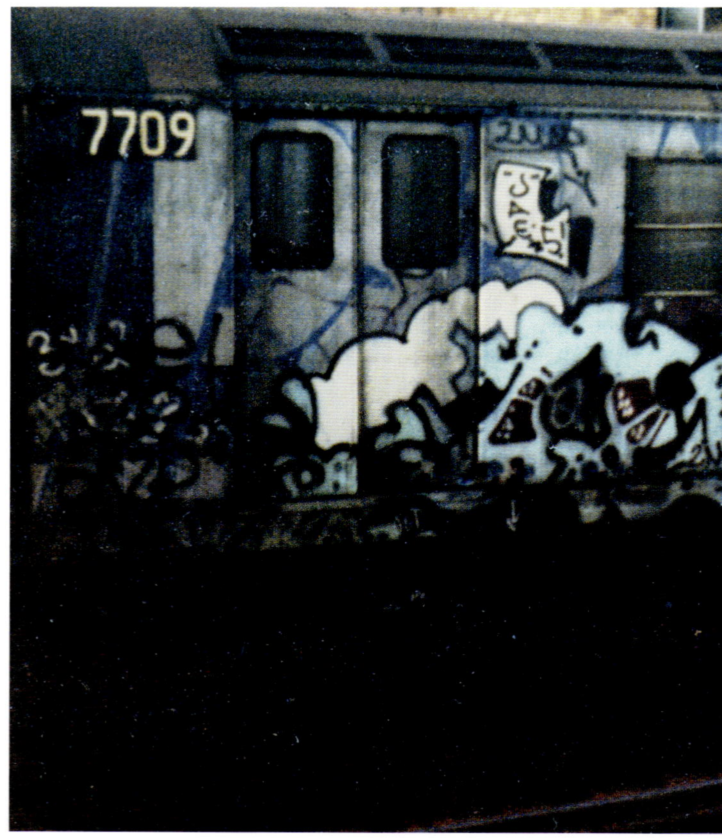

CYA (2Mad)-Daze, 1977
Photo courtesy of the artist

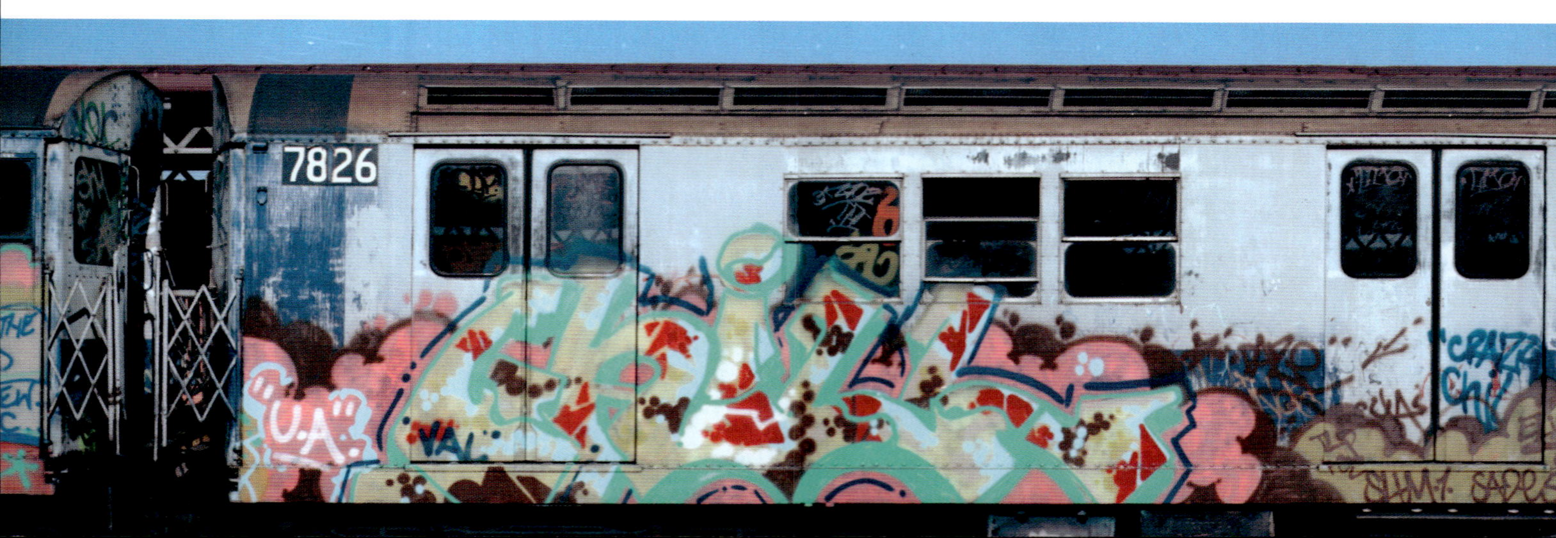

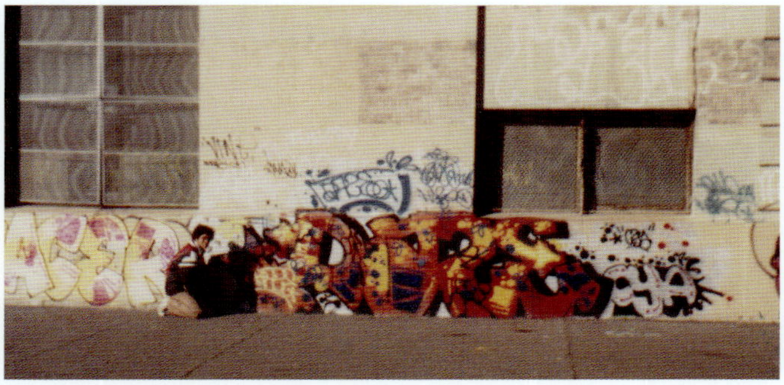

Daze, East Tremont school yard
Photo © Jean13

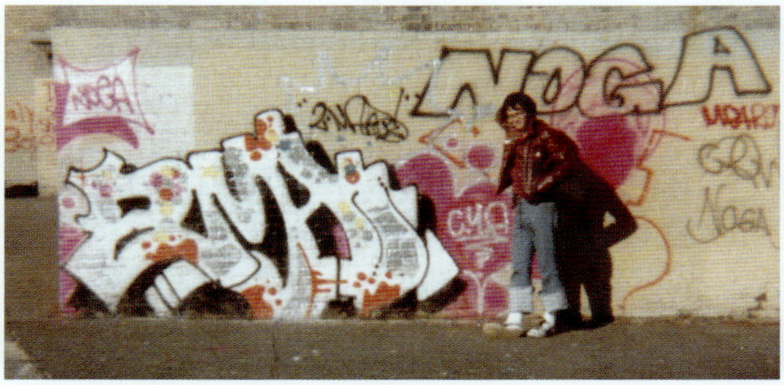

2Mad, East Tremont school yard
Photo © Jean13

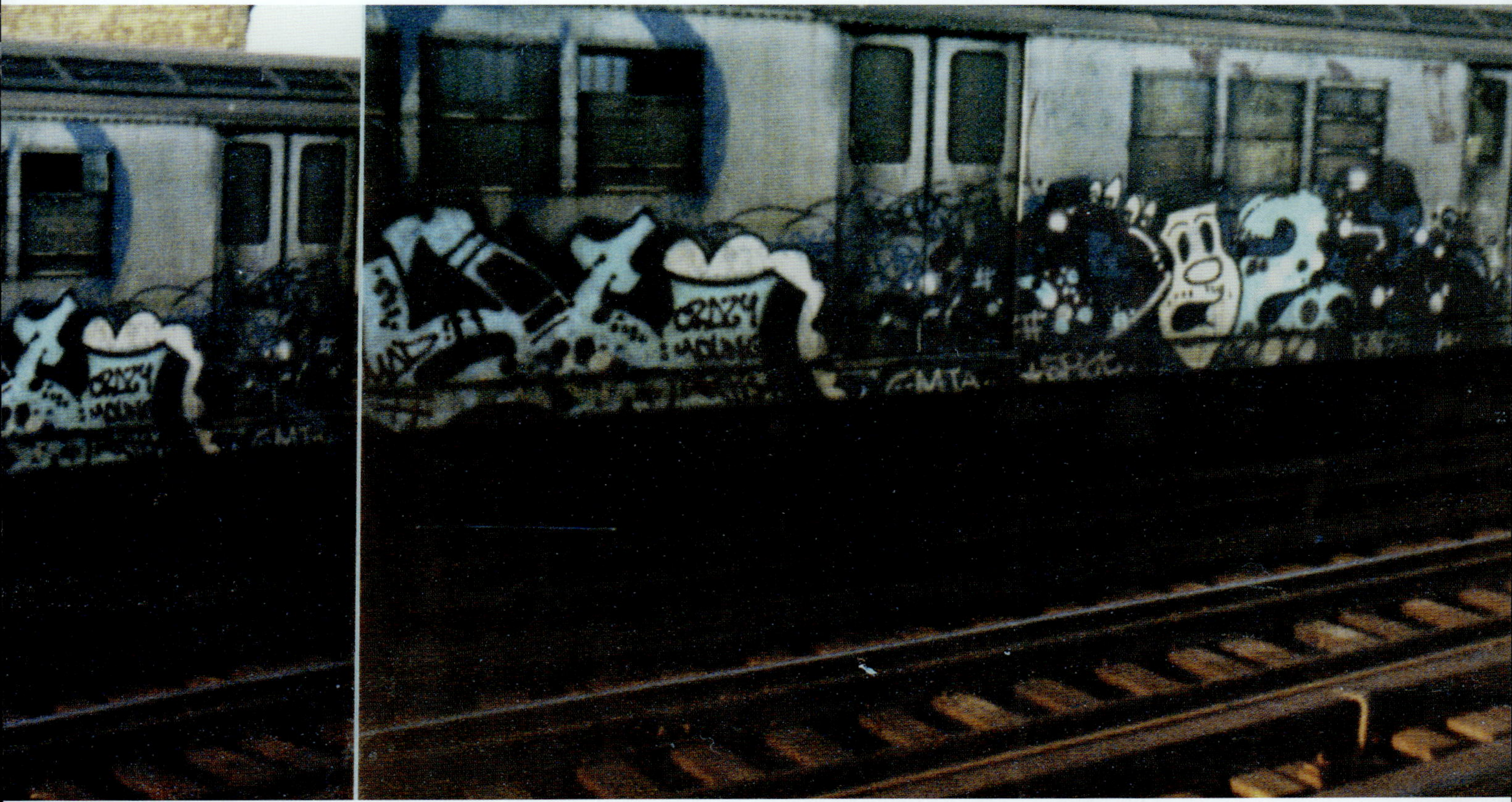

Chill2 (Daze)-Keith (El Kay)
Photo © Henry Chalfant

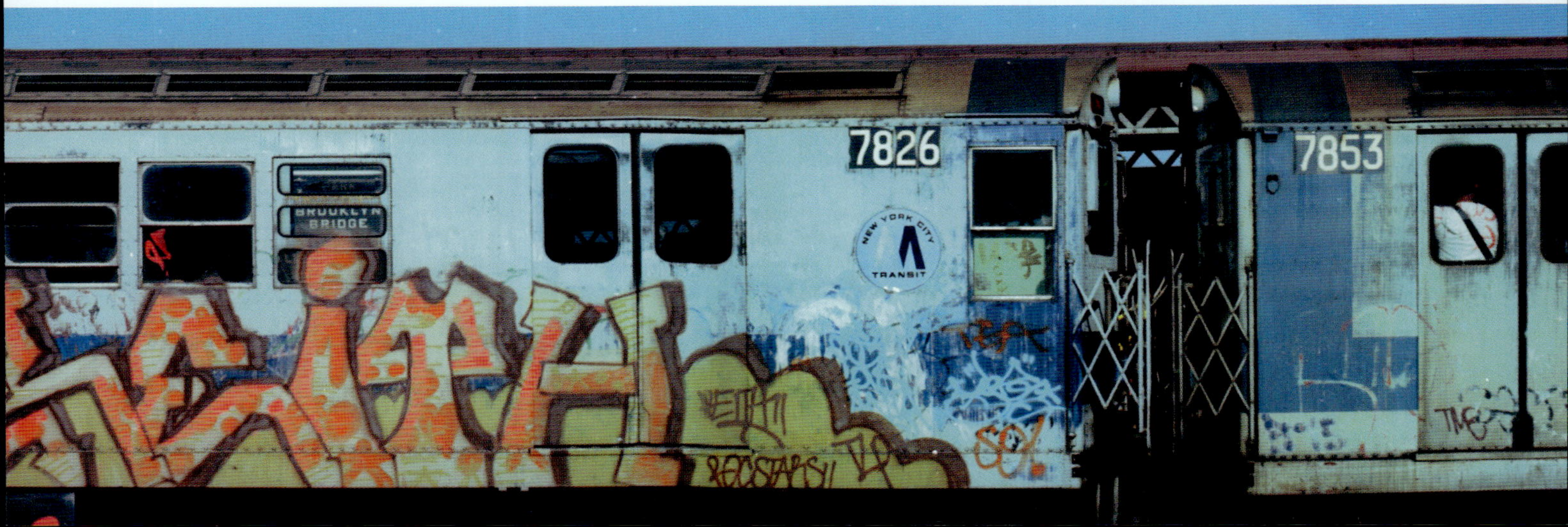

CHAPTER 3
TRANSIT(ION)

BY JAY J.SON EDLIN

The name Daze did not appear on Christopher Ellis's birth certificate. The transformation began in Crown Heights, Brooklyn, where Ellis spent the early part of his childhood. Ellis recalls most of his friends' parents being of Caribbean descent. Rampant crime, gang activity, and a general lack of opportunity spurred his family's search for greener pastures that equated to an exodus to Roosevelt Island in 1976. The new apartment complex situated between Queens and Manhattan provided Ellis with a broader, safer, more ethnically diverse environment. The development, although part of the fiber of NYC, retained a small-town feel and provided easy access to Manhattan via the island's tramway. An innately artistic child, Ellis began drawing characters gleaned from the *Daily News*'s Sunday funnies, in particular *Dick Tracy* and *Terry and the Pirates*. Marvel comics also informed his earliest work, as he envisioned himself becoming the next Jack Kirby or John Romita. In the late '60s, a relative gave Ellis the greatest present he'd gotten to date: a subscription to *MAD* magazine. Each week a new issue arrived and an inspired Ellis began channeling his inner Mort Drucker.

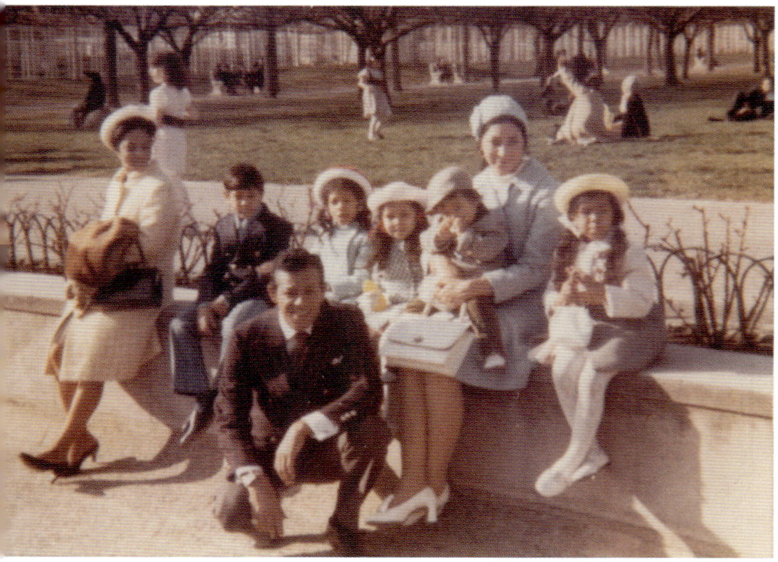

The Ellis family on Easter Sunday.
Botanical Gardens, Brooklyn, 1969

By 1974, Ellis began to notice graffiti on the streets, which he attributed to the territorial markings of gangs. Ominous names like The Vanguards, Ex Vandals, and The Last Survivors screamed from local walls conjuring up images of kids rumbling in painted denim jackets, but Ellis never met any of these urban outlaws. As the writing culture exploded and individual names appeared in abundance, Ellis realized that a war against the system raged on stressing individual glory with the promise of fame to its victors. Utica Avenue, Ellis's home station, housed a lay-up that served as one of graffiti's most active studios. In 1975, Ellis observed a subway masterpiece that changed his mindset on illegal art. A Blade whole car with top to bottom dancing girls, their flowing hair extending onto the subway car's roof, rolled into the station gradually slowing and finally stopping in front of him. Not yet savvy enough to decipher the name, he instantly recognized the women as the recreated work of *MAD*'s Don Martin.

In a defining moment not unlike when a kid realizes what he wants to be when he grows up, Ellis's perspective on illegal art changed from one of casual observation to one of impending participation. Although he left Brooklyn never having touched a spray can or marker, graffiti just wouldn't leave Ellis alone.

In 1976 Ellis enrolled in the High School of Art and Design. The bathrooms, cafeteria tables, and gym lockers looked more like the inside of a subway train than a school. All of the students carried sketchbooks and the passion that would become an addiction for the next decade of Ellis's life overtook him. The multi-racial, multi-geographical student body gave Ellis his first taste of going all-city.

Art and Design's alumni included a who's who of graffiti's illuminati. Ellis soon found himself in the

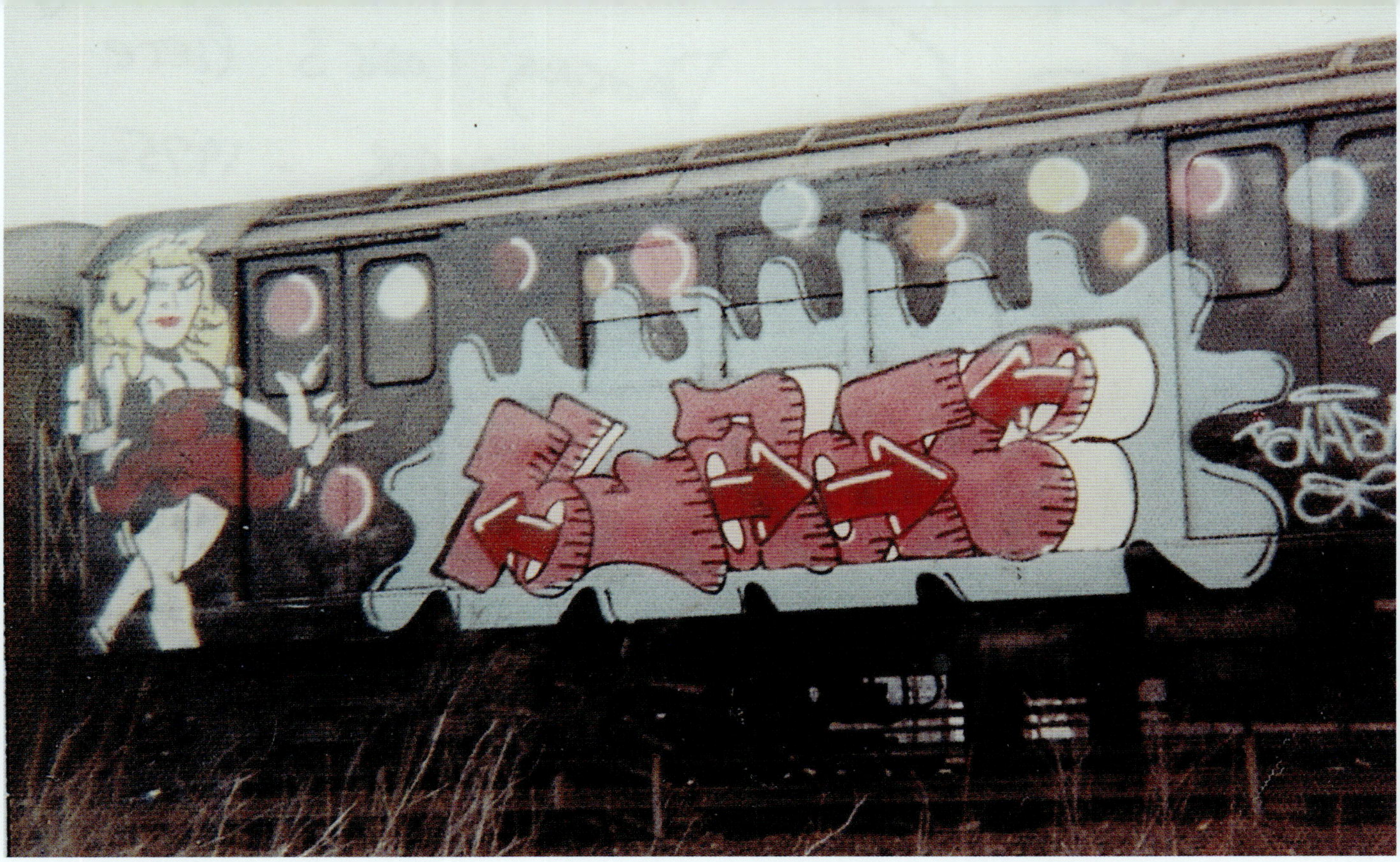

Blade TC5 piece, 1975
Photo © Blade TC5

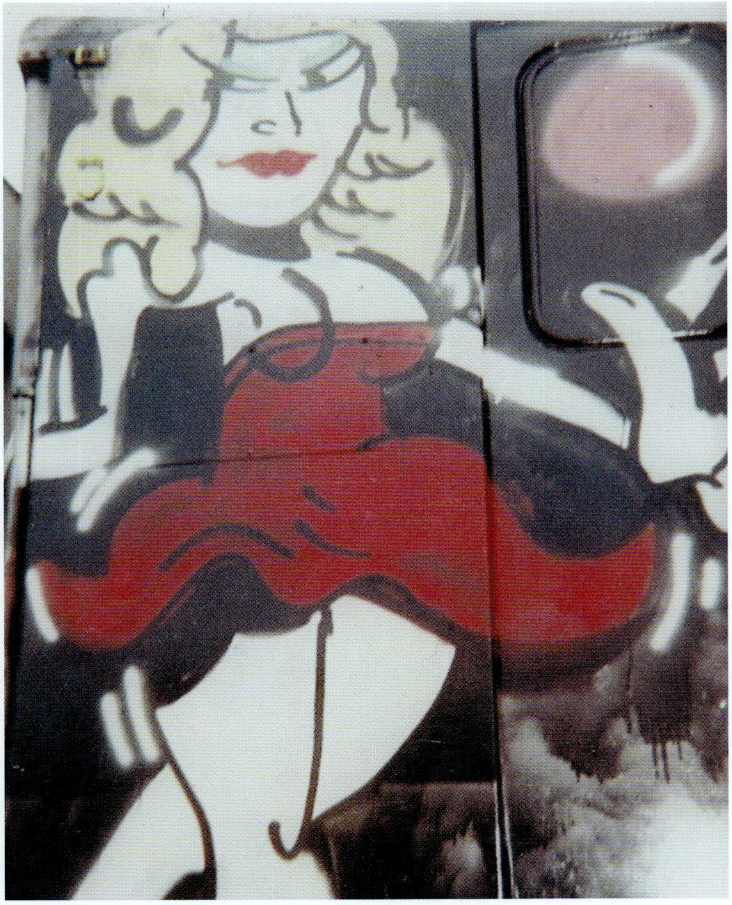

Detail of dancing girl, 1975
Photo © Blade TC5

Sketchbook page from 1979

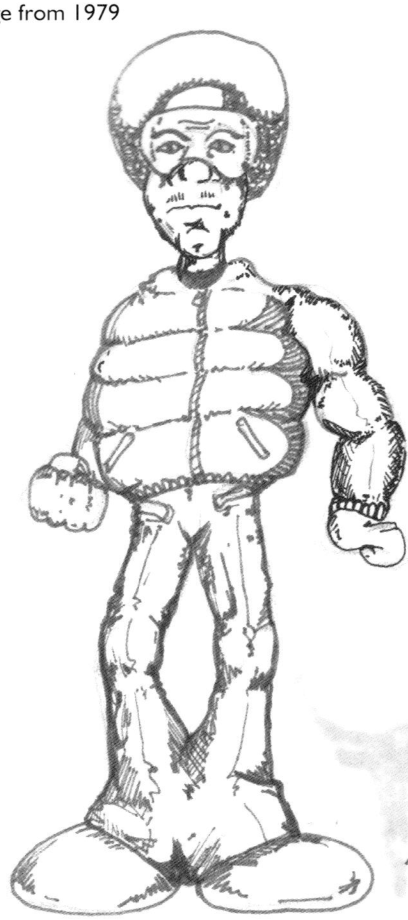

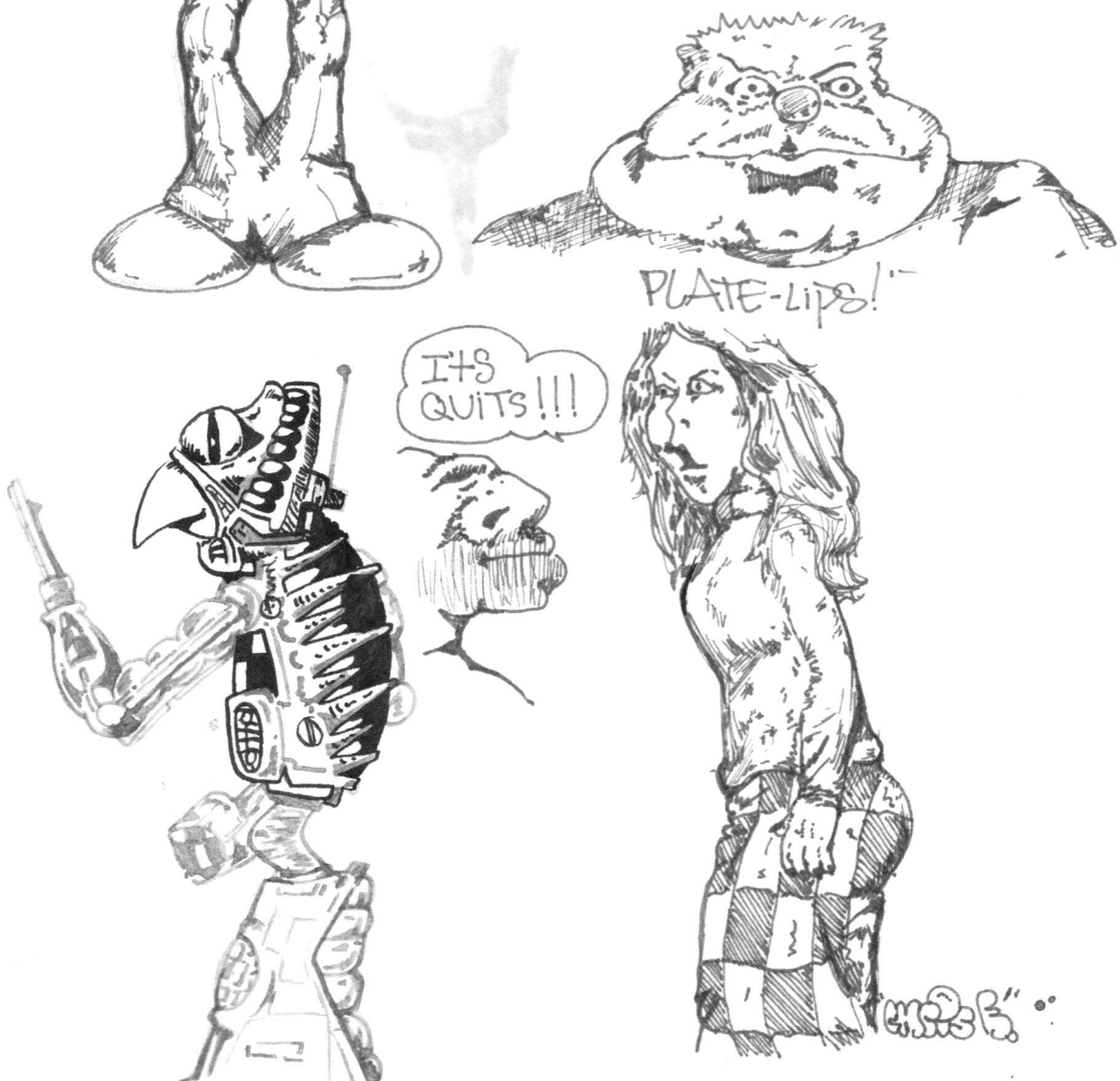

company of Don 1, King of the RRs, and Chino Malo, a recently retired style master, and his partner Inca. They had all mastered the art of graffiti, but being a couple of years older, had shifted their focus towards women and careers. Tales of their experiences and the black book sessions they presided over in the cafeteria provided Ellis with more than enough knowledge and inspiration to forge his own path to subway glory.

After hearing the call of the wild and figuring out how to answer it, Ellis (now known as Daze), along with classmates DEA 2 and 2Mad, ventured up to the 4 yard in the Bronx. Lady Luck never got the memo and their mission was curtailed by a raid. The hapless rookies narrowly eluded capture, having to separate themselves from jagged rusty fencing in effecting their escape. Failing to make his mark, an undeterred Daze returned to the cafeteria sporting fresh scabs like badges of honor as he spun his tale of woe to a captive lunch crowd. The experience made Daze hell-bent on vanquishing the subways in the same fashion established writers like Tracy 168, Blade, Cliff 159, and Stay High 149 had.

Daze began traveling to formerly unknown parts of the city to spread his newly minted moniker and secure the necessary tools for the job. The characters he'd practiced copying from *MAD* magazine for the past several years took on a new life. In addition to attending Graffiti High (Art and Design), Daze networked by making pilgrimages to the newly relocated Nation of Graffiti Artists HQ located near Crotona Park in the Bronx. Style masters like Chain 3, Tean 5 and his brother Kade, Kase 2, Noc 167, and Ree2 would often pass through, and Daze's social prowess and ambition carried him far. Not the type to wait for an invite to the most prestigious crews such as TDS, TFP, or CIA, Daze formed an internal alliance with fellow Art and Design classmate 2Mad, who had just founded the crew Crazy Young Artists. 2Mad, a tough-as-nails Spanish kid from the Bronx, had vicious lettering and character skills. CYA's other early members included Doze, Jean 13, Nak 143, and Base 2. The crew made some noise on the IRTs, garnering a good deal of attention and respect from other, more established crews. Broader recruitment followed, but CYA's longevity fizzled when 2Mad joined the military and its more talented writers enlisted in other crews.

Although Daze claims no mentors, he admittedly set out to write with the greatest artists of his era. Iz the Wiz, Dondi, Zephyr, Noc 167, Mitch 77,MED 167, PJAY ONE, Cos 207, CRASH, KEL FIRST, NAK 143, SKEME, and DEZ highlight a long list of formidable collaborators. Daze credits painting with superior writers as an infectious process that enhanced his skill set through osmosis and stirred his competitive juices. Many style masters used a multi-name approach, citing boredom with the letter restrictions of a single name. Going with that flow, Daze's other aliases included Chill 2, Wind 2, and Bode (after Vaughn Bode, graffiti's most sampled artist).

Daze credits Repel, a writer whose fame remained underground, with teaching him mechanical styles and fondly reminisces about returning to Brooklyn to

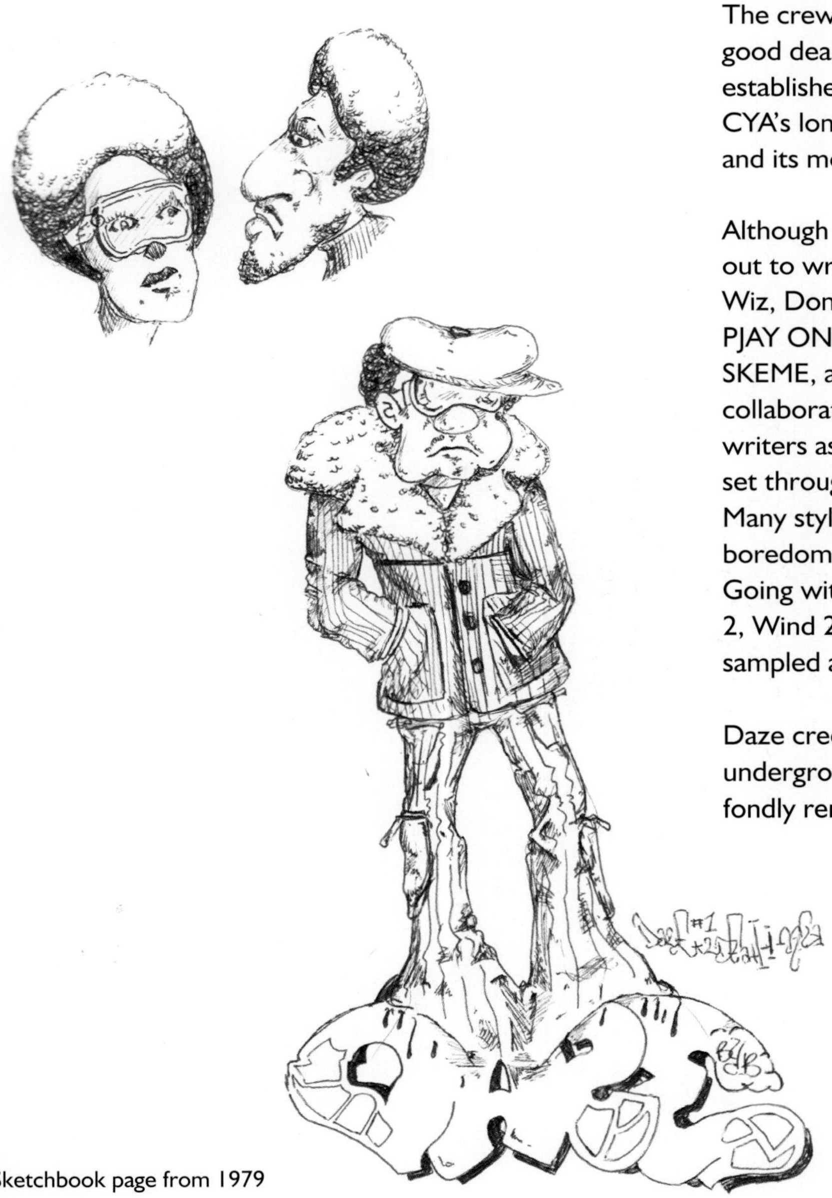

Sketchbook page from 1979

scrutinize Repel's photo albums. Straight up shots of works by The Fabulous 5 and a vast selection of cars by Bronx IRT style master Billy 167 highlighted the collection. Daze never focused on throw-ups or insides, activities that required hitting an entire yard for effectiveness. Instead he concentrated on quality, executing the most artistic pieces he could, feeling that he'd get more shine that way. As his reputation grew, he began to envision art as a livelihood.

In 1980 Daze attended Soul Artists meetings with the likes of Futura 2000, Dondi, Zephyr, Ali, and an unknown art student named Keith Haring. That same year he cut his teeth on canvas when he participated in The Esses Studio project. Art-loving businessman Sam Esses loved the work he saw on the subways and yearned to put the brakes on the moving masterpieces by capturing them on canvas. The project curated by Zephyr and Futura 2000 included Cos 207, Kel 139, Crash, Dondi, Seen, Noc 167, and other notable writers of the period.

By 1981 Daze had become a fixture at Fashion Moda, an alternative art space located in the South Bronx. The space that was founded by Stefan Eins and Joe Lewis had recently allowed Crash to curate a graffiti-themed exhibition called *Graffiti Art Success*. Crash and Daze soon started getting commissions to paint signs and backdrops. In 1981, Daze participated in the *Beyond Words* show at The Mudd Club, curated by Futura 2000, Fab 5 Freddy, and Keith Haring. The show was considered groundbreaking for bringing uptown and downtown together, and resulted in Daze's first sale. Ironically, the several small paintings Daze contributed failed to sell. But an impromptu tag he took alongside a tag by Jean-Michel Basquiat on a piece of newspaper that covered a refrigerator caught a collector's eye. The purchaser, renowned art critic Rene Ricard, would later lose the piece in a fire. The fifty bucks Daze got from the sale made him feel like a million and hear the beat of a different drum. In the early '80s he and Crash rented a Bronx studio together and have maintained various spaces in the borough ever since.

Daze at Esses Studio, 1980
Photo © Henry Chalfant

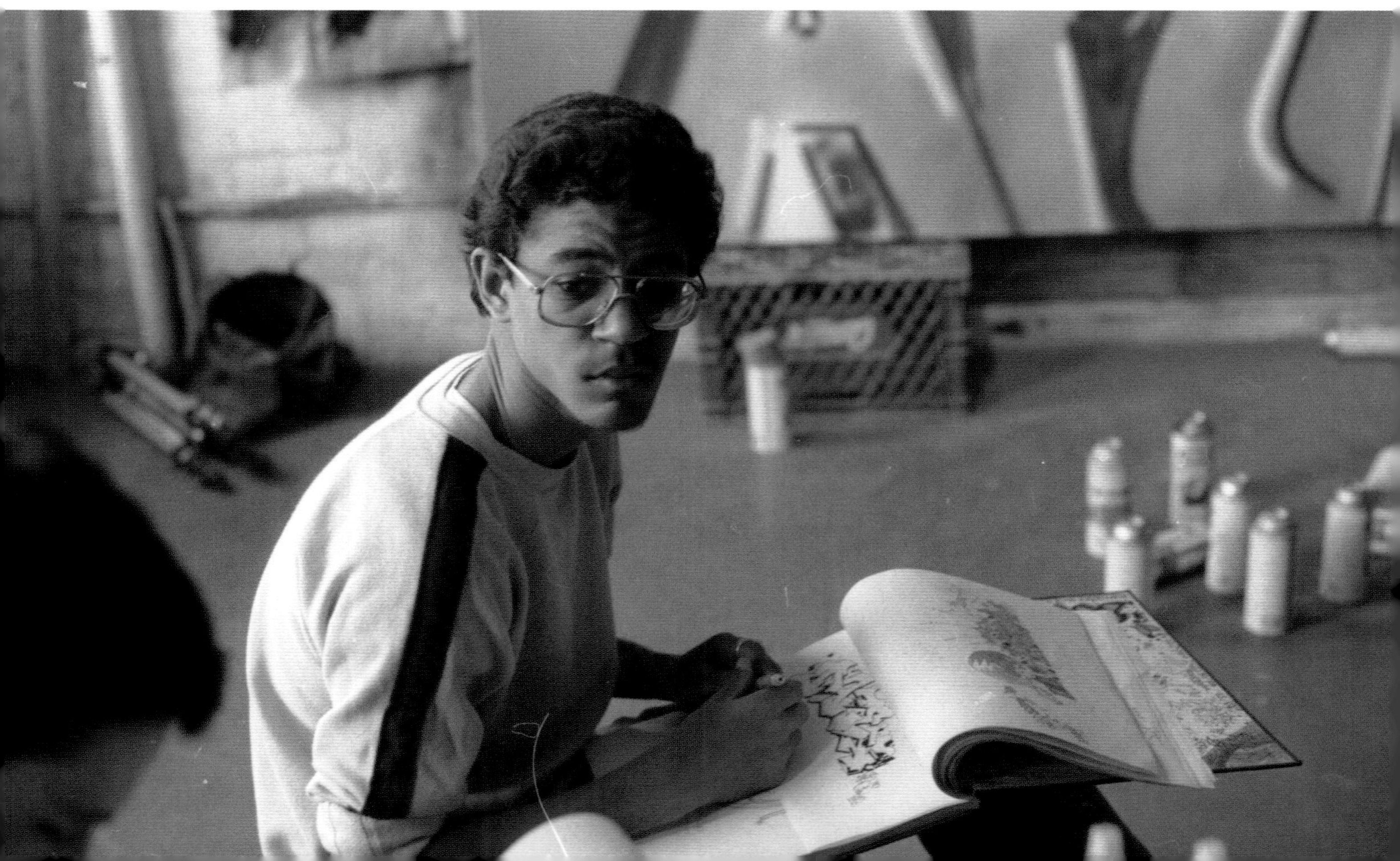

In an effort to capitalize on graffiti's growing commercial momentum, Mel Neulander, a fur salesman with a fierce mercenary instinct, and partner Joyce Towbin, who came from an art background, enlisted Crash as a recruiter for their new gallery venture. Crash, excited by the idea of bringing the Fashion Moda experience to a downtown audience, recruited a lineup comprised of old-school graffiti legends such as Tracy 168, Wasp 1, Iz The Wiz, and Caine 1 and paired them with current writers such as Daze, Erni, Cey, Freedom, Noc 167, and Lady Pink. The gallery, known as Graffiti: Aboveground (also known as GPI), was in the Meatpacking District and attracted media attention and well-heeled collectors, enabling many artists the opportunity to create and sell canvases for substantial prices. GPI folded after a two-year run but provided valuable access and training for artists to cash in on the feeding frenzy for graffiti art. Finding himself at a crossroads, Daze grew weary of splitting his time between creating pro bono masterpieces in train yards and lounging in clubs with the likes of Madonna and John Lurie while galleries beckoned.

In 1984 Daze retired from the exhausted medium of the subways to pursue his dream of becoming a fine artist. He draws a couple of parallels between subways and galleries. First and foremost, the obsessive work

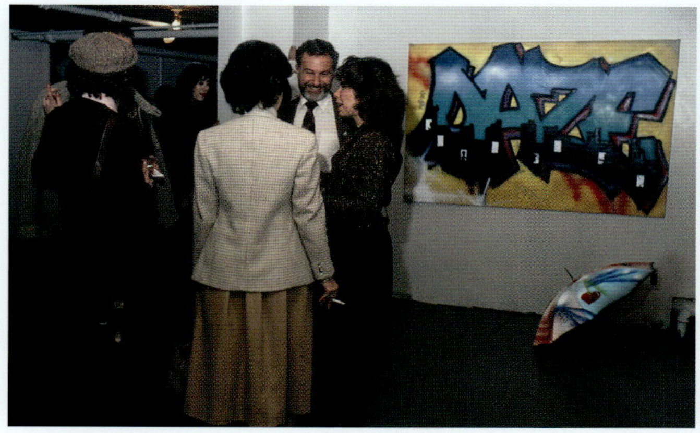

Opening at Graffiti: Aboveground gallery, 1981
Photo © Martha Cooper

Opening at Graffiti: Aboveground gallery, 1981, featuring paintings by Crash and Daze
Photo © Martha Cooper

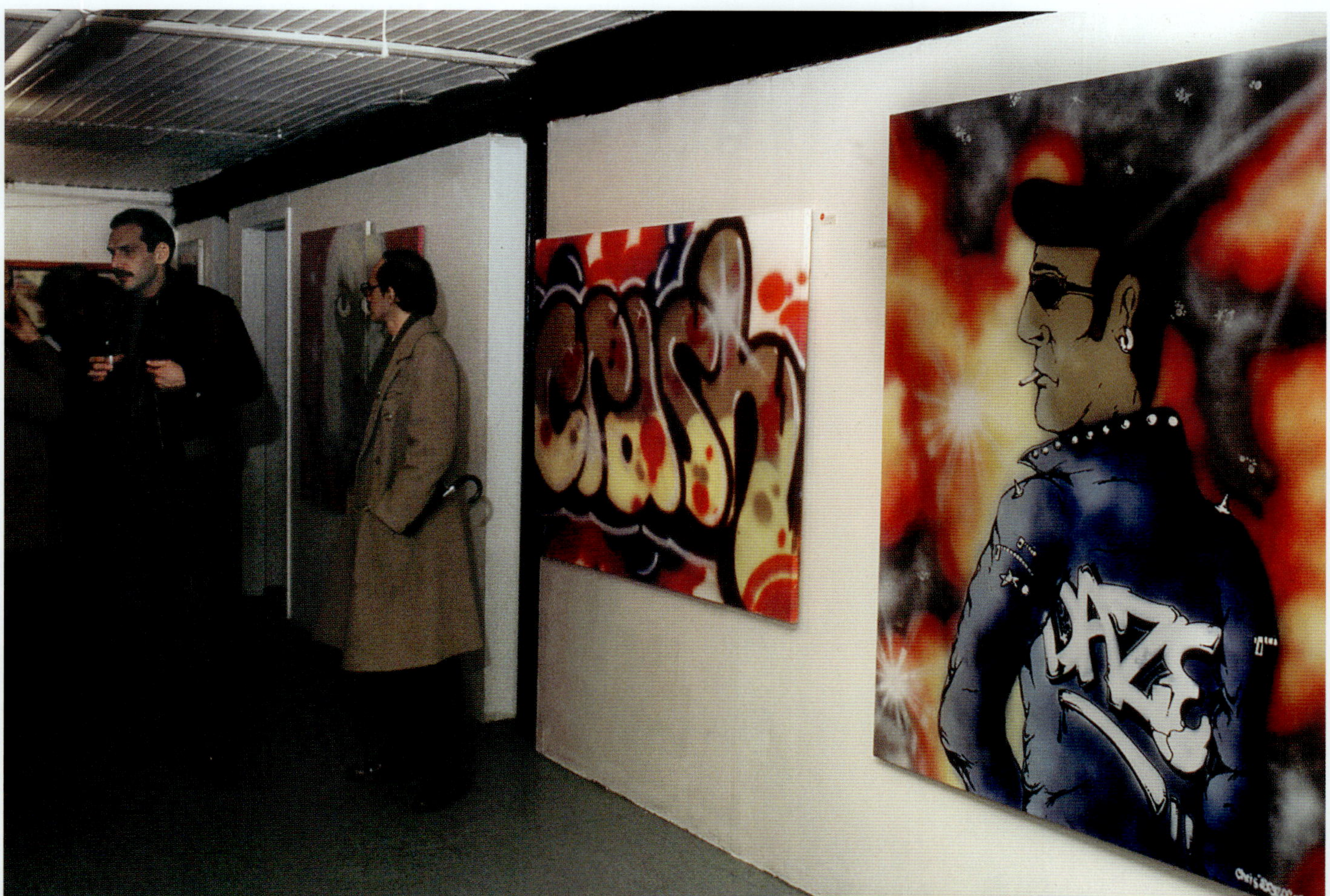

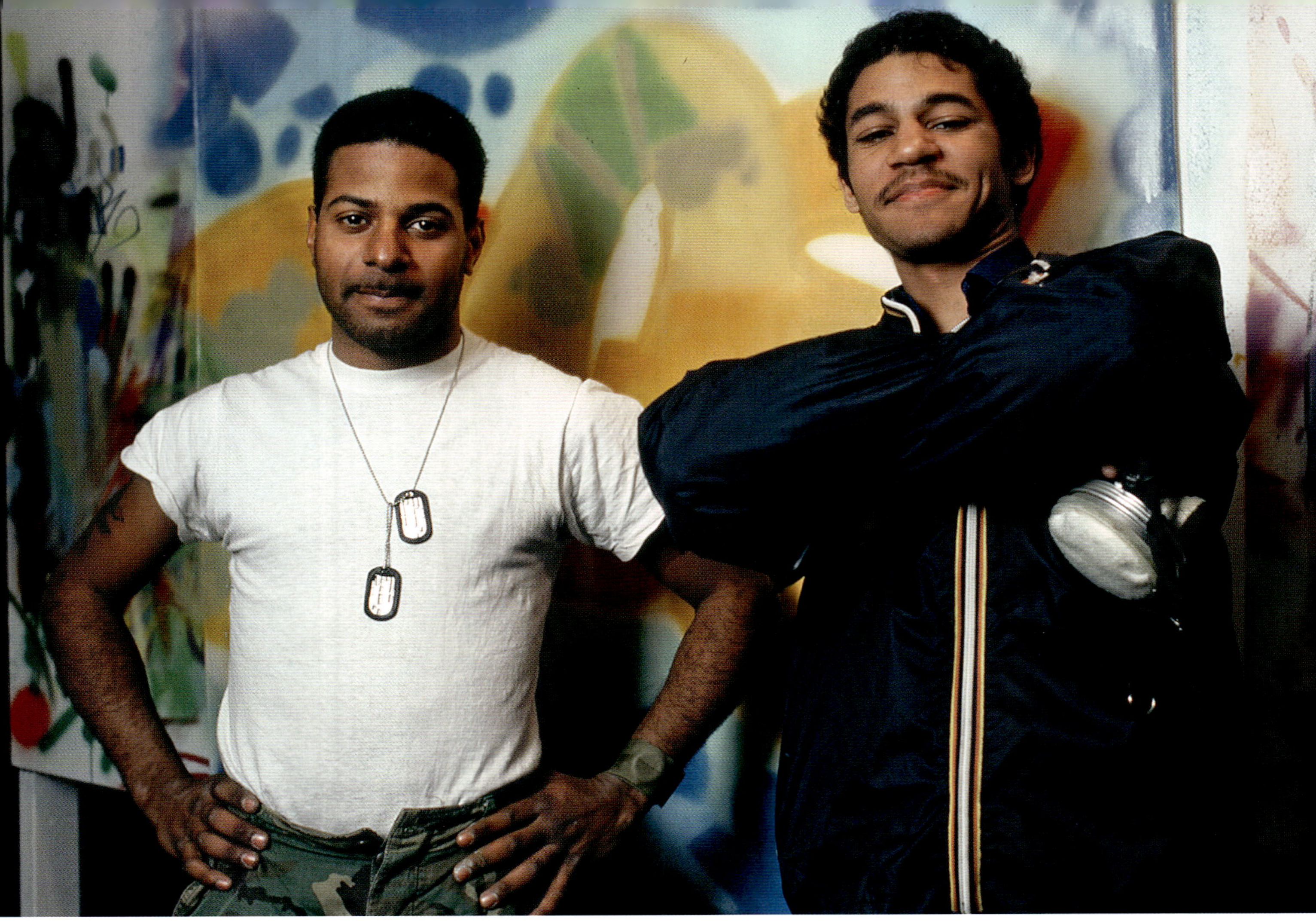

Cos 207 and Daze at Graffiti: Aboveground gallery, 1981
Photo © Martha Cooper

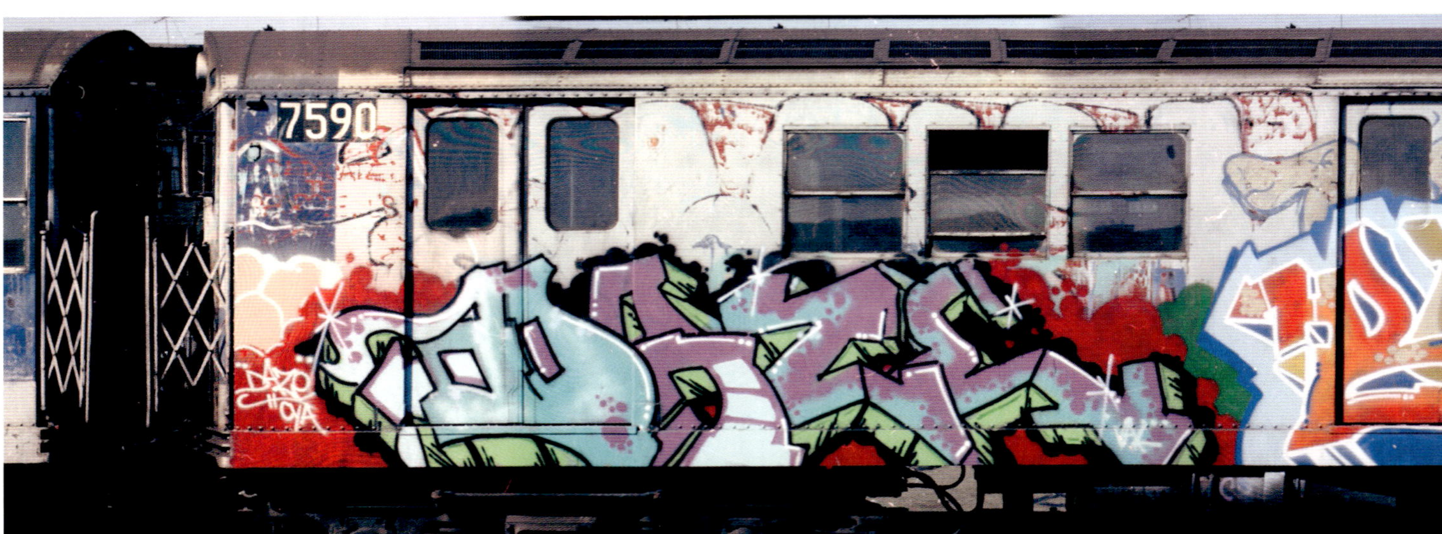

ethic he employed while attempting to dominate the trains has remained with him. Secondly, although his work became more figurative, he credits the makers of Krylon, Rustoleum, and Red Devil for the development of his formidable color sense.

Daze rocked trains from 1976 to 1984—years he considers graffiti's greatest. Whole cars got painted every night, with writers going all out in their attempts to burn each other. During this time Daze participated in the films *Style Wars* and *Wild Style*, and photos of his pieces appeared in Martha Cooper and Henry Chalfant's book *Subway Art*; these projects blurred the lines between graffiti and hip-hop cultures. Although he acknowledges both cultures share a mutual place of origin, Daze believes that's where the similarity ends and that they are in fact autonomous.

Daze's artwork has put bread on the table since the mid-'80s, and though he would prefer to be remembered as a fine artist more than as a subway painter, he recognizes the value of both. The subway paintings inspire kids in a way that museums never could. Museum paintings offer an artist permanence, mainstream exposure, and respect.

A portrait of John Coltrane, a saintly image of Stay High 149 floating in a subway tunnel, swimmers frolicking in the Coney Island surf, and painted women of all varieties line the walls of Daze's South Bronx studio. Bound for the Brooklyn Museum, the Museum of the City of New York, or a collector's home, the paintings pull in and out like the trains at Utica station. The racks of vintage spray paint and a few stored burners from the '80s, which Daze remains attached to and has kept, serve as the only bridge between past and present.

After attending 2015's Basquiat notebook exhibition at the Brooklyn Museum a few blocks away from his old apartment, Daze had an epiphany as he waited for the subway home. A train disguised as a Target ad pulled into the station—Blade's dancing girls, now septuagenarians, nowhere to be found.

Jay J.SON Edlin (born Bronx, New York, 1958) started writing graffiti in 1973 under the names TERROR 161 and later, J.SON. In 1975 he founded the Broadway-based writing crew The Masters of Broadway (The MOB). He has been documenting the graffiti scene for over two decades and published his first book, Graffiti 365 *(Abrams), a global survey of street art and graffiti, in October 2011.*

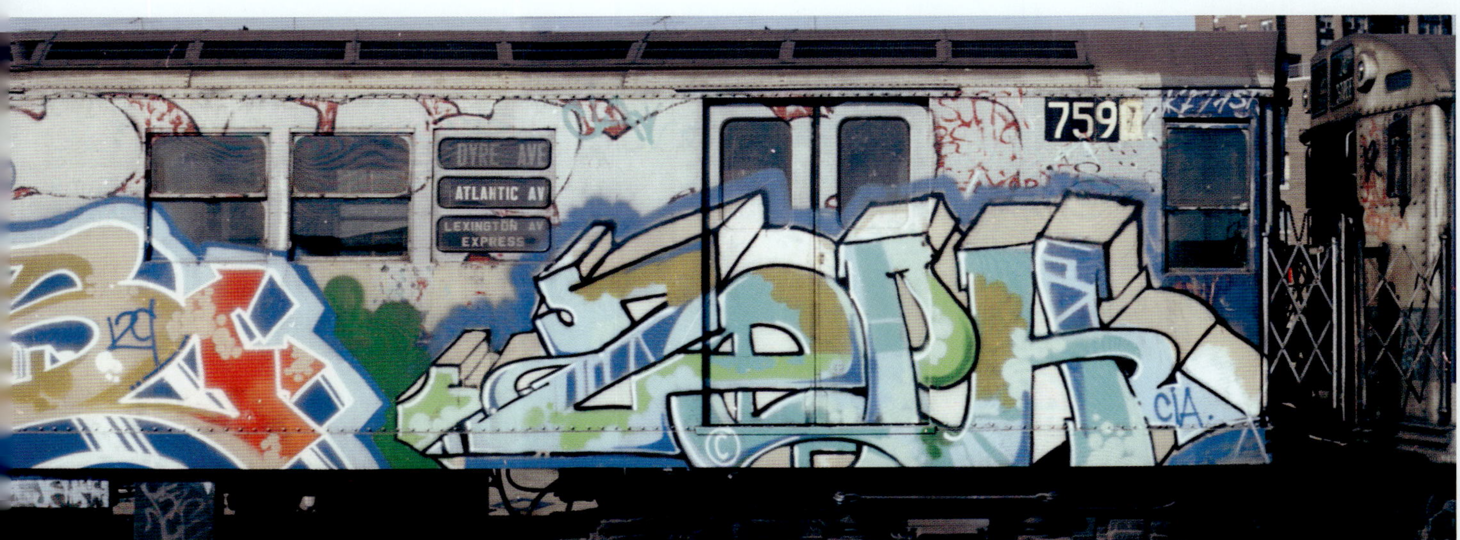

Daze-Bus129-Zeph
Photo © Henry Chalfant

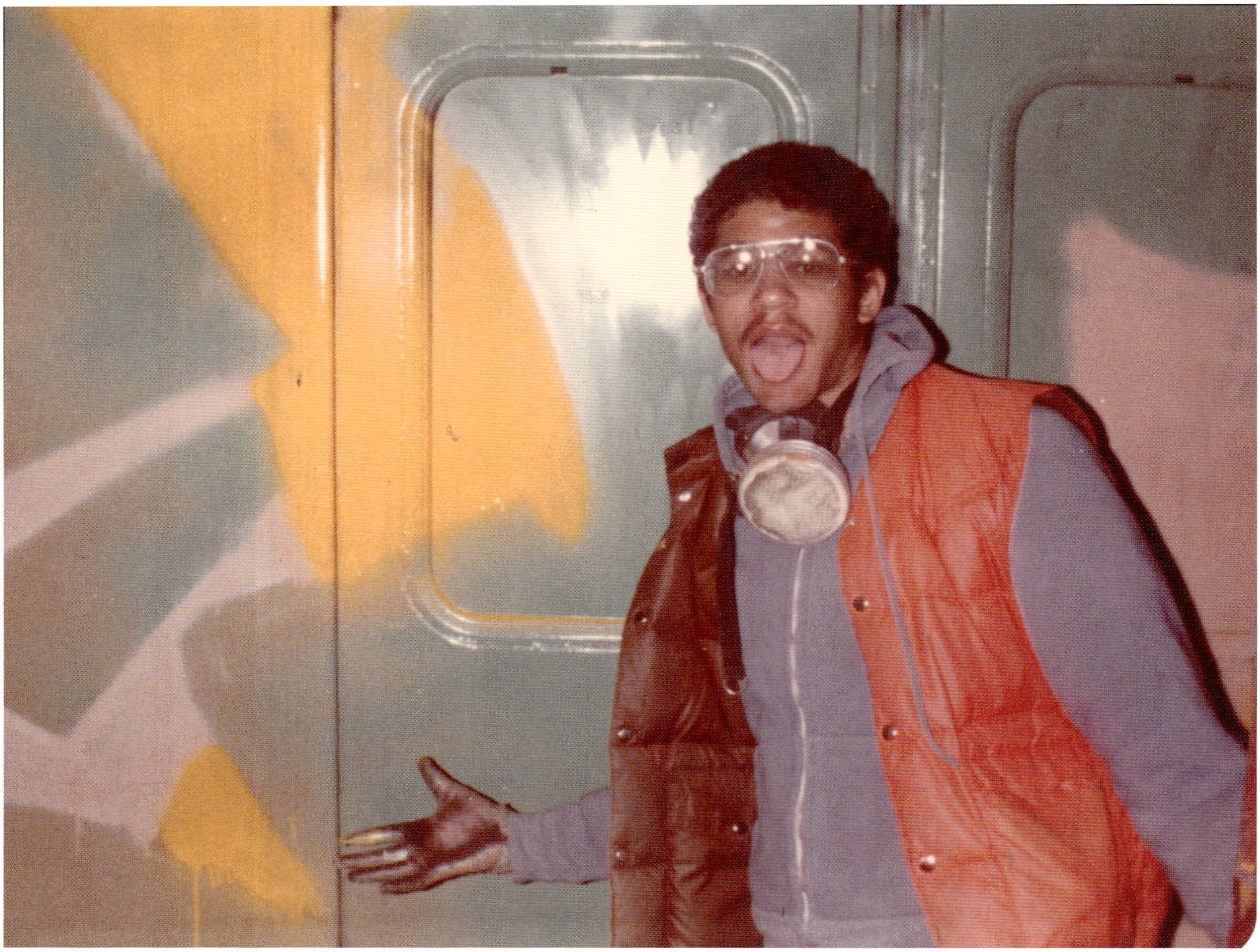

Tunnel action
Photo courtesy of Iz The Wiz

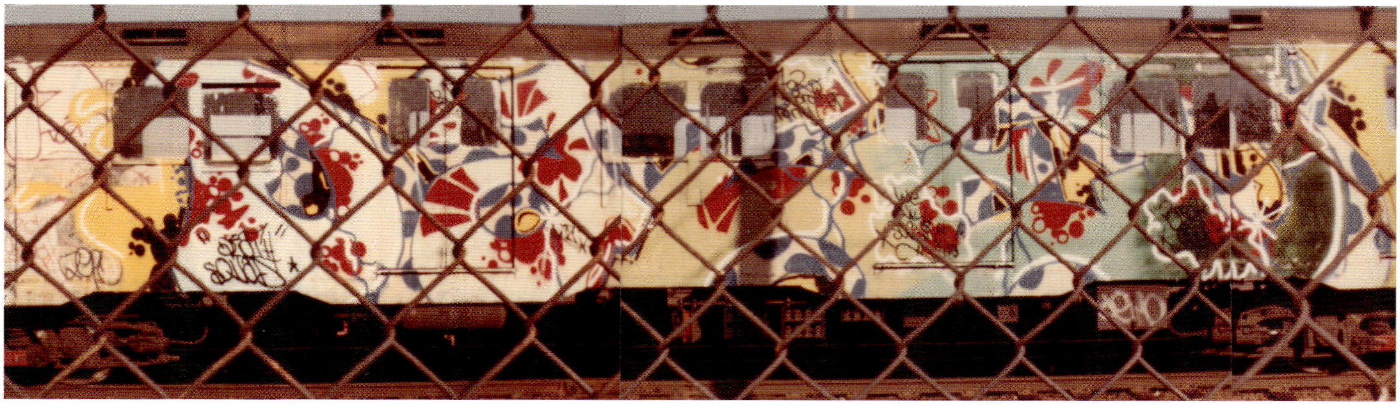

Daze, top to bottom
Photo courtesy of Iz the Wiz

CHAPTER 4
THE EARLY '80S

My initial introduction to the art world of the early '80s was a slow but steady one. People tend to reminisce over the events that took place during that period as if they encompassed the entire decade, but in actuality most of the key events that transpired happened between 1980 and 1984. I think that period becomes a bit elongated in memory because so much was condensed within a small period of time. Week after week, art events, parties, happenings, press, and media attention both national and international took place. By 1984, however, a lot of that attention started to die down quickly and only the most stalwart were able to acclimatize themselves to the new conditions that surrounded them.

During 1980 I was still immersed in the world of subway painting. I painted trains on a regular basis with my partner Crash and others such as Base2, Nac, Mitch77, and Repel, to name a few. At this time Futura 2000, Zephyr, and Ali had reformed the Soul Artists under the auspices of a storefront workshop on the Upper West Side. One of the good things about the workshop was that it gave people a place to find us if they needed to. Eventually a man named Sam Esses made the foray uptown to the workshop. Encouraged through his daughter's friendship with Zephyr and Haze, he became smitten with the work he saw there and with the high quality of work being done on the trains. With Futura

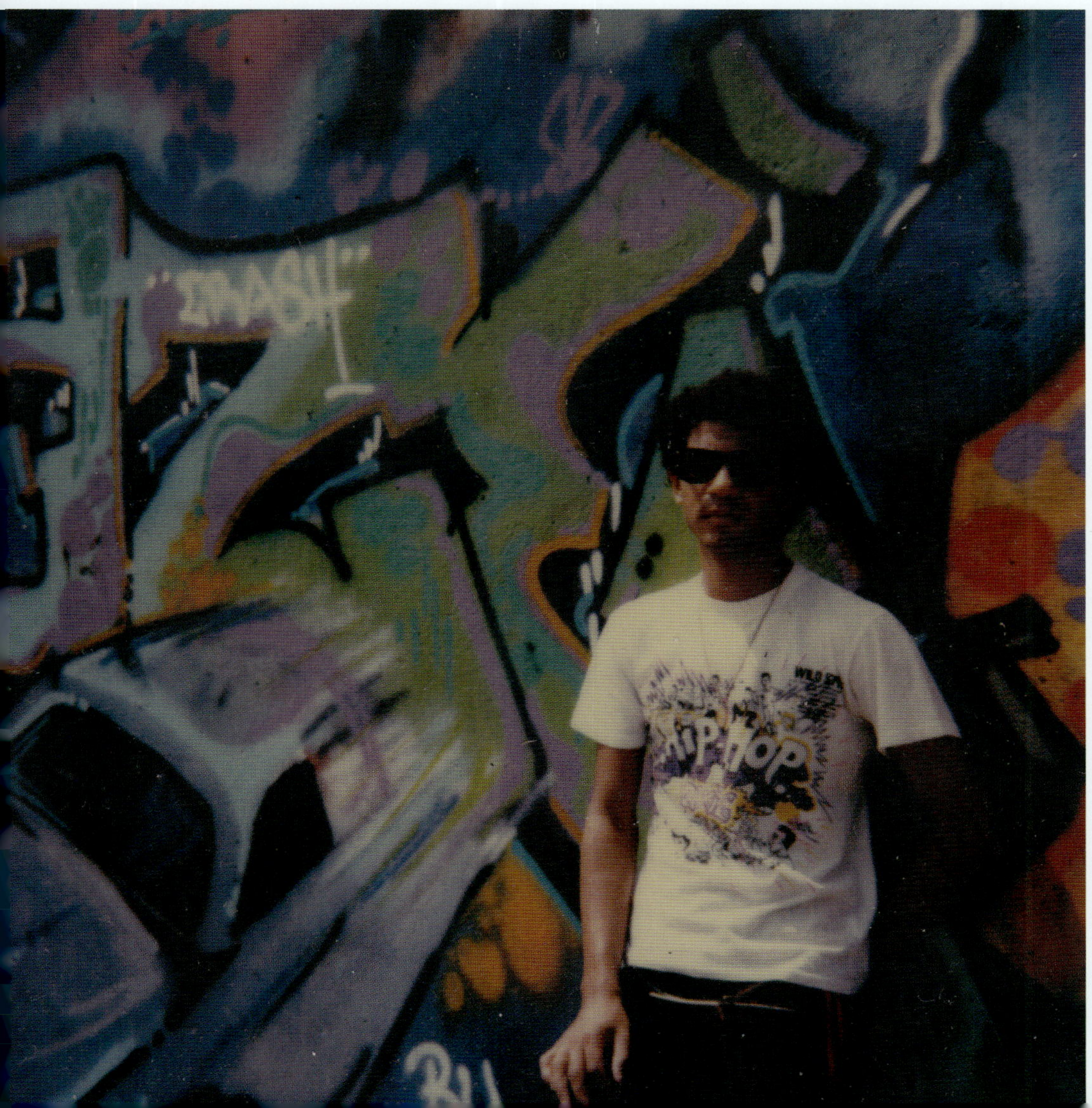

South Bronx, 1984
Photo courtesy of the artist

2000 and Zephyr at the helm, a graffiti painting workshop was set up in a space on the Upper East Side, and many of the city's best writers were invited to paint canvases. Sam's original idea was to preserve some of the best work being done on the trains. In essence I think he was almost trying to create a kind of art time capsule. At any rate, I was invited to participate in this event, and it was my first initial foray into painting on canvas. It was the first time that I used spray paint without looking over my shoulder for a work bum, a cop, or other writers. Unfortunately Sam Esses's heirs did not share his artistic vision. Ultimately they sold the entire collection for an undisclosed amount, giving the artists absolutely nothing for their work. This example serves as a glaring form of exploitation on the part of the heirs who profited 100 percent from the sale.

Daze-Tue, Latin action comes to the RR line
Photo courtesy of the artist

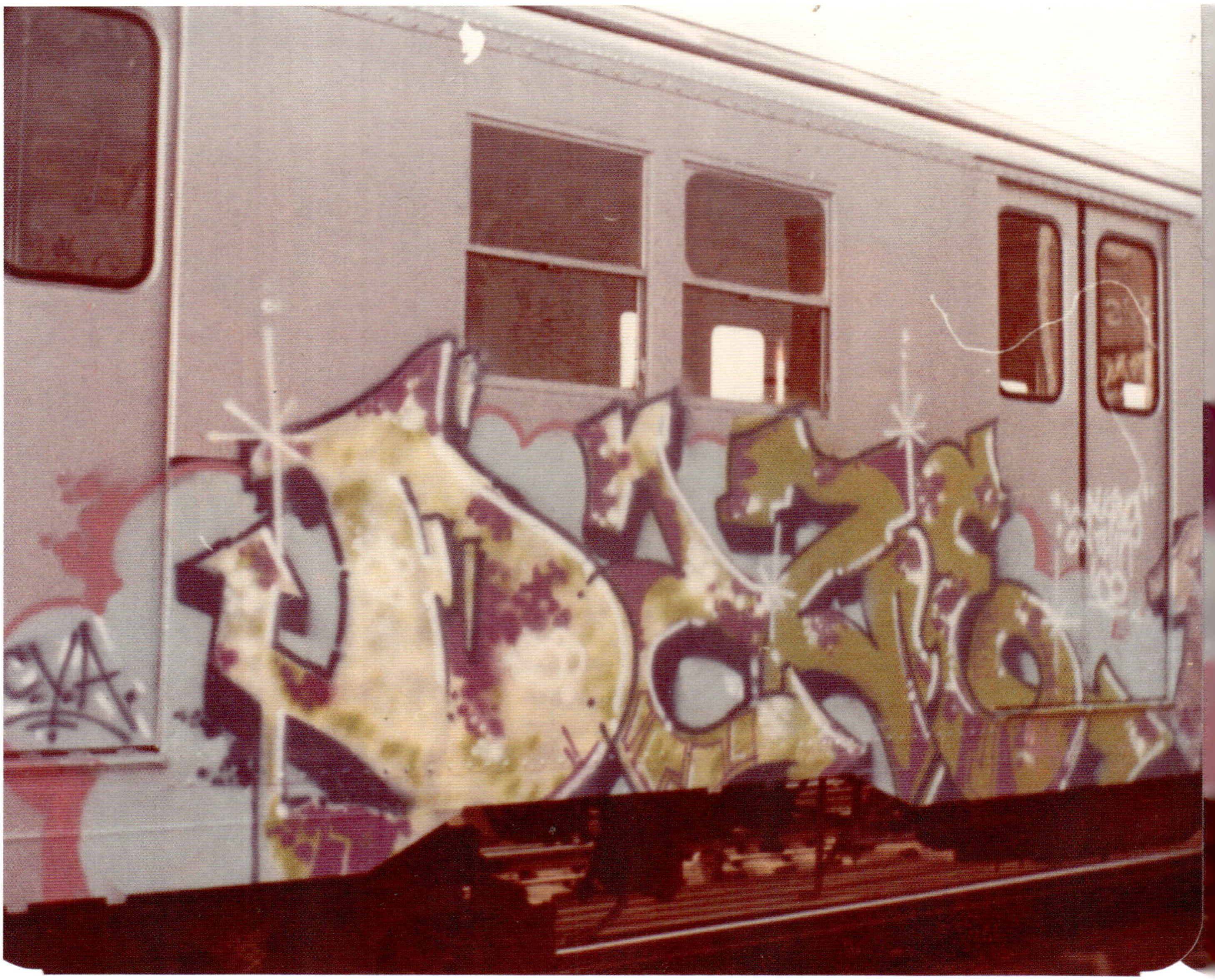

I think that anyone who's truly artistic allows room for development and evolution. Without such, one cannot excel and the work eventually becomes stagnant. I always allowed room in my development for inspiration and experimentation in other mediums. When I began making my first paintings at the Esses studio, both of those elements came into play. I looked at painting on canvas as a new and challenging medium in which to

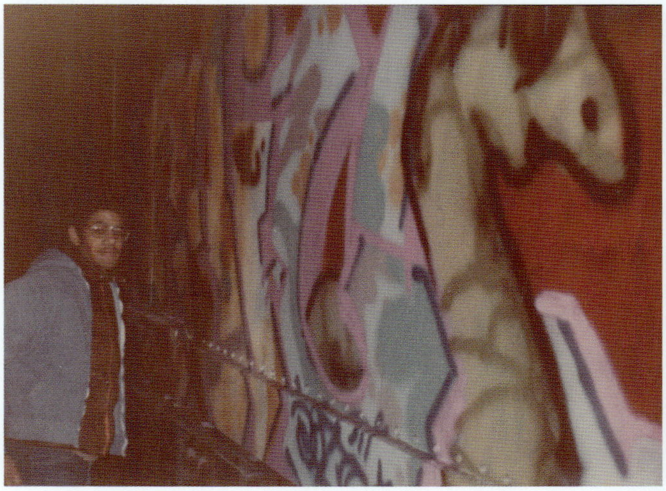

Self-portrait next to Chill2 piece
Photo courtesy of the artist

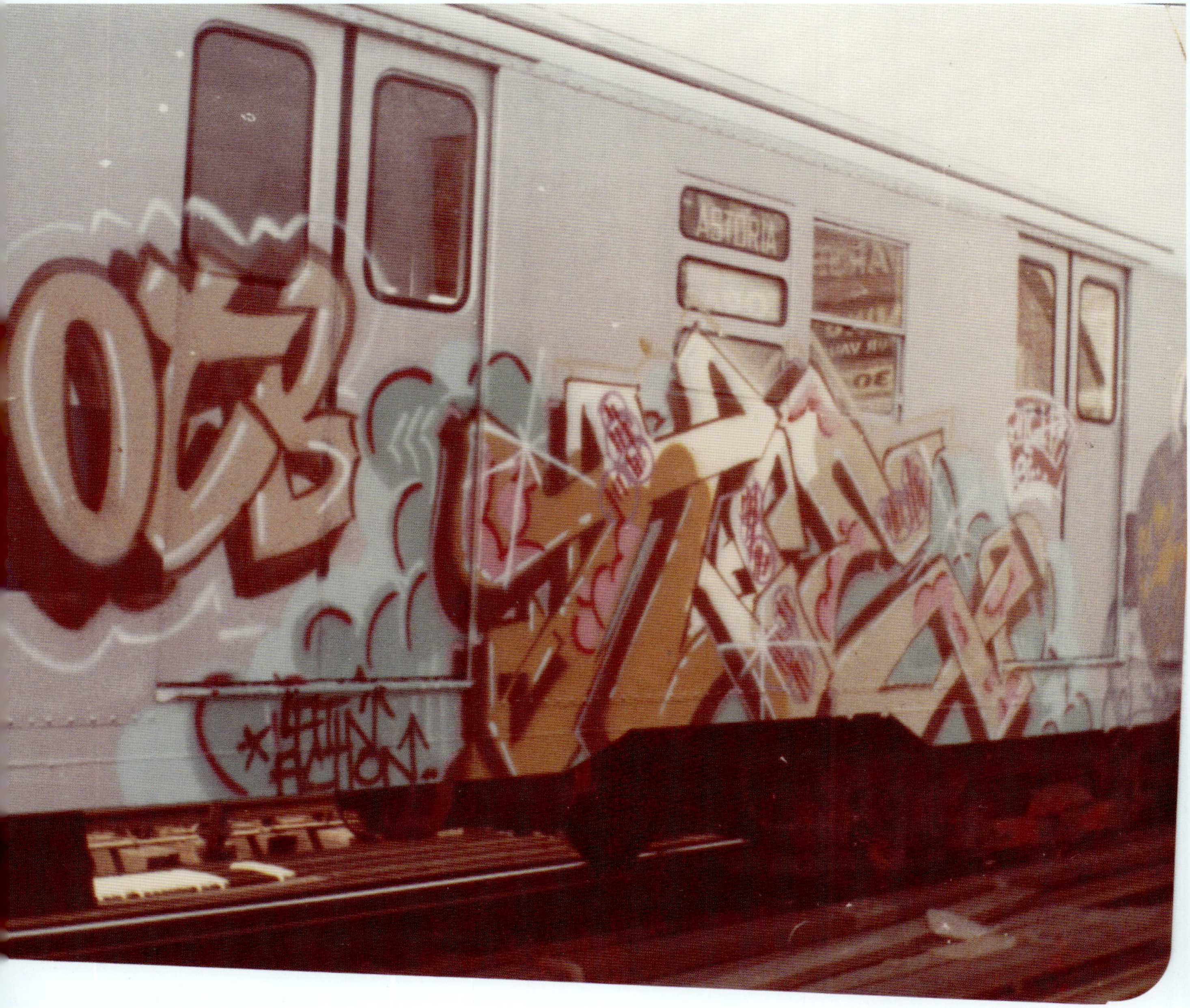

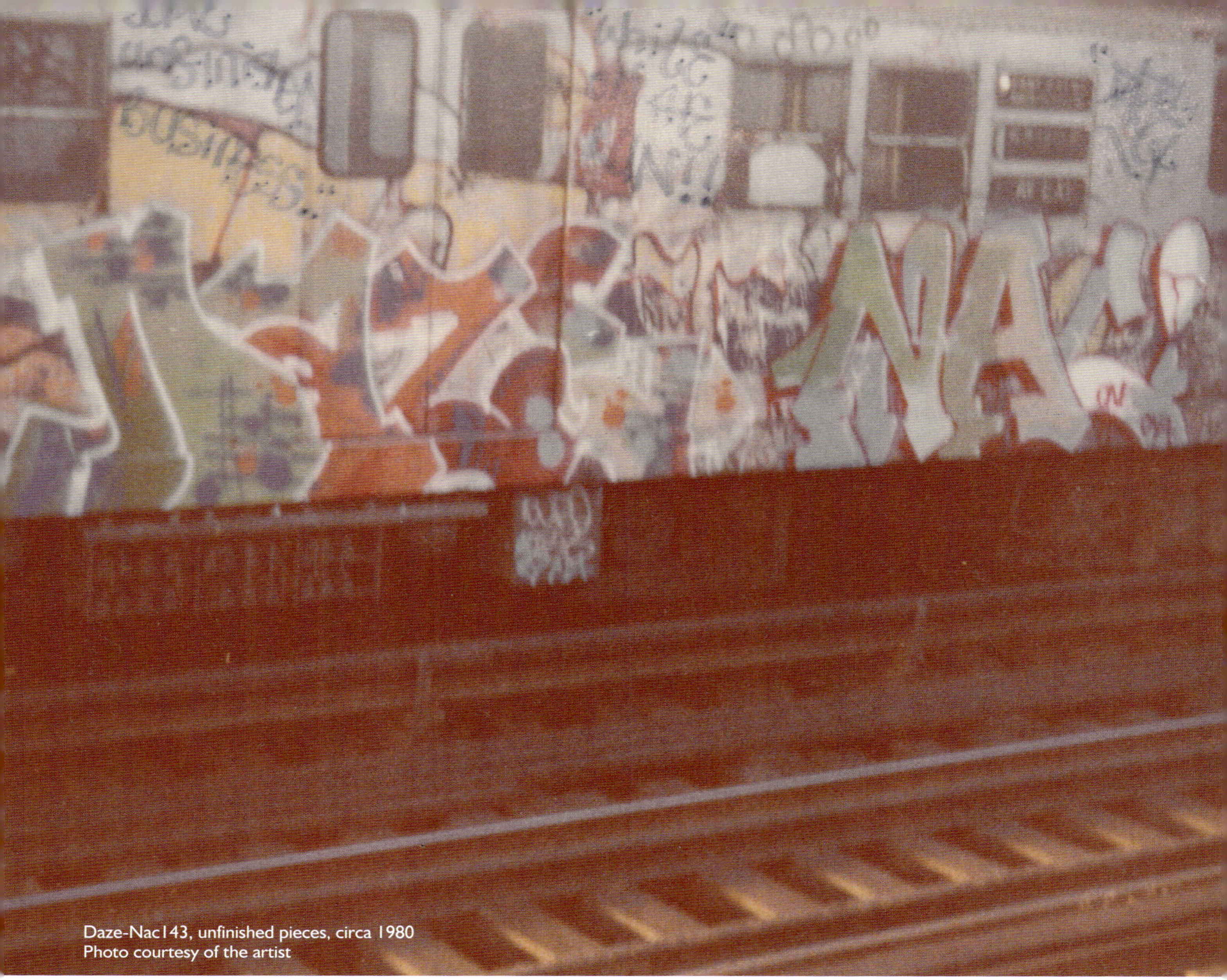

Daze-Nac143, unfinished pieces, circa 1980
Photo courtesy of the artist

express myself more clearly. At the time I had no professional aspirations to enter the gallery world. I was just interested in spray paint on canvas as a medium in which to express myself.

The Esses studio was a huge success in many ways. Many writers who didn't have access to each other met for the first time, and the studio became yet another place for the media to find us. Once the media started to get a hold of this new formerly underground story, things took off like an express train between Hunts Point and Parkchester Avenue. Through all of that and the eventual end of the Esses studio, I continued painting canvases by day and trains by night.

The next series of events happened so fast that in hindsight it seems like a runaway thoroughbred with the rider holding on for dear life. Crash was invited to curate an exhibition at Fashion Moda called *Graffiti, Art, Success,* which eventually traveled to the New Museum. Soon after, P.S. 1 in Queens held an exhibition curated by Diego Cortez, called *New York, New Wave*, that featured many of the top writers including Dondi, Lee, and Zephyr alongside the likes of Jean-Michel Basquiat, Keith Haring, Nan Goldin, and many others. Another pivotal exhibition was the *Beyond Words* show that was curated by Fab Five Freddy and Futura on the fourth-floor gallery space of the Mudd Club. Actually it was during this show that I

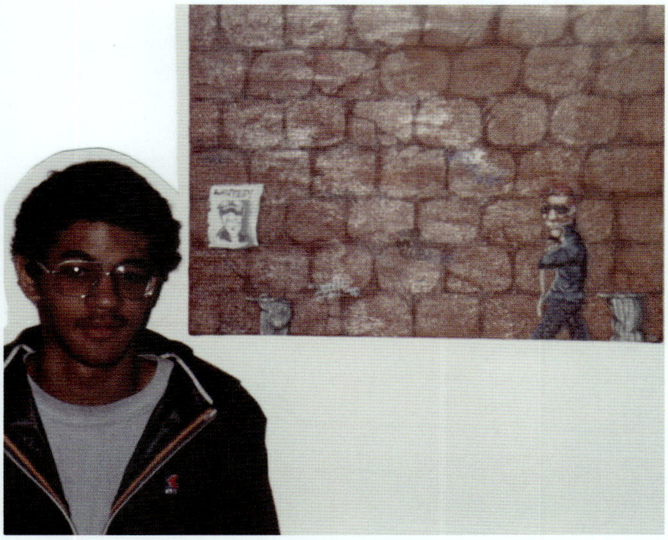

Self-portrait at the *Beyond Words* show at The Mudd Club
Photo courtesy of the artist

sold my first work of art, a piece of newsprint wrapped around a refrigerator tagged by Jean-Michel Basquiat, Poke, and me. Influential art critic and poet Rene Ricard bought the piece and simultaneously wrote an article for *Artforum* magazine called "The Radiant Child," in which I was mentioned.

I think one of the most exciting things that took place in those initial early years was the mixing of opposite ingredients such as the downtown/uptown scene, and the punk/hip-hop scene, and fusing those elements together. This cultural mash-up was the impetus for many influential trends in music, art, and fashion years later. The climate in those early years was one of inventiveness and inclusivity and many artists were given their first few rays of exposure in this new world. For me, this new scene was exciting and at times intimidating. I felt, even at that time, that a lot of the attention that was being given was almost of a sensationalistic nature and did not delve too deeply into

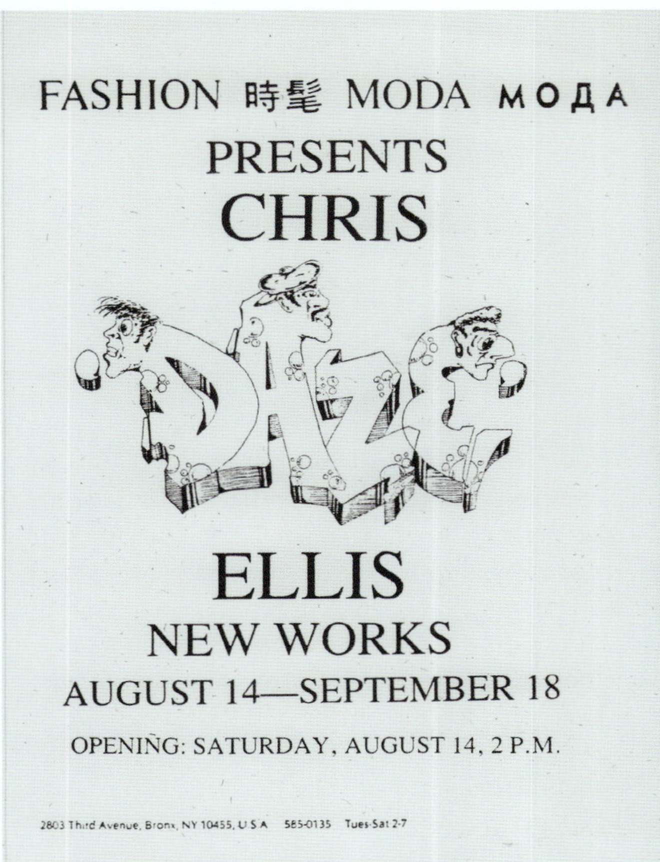

Fashion Moda invitation for my first solo exhibition
Bronx, New York

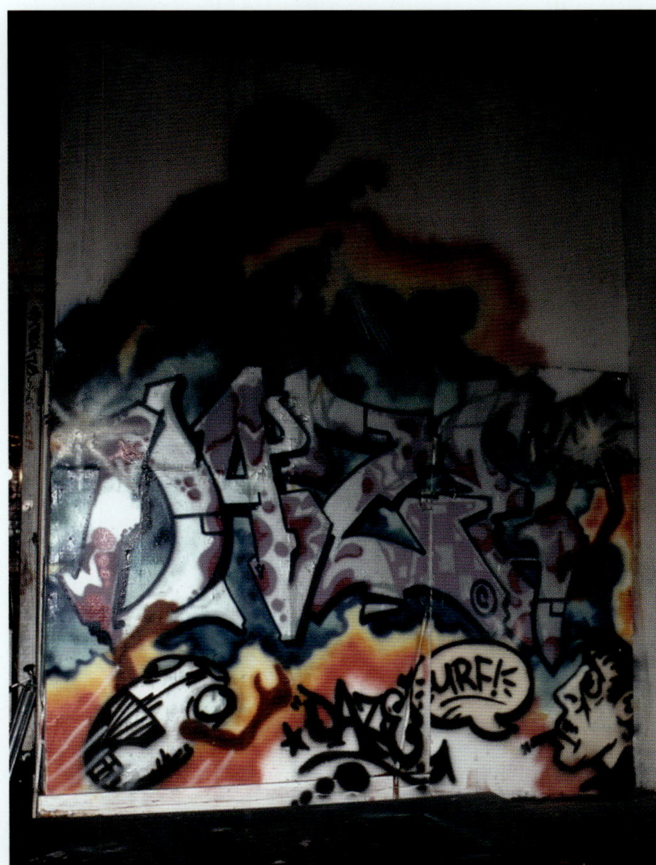

Fashion Moda installation
Bronx, New York, 1982

trying to understand the artists or the movement. Still, I looked at it as a challenge and an opportunity, and soon Crash and I were having exhibitions on an international level in galleries and museums worldwide. Even at a young age both of us seemed to have a similar work ethic, so with the first inklings of money received from painting sales we pooled our resources and rented a painting studio on 149th Street in the Bronx where we remained for the next seventeen years. This proved to be a crucial decision for us as it gave us our own place to work without interference from anyone. It also gave dealers and collectors a place in which to view both finished and unfinished works in progress. The studio was a place where we could create our own dialogue among paintings. We were able to spend weeks working on a painting for the first time instead of mere hours.

It's hard to believe, but at that time I simultaneously kept a foothold in the underground train-painting scene. During the early '80s I painted some great cars with Skeme and Dez, who later would come to be known as the famous DJ Kayslay. Skeme and Dez enabled me to

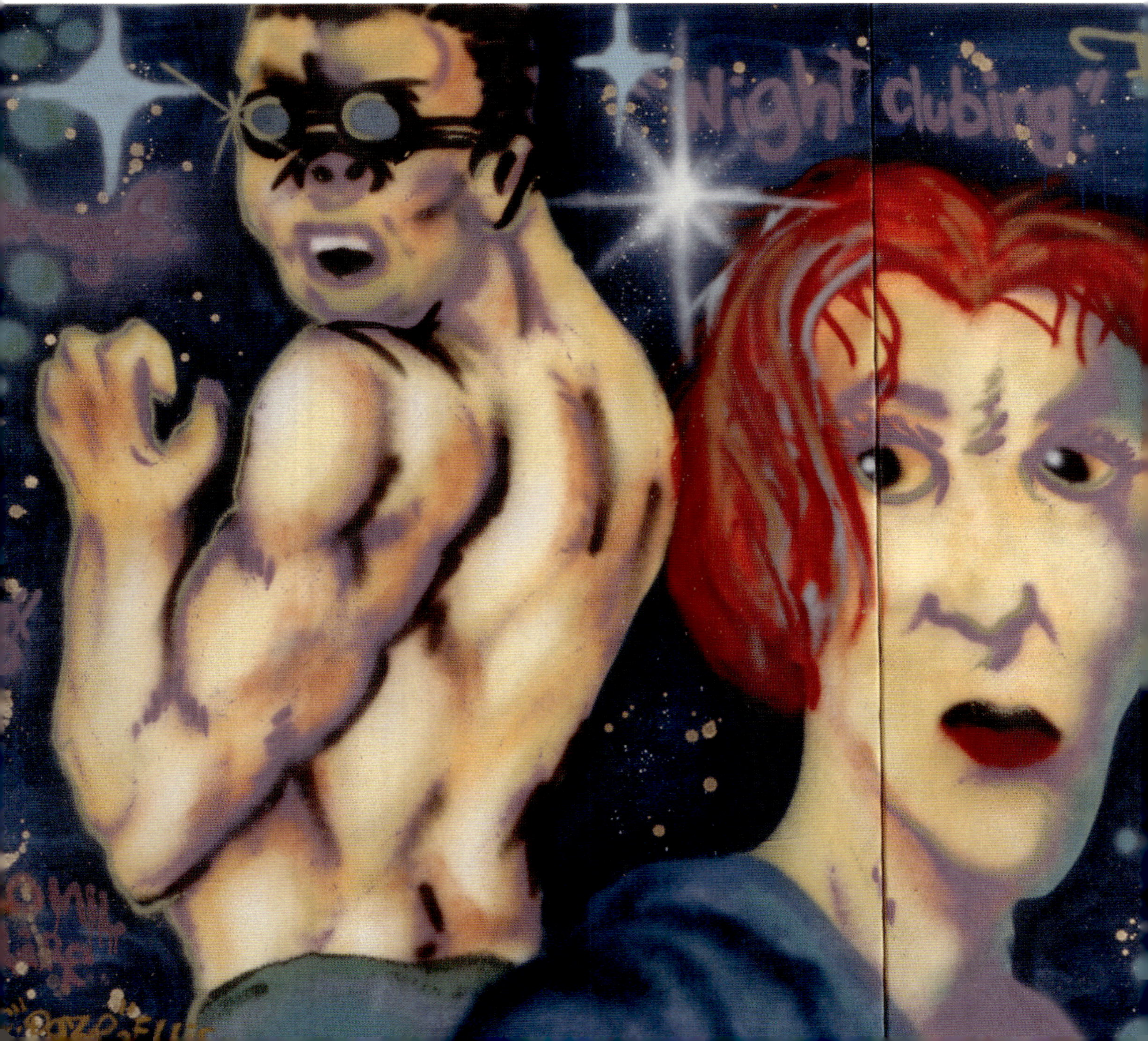

have my last hurrahs in the New York City transit system. Most of the cars that we pulled out were courtesy of the 3 yard, which was a great place to paint but was a difficult line to photograph because the whole line remained underground. Nevertheless those cars were eventually transferred to the 1 line and we'd get great photos on 125th Street. At one point I thought about those amazing photos that Martha Cooper had taken of Dondi in action in the 2 yard. I invited her to document Skeme, Dez, and me in action, and she jumped at the chance. I couldn't believe how courageous she was inside the yard. She was amazing! After climbing through a hole cut in the fence, she lowered herself down to the track and followed us across the many lanes of laid-up trains. Eventually we found the perfect row of cars, and we each staked out a car. Dez and Due 2 executed a top-to-bottom whole car, while Skeme painted a window-down whole car that read "Skeme-O-Matic." Our boy Con did a piece and bombed insides while I set out to do a memorial car for the recently deceased Caine One that read "Daze and Caine." Martha documented it all from start to finish, even

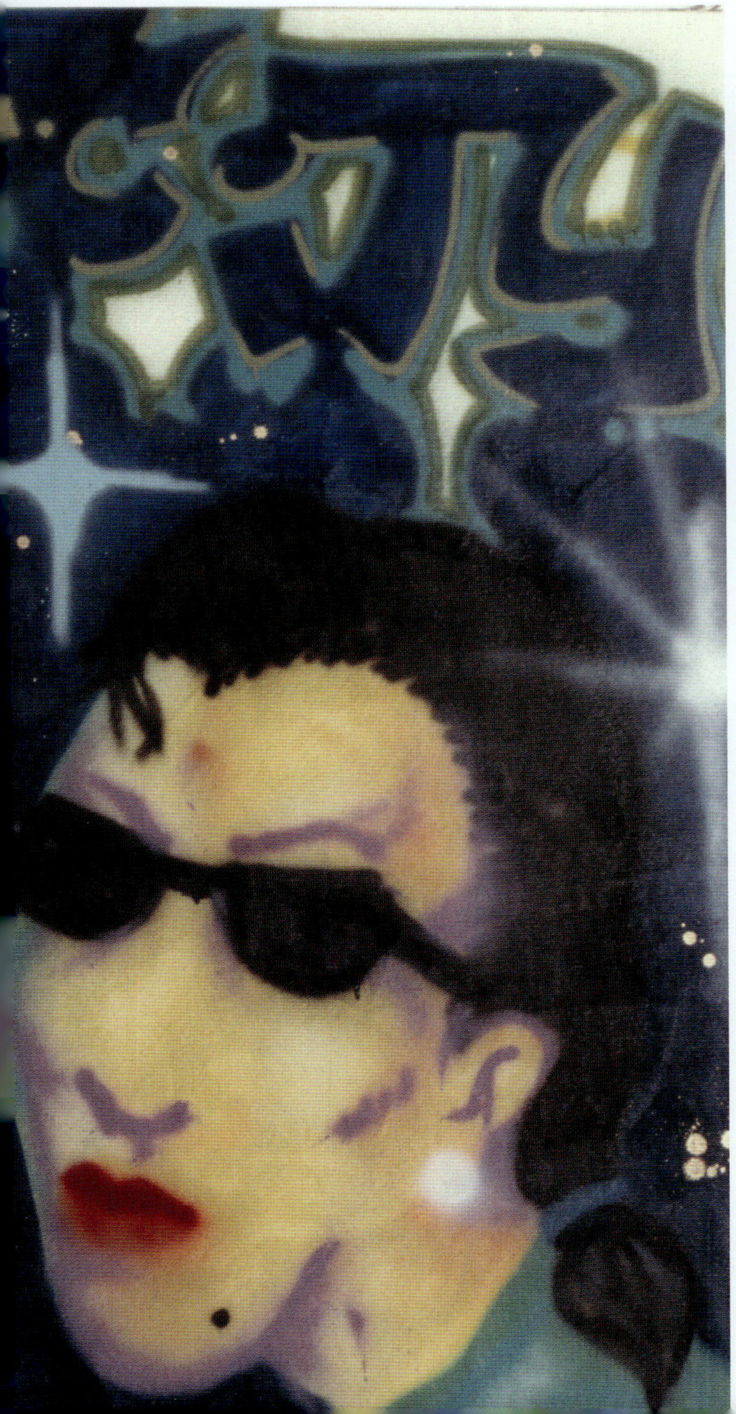

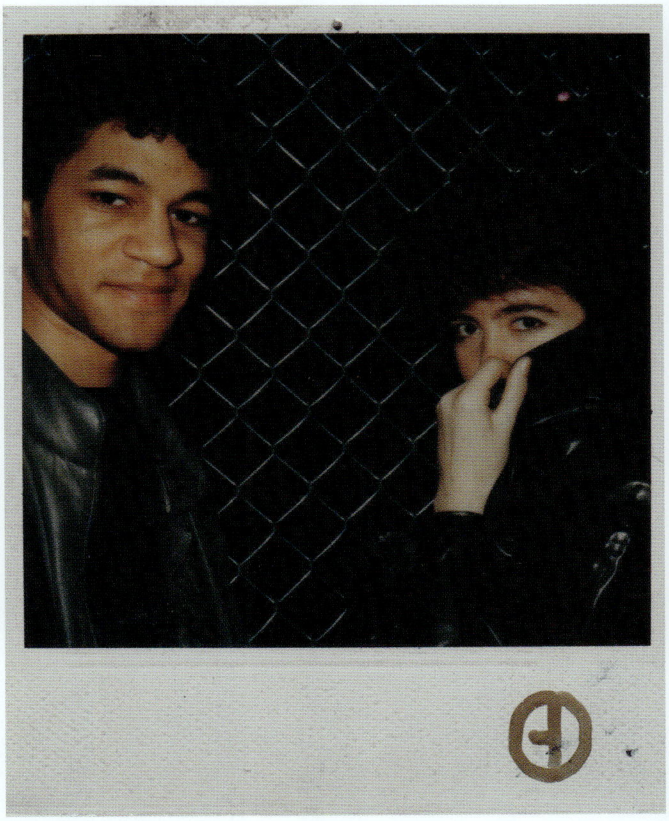

Area Club, 1983
New York, New York

Night Clubbing, 1984
Spray paint on canvas, 72" × 120"
Collection of the artist

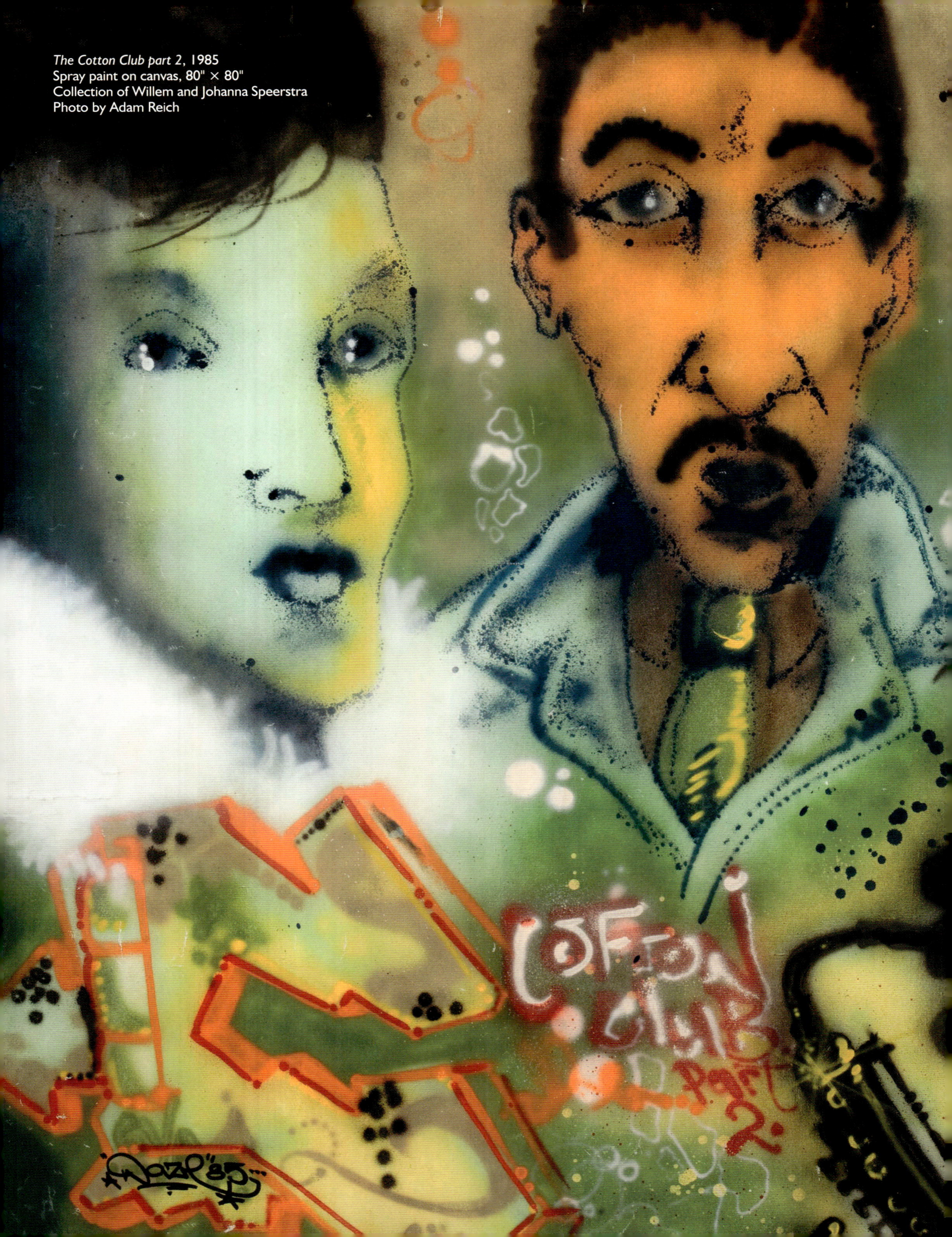

The Cotton Club part 2, 1985
Spray paint on canvas, 80" × 80"
Collection of Willem and Johanna Speerstra
Photo by Adam Reich

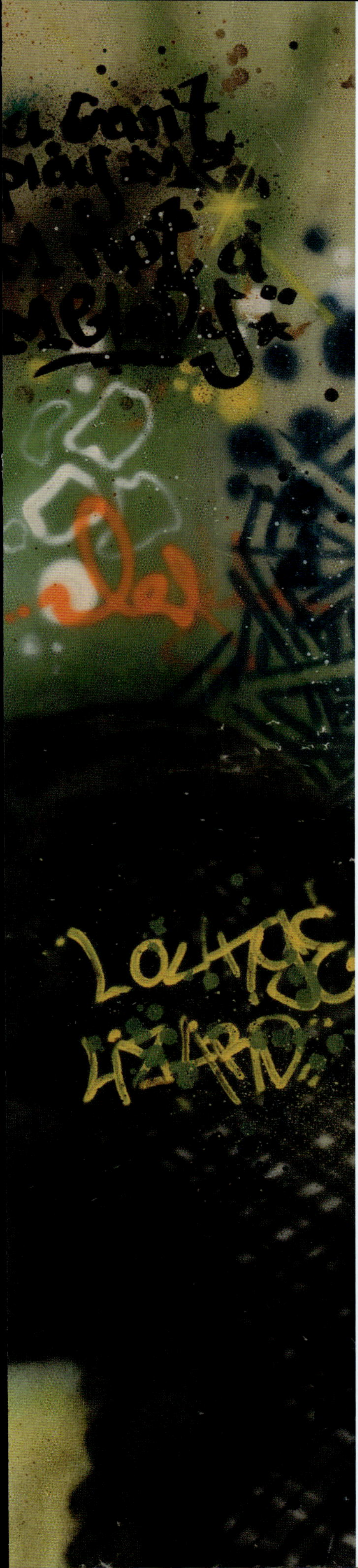

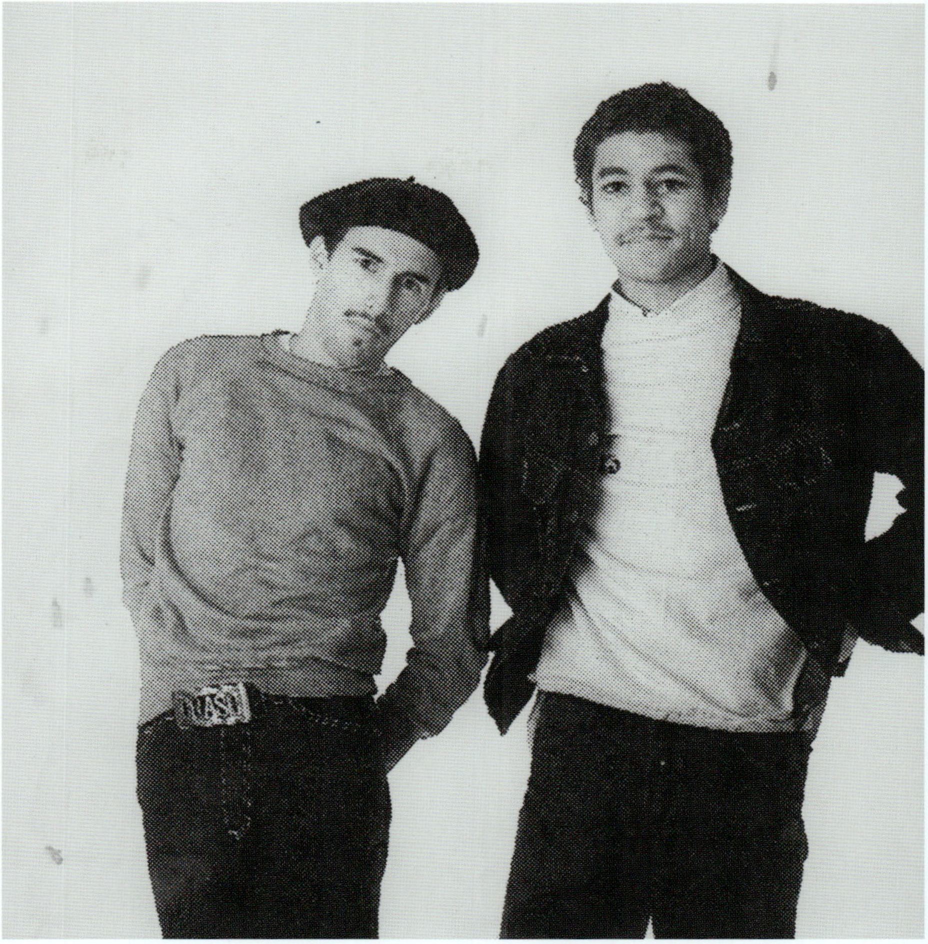

Crash and Daze
Photo shoot for *Per Lui* magazine

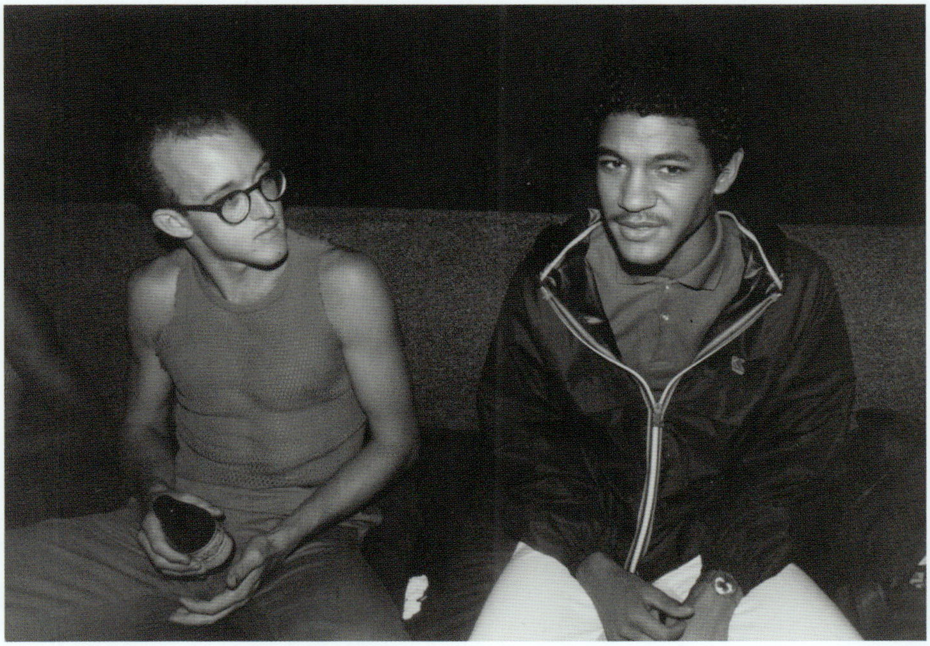

Keith Haring and Daze at The Roxy, 1984
Photo © Fatima Ingraham

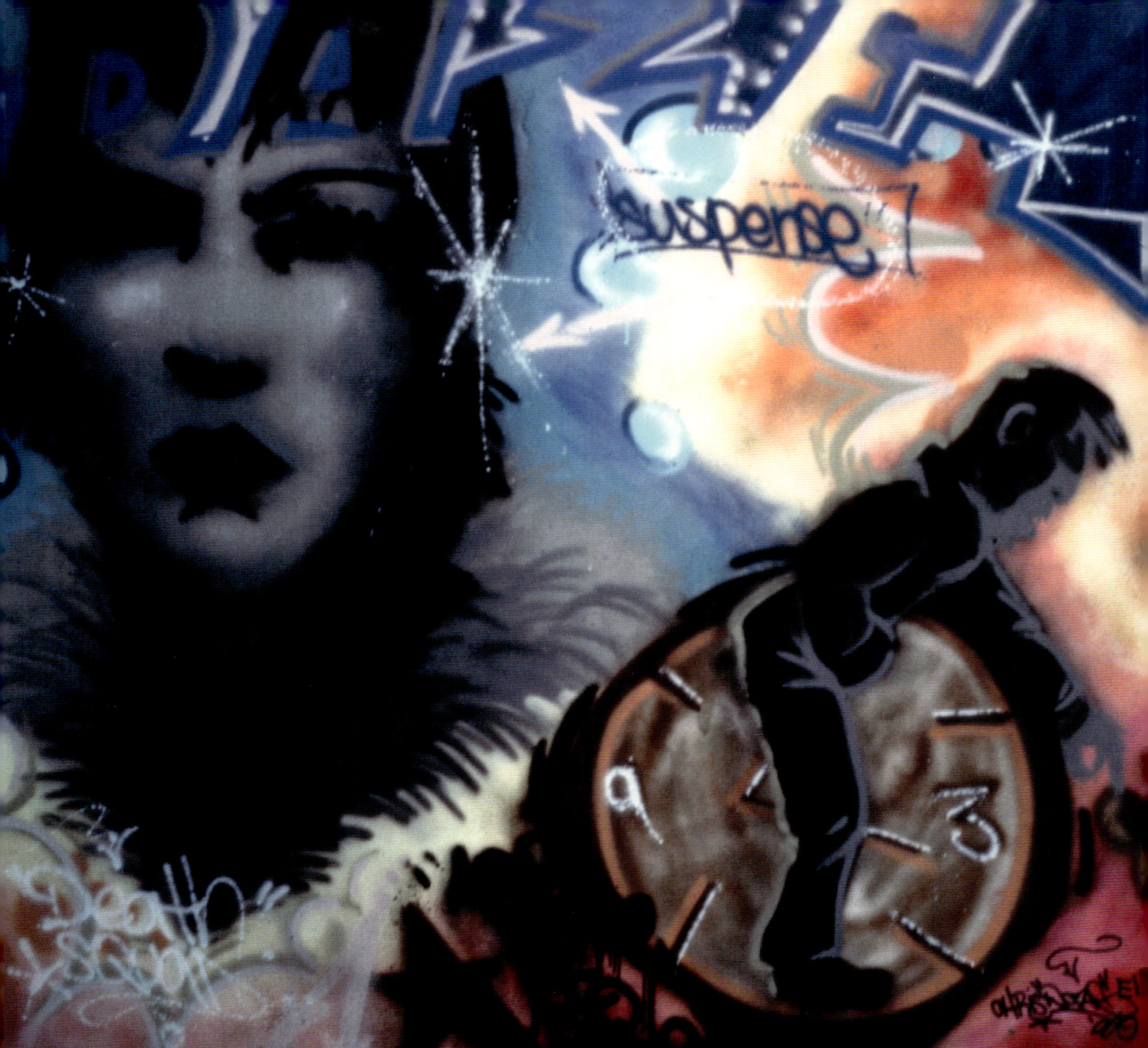

Captivator, 1983
Spray paint on canvas, 80" × 80"
Private collection

climbing on top of the train to get the right shots. She was and remains an amazing photographer and I'll always look at the resulting photographs of that night as the perfect documentation of a typical night for us. I should also mention that photographer, sculptor, and filmmaker Henry Chalfant's SoHo studio was yet another place where writers could congregate and view some of the amazing photographic documentation of trains he had amassed. His studio acted as a catalyst for exchanging information within the movement. All this was captured in several scenes in his incredible documentary *Style Wars*. Henry's studio was the ground zero of inspiration for many of the whole-car productions that proceeded to pull out during that period.

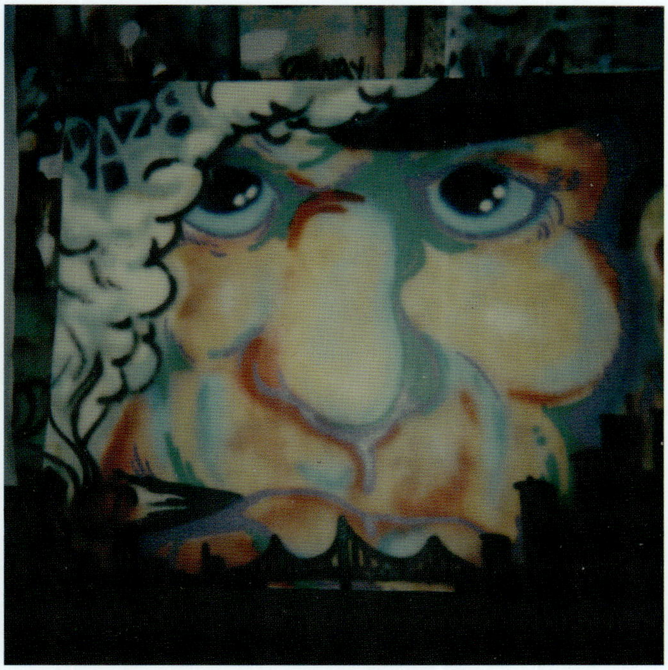

King of the City, 1984
Spray paint on canvas, 46" × 50"

At the same time all of this underground aerosol activity flourished, above-ground interest and opportunities continued to present themselves. This spawned the formation of The Graffiti: Aboveground (GPI) gallery. Formed by Joyce Towbin and Mel Neulander as a workshop and exhibition space, GPI flourished for two years despite criticisms of exploitation of the culture by some. Crash, Pink, and I were the first artists to be approached by Joyce and Mel, but quickly the core group grew to include Erni, Cey, Wasp, Tracy168, Caine 1, Noc167, and Freedom. Other artists were invited intermittently to participate in exhibitions and projects. Whether or not GPI actually exploited the culture is debatable, but one thing that I'm certain of is that it served as yet another place for artistic opportunities to present themselves and for us to work on paintings in peace. Many journalists flocked to the workshop, which was located in the Meatpacking District in Manhattan, to interview and photograph us at work.

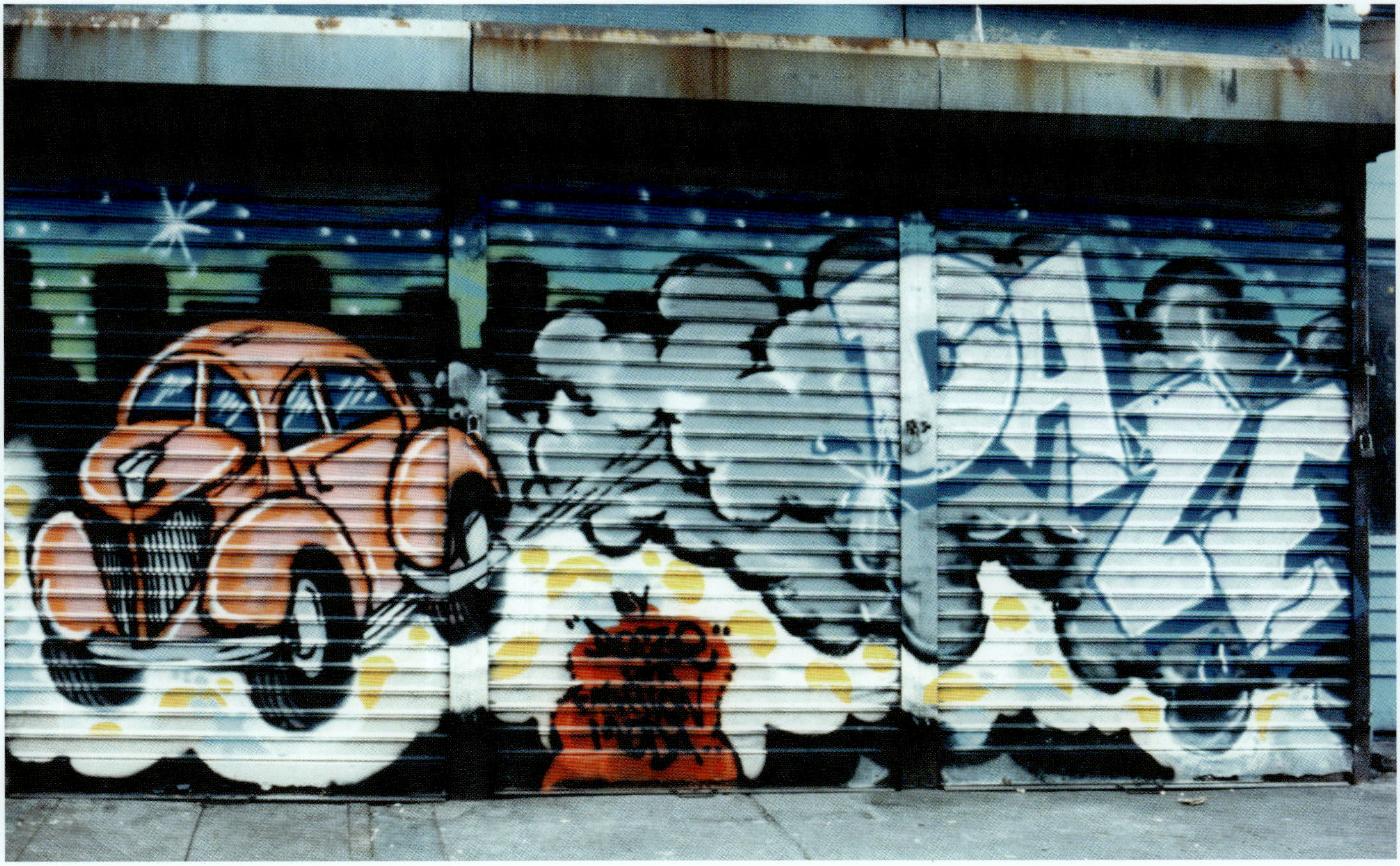

Daze, Brook Ave., 1982
Bronx, New York
Photo © Lisa Kahane

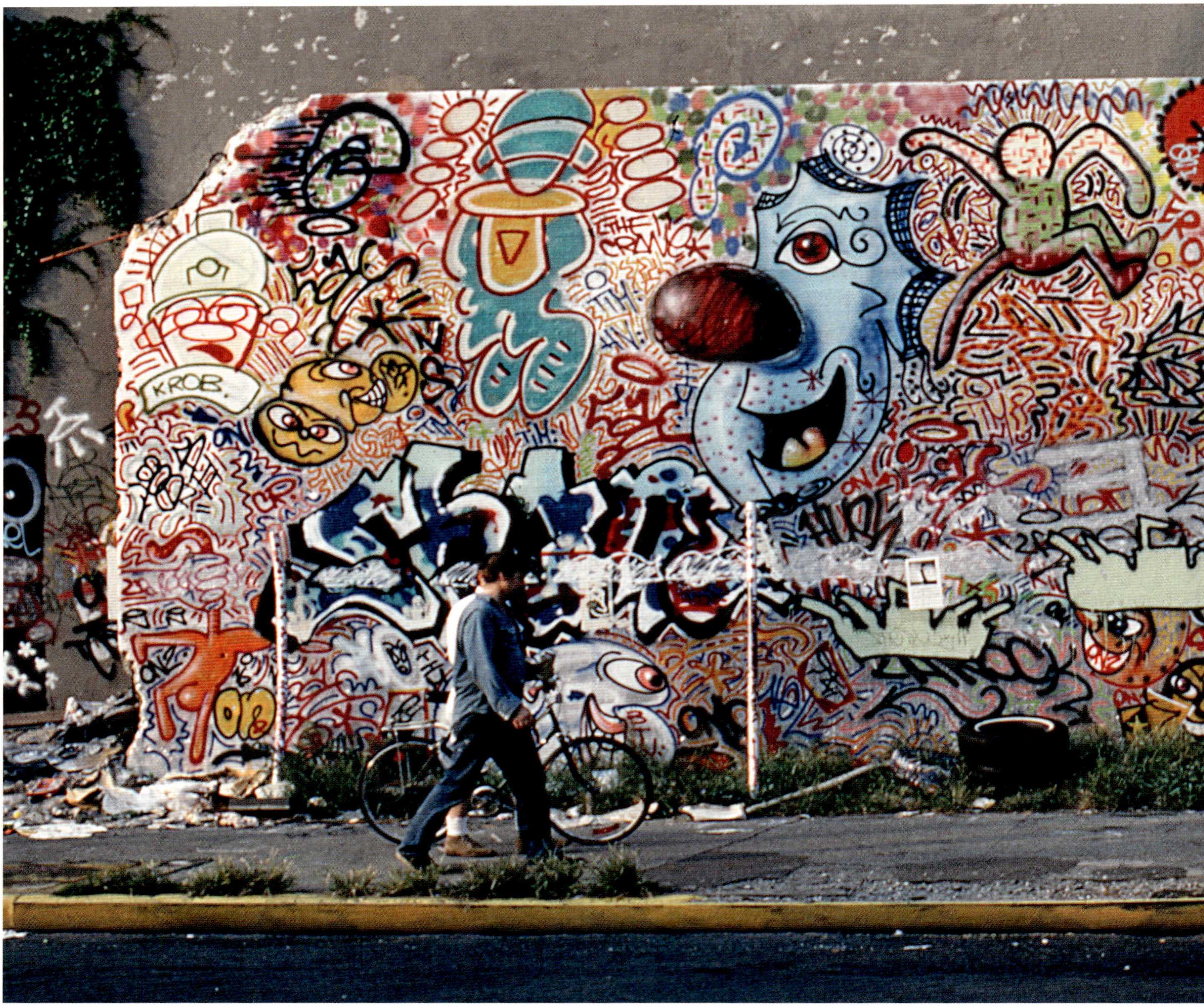

Houston Street wall, 1982.
This collaborative wall was painted with Kenny Scharf, Noc167, On2, Shone, Crane, Ero, La2, Keith Haring, and myself.
Photo © Martha Cooper

Crash and I in particular took advantage of the free studio space and worked on our paintings daily. If nothing else, the GPI workshop provided a place for us to work and encouragement to continue. Through all of this my work on canvas continued to advance. I was not afraid to experiment and I could feel the work evolve and my personal vision take shape. The work that I did on the trains with Skeme and Dez was still style based—that is to say it focused on letters exclusively. My paintings on canvas, though, reflected other interests I had in film, music, comics, and the city itself. I felt that whatever it was I had to say, in this new medium my vision had to become more personal. I think that a lot of the paintings I made during this period reflected the journey I was on. My work was growing and a lot of that growth was under the scrutiny of the public eye. Needless to say, in hindsight that was a double-edged sword. On one hand it felt great to receive attention for something that had been done for so long underground without any

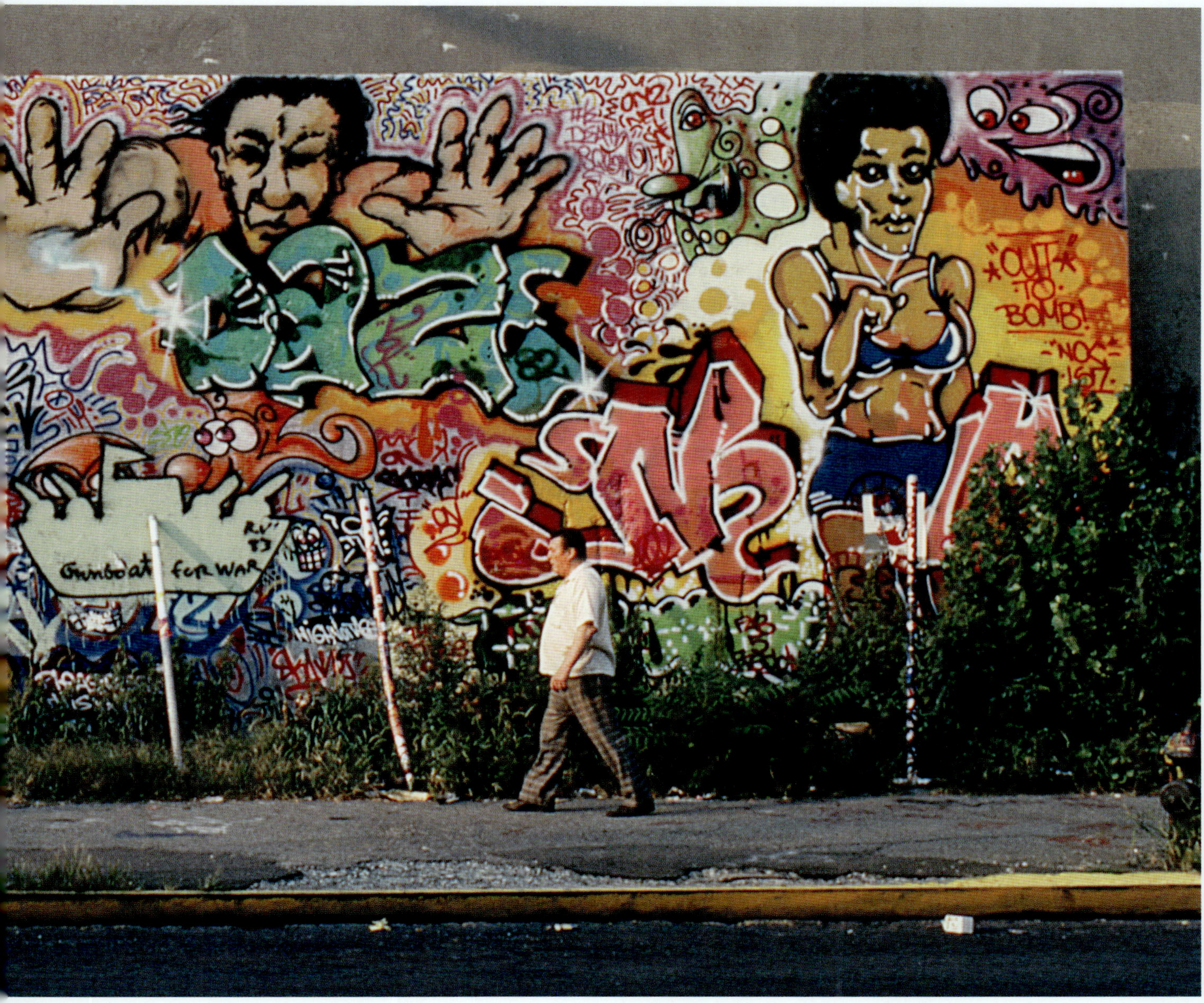

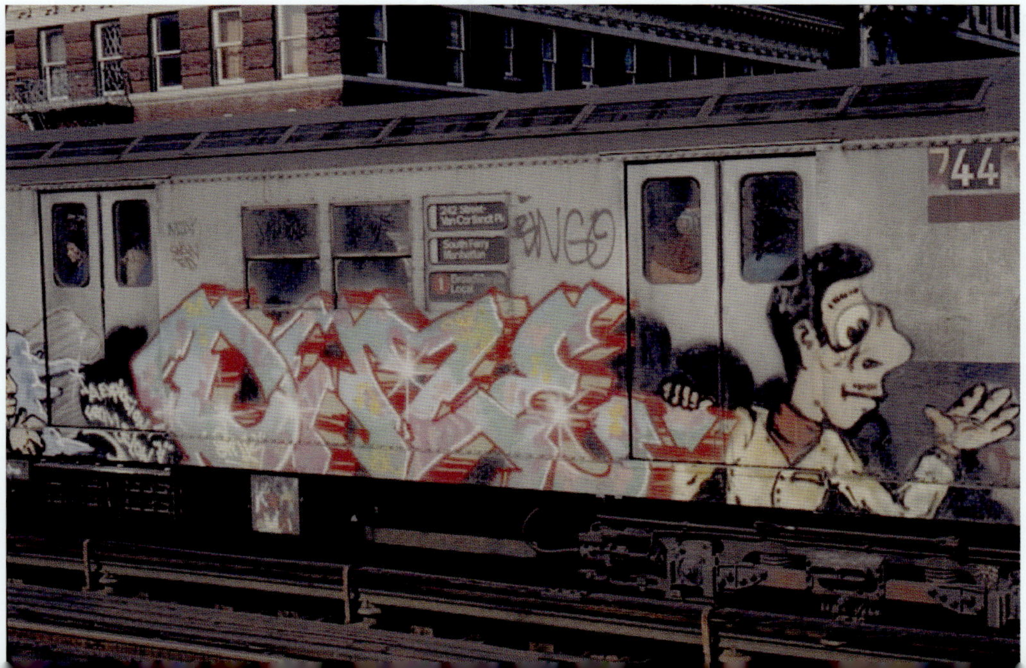

Broadway local.

This incredible wall was also painted in 1982 at The Graffiti Hall of Fame. It was painted by Dez, Skeme, and myself.
Photo © Martha Cooper

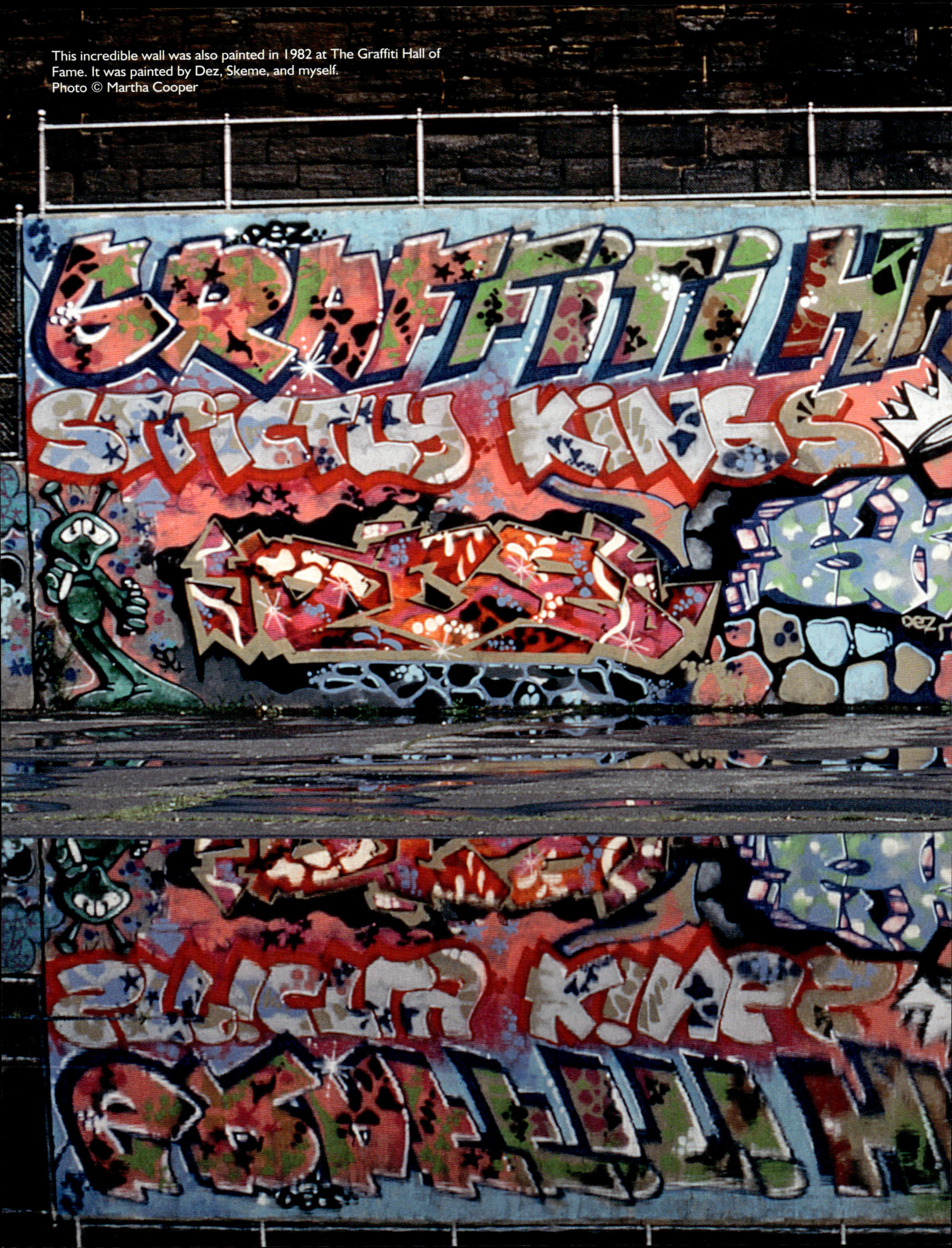

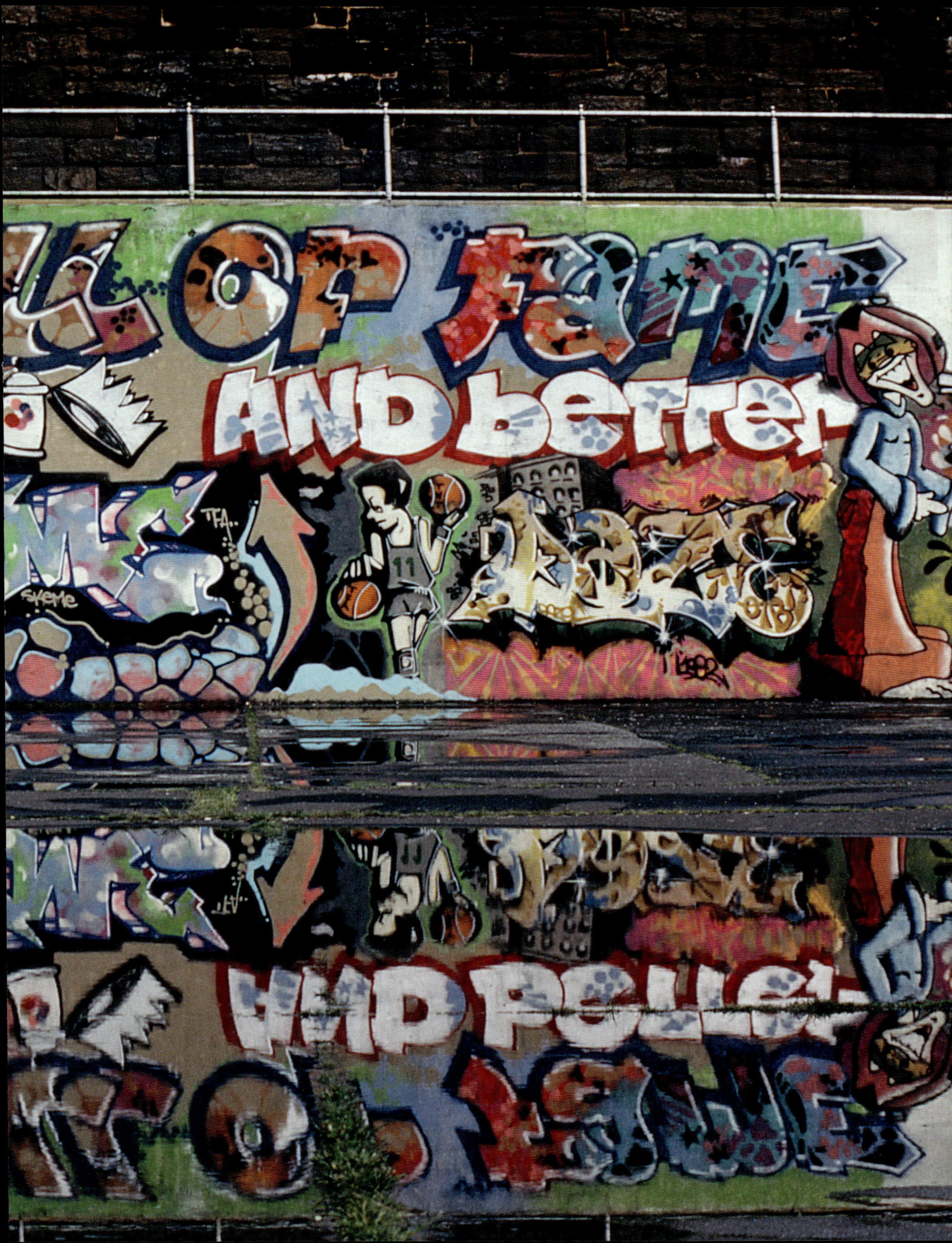
of fame
AND better

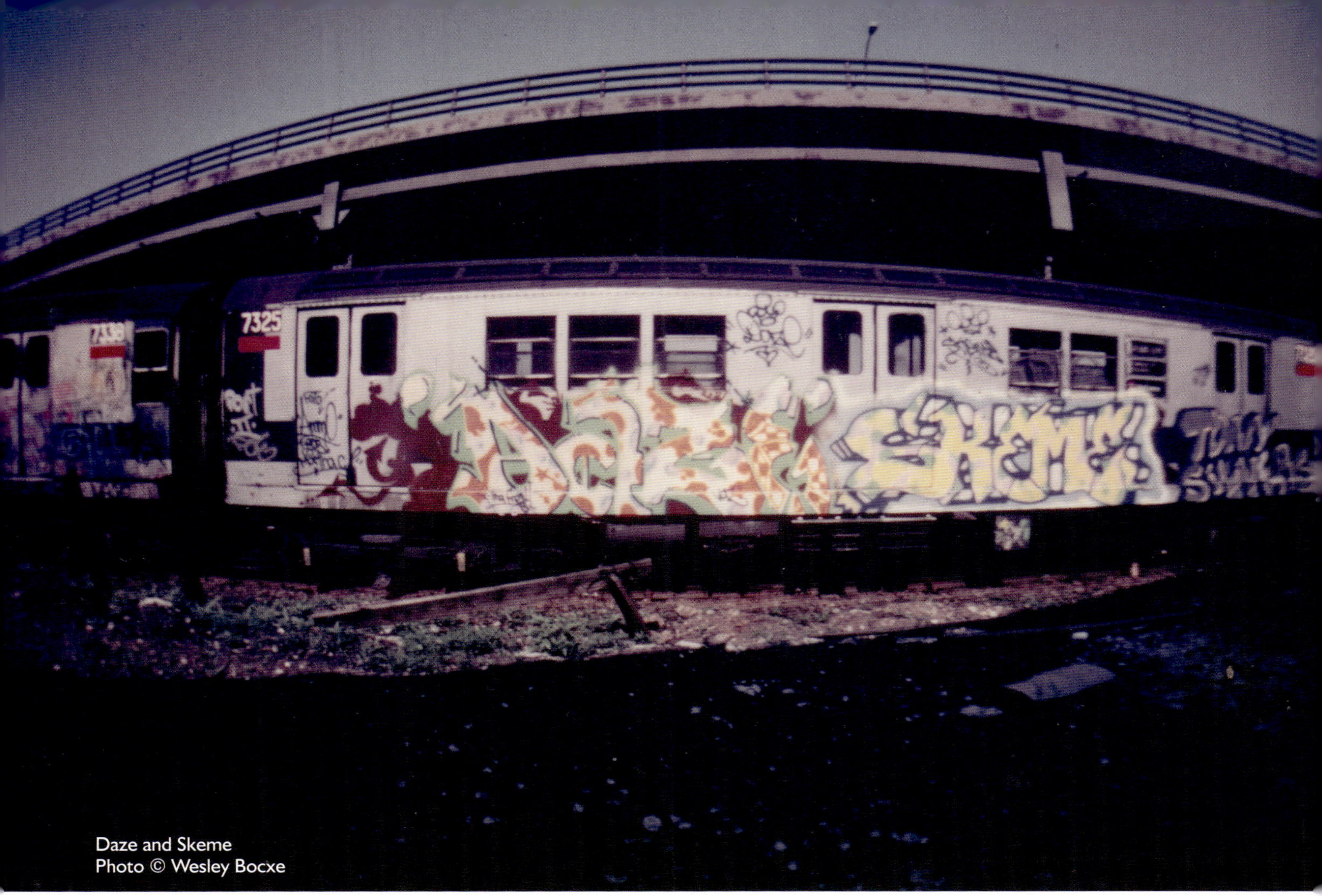

Daze and Skeme
Photo © Wesley Bocxe

Photo © Martha Cooper

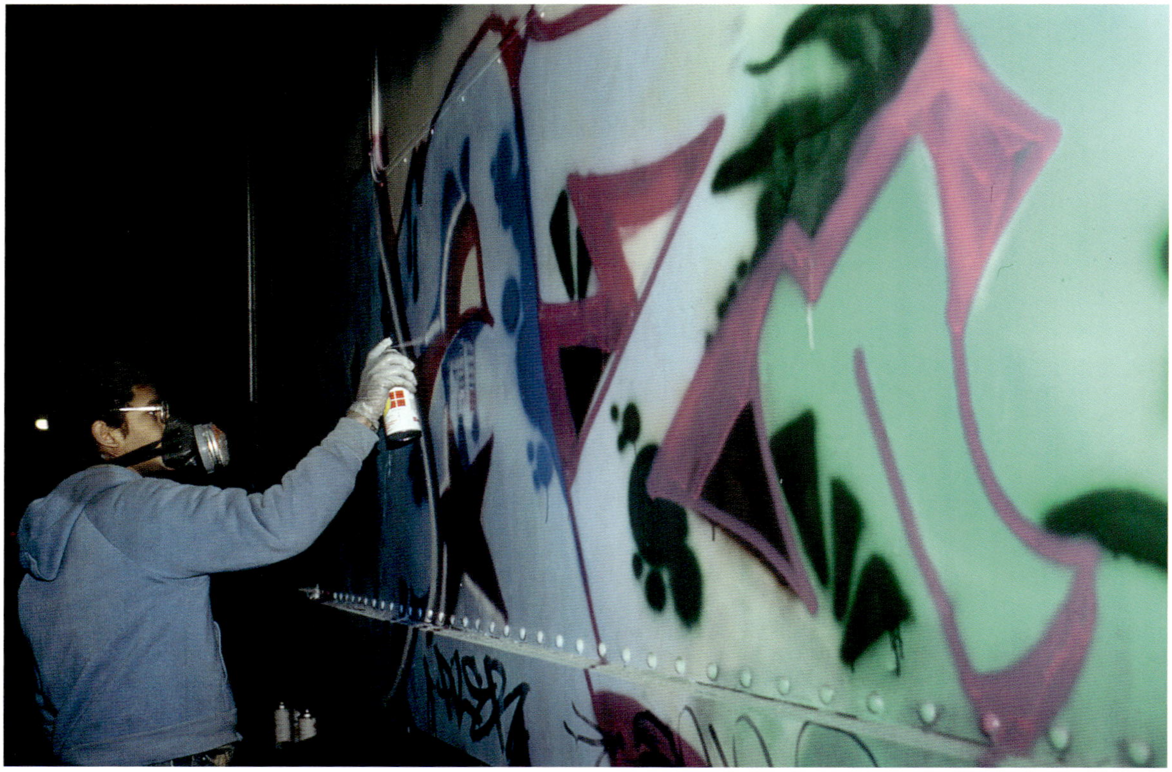

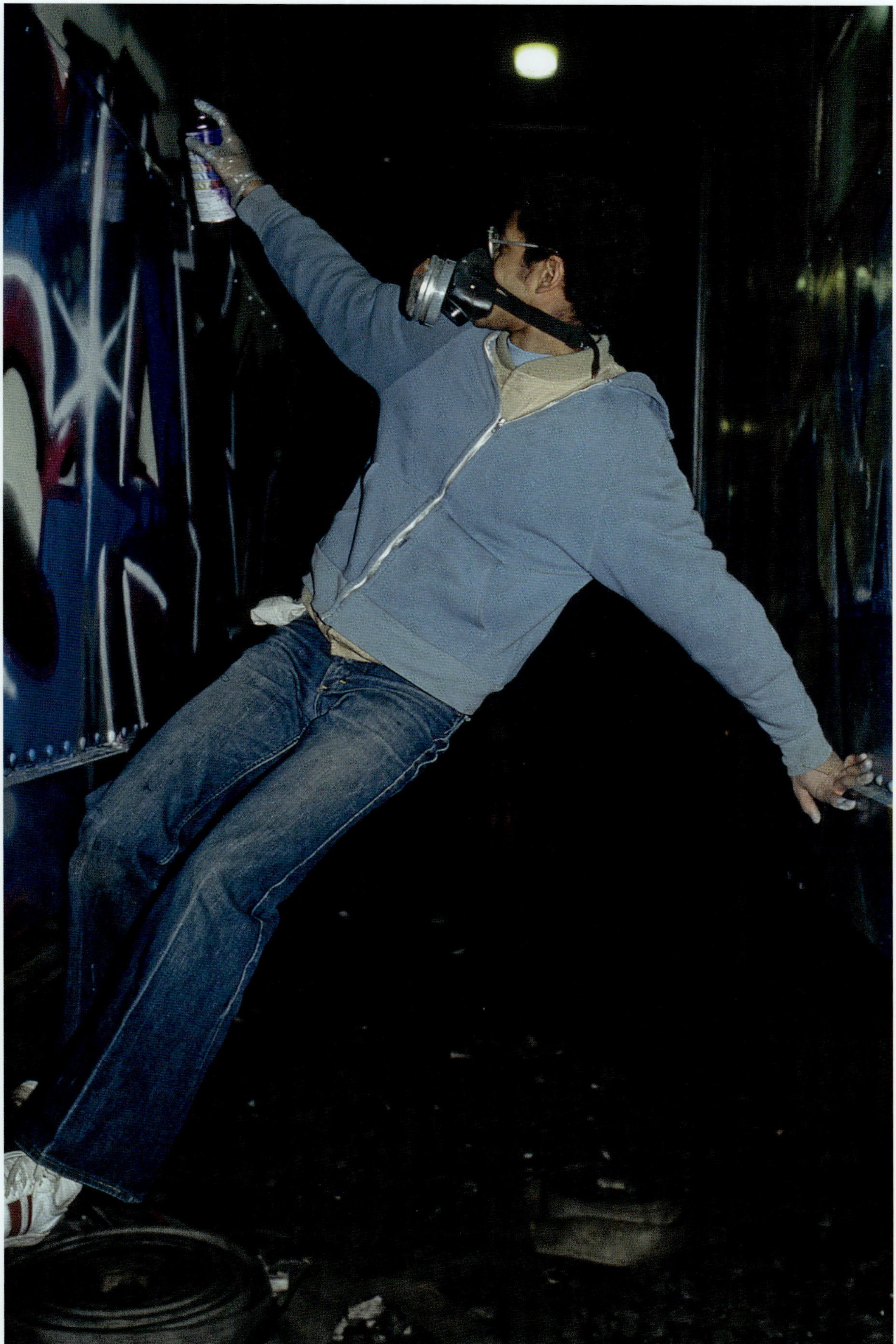

Photo © Martha Cooper

mainstream attention. Because it had been underground, the growth and evolution of the culture proceeded rapidly without any outside intervention. On the other hand, once recognition and opportunity presented itself, many were unprepared to actually succeed as artists. Thus began the great contradiction of writing as a part of culture versus the established culture of the commercial and fine art world. This was the period when many were forced to mature as artists and individuals in order to compete with the outside world.

I could not complete discussion of the early '80s without noting the role that New York nightlife played in all of this. One of the most amazing things about this particular period was the way the disparate cultures of

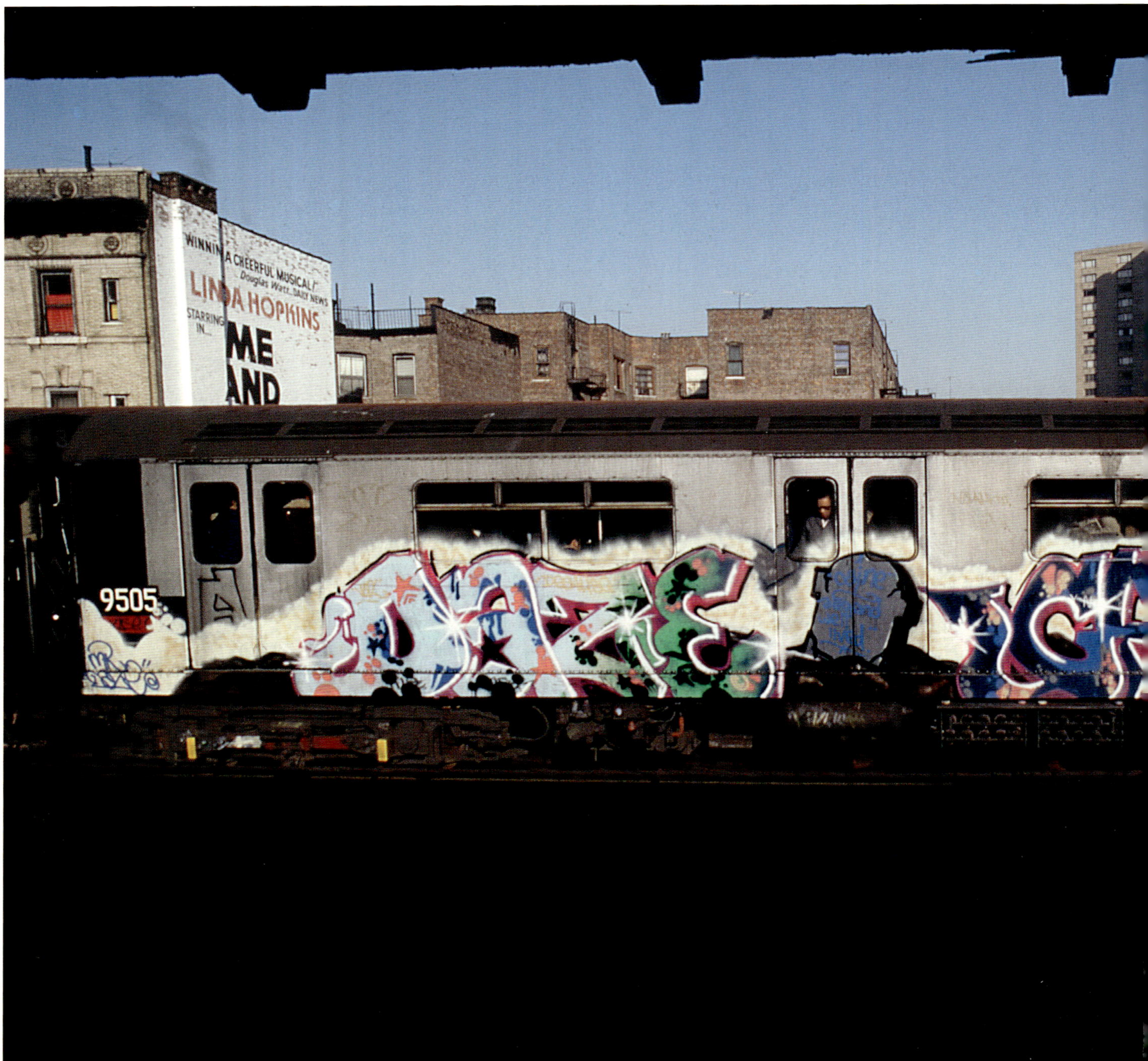

uptown and downtown found themselves occupying a common ground within the New York nightlife. Places like the Roxy gave hip-hop culture a chance to congregate within the downtown scene that was largely punk rock and new wave. You can't overemphasize the impact of walking into the Roxy on any given Friday night to watch Africa Bambaata and Jazzy Jay spin while the Rocksteady Crew took out all toy comp to an audience that consisted of denizens of the downtown scene and heads from uptown. Soon the word was out that the Roxy was the place to be on a Friday night, and celebrities started to make the scene. I remember one night hanging with Aone in the VIP lounge upstairs and watching him step to Mick Jagger as if they were old friends or something!

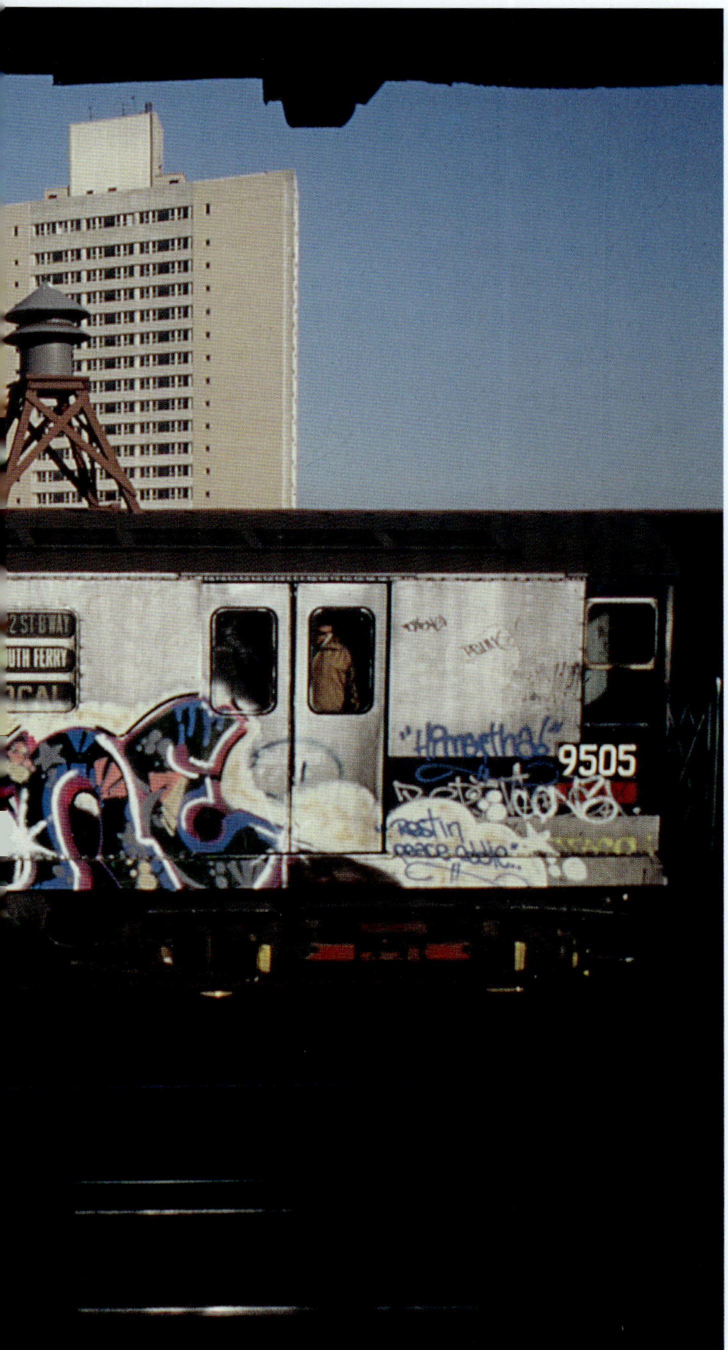

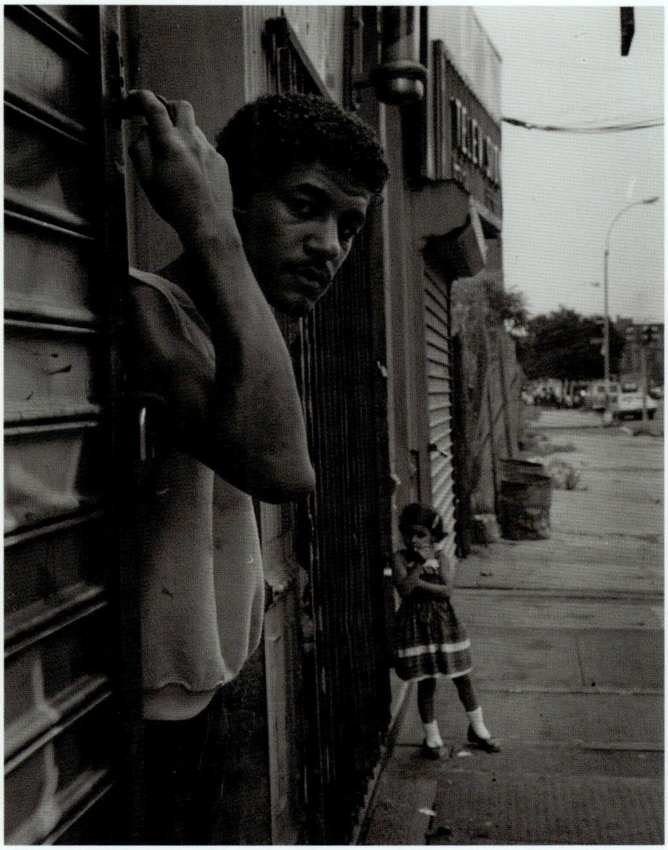

Daze, Brook Ave., 1982
Bronx, New York
Photo © Peter Bellamy

Photo © Martha Cooper

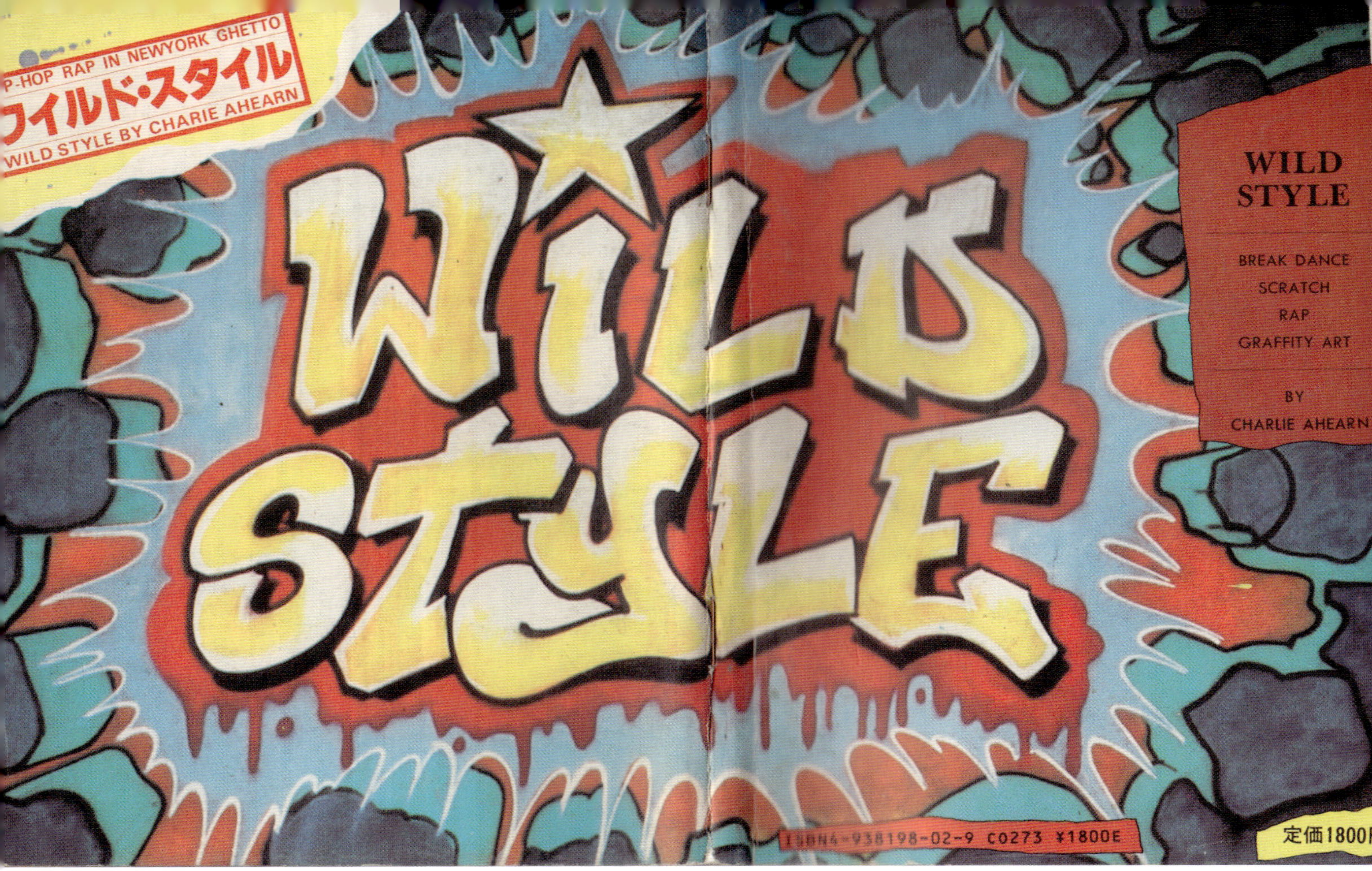

Wild Style, Japan tour

On other occasions I would see Matt Dillon, Madonna, Lauren Hutton, Richard Gere, and various other celebrities meandering through the thick crowd of uptown and downtown constituents, listening to the beat of "planet rock" and watching the Rocksteady Crew take over the dance floor.

Danceteria was another spot downtown located in the west 20s where one-night art shows took over the fourth-floor space while rap music took over the turntables on special nights. I remember seeing Run DMC perform there to a half-empty room of curious onlookers. A year later, after their first album rocked the airwaves, I saw them play to a first-floor packed audience whose excitement was barely contained. The movies *Wild Style* and *Style Wars* were screened in the club, turning the participants into overnight celebrities. I remember Crash and I were asked to paint the walls of the fourth-floor space with pieces and tags for a special *Wild Style* event. I don't think that anyone stopped to consider that history was in the making. At the time we were all caught up in the excitement of the moment.

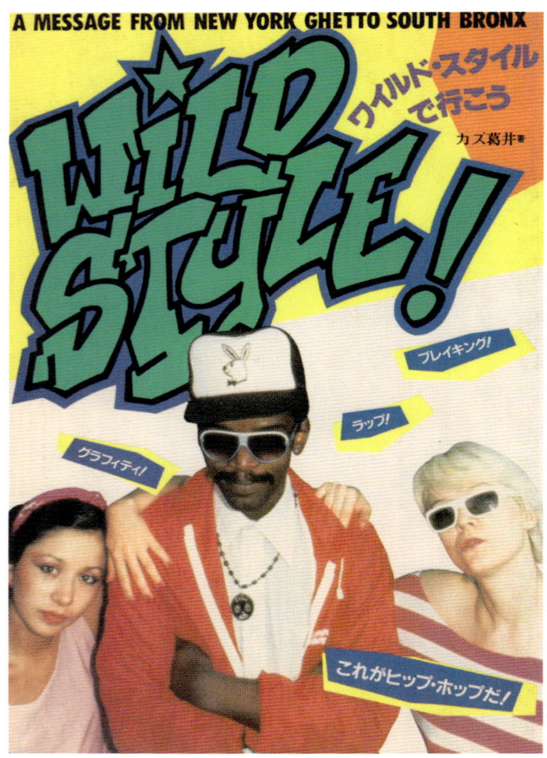

Catalogue cover for *Wild Style* Japan tour

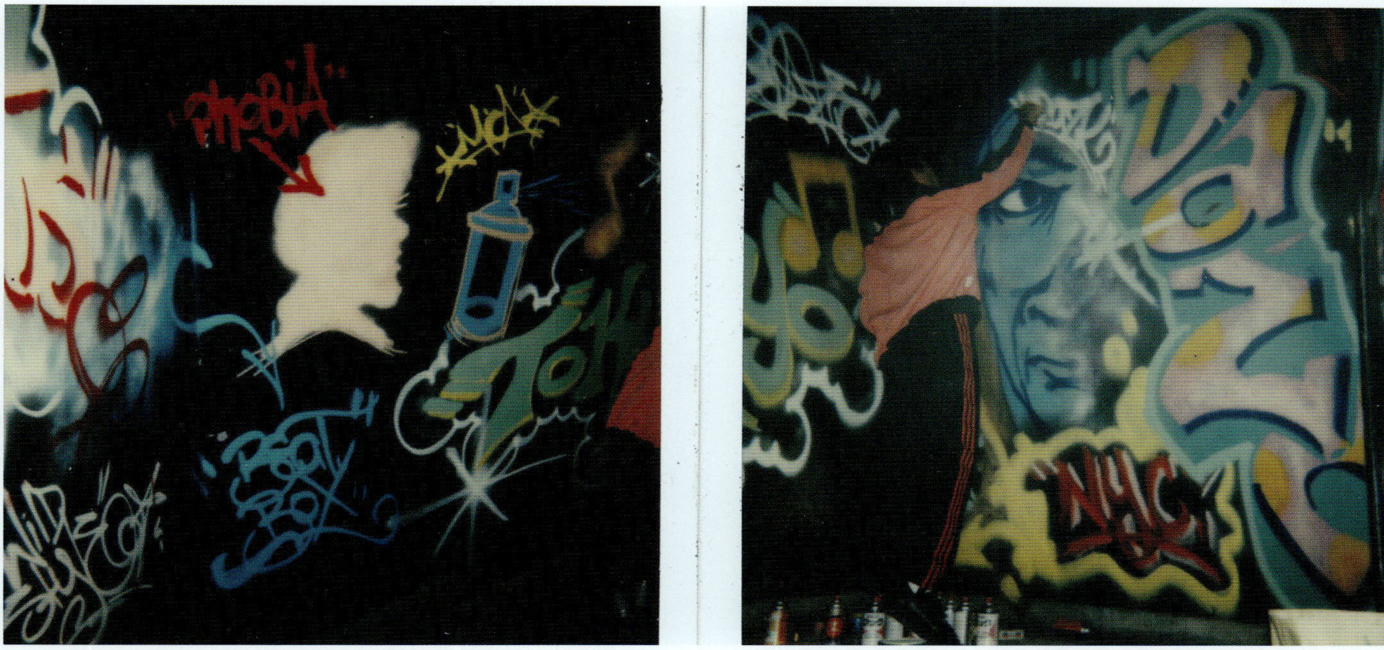

Painted installation in Tokyo for the Japan *Wild Style* tour, 1983

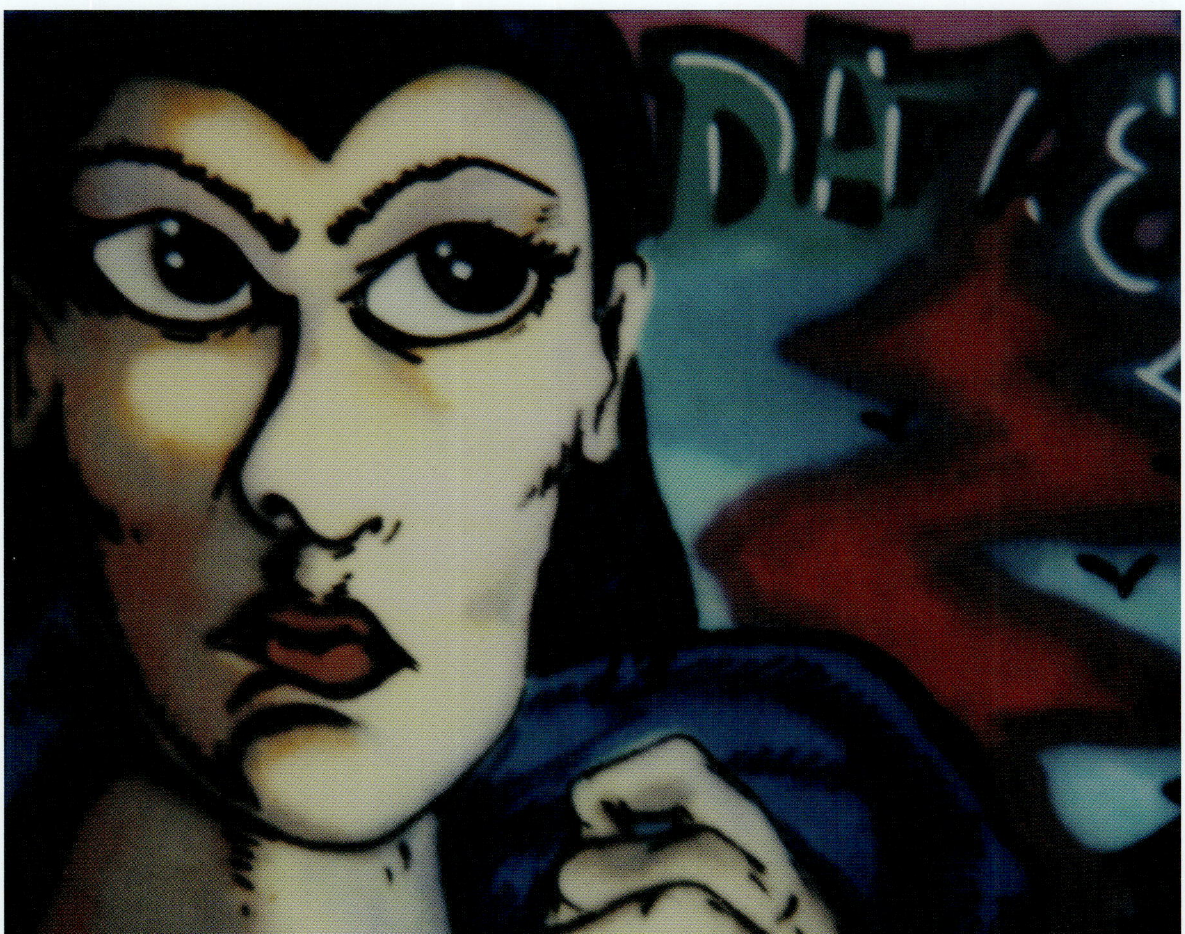

Tokyo Queen, 1983
Spray paint on canvas, 68" × 52"
Private collection, USA

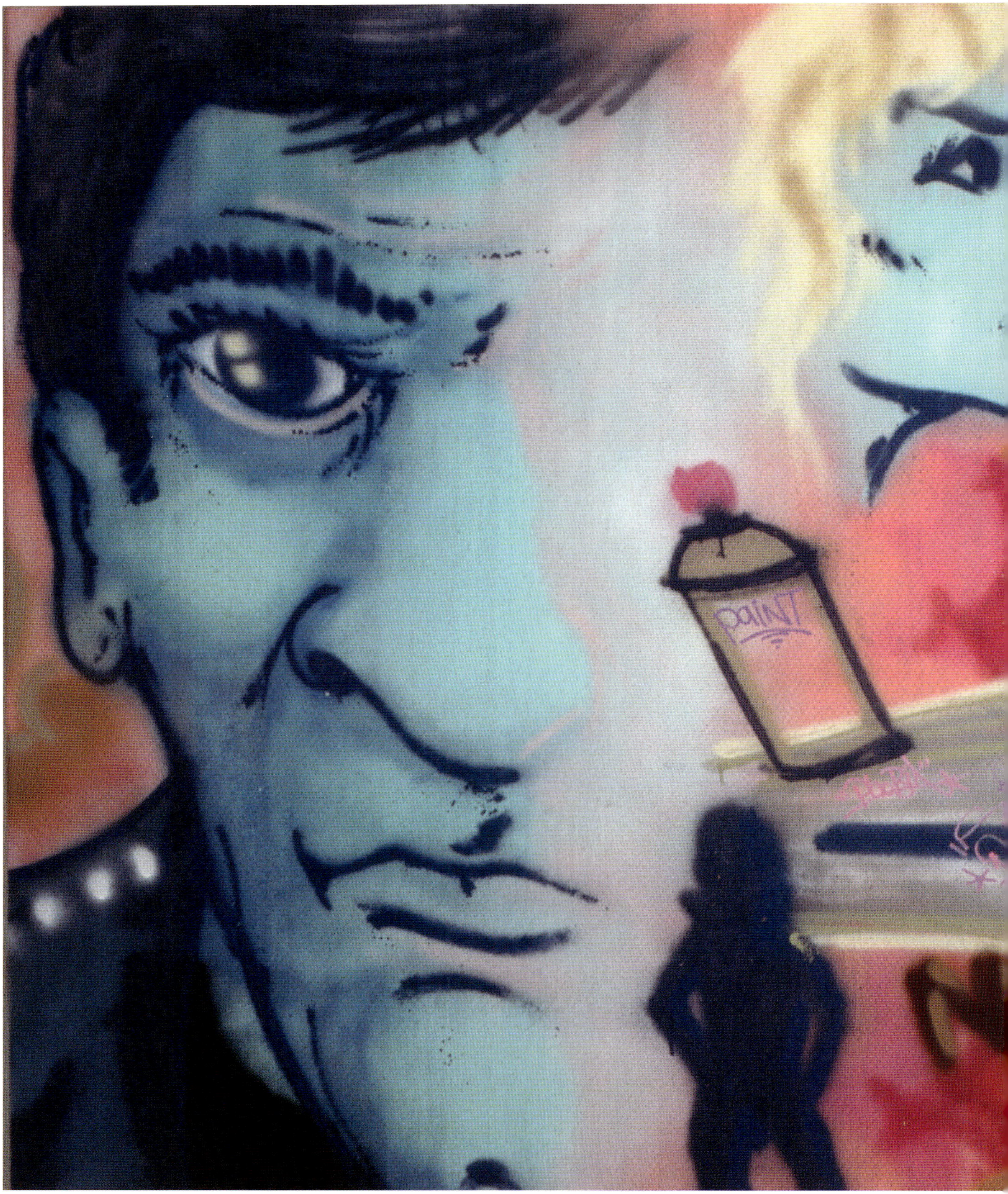

Japanese Subways, 1983
Spray paint on canvas, 53" × 93"
Collection of The Brooklyn Museum, Brooklyn, New York

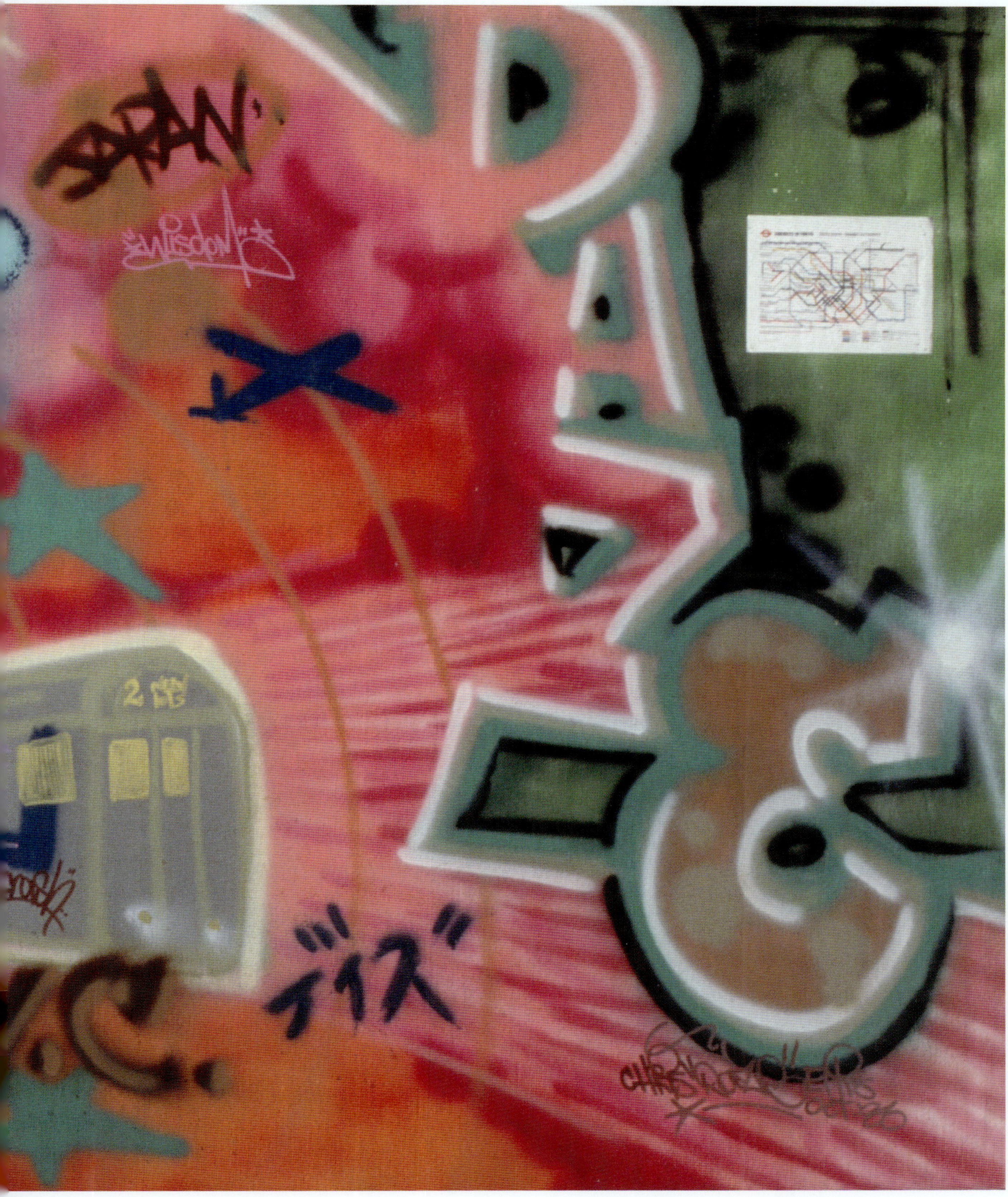

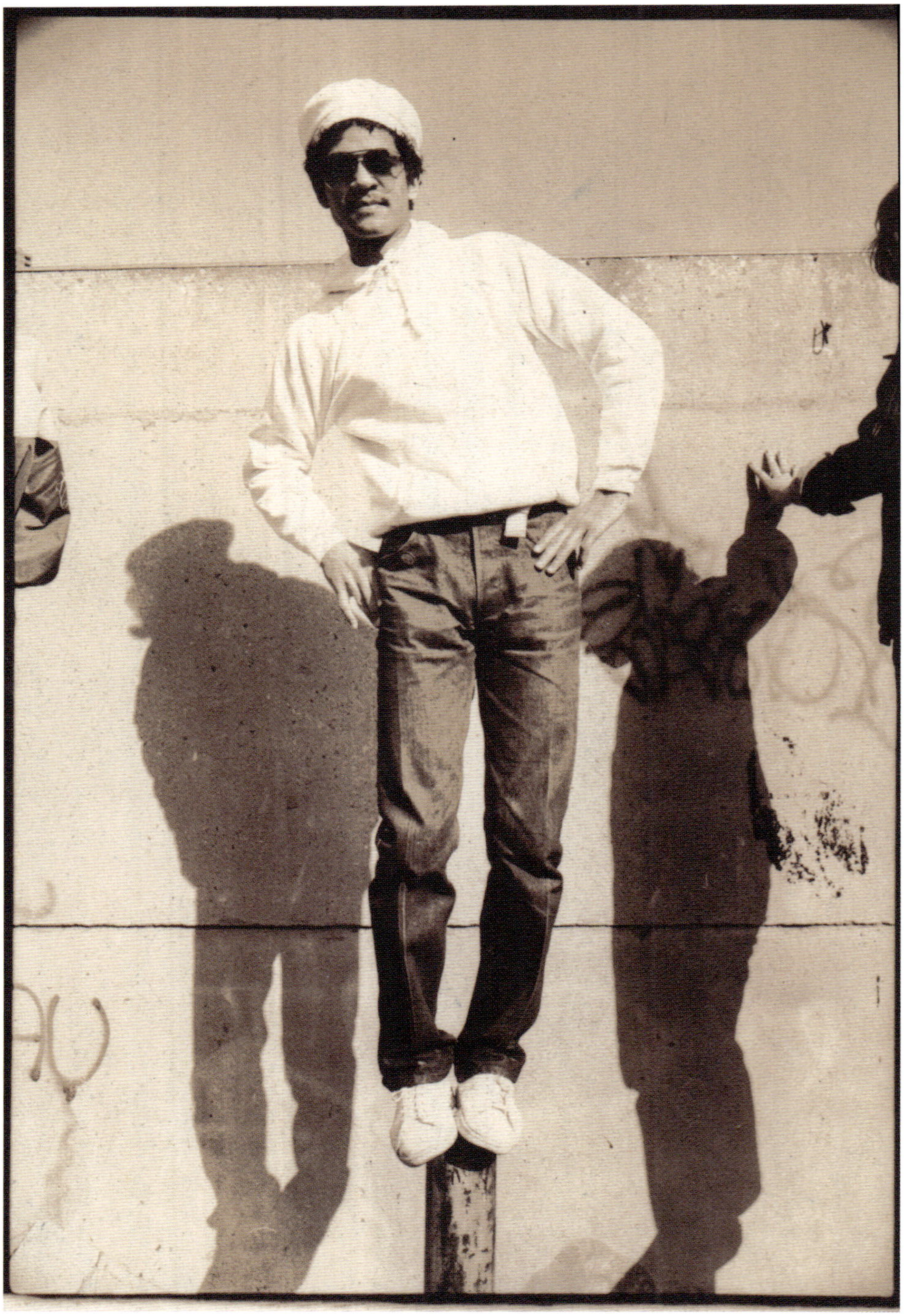

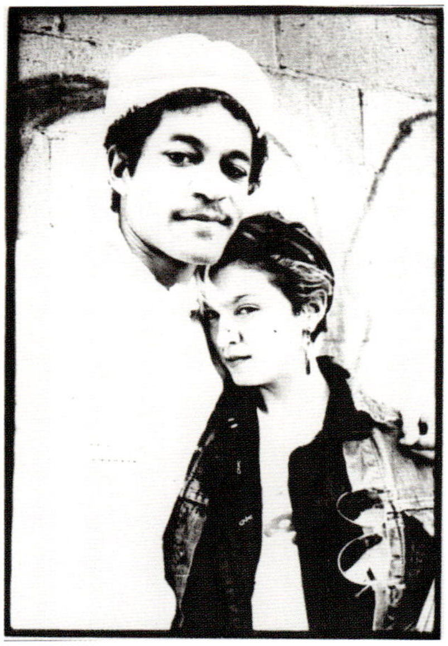

Daze and Madonna, 1984 photo shoot
Photo © Beth Baptiste

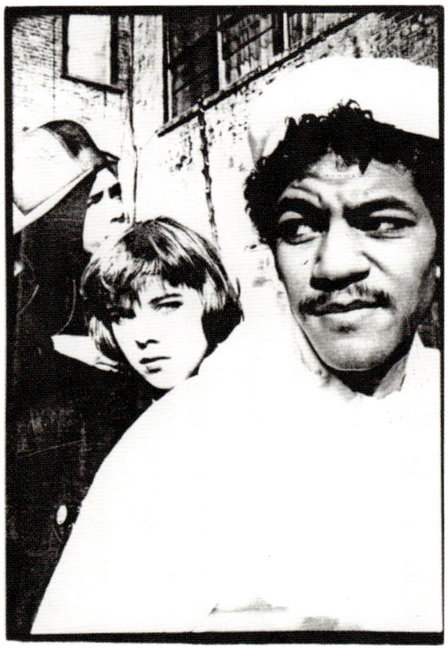

ON2, Debi Mazar, Daze, 1984 photo shoot
Photo © Beth Baptiste

1984 photo shoot
Photo © Beth Baptiste

We were just beginning to catch a glimpse of possibility that perhaps we could actually make a living from all of this—that perhaps this could be our life's work, that it didn't have to end. Wouldn't that be worth it all? None of us had any idea that this culture to which so many had devoted themselves would one day spread to urban communities worldwide. I don't think it's an exaggeration to say that many of the events that transpired in New York at that time—graffiti, punk, hip-hop, the East Village art scene—opened the doors for what we see and hear today. I feel extremely lucky to have been a part of that and to have contributed. It was an amazing whirlwind of nonstop activity in the clubs, galleries, train yards, and streets that blew the lid off society and set the stage for what was to come after.

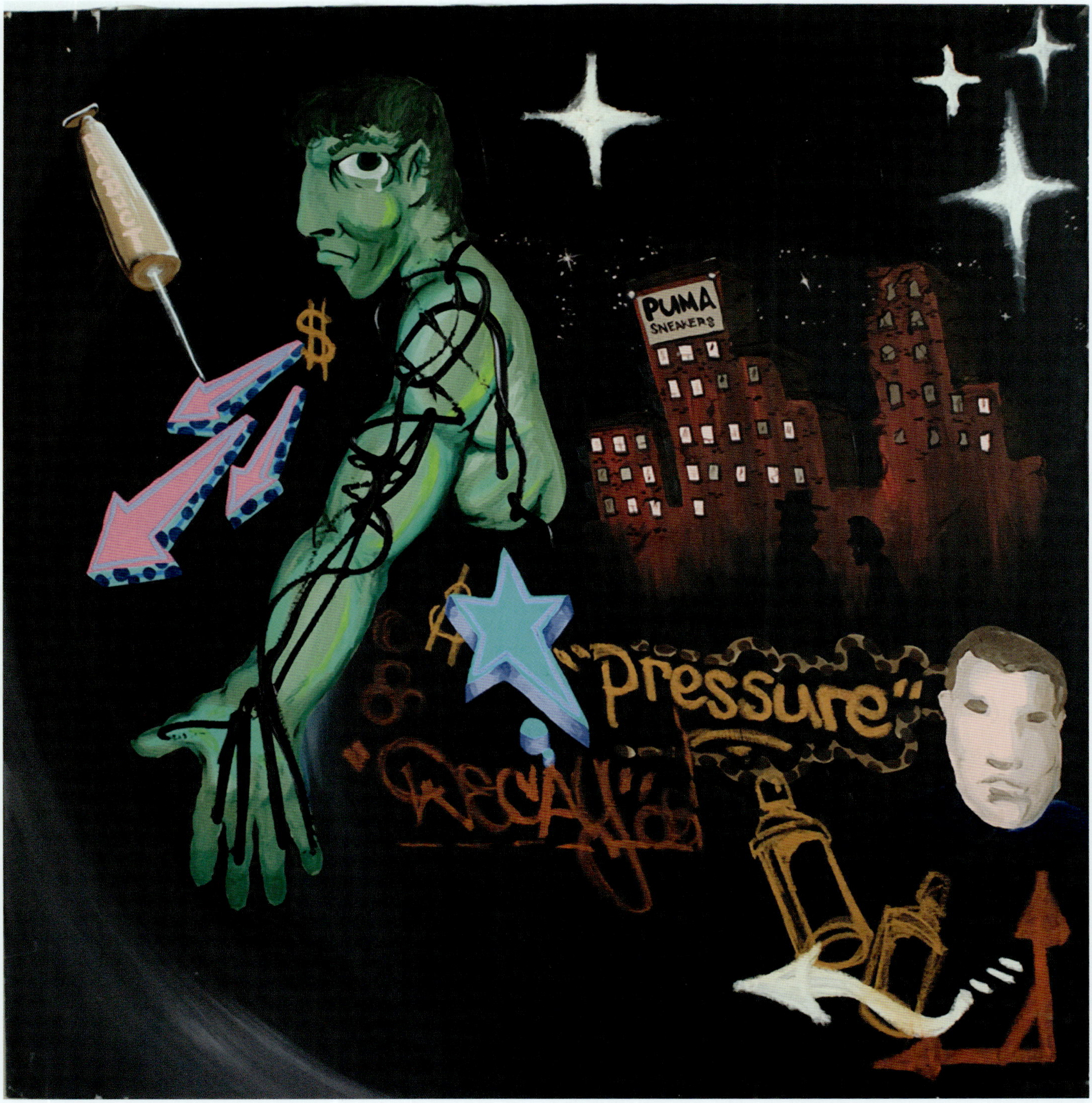

Pressure, 1981
Acrylic and oil stick on canvas
Collection of John Axelrod

CHAPTER 5

FROM CITY AS CANVAS TO CANVAS AS CITY:

THE URBAN AS SUBJECT & STRATEGY IN DAZE'S PAINTINGS

BY CLAIRE SCHWARTZ

Look in the window. You know this scene: the interior of a New York City subway car. Bathed in fluorescent light, the car looks clean, almost sterile. See the long red bench that people vie for at rush hour and the metal overhead bar that they clutch when there are no seats left. See the panels of multicolored advertisements that compete for the passengers' attention. Faced with the promise to *Save More* and the declaration that *This Is the Season*, you can't quite make out the specifics of the money-making scheme or the details of the latest trend. The text on the double doors that open onto the platform as people rush out and then crowd in is, by contrast, perfectly legible: PLEASE KEEP HANDS OFF THE DOORS. Constructed to organize bodies in space—to chart sightlines, to control the chaos of crowds that is New York's eternal promise—this familiar urban vocabulary is markedly missing a key component: People.

Look again. See, this time, not only the view through the window, but the window itself. The ovular glass is framed by a bright red swath of door punctuated by spots of white. The precise shading to the right of the window rhymes with the realism of the car's interior, calling the viewer to imagine a light outside the frame cast onto the door. In the upper right corner, there is another patch of white. This white relinquishes memesis. This white is instantly recognizable as dripping spray paint. There are graffiti tags on the door—writing in deep pink on either side of the window that fades partially into the red acrylic—but this white drip of paint is something else, a tag less on the subway door than on the canvas itself. An interface between the world of the painting and the painting in the world, this mark calls the viewer into the material realm of the process of making. The painted subway door—the frame of this urban scene—is itself a material artifact, a theater of varied representational practices that do not simply depict urban space, but perform it. If the subway car hosts no bodies, the canvas registers the body's trace through the record of the creative gesture.

Untitled, this painting by Daze (b. Chris Ellis) manifests the artist's profound engagements with the medium. Never simply an illustration of urban space, Daze's canvases develop a grammar of painting that presents us with familiar scenes while demanding that we look anew. A prolific artist who has worked across medium and site, Daze is perhaps best known as a member of the second generation of New York graffiti artists. Lauded as one of the most important "writers" of our time, Daze began painting the New York City subways alongside such notables as Crash, Futura, Lady Pink, and Seen while a student at the High School of Art and Design in the mid-1970s. Dissatisfied with his teachers, many of whom were not practicing artists, Daze supplemented the school's curriculum by immersing himself in the city's multitude of art institutions. While taking the city as his canvas by writing on trains and other public spaces, Daze simultaneously honed a painterly vocabulary through time at museums and galleries. Indeed, Daze's work is informed by a capacious range of influences from Gordon Parks's 1971 film *Shaft* to Japanese photographer Daido Moriyama. The dynamic interplay between stillness and motion that animates many of his paintings manifests Daze's longstanding engagement with comic strips and films. His work mines these genres for lessons on angle, perspective, and motion, while foregrounding the material specificities of paint and canvas.

Reflecting on an early encounter with Jean-Michel Basquiat's paintings, Daze says, "I was initially kind of disappointed by his first attempts at making paintings. Yet, he evolved really quickly and built up this whole

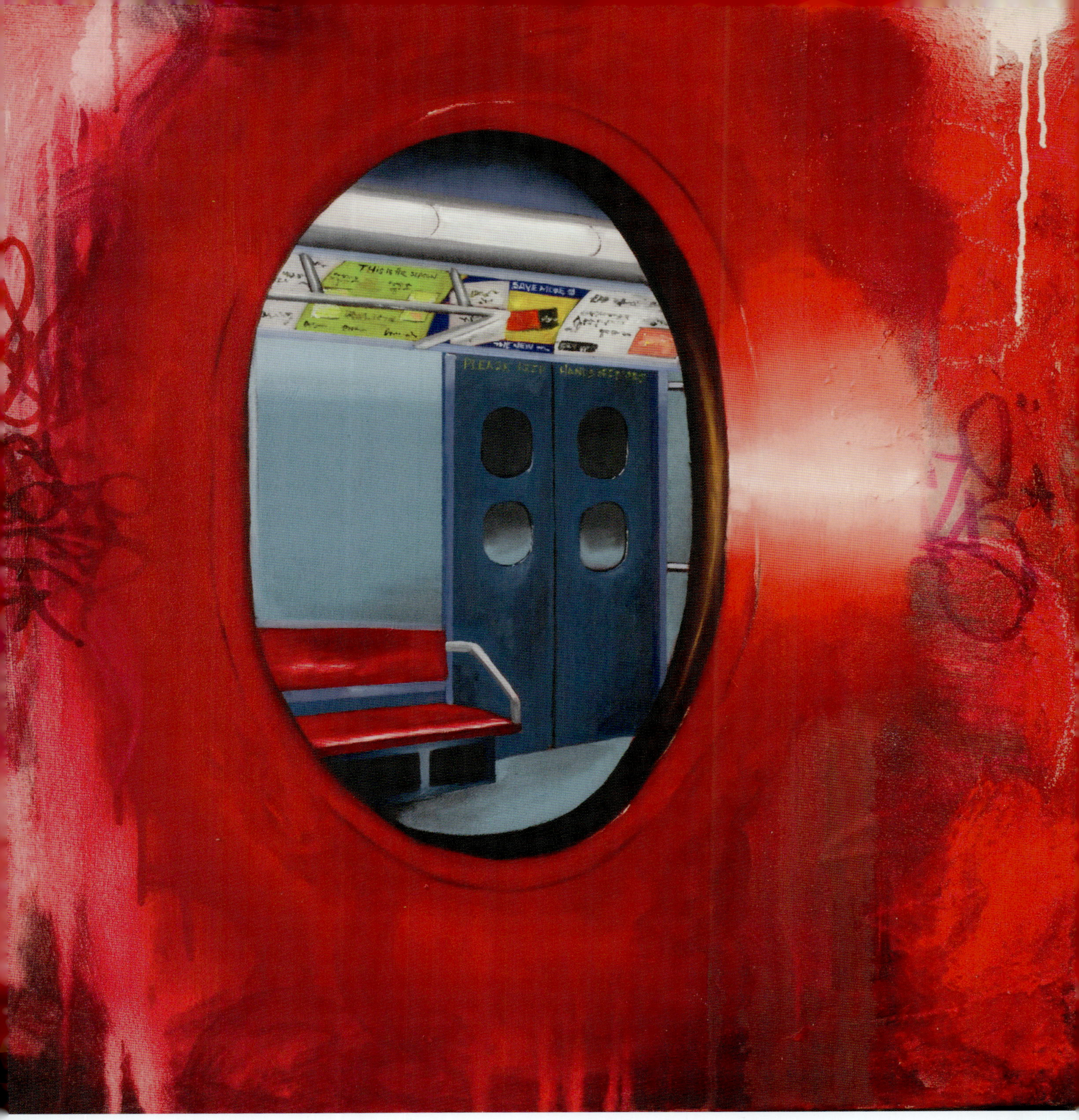

Untitled, 2009
Spray paint, oil and acrylic on canvas, 30" × 30"
Collection of the artist
Photo courtesy of Adam Reich

language. He started to make the paintings that continue to intrigue me to this day."[1] This studied attentiveness reflects Daze's concern with an artistic transition that didn't simply substitute the train with the canvas but, rather, leveraged the canvas and the world of the gallery to enhance his investigations of urban space, while pushing the boundaries of studio practice.

As first a viewer of work by and then shown alongside artists like Basquiat and Keith Haring, Daze has long been critically engaged with the navigations of street-to-canvas. Attentive not only to his contemporaries, Daze reaches back through art history, citing the WPA as an apt site for considering artists who navigated the creation of public works alongside studio practice. While Daze's public works have received significant attention, there is much to be said about his studio practice.

Though he did not set out with the aim of placing work in galleries or museums, Daze's paintings have been shown in galleries from Singapore to SoHo and have been acquired by such museums as the Groninger Museum (Groningen, Netherlands), the Museum Ludwig (Aachen, Germany), the Museum of Modern Art (New York City), and the Brooklyn Museum, the institution only a few blocks from Daze's childhood home. This brief essay builds on the work of curators such as Kelley Tialiou and Maurizio Vanni in seeking to elaborate a conversation around Daze's paintings. Without divorcing Daze's studio practice from his multi-media career, this essay considers Daze's innovations specifically in painting.

Drawing on his graffiti practice, Daze's first paintings—made in the early 1980s—were entirely in spray paint. Yet he quickly began to expand in both material and vocabulary, and a brief glance across his oeuvre evinces rigorous experimentation underwritten by an enduring interest in urbanity. He often paints in the context of series, a strategy that both allows for the development of his vocabulary as the paintings rhyme with and diverge from one another, and underscores the studied character of his practice. Certain series—like *Elevated Stations* (2000–2013), *Coney Island* (1995–2011), and *Staten Island Ferry* (1997–2014)—call up iconic New York City sites, while others are more avowedly conceptual. The paintings in the *Geometric* series (2010–2013), for example, exemplify this latter category as they marry Daze's longstanding engagement with graffiti with the stripped vocabulary of minimalism.

Like the *Geometric* series, *Grey Scale* (2010–2012)—canvases rendered nearly entirely in shades of gray—departs from popular conceptions of graffiti. Eschewing notions of graffiti as a bright addendum to the concrete jungle of the city, *Grey Scale* makes space for an investigation of graffiti's formal qualities. As artist and writer David Batchelor opines in his pithily titled essay "Chromophobia": "If colour is not a contaminant, then it is more often than not treated as an addition, embellishment or supplement, relating to 'mere' appearances rather than to the essential structure of things."[2] In the *Grey Scale* paintings, nothing can be trivialized as simply "embellishment or supplement." By fixing the cityscape in this stringently limited palette, these paintings visually insist on graffiti as a structuring language alongside more traditionally conceived components of urban infrastructure, such as streets and subways. Consequently, the binary between essence and appearance, structure and surface, is thrown into crisis, as these elements dissolve into the broader category of experience.

Yet, this distinction I have drawn between series grounded in external urban referent and those that function more as self-reflexive studies is a crude one, as Daze's work disrupts this kind of dichotomous construction. For example, the paintings that comprise the *Elevated Stations* series may image the iconic elevated subway platforms in New York City, but they also call on the particular properties of paint to achieve their effect. Several of the paintings from this series feature a solitary black male figure of uncertain presence. Here Daze uses not the horizontal blur that signals movement in the language of photography—a medium with which he is deeply engaged—but a vertical blur or drip. The top of the figure is fleshed in a realist style consistent with the rest of the canvas before dissolving into an abstracted painterly gesture, a translucent swath of color through which the urban background can be glimpsed. The result is a haunting suspension that swiftly calls up the underside of the city's fast-paced compulsion. These figures hover in ambivalence between appearing and disappearing. Here it is not the buildings erected and demolished in the dizzying urban rhythm, but the person—especially the black male figure—whose status as present is not to be taken for granted.

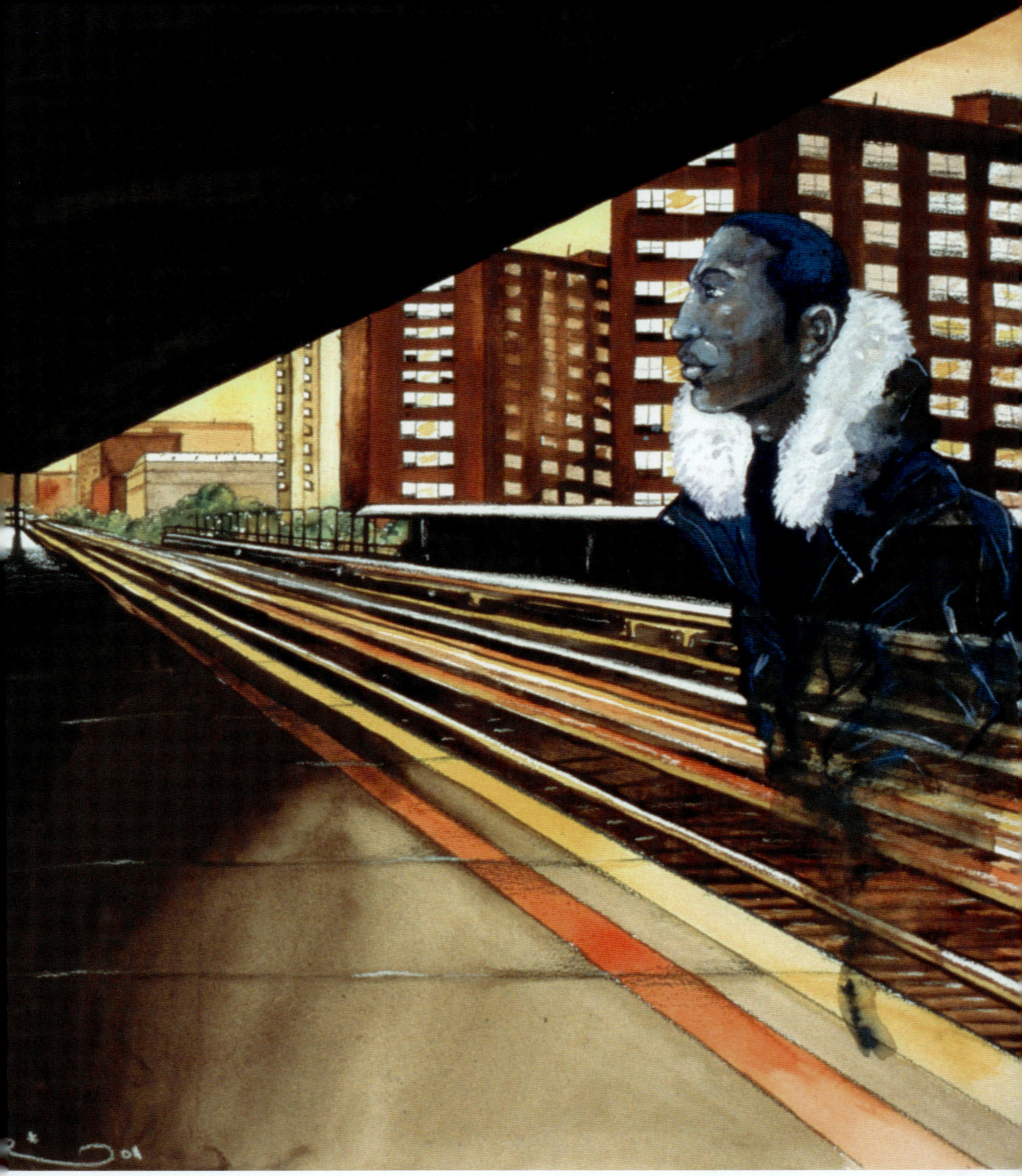

Jackson Avenue, 2001
Gouache on Arches paper, 18" × 24"
Private collection

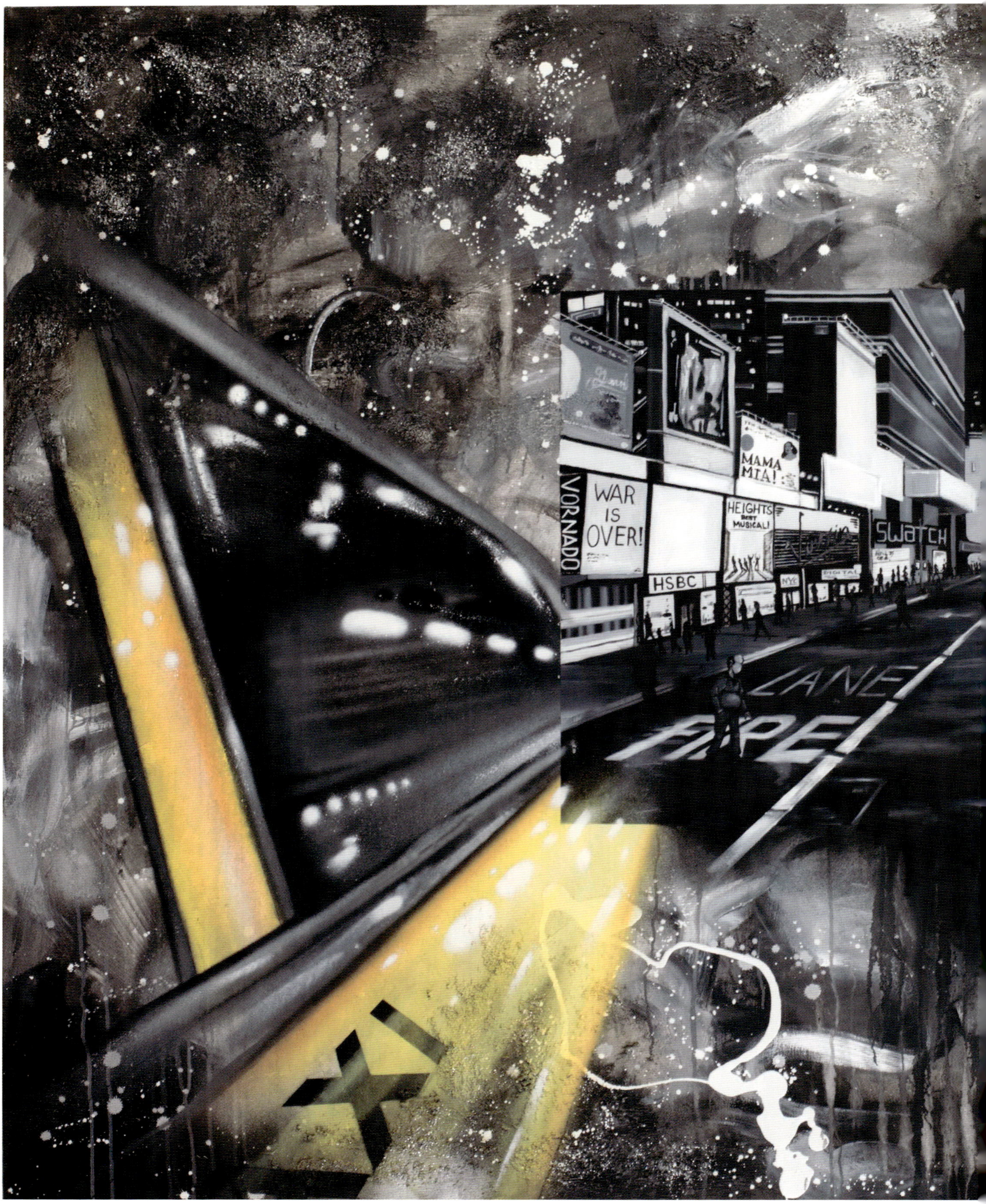
VORNADO
WAR IS OVER!
MAMA MIA!
HEIGHTS BEST MUSICAL!
HSBC
SWATCH
LANE

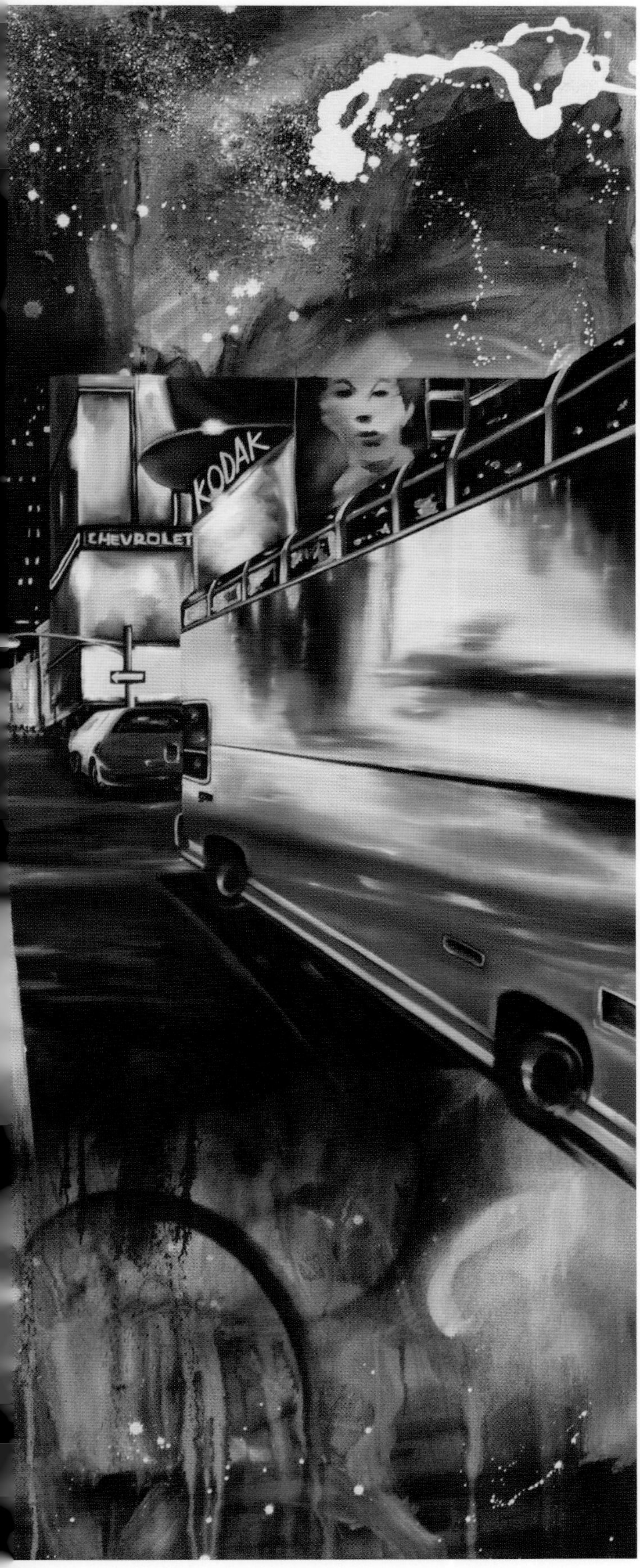

Life in the Fast Lane, 2012

Spray paint, oil, acrylic, and pumice on canvas, 66" × 82"
Collection of The Addison Gallery of American Art, Phillips Academy, Andover, Massachusetts
Purchased as the gift of The Addison Contemporaries, John Axelrod (PA 1964)

With reference to *Life in the Fast Lane* (2012) from a series on Manhattan's imminently recognizable Times Square, Kelley Tialiou remarks on the composite perspectival innovation that animates the painting. Tialiou notes: "The one-point perspective he uses to capture this cityscape is not only a nod to historical painting traditions, but also, combined with the speeding streaks of motion, a way of conveying the character of New York City street life and—perhaps—a reference to the origins of graffiti on the city's subway cars."[3] Tialiou's observation underscores that Daze's canvas functions not as a disorienting multi-perspectival experience, but as an act that—like the conspicuous drip of white paint on the depiction of a subway door—calls attention to competing representational practices that contour urban space. Like the city itself, Daze's paintings hold together the strange and the familiar, the past with the future, demanding that we look closely and anew.

Endnotes

1. Author's interview with Daze, 5 March 2015.
2. David Batchelor, "Chromophobia: Ancient and Modern, and A Few Notable Exceptions" (Leeds, UK: Henry Moore Institute, 1997), 2.
3. Kelley Tialiou, "Object Information: *Life in the Fast Lane*," Addison Gallery of American Art (2014), http://accessaddison.andover.edu/Obj24653?sid=42355&x=630034.

Claire Schwartz is a PhD candidate in African American studies and American studies at Yale. Her research focuses on representations of urban space in visual art and poetry of the African diaspora. In 2014, she was a student curator of Contemporary Art/South Africa, *an exhibition at the Yale University Art Gallery.*

CHAPTER 6
FROM HERE TO . . .

Over the years many younger artists have sought my advice on getting started professionally. I don't have all the answers but I do know that having a good work ethic has helped. I've never been the type of artist who sits around waiting for some eternal lightning bolt of inspiration to strike. In fact I am very working class in my approach. Whether I'm in the mood or not, I work everyday. As I work ideas and inspiration emerge. My work is very much a timeline in this way. One painting leads me to another and so on. My ideas and inspiration come through work and experience.

I would not say my life has been a sequence of carefully calculated career moves, but I will say one of the smartest things I did early on was to get a studio. Over the years I've seen many artists make money from their work and not put a single penny back into the work itself. This is ridiculous. When I began to consistently make money from my paintings I got a studio with Crash. This was about 1983. To this day we still maintain a studio together. The studio has given us a center of operation. It is the nucleus from which new work can be developed and created. It is also a place where people can view both finished works and works in progress. Wherever my travels have taken me, it's always been nice to come back to work in the studio. If that was a career move, it was the right one.

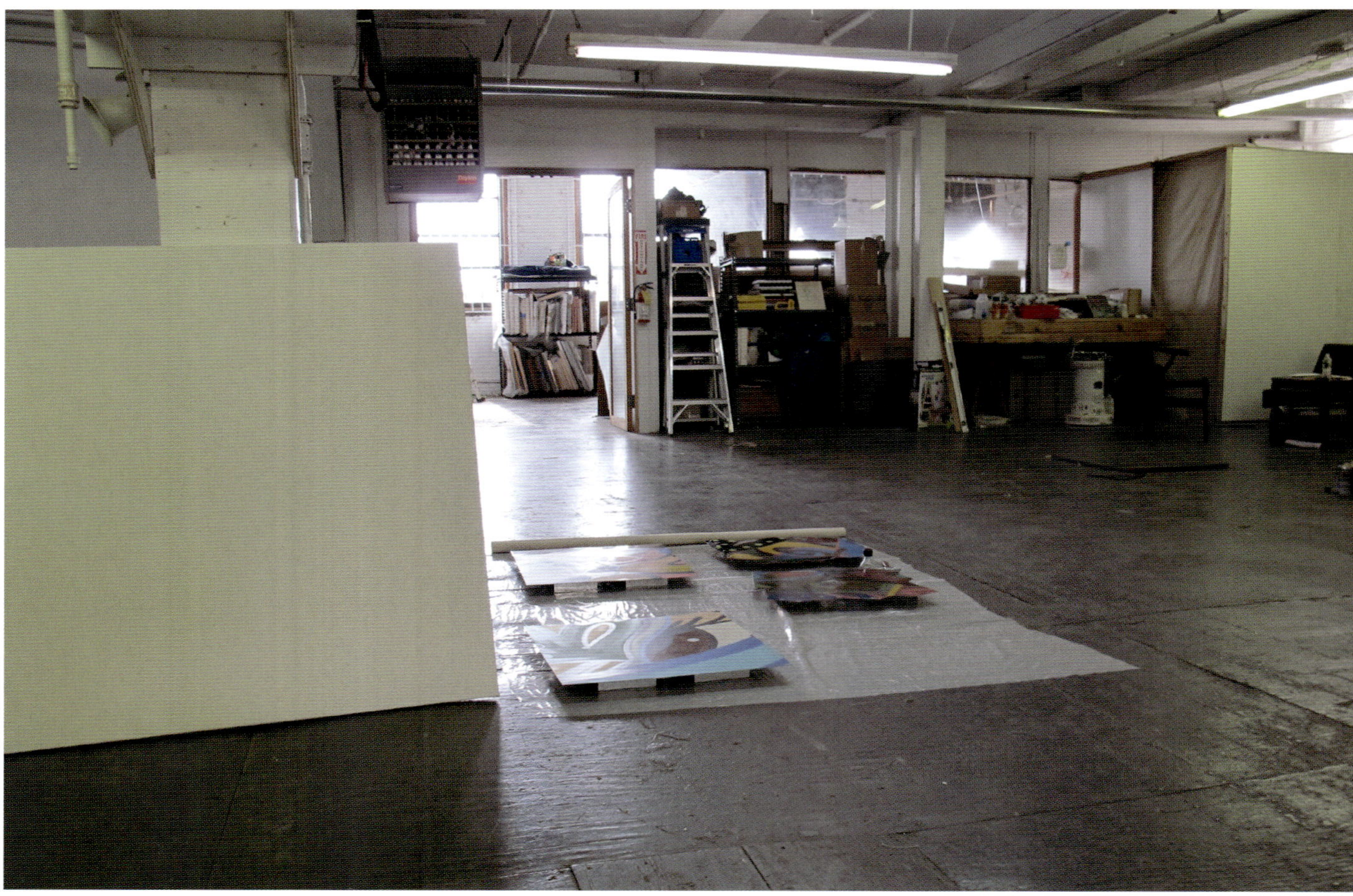

Studio 2015
Photo courtesy of the artist

Cover of *Arte Di Fronteira* catalogue
Bologna, Italy, 1983

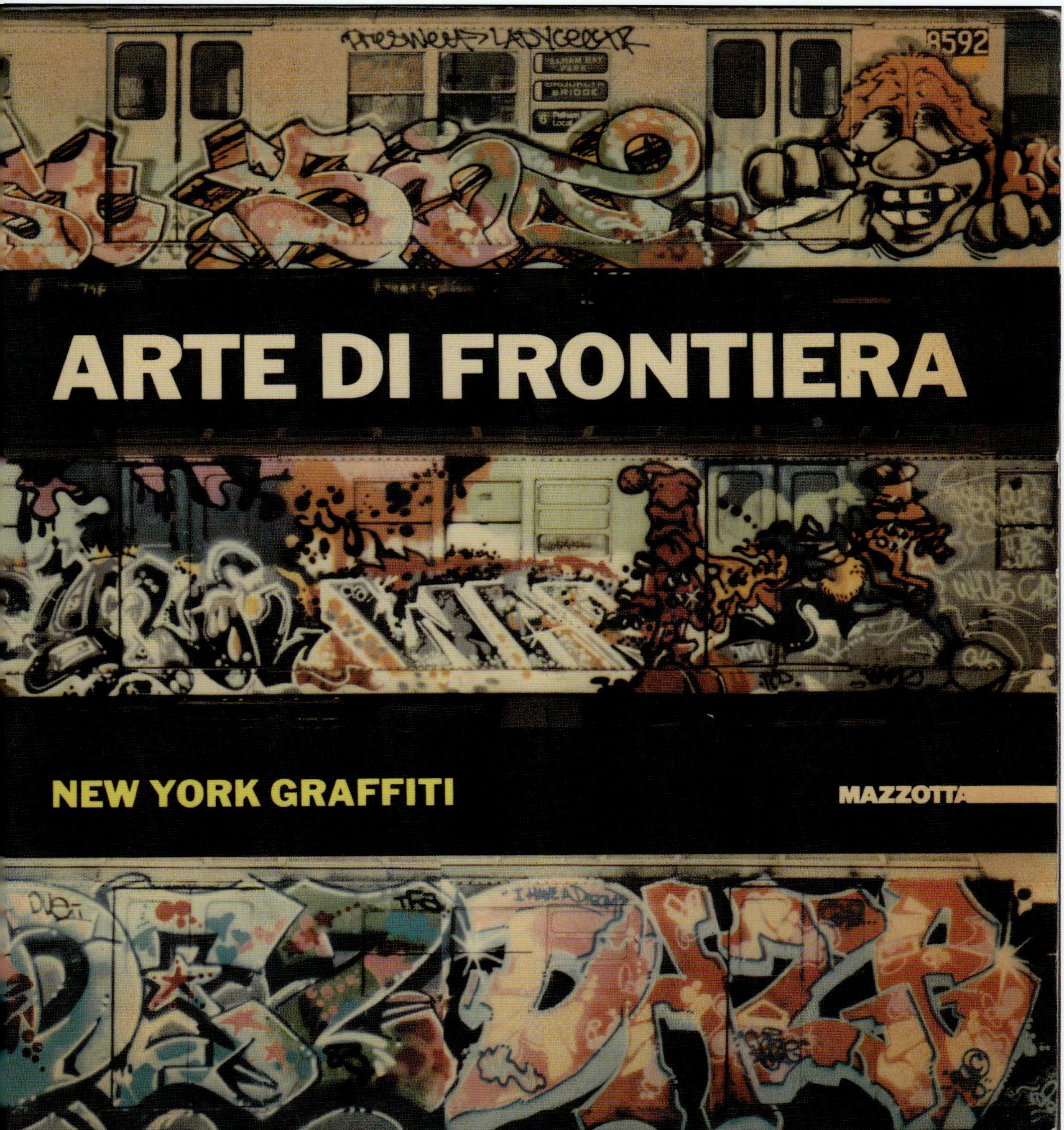

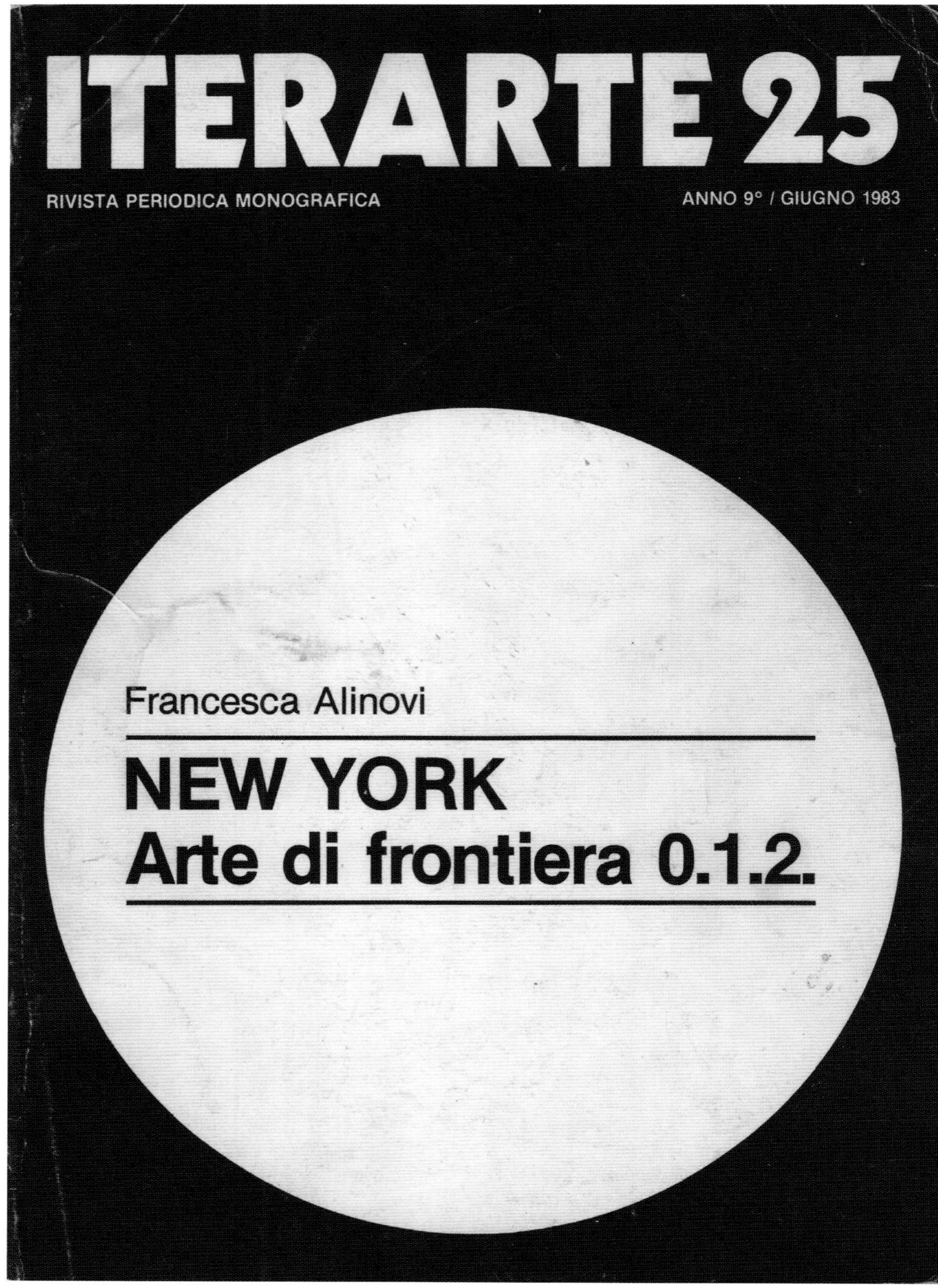

Cover of *Iterarte* magazine, 1983

In 1982 I took my first trip to Europe to participate in the exhibition *Arte de Frontiera*, curated by Francesca Alinovi. This groundbreaking exhibition took place at the Galeria Communale d'Arte Moderna in Bologna, Italy. It introduced for the first time artists such as Keith Haring, Kenny Scharf, John Ahearn, Jean-Michel Basquiat, Rammellzee, Crash, Lady Pink, and myself to a European audience. I remember taking the flight over and then the train from Milan to Bologna. I felt as if I were in a movie by Roberto Rossellini. The exhibition pulled together not only what was going on in galleries downtown but also what was beginning to emerge in alternative spaces such as Fashion Moda in the Bronx. It perfectly captured the climate and sense of community that was prevalent in New York in 1984. Sadly Francesca Alinovi did not live to see the opening.

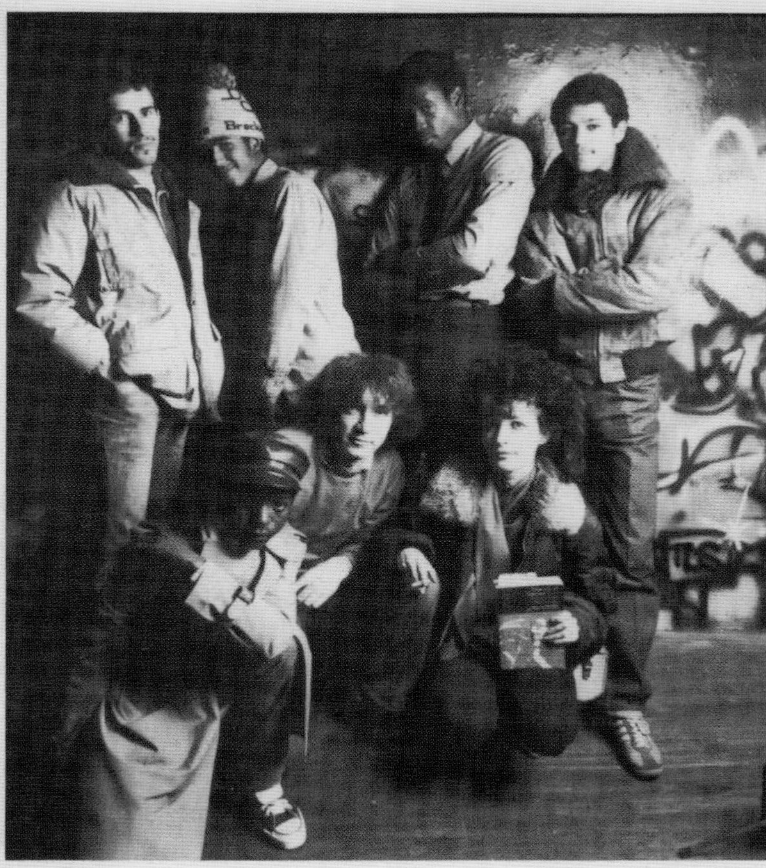

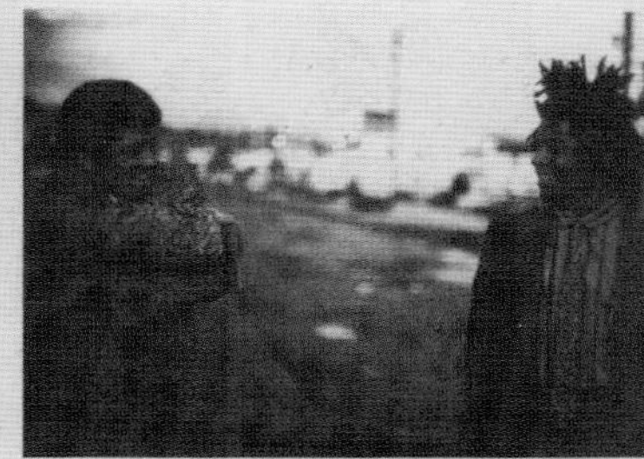

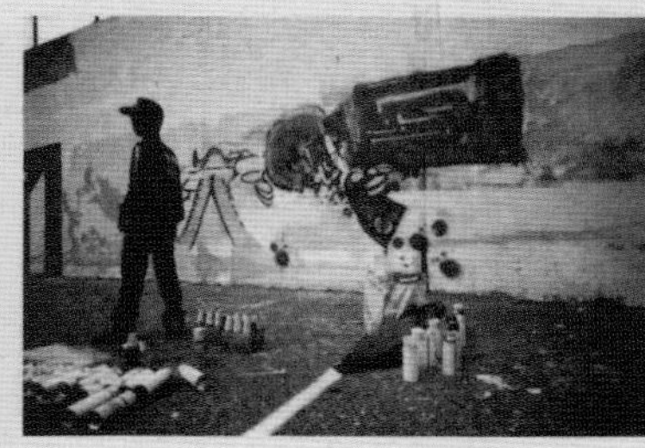

Rammellzee e Jean Michel Basquiat, Los Angeles, 1982, foto Torton

A One mentre spruzza la vernice spray sul muro di una scuola nel South Bronx

Da sinistra a destra, dietro, Crash, Toxic, Koor, Daze e, davanti, A One, Stefan Eins, Francesca Alinovi, all'inaugurazione della mostra del Panzerismo Iconoclasta a Fashion Moda, novembre 1981, foto Michael Transue

mato e militare: è lo stile di un nuovo linguaggio atomico e nucleare che spara i propri missili linguistici dritti a colpire il bersaglio della civiltà del 2000.

Da A One, una sera, assieme a Toxic, vengo iniziata segretamente alle teorie fantapocalittiche e medievalfuturologiche di Rammellzee, l'occulto capobanda di questi guerriglieri delle lettere armate, l'inventore persuasivo, e fascinoso, dell'iconoclastia combattuta a colpi di panzer di immagini, di carri armati di segni, mimetizzati sotto le vesti protettive del linguaggio dell'arte e della pittura. A One, sempre quella sera, mi fa leggere con aria da gran complotto il primo pamphlet d'assalto di Rammellzee, in cui Rammellzee profetizza, come un Nostradamus, per messaggi criptici e sibillini, la fine del linguaggio, dell'arte e della comunicazione occidentale.

Rammellzee è introvabile, inavvicinabile e, scoprirò poi, anche incomprensibile. Rammellzee è un senzatetto, non ha dimora, vive qua e là e spesso si rifugia nel suo ghetto nero di Far Rockaway, vicino a East Hampton, a due ore di treno da New York. In più è sempre in giro con la sua banda di rappers (lui parla al microfono, fa il Mic-Controller, con una splendida cantilena di parole inventate, e dà il ritmo agli electric boogie dancers). E quando finalmente lo incontro, lu parla una lingua slang slegata da ogni logica e da ogni grazia di dio. Dopo aver imparato l'inglese mi accorgo che con questi artisti neri l'inglese non serve più: non serve la grammatica, ma la lingua dell'affetto, della simpatia e dello «stonamento». Incontro Rammellzee davanti a un tavolo. E non riusciamo a dirci una parola. Ci rincontriamo davanti a un drink. E da lì nascerà un'intervista straordinaria.

Dopo aver incontrato i mostri del gusto, di natura e dell'arte, ora finalmente trovo i mostri del linguaggio. Comunicare con Rammellzee è come comunicare col quartomondo extraterrestre. Al mio ritorno scrivo, sempre su «Flash Art», le mie prime esperienze con lo slang del Duemila. *«Penne nere e visi pallidi», i kids sul piede di guerra, ultima generazione dell'arte newyorkese, musi neri bianchi e caffelatte, di cui raccontavo i primi tam tam d'assalto l'anno scorso, oltrepassate le frontiere geografiche di Manahattan e conquistata l'isola del dollaro, lanciano ora sofisticati missili linguistici diretti a sfondare le barriere del linguaggio.*

I kids hanno elaborato un inintercettabile gergo linguistico subdolo e criptico, barbaro e futuribile. Un gergo dalla forza insidiosa, che disarticola la lingua convenzionale conosciuta e spezza le linee di associazione pattuite dai regolamenti della comunicazione ufficiale.

È questo lo slang del Duemila, il gergo privato e indecifrabile coniato da gruppi eccentrici di cultura che legittimano le loro violazioni di minoranza sulla conquista largamente garantita di una consolidata lingua di maggioranza: la lingua dei mass-media, la lingua della economia e della produzione, la lingua degli armamenti militari, la lingua della colonizzazione dello spazio, la lingua dei computers e dell'informatica. Assicurato lo scorrimento fluido e facile del linguaggio funzionale universale, lo slang si inventa la lingua dell'affetto, dell'arte e del complotto.

I kids hanno coniato slangs personali che confondono i sistemi della comunicazione attuale, perché provengono loro stessi da una personale condizione di confusione naturale e

28

Iterarte magazine, 1983

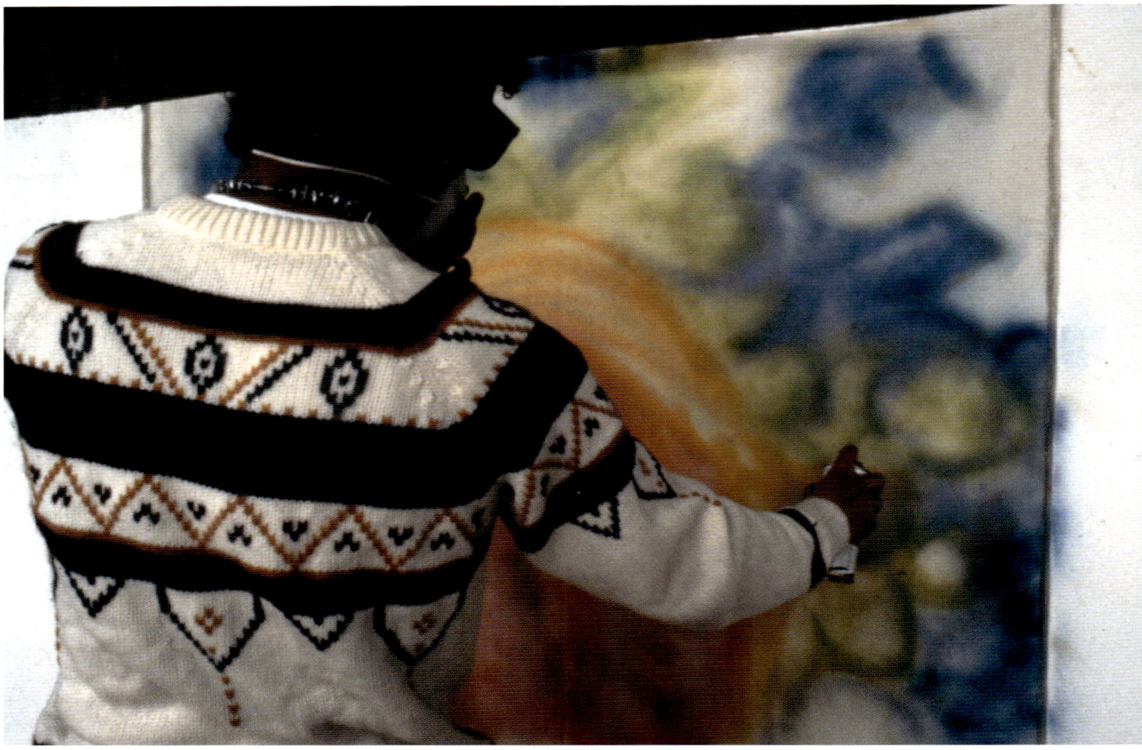

Painting on the terrace of the Galleria Communale d'Arte Moderna
Bologna, Italy
Photo © Gian Franco Mantegna

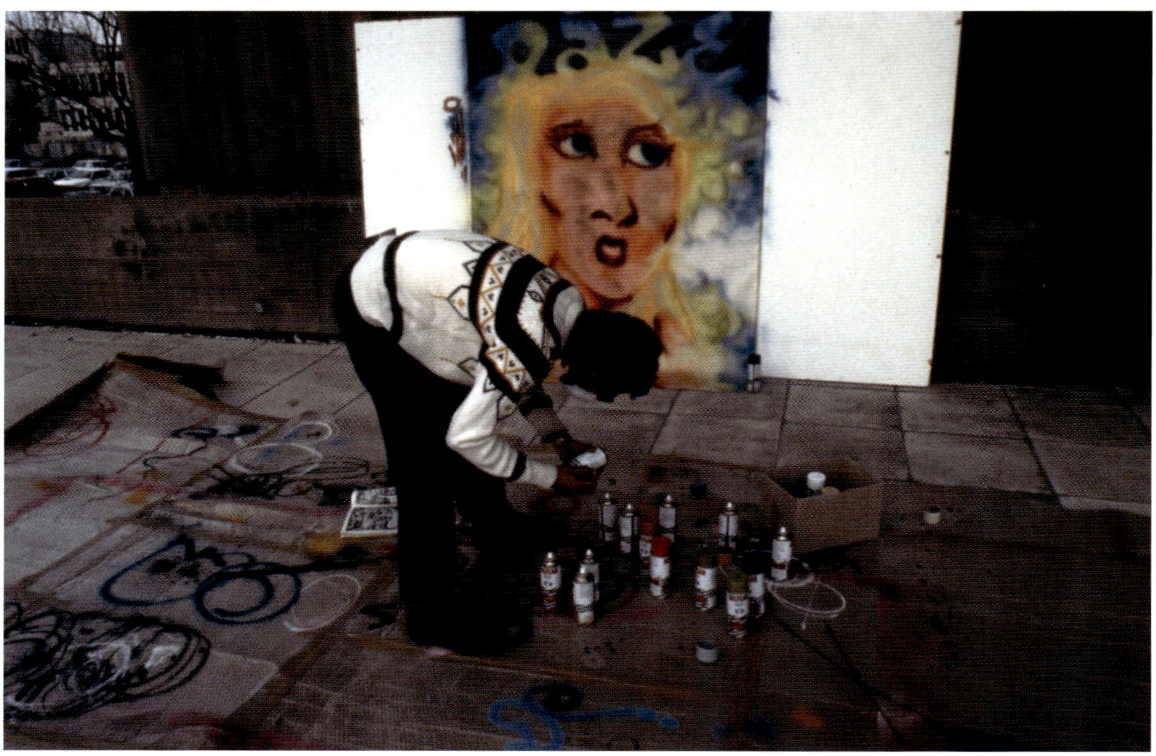

Photo © Gian Franco Mantegna

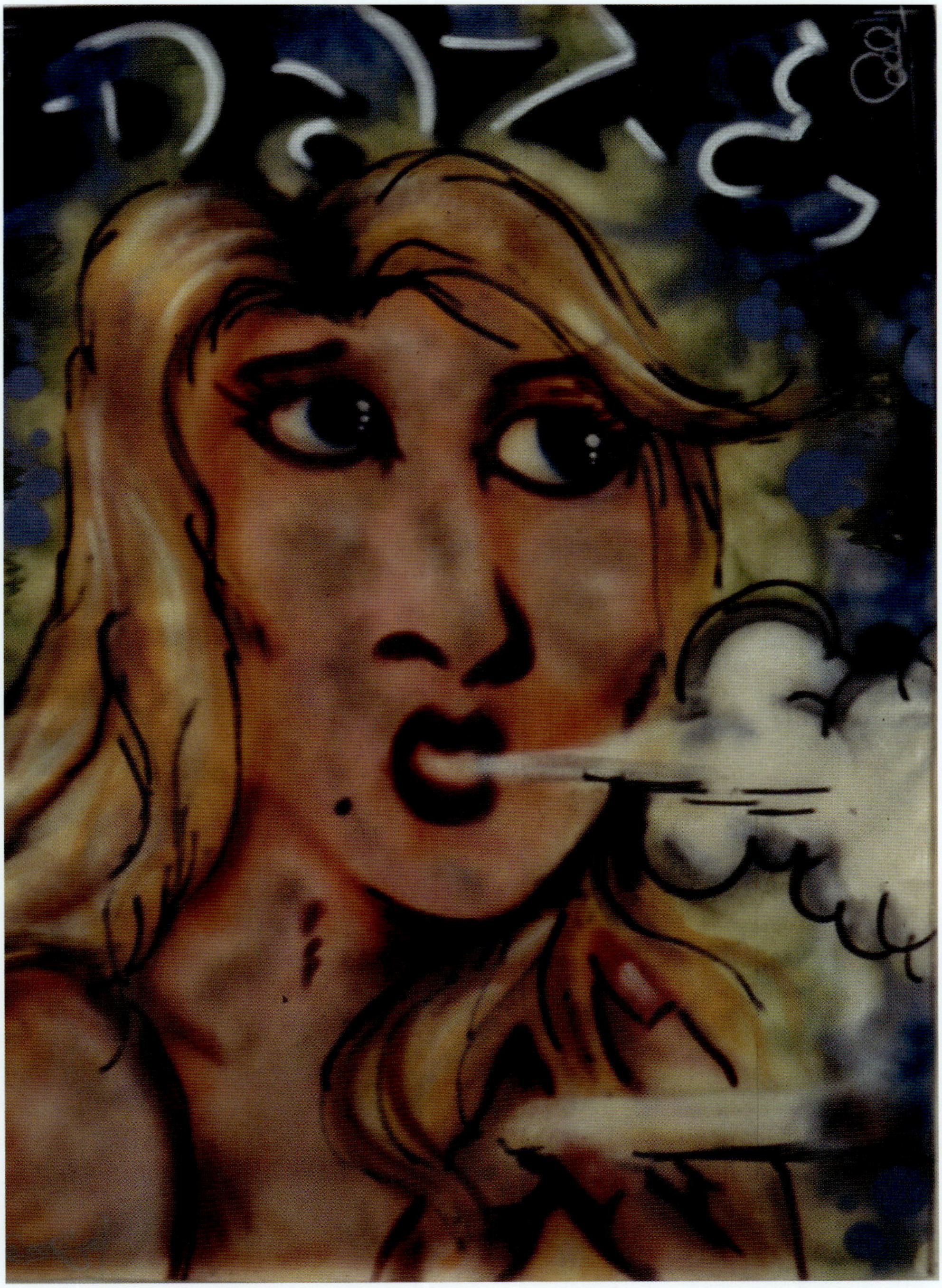

Photo © Gian Franco Mantegna

This exhibition was the launch point for many artists' careers in Europe. I remember Crash, Toxic, and I making paintings on the terrace of the museum, taking interviews, and befriending local artists. The audiences in Europe seemed to be able to appreciate what we were doing as art without all the social stigmas that American audiences seemed to be so fond of. That was the first of many subsequent European trips to follow.

At that time much of the attention was coming from countries such as Germany, Italy, France, and the Netherlands. These countries embraced not only the paintings that I made at the time but the culture as a whole. One of my fondest memories from that period was having a solo exhibition in 1989 at the Galerie B5 in Monte Carlo. To be flown to this chic destination and have an exhibition was an honor. The opening was well attended and that night the gallery hosted a dinner for me in a restaurant overlooking the French Riviera. Another cinematic experience!

Traveling to Europe, I would completely immerse myself in the culture of whatever country I was in. I was excited to visit world-class museums such as the Centre Pompidou in Paris, the Prado in Madrid, the Uffizi in Florence, and the Museum Ludwig in Cologne. These experiences found their way pretty quickly into my work.

My world view was expanding and so was the content of my painting. The painting *Japanese Subways* was about my first trip to Japan and feeling very much like

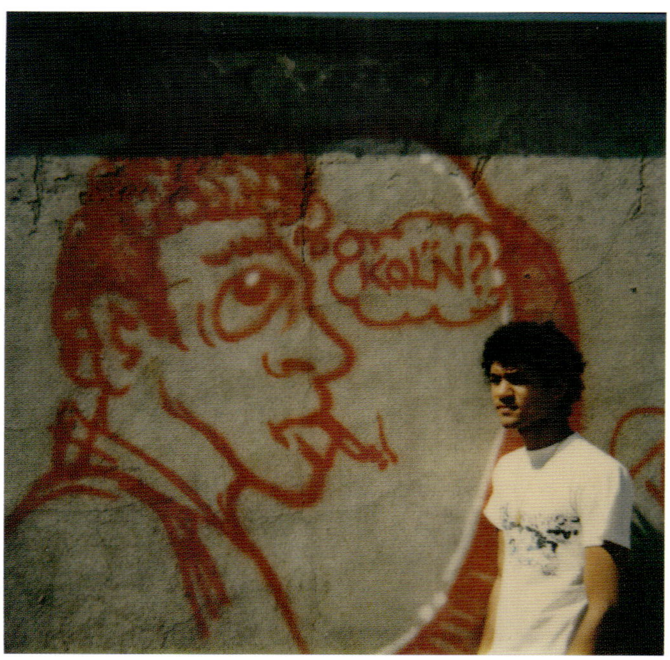

Self-portrait in Cologne,
Germany, 1984

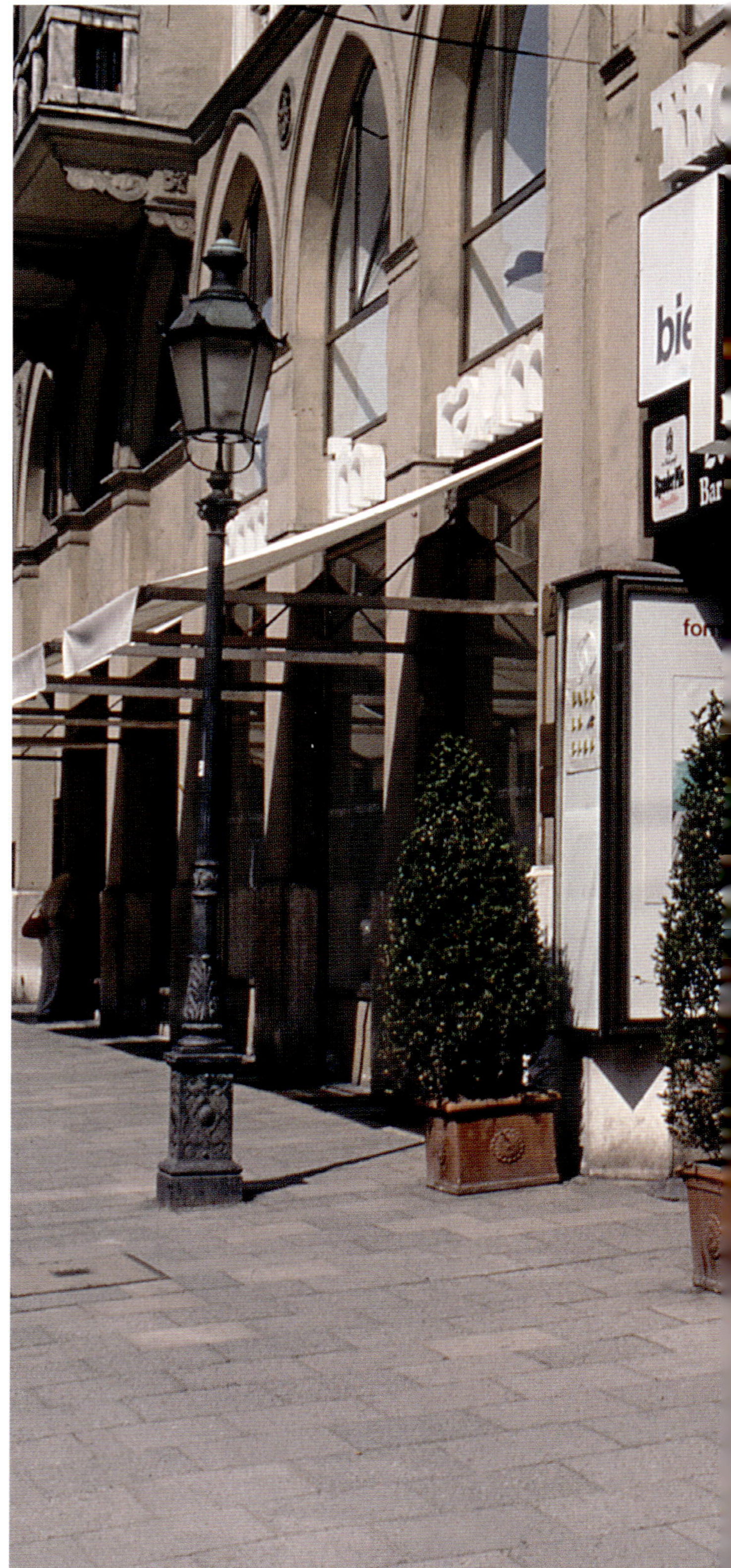

Painting I did for the façade of Galerie
Thomas in Munich, Germany, 1984
Photo ©Martha Cooper

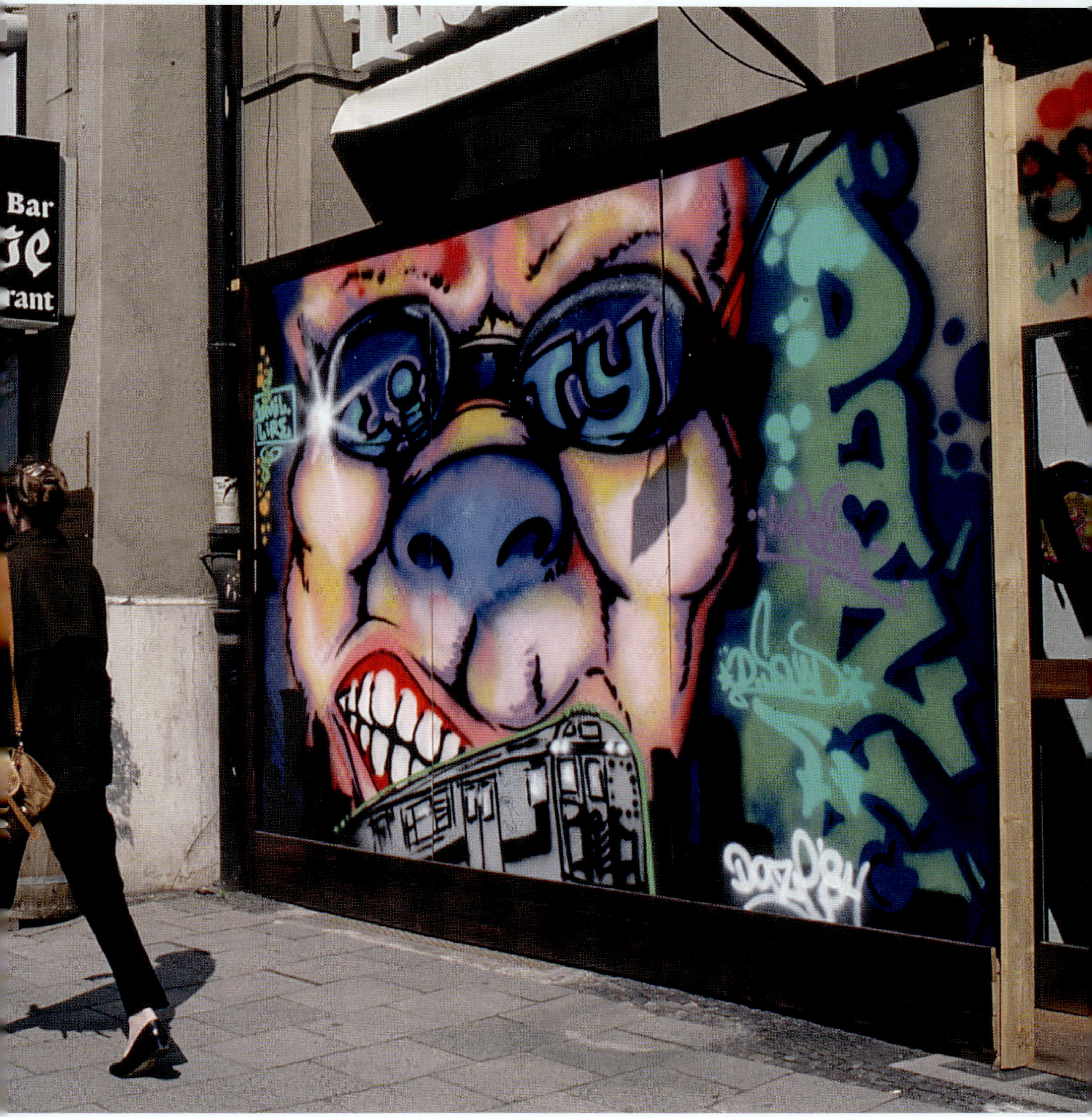
Bar
rant
TY

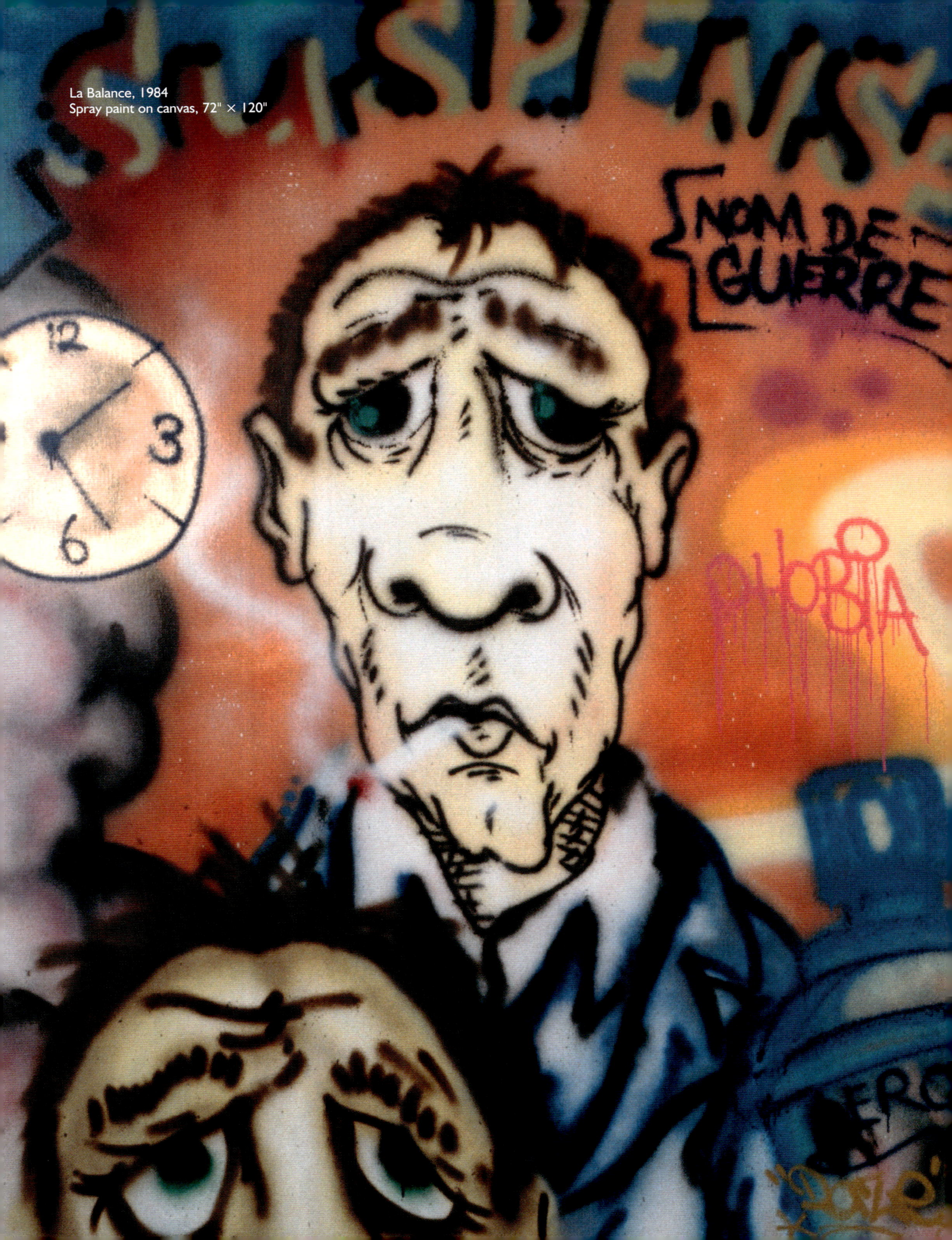

La Balance, 1984
Spray paint on canvas, 72" × 120"

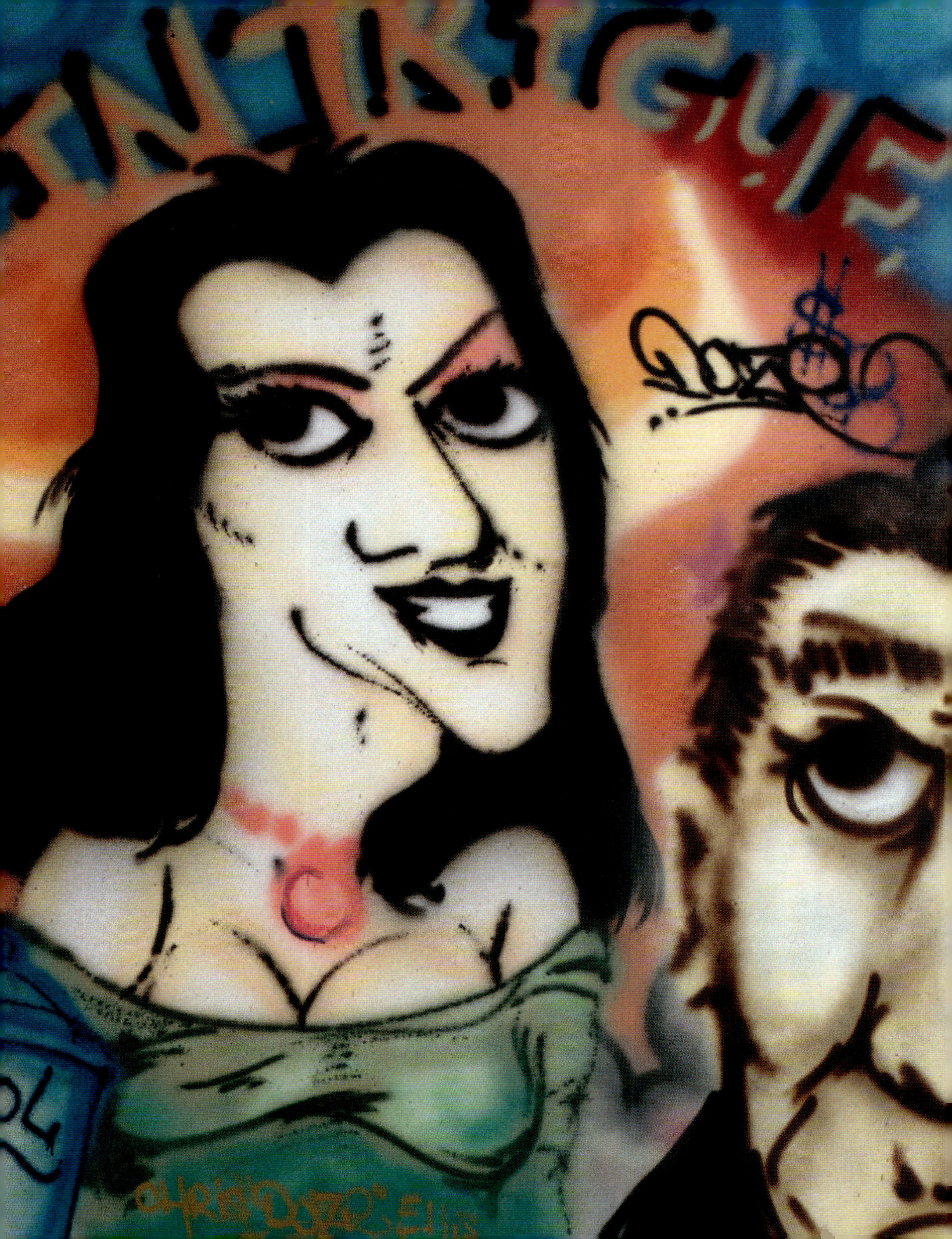

the outsider there. It was about the long flight to Japan and trying to navigate my way around Tokyo once I arrived. The painting *La Balance* was based on a French detective movie directed by Bob Swain. Even when I wasn't in Europe I began to immerse myself in films directed by such masters of cinema as Goddard, Truffaut, Fellini, Rossellini, and Fassbender. It is by no coincidence that many of my paintings from this period are composed to look like film stills.

In contrast to what was going on in Europe I was still having a difficult time getting my work shown in America. I would meet dealers that would selfishly want to represent, and in fact control, the entire movement. By 1985 the art world's love affair with graffiti had ended. In retrospect I think once the dealers realized that it was not going to be an easy task to manipulate and control the culture, they were out. I was lucky enough to have an audience in Europe. For this I am eternally grateful.

In 2010 I was invited by Mary Dinaburg and Howard Ruttowski of Fortune Cookie Projects to have an exhibition in Singapore. I had never before shown in Southeast Asia and was really excited about the prospect of showing in a completely new environment. The exhibition was not a retrospective in the traditional sense but instead focused on summing up my world until that point. In addition to the exhibition the Vivo City shopping center commissioned me to paint a large mural in the atrium of one of their buildings. Howard and Mary were both really amazing to work with and they planned the exhibition to tour additionally to Beijing, China, and Seoul, South Korea. Although I had briefly shown in Japan and Hong Kong before, these exhibitions were more of a proper introduction of my work to Asia.

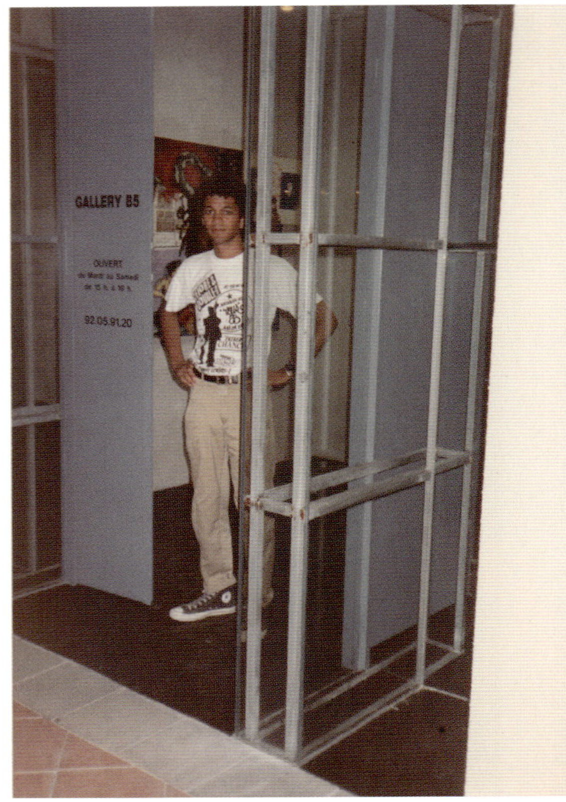

The Galerie B5, Monte Carlo

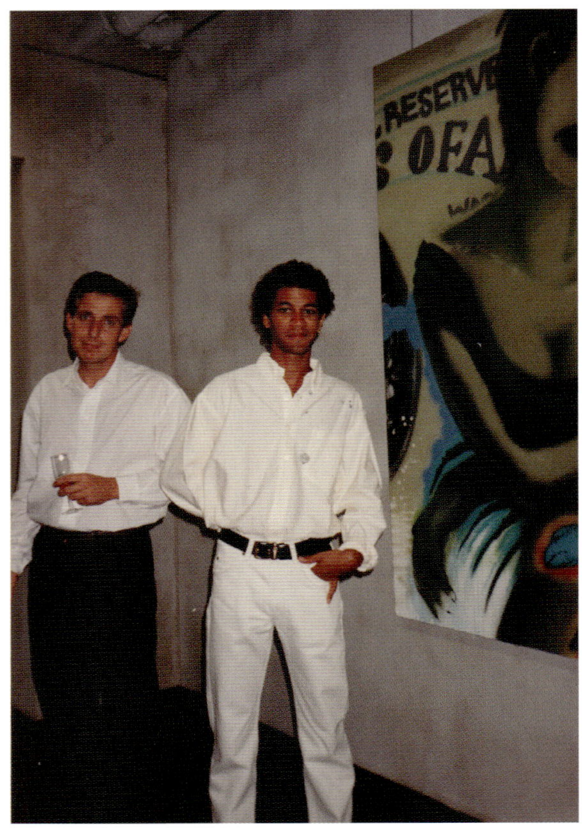

Mr. Willem Speerstra and I enjoying the opening
Monte Carlo, 1989

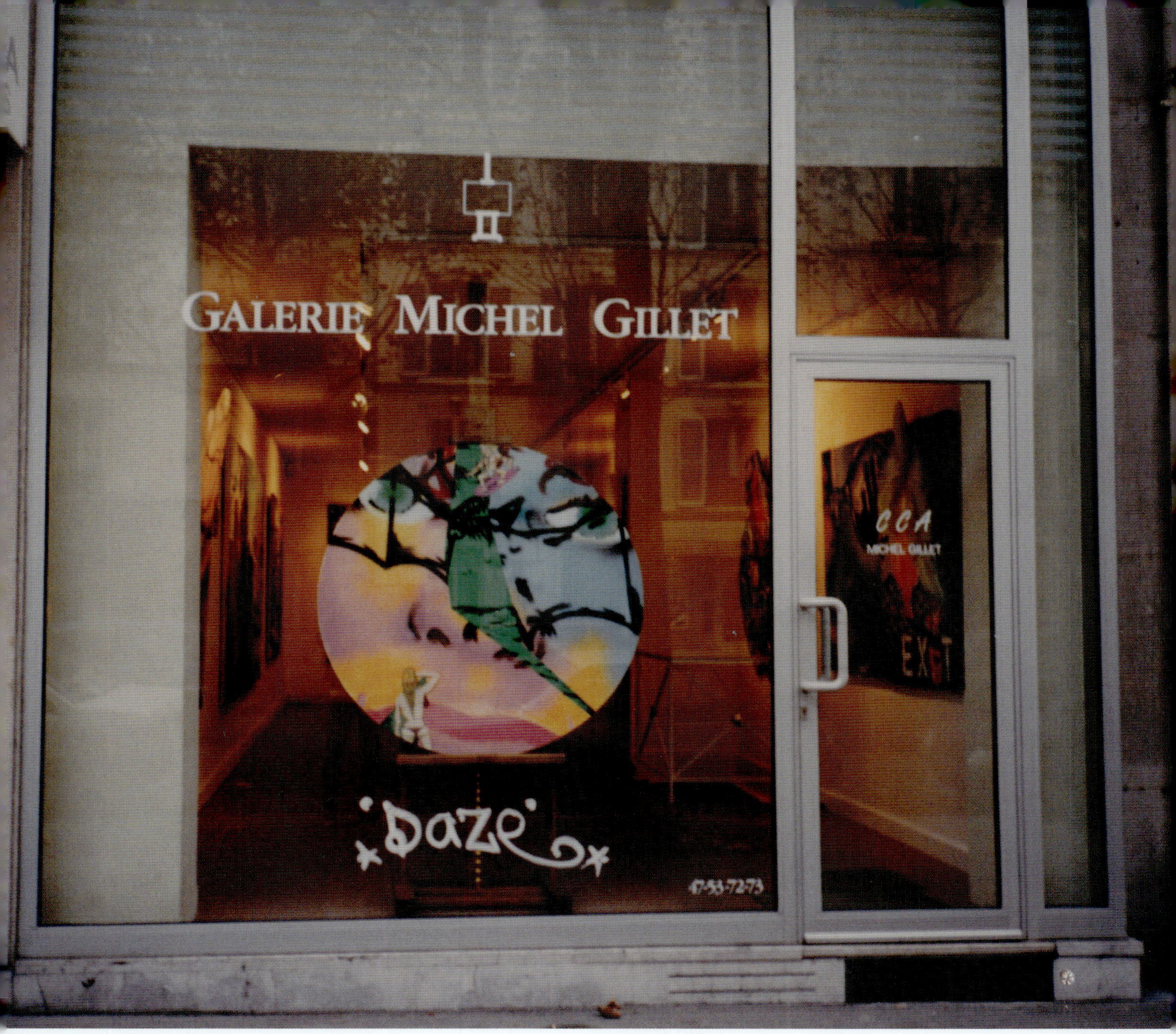

Galerie Michel Gillet
Paris, France, 1990

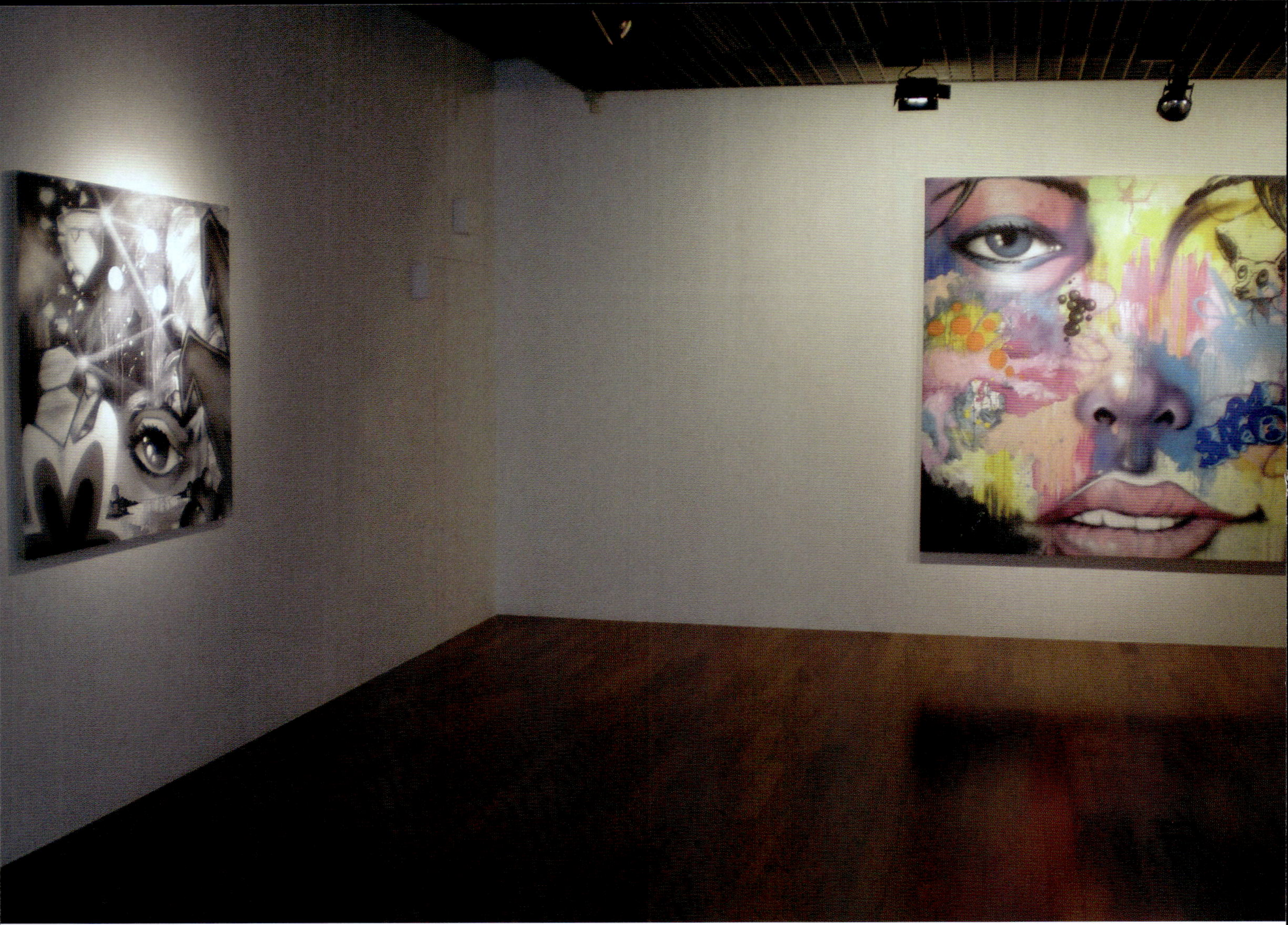

Installation photo of my show at The Watergate Gallery, Seoul, South Korea, 2010

It is important to note that in addition to all the other elements that comprise my work as a whole, an important new chapter would emerge: art education. In the mid 1990s I began working with kids on small mural workshops. Typically they would last for a few days to a week at most. The workshops would begin with me doing a simple slideshow presentation of my work, having a discussion after, then moving on to either working on drawings or a mural directly. I did at least one or two of these a year for the next five years. At first it was just something to do on the side to supplement my income. Usually these projects were funded by some kind of city council or came out of a school budget. However, from the beginning, my approach to it all was different. No matter what the size or scale of the project, I wanted to encourage the kids to do some kind of thinking on their own. I didn't want to look at them as my assistants, telling them

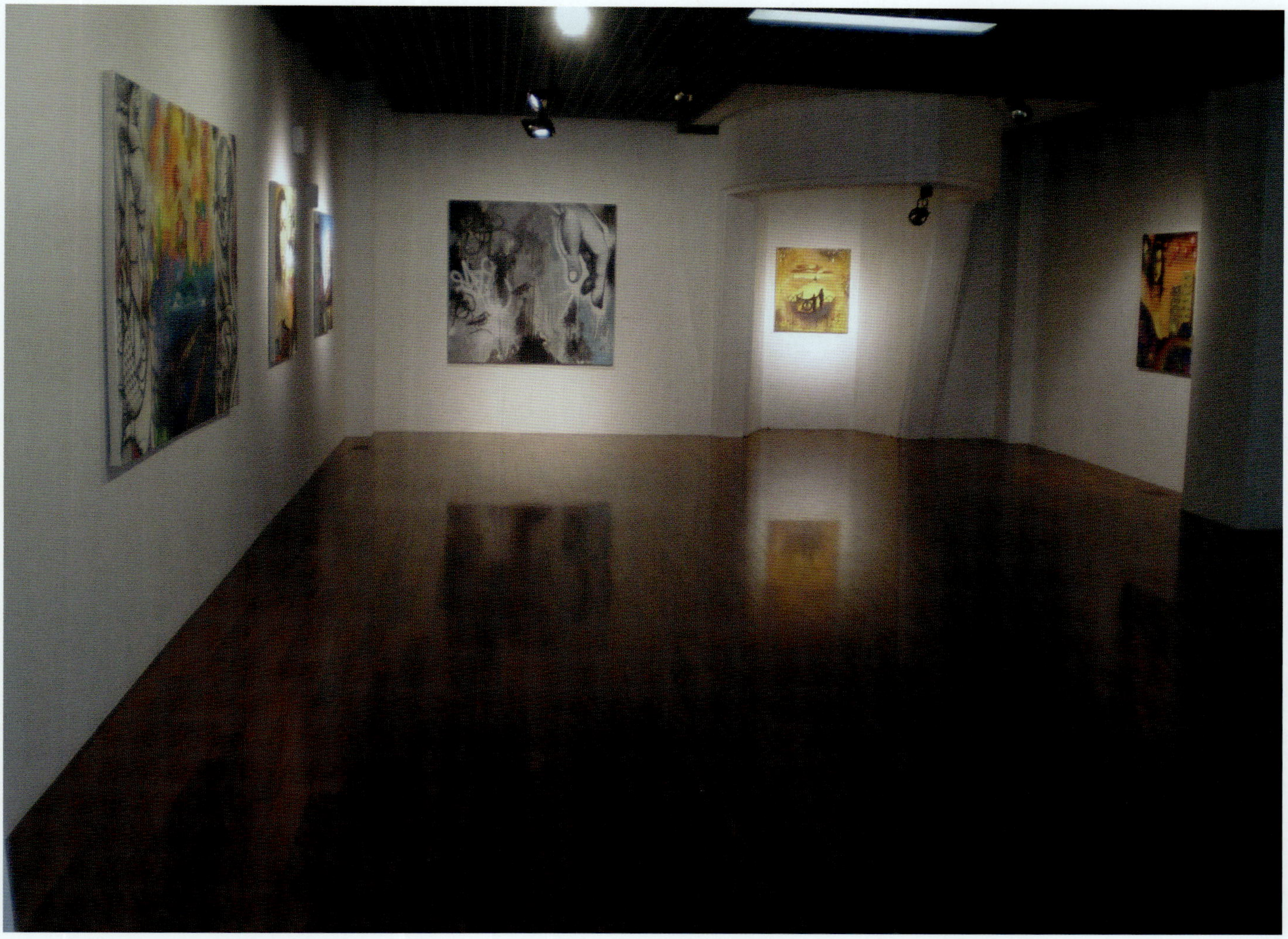

The Watergate Gallery exhibition
Seoul, South Korea, 2010

when and where to paint. I wanted them to gain knowledge through the experience of working with me. My goal was to build confidence in them and to teach them the importance of teamwork. I realized early on that I had the one thing so many teachers fight for: I had their attention. I realized that no matter the economic background or cultural difference, most kids were interested to some degree in graffiti. In coming to this realization at least half the battle was won.

These mural workshops were a win-win for everyone; they were those rare occasions when everyone gets something out of them. Sponsors were happy because the projects were a success, and children and their parents were happy with the outcome. In 2001 I began to take the project worldwide by working with Christian Schneeberger and the city council of Kruezlingen, Switzerland. I was unsure about how this type of program would go down in Europe. I didn't know whether or not kids from a relatively small area in Switzerland would be able to relate to my experiences as an underground urban explorer. My fears however were unfounded as that project was a complete success. The students embraced both my presentation and the project as a whole. During the first year we completed a large mural on the main street of Kruezlingen, and a huge multi-paneled work just outside of the city. This program was so successful that I was invited back a second time a year later to continue the program.

Following the success of that workshop, in 2004 I was invited to Brazil by the United States Consulate and the organization CUFA to work on murals, lectures, and youth workshops in several *favelas* [urban slums] in Rio de Janeiro. Working in these areas was a bit more of a challenge, mostly due to lack of financial responsibility on the part of the government, but also due to language barriers. But I was able to overcome both obstacles and provide a youth program that all were able to participate in. From these experiences I was able to see first hand how resourceful people in these communities could be, working with very little or no aid from government agencies. I viewed myself as someone contributing a positive element to the local community and respectfully approached it as such. I was invited back four years later to repeat the program.

Through these diverse experiences I realized that I had a young audience worldwide whom I could collaborate

Painting with kids' workshop in Rio de Janeiro, 2004

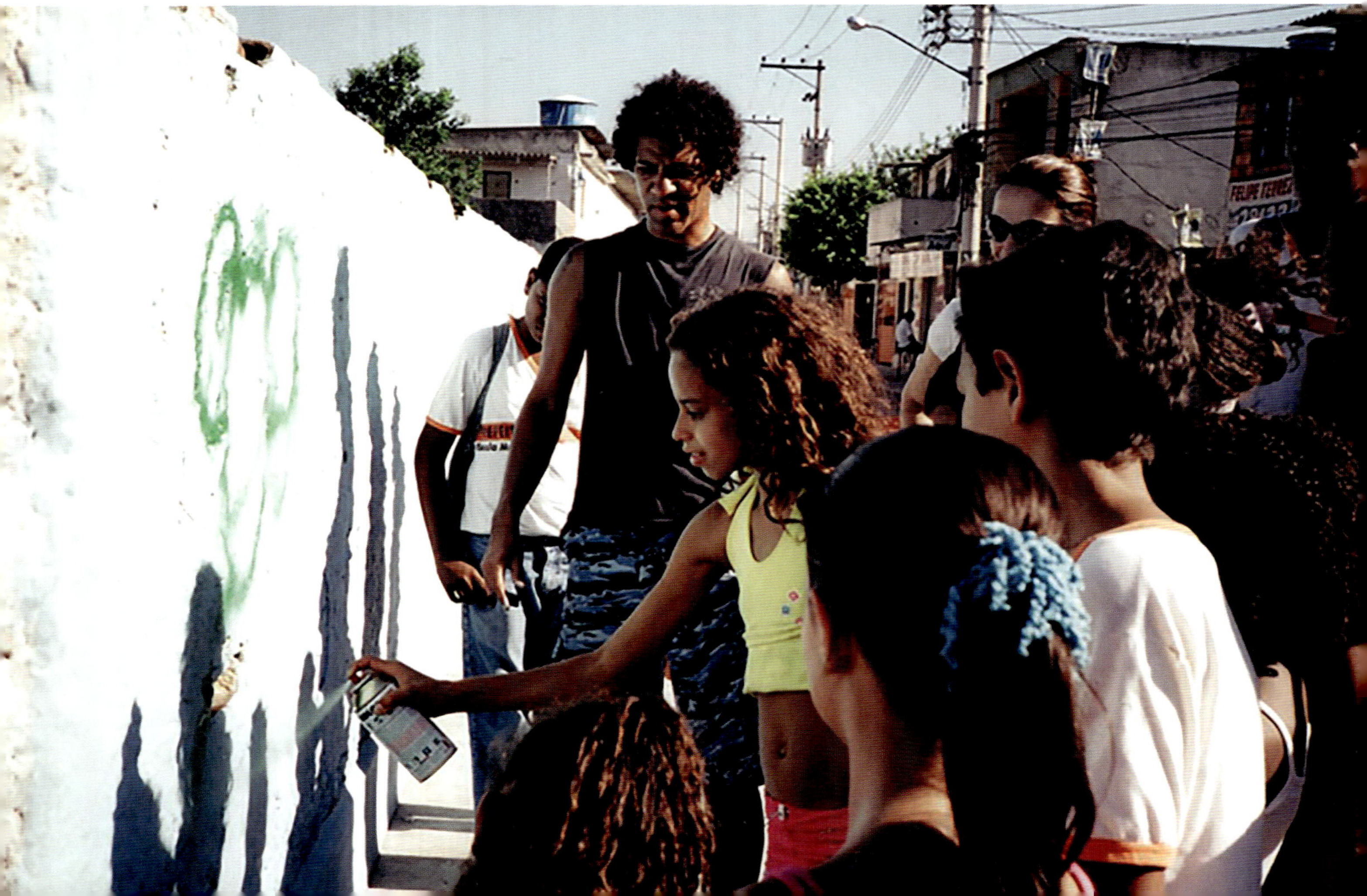

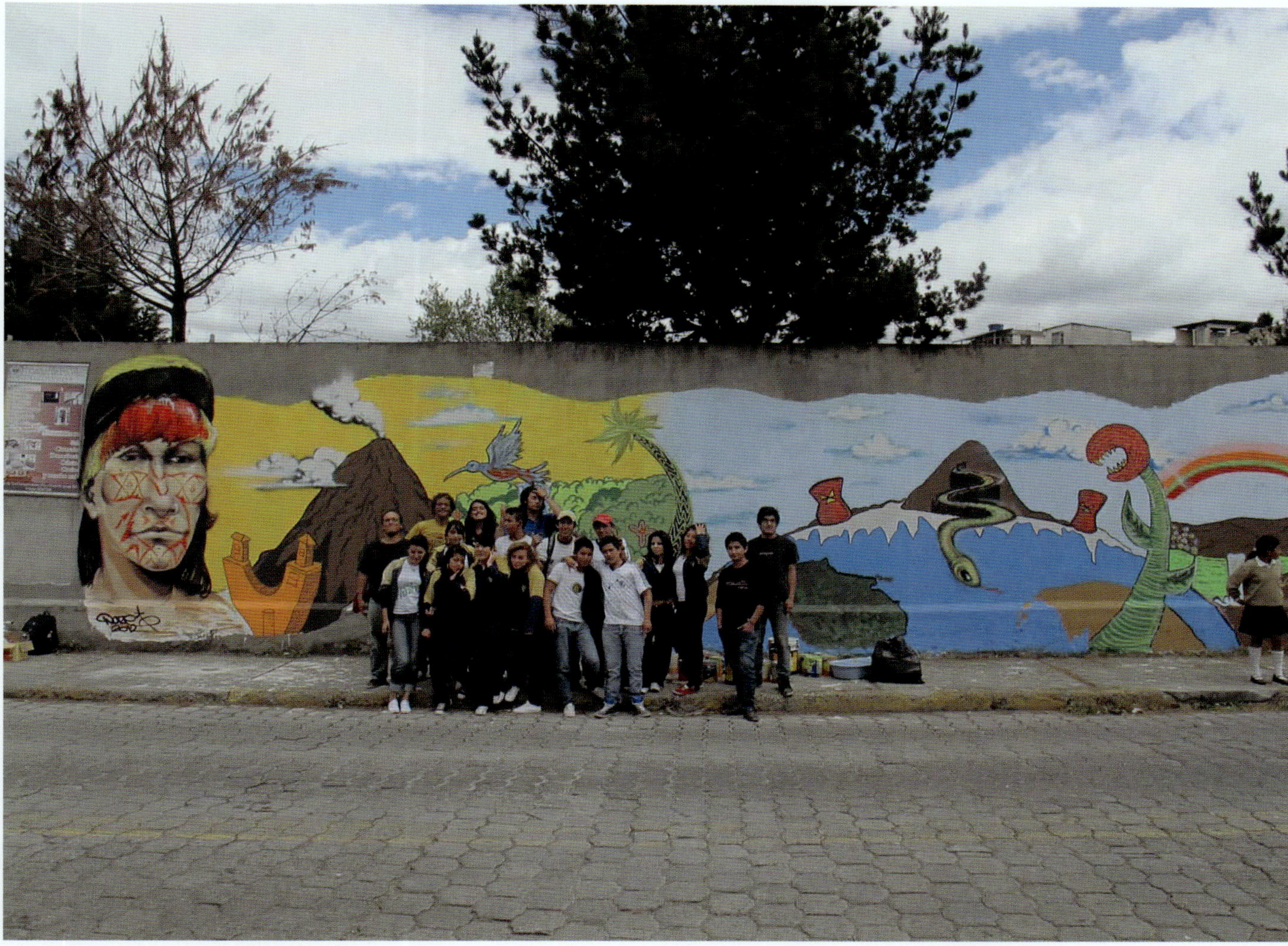

Collaborative mural with students from Quito, Ecuador smARTpower initiative of the State Department and the Bronx Museum, 2012

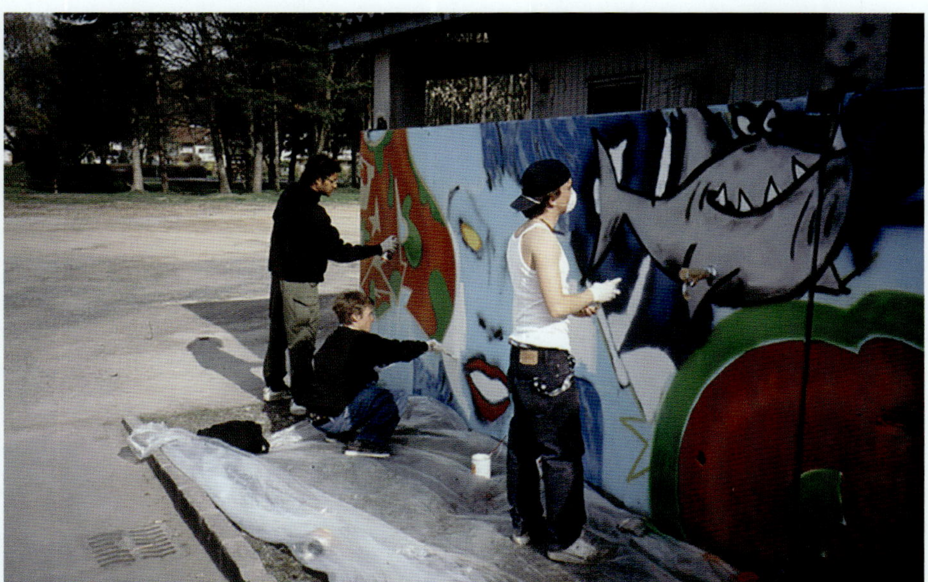

Painting with kids from the Urban Art Project, Feldkirch, Austria, 1999

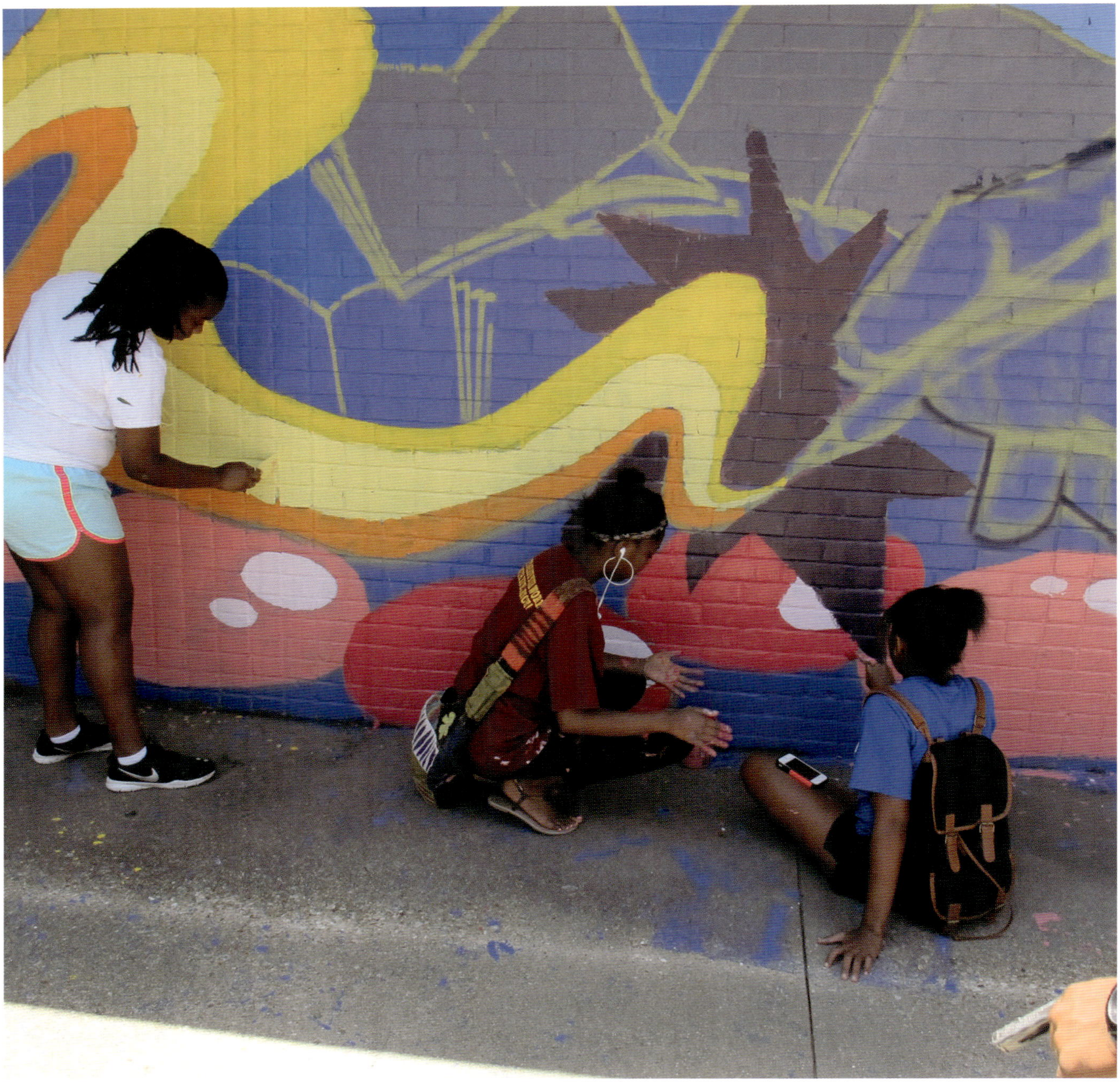

Students painting mural as a part of the 2014 Museum of Public Art Initiative
Baton Rouge, Louisiana

with regardless of social, economic, and cultural differences. These experiences were very far away from the tony galleries and museums of New York, Paris, and London, but no less important.

I've painted all over the world but there is nothing quite like working in New York. The difference is that whether I am working in my studio, or on the street, the stakes here are always high. Whenever I'm painting something on the street there are all sorts of intrinsic factors that come to mind. I am always aware of the work of my peers and how what I'm doing will stand up to critics. At the same time I'm aware not only of the history of the culture but where it's going and how I can take it to the next level. I have a deep respect for history but at the same time it's not some place I want

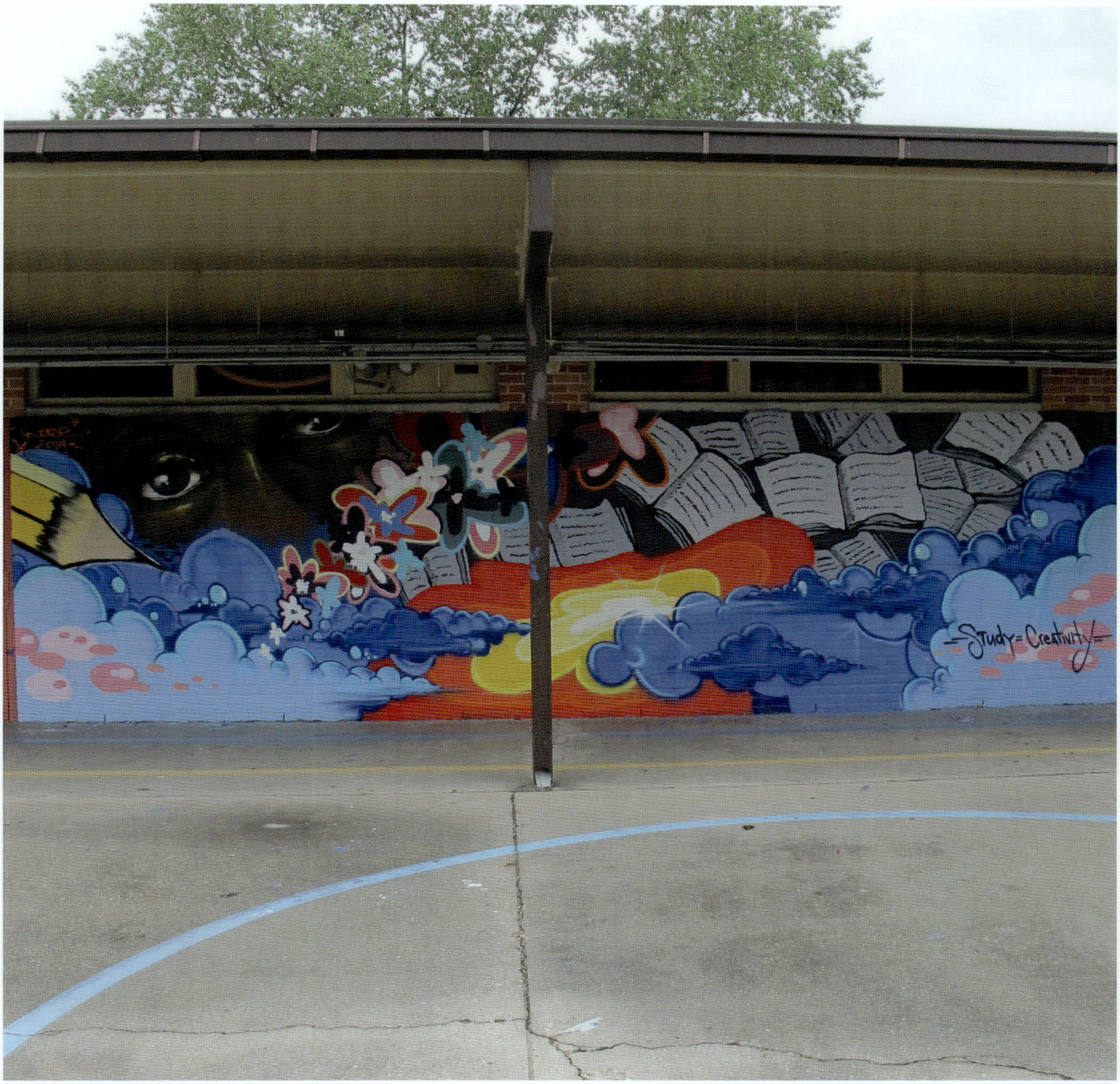

Completed mural with students
Museum of Public Art, Baton Rouge, Louisiana, 2014

to dwell. When I'm painting at the studio I'm less aware of the work of my peers and more conscious of my place in history. I've always felt that painting in public is more of a physical act and painting in the studio is more cerebral. In both instances I've always left the element of chance to rear its head and play a part. I would not be so arrogant as to suggest my work is superior to what I've seen in museums but I'd like my work to be able to co-exist in the same room. If I can do that, then I've accomplished something.

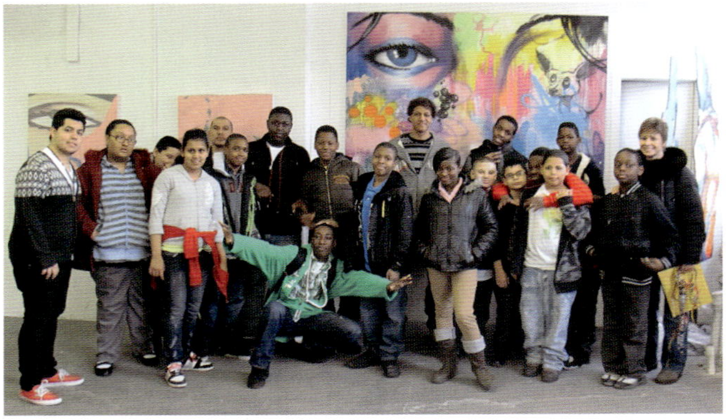

Studio visit with students from the Leap Arts organization

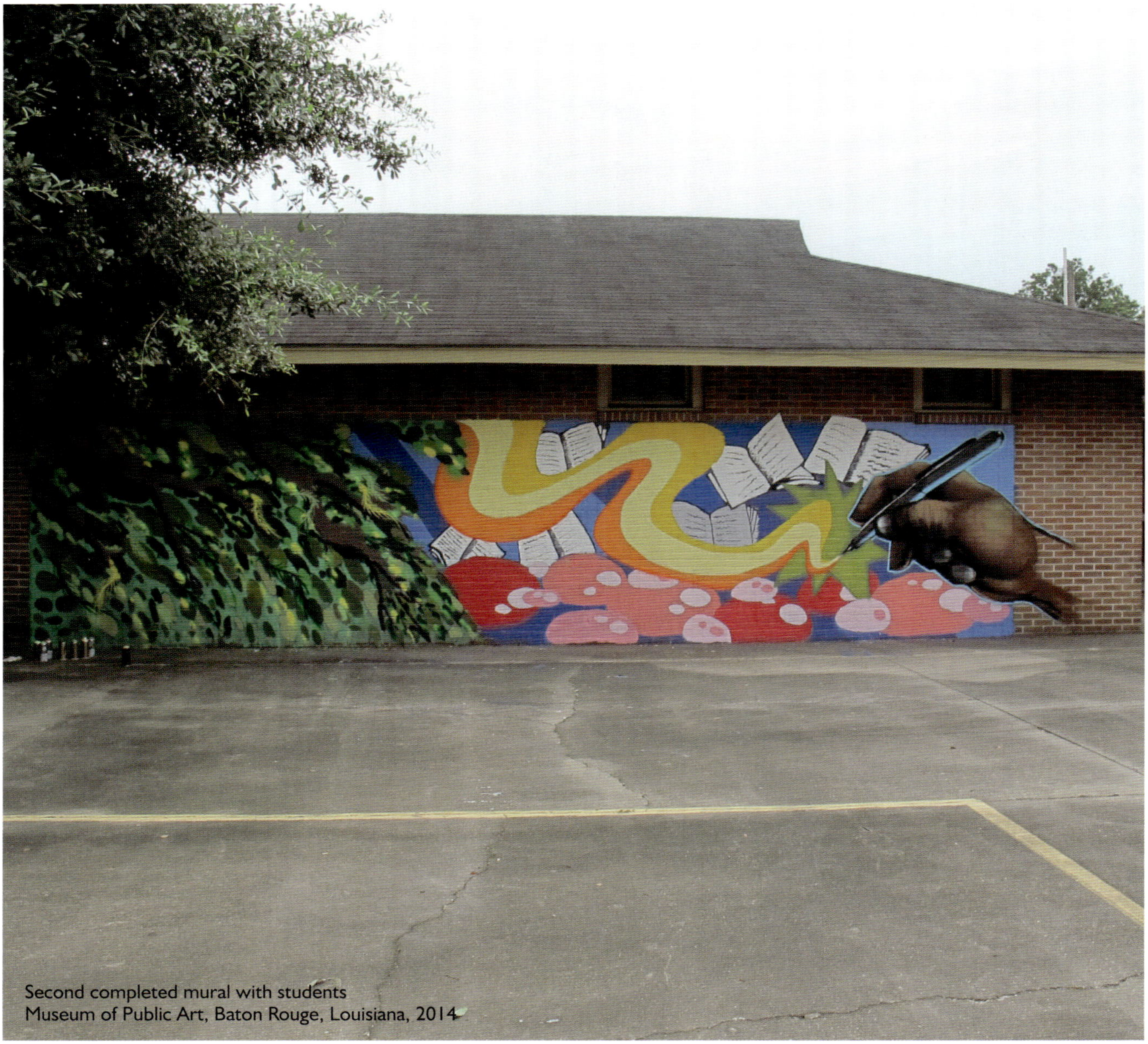

Second completed mural with students
Museum of Public Art, Baton Rouge, Louisiana, 2014

I've been fortunate to have had the opportunity to paint walls in countries as diverse as Brazil, Ecuador, Beijing, Germany, Paris, Italy, and Australia, to name a few. In the last fifteen years I've seen the landscape of New York change in a way that's made it less conducive to painting outside. Each year there are fewer and fewer walls to paint. I think this is due to many conditions but the main one is simply that old buildings are being torn down and replaced by monolithic architecture made of glass and steel. The city is losing a lot of its once-interesting and historically diverse buildings. What they are being replaced with is slick and soulless. Though there is nothing quite like painting in New York, in recent years I've preferred painting murals in other countries. Since 2002 I've painted a large majority of my walls in Brazil, Sao Paulo, and Rio, in particular. I've painted some amazing murals in collaboration with artists such as Binho, The Fleshbeck Crew, and Os Gemeos, to name a few. I have a deep respect for their work and found a new kind of creative freedom there that I had not experienced since the early 1980s in New York. The Brazilian artists work together in a way that is both very free and creative. They are not afraid to experiment or try new ideas. I found their approach to painting really inspiring and fresh and tried to contribute as much as I could to this spirit.

In addition to painting in Brazil I've always enjoyed painting in Europe. I've always found the scene in such countries as Italy and France to be quite refreshing. It seems as if artists in these countries really studied what was historically going on in New York. They wanted a complete knowledge of what was happening from the early 1970s onward. Whenever I traveled to Europe I was always met with a host of questions about what it was like painting from the mid-1970s until the early '80s. In addition to wanting to acquire as much factual knowledge as possible, there is a real sense of community in Europe that is very positive.

Rio de Janiero, Brazil, 2004

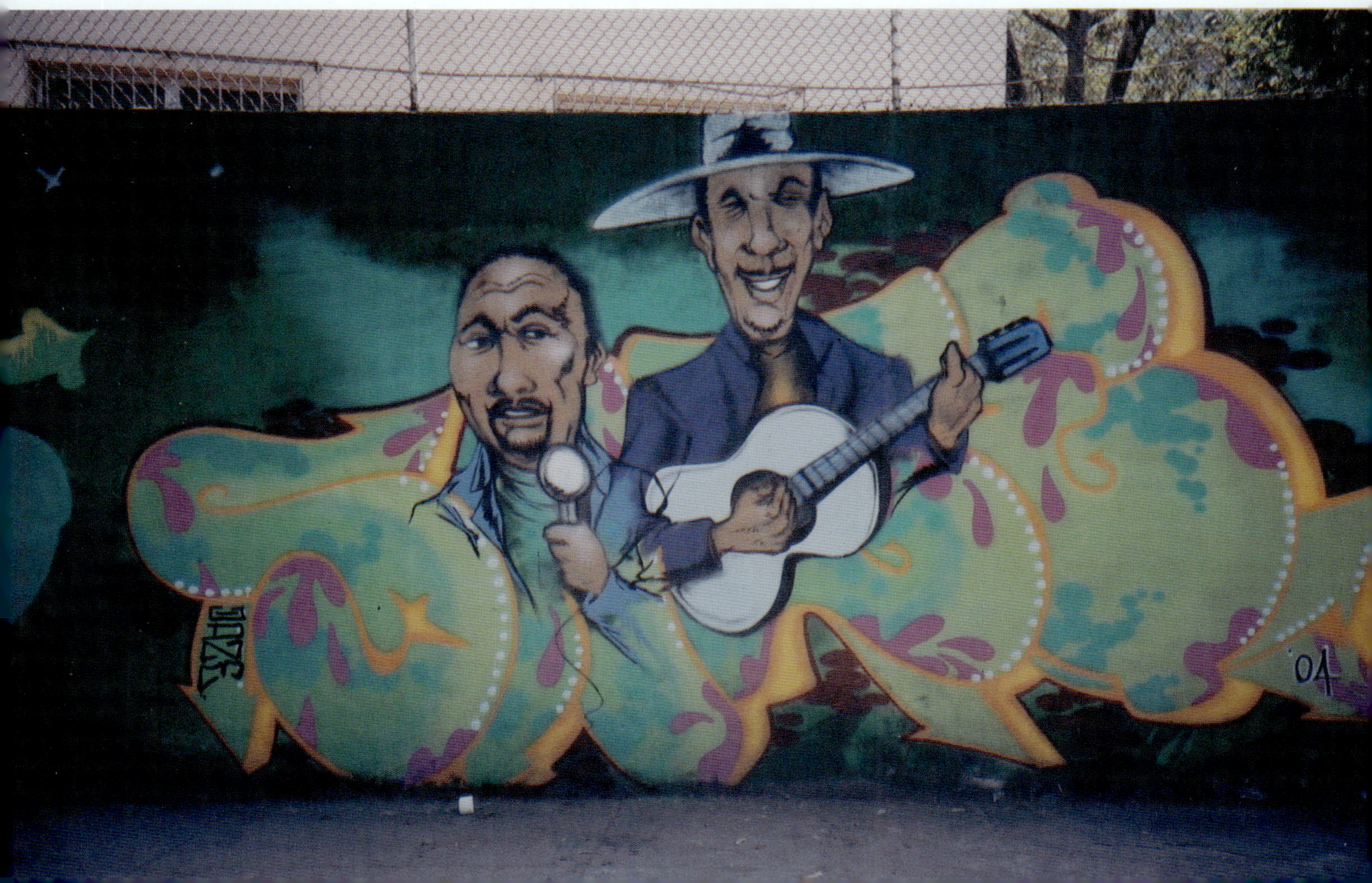

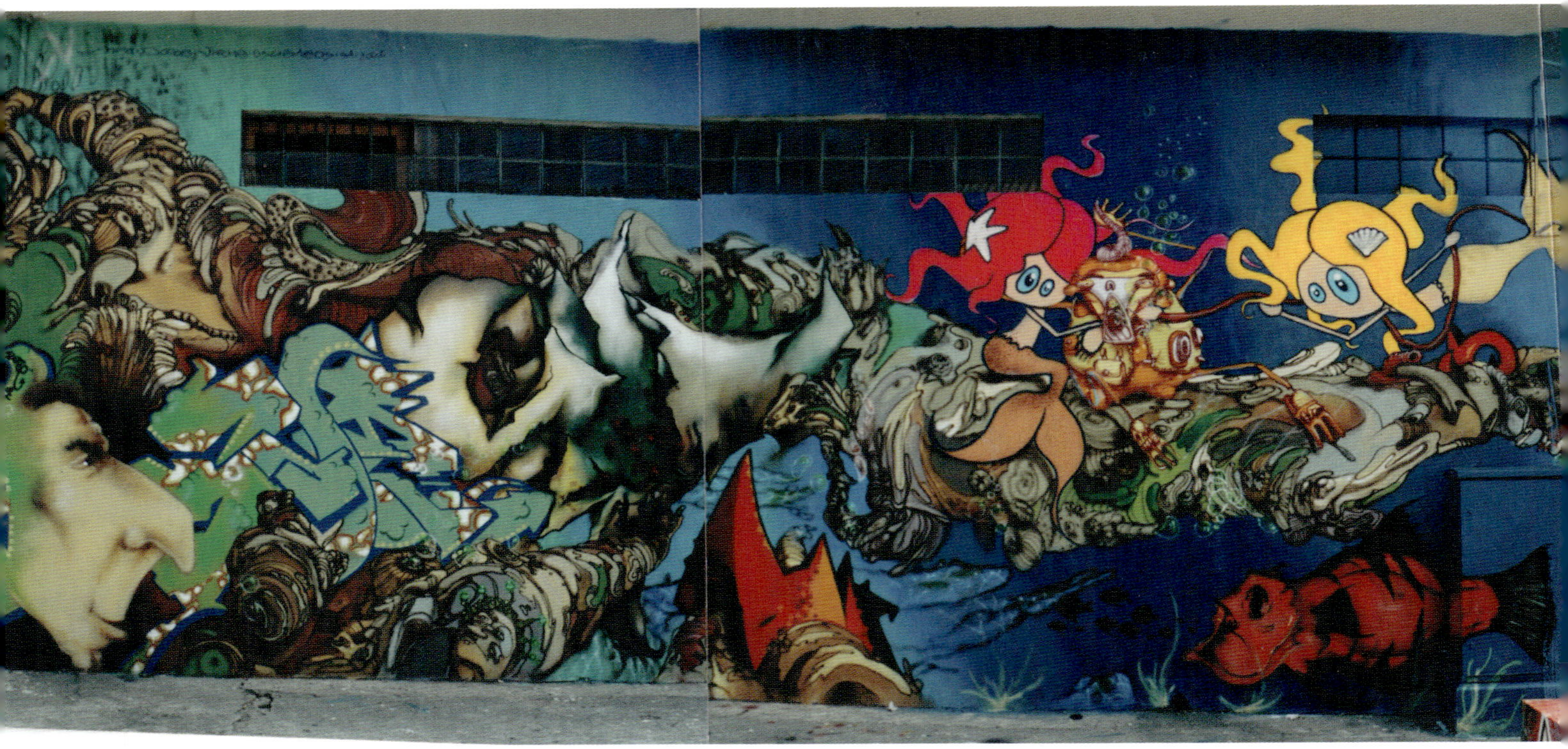

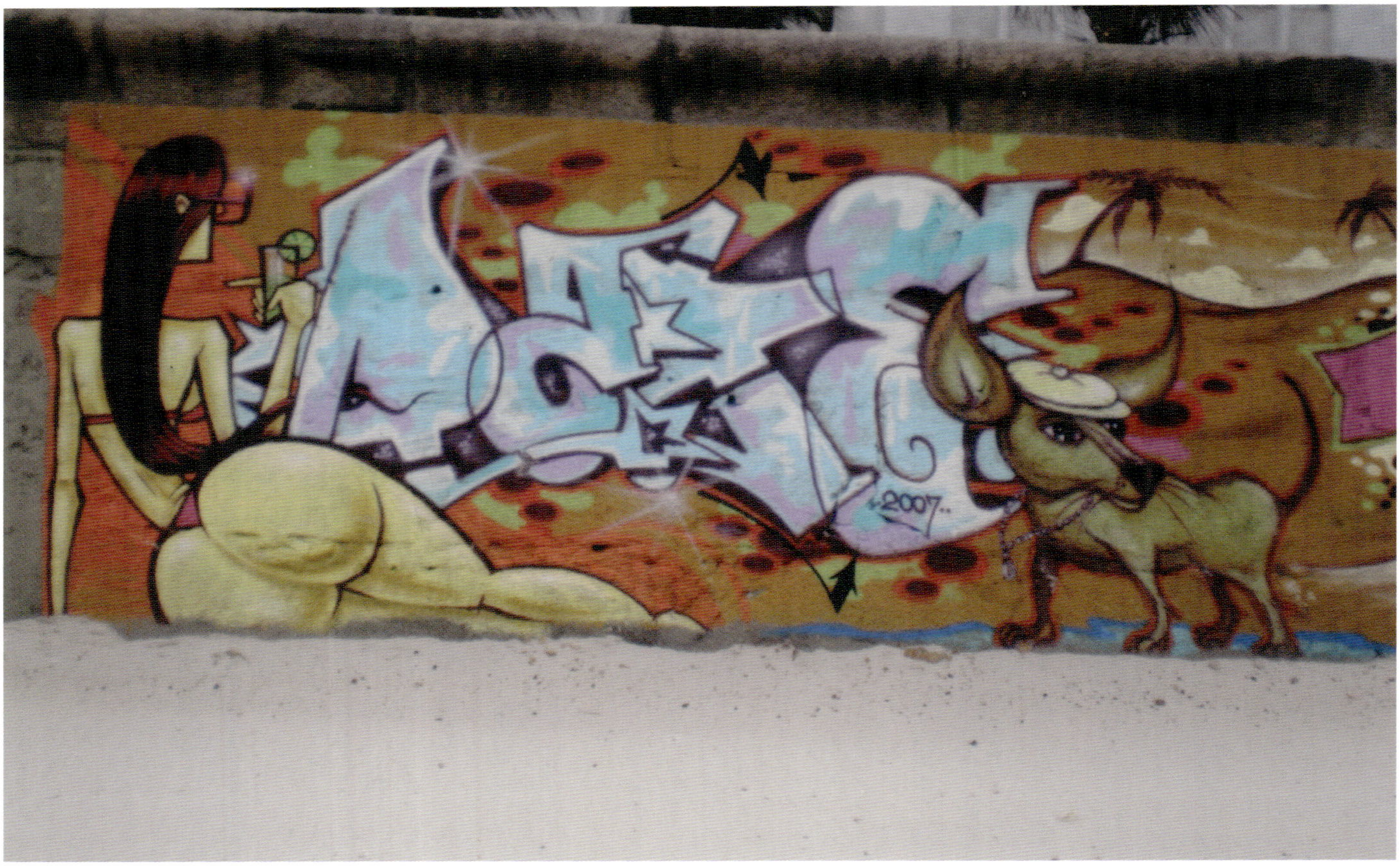

BR, Daze
Ipanema beach, Rio de Janiero, 2007

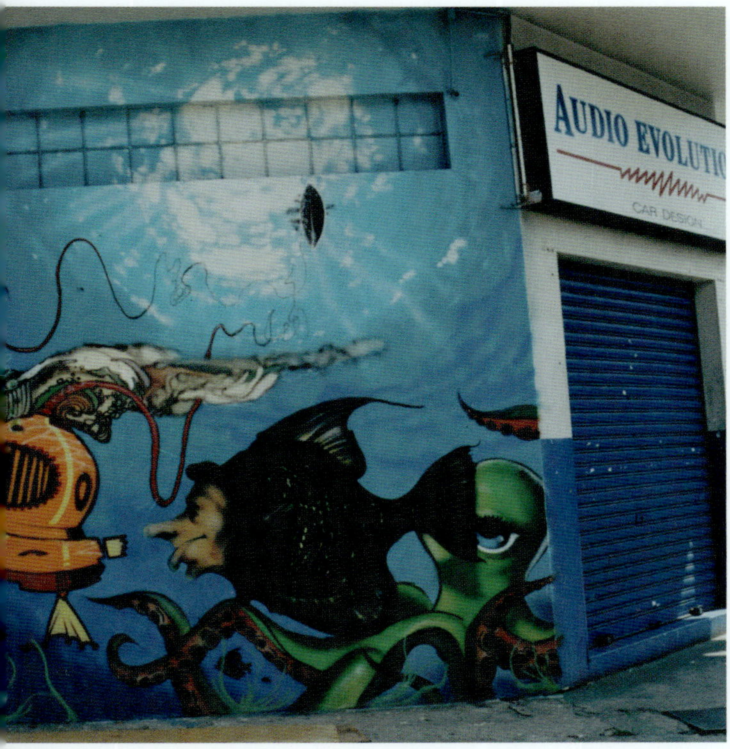

The decision to become a full-time artist requires one to take a huge leap of faith. You must have enough confidence in yourself to be able to confront challenges full on. There will be peaks in which you'll fully appreciate the rewards of all your hard work. More than likely though you'll have to learn to traverse the deep valleys of disappointment that will be full of obstacles. How you learn to navigate through and deal with adversity is what will define you. I made the decision long ago that my journey will be a long one with many stops and a few detours along the way. Armed with the tools of knowledge and the realization that I can face any challenge, I'll be ready for the future.

Painting with Os Gemeos, Vitche, Nina
Sao Paulo, Brazil , 2001

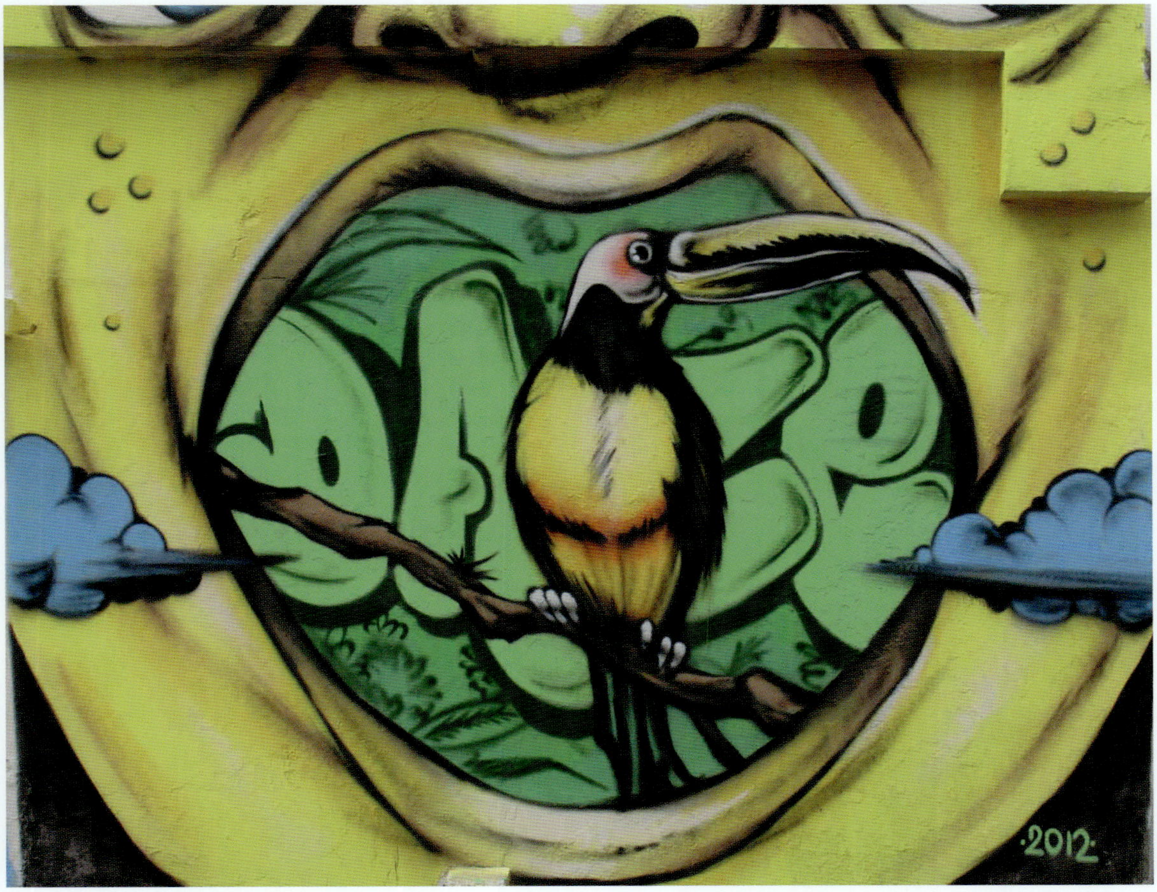

Quito, Ecuador, 2012

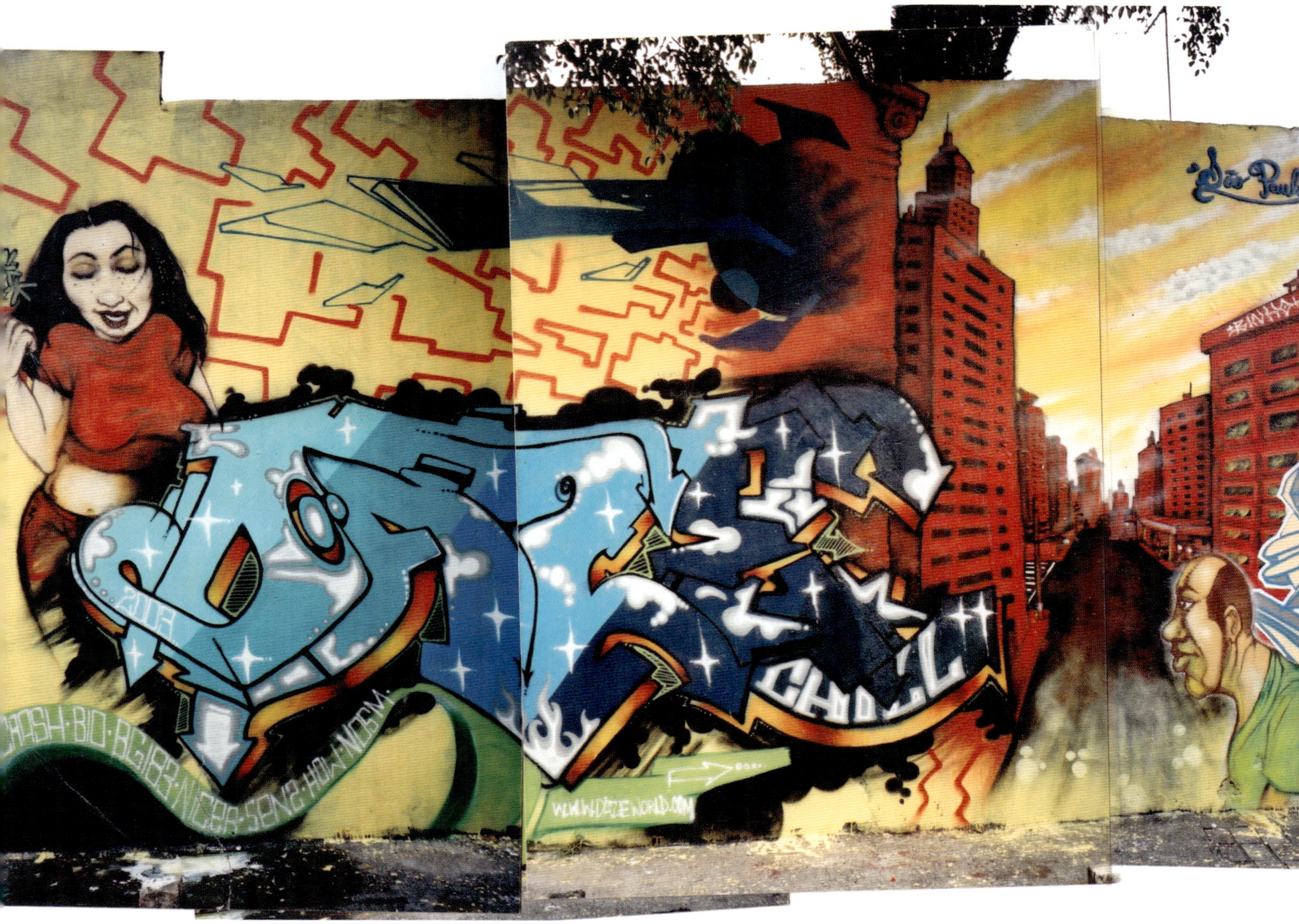

Daze, Binho, Ciro, Does, Fuk,
Sao Paulo, Brazil, 2003

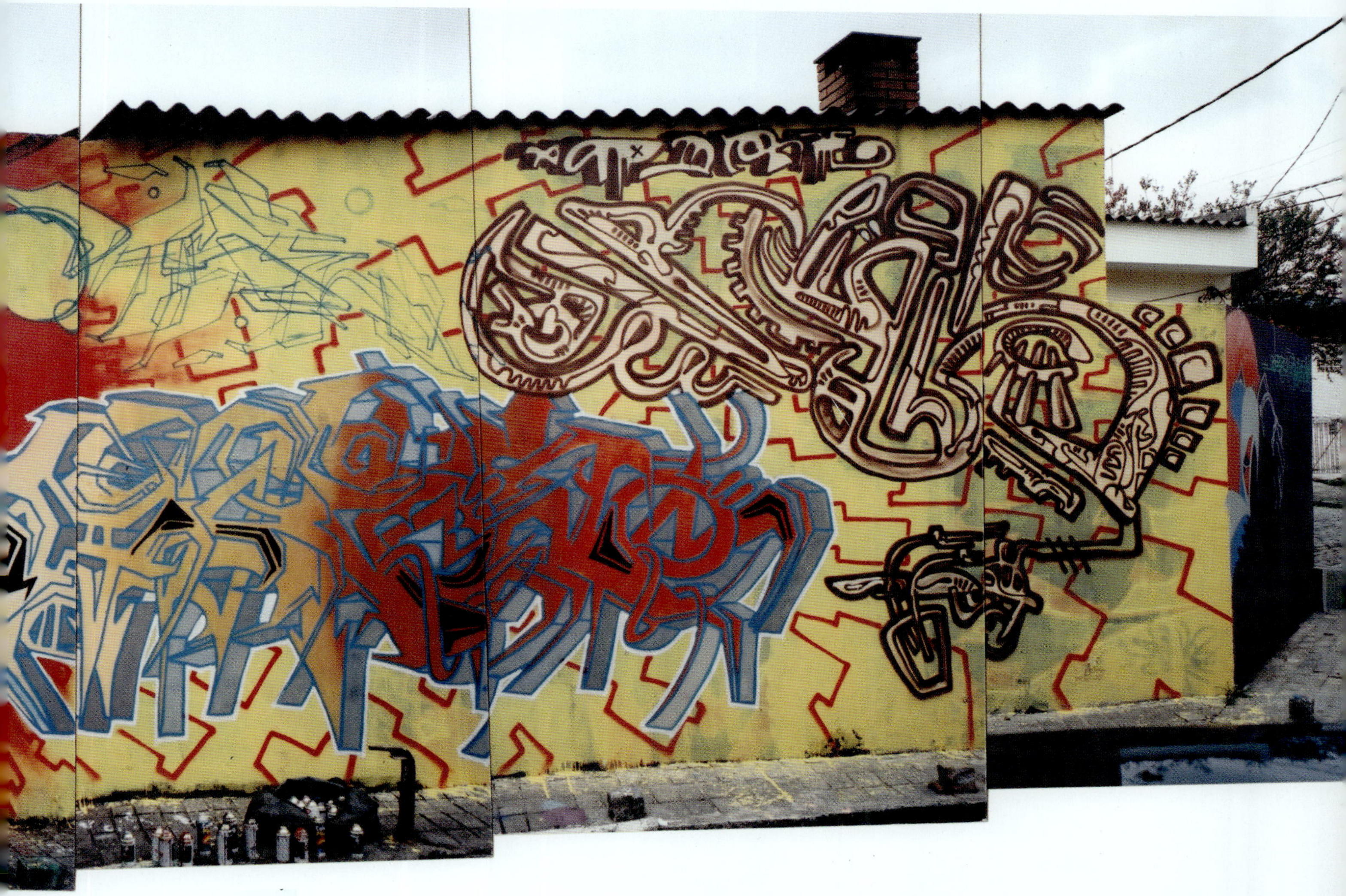

CHAPTER 7
GALLERIES

PROJECTS

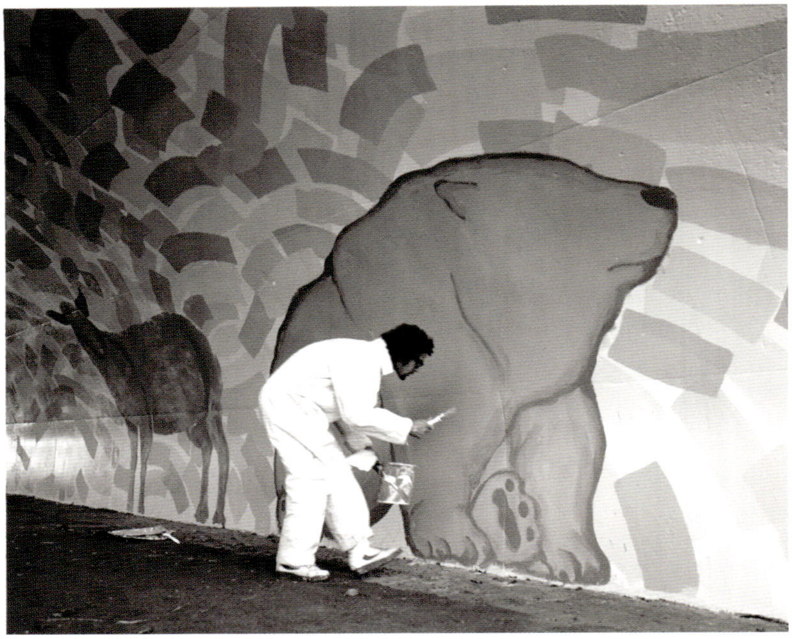

Bronx Zoo mural project with
Crash and Lee, 1994

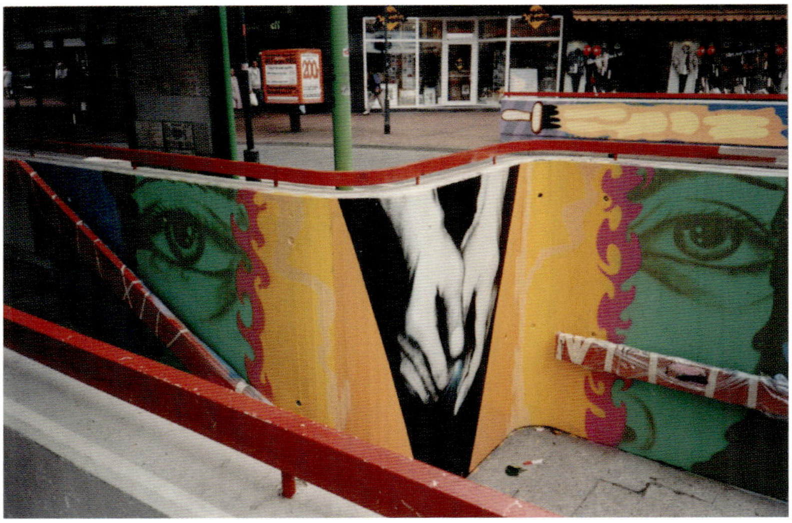

Entrance to Sedanstrasse/Lister Meile station
Hannover, New York Express project with
Crash and Lee, 1995
Hannover, Germany

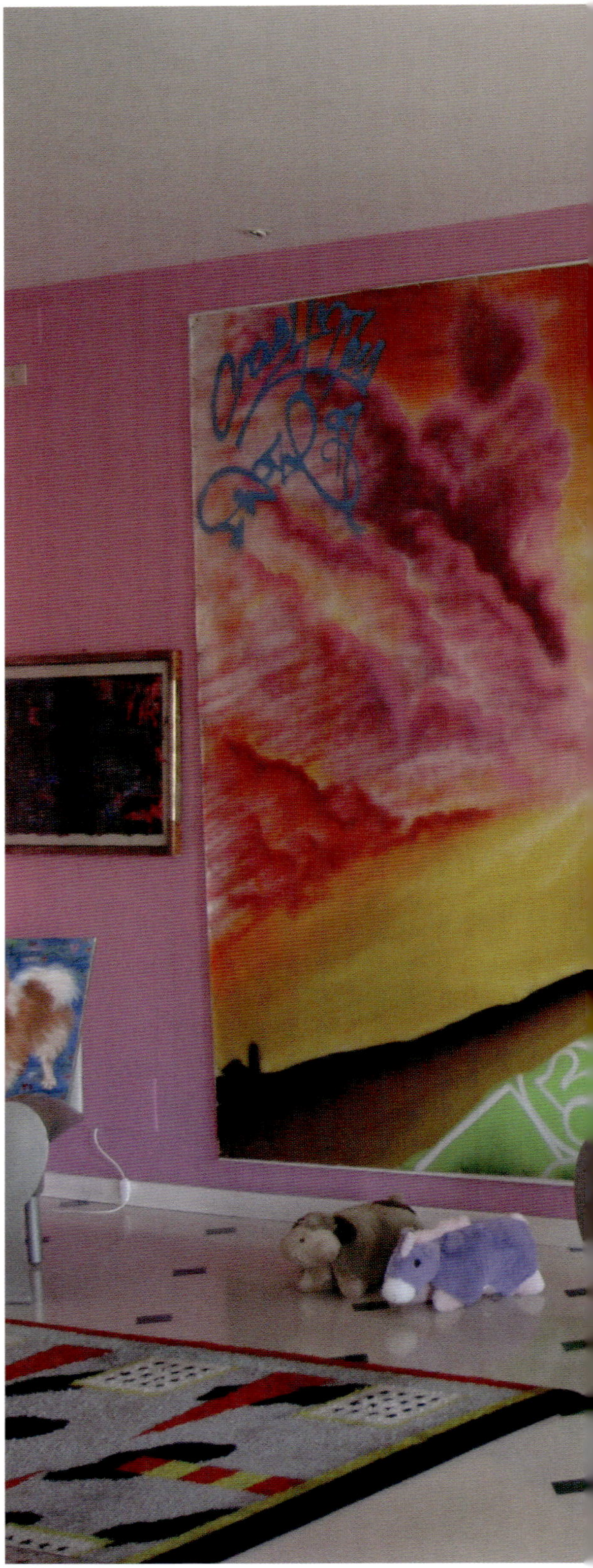

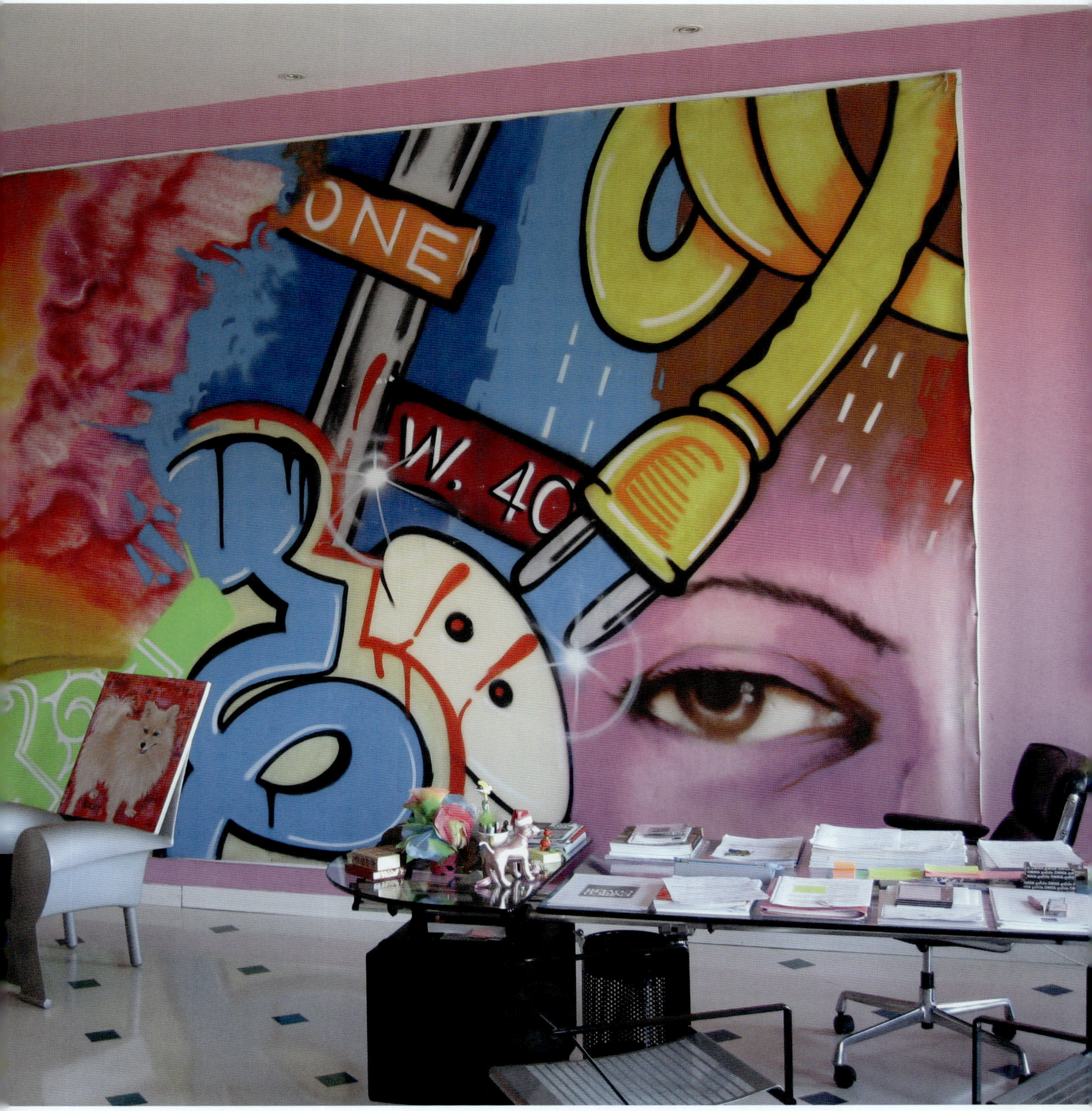

Daze, Crash collaborative painting, 1997
Private collection, Florence, Italy

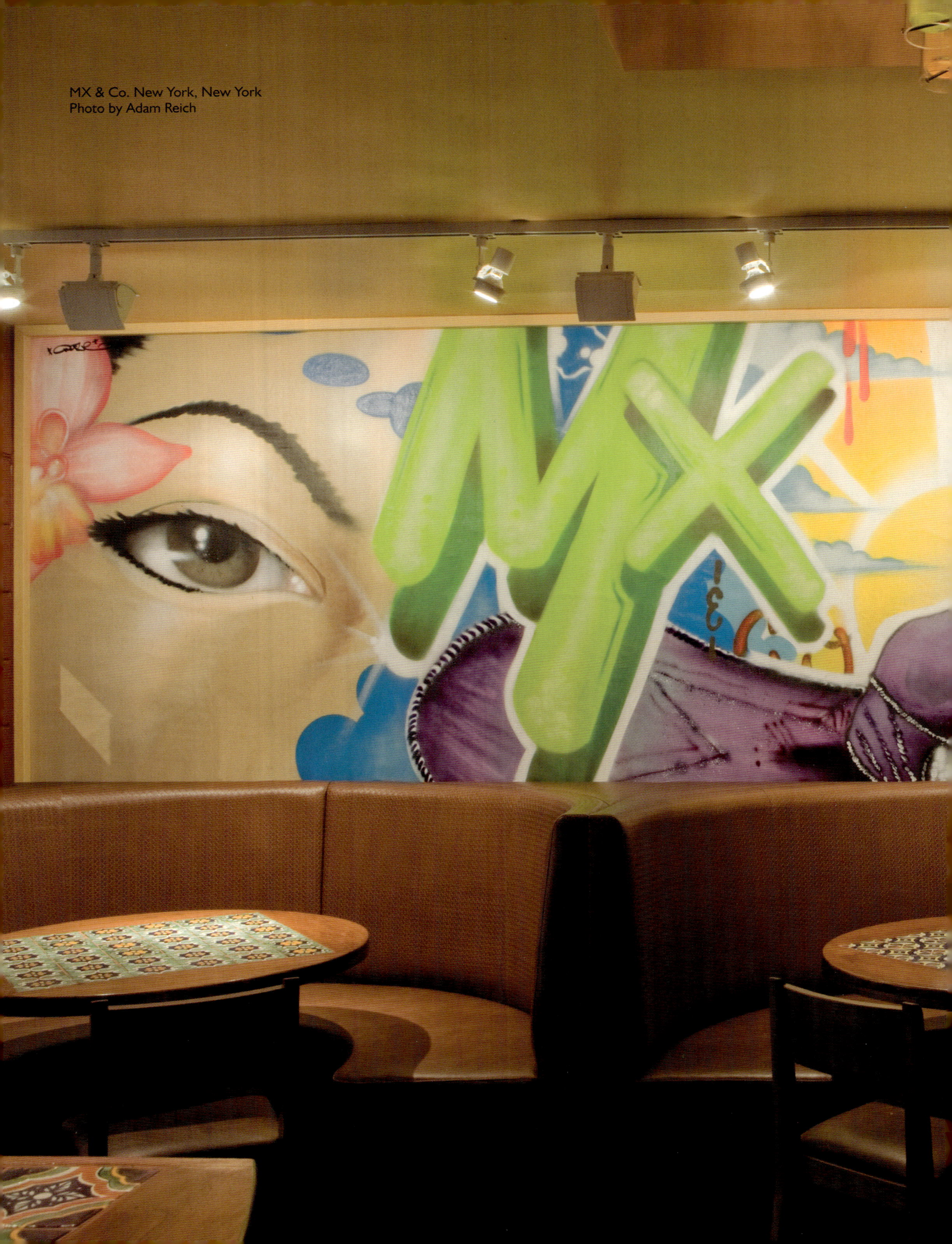

MX & Co. New York, New York
Photo by Adam Reich

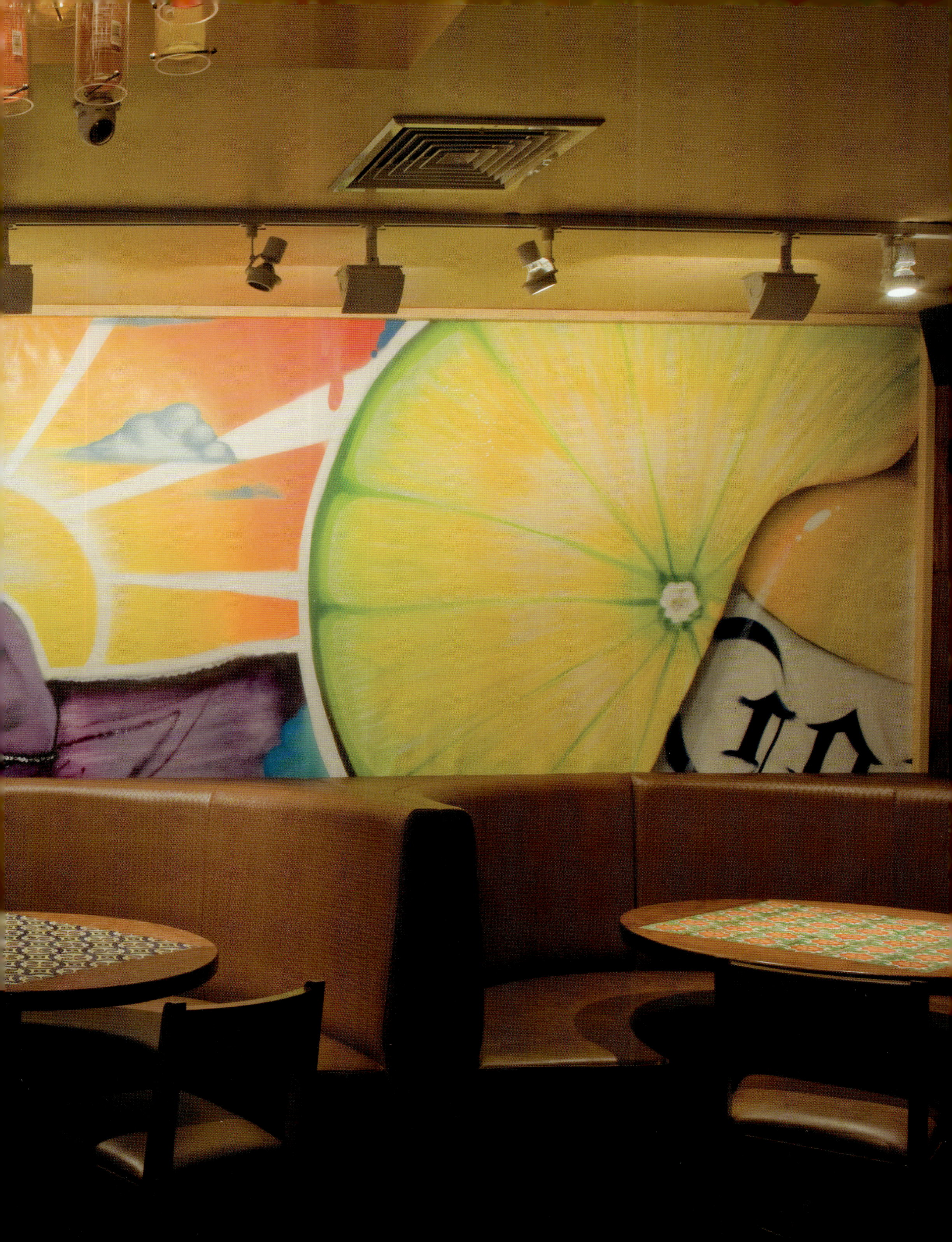

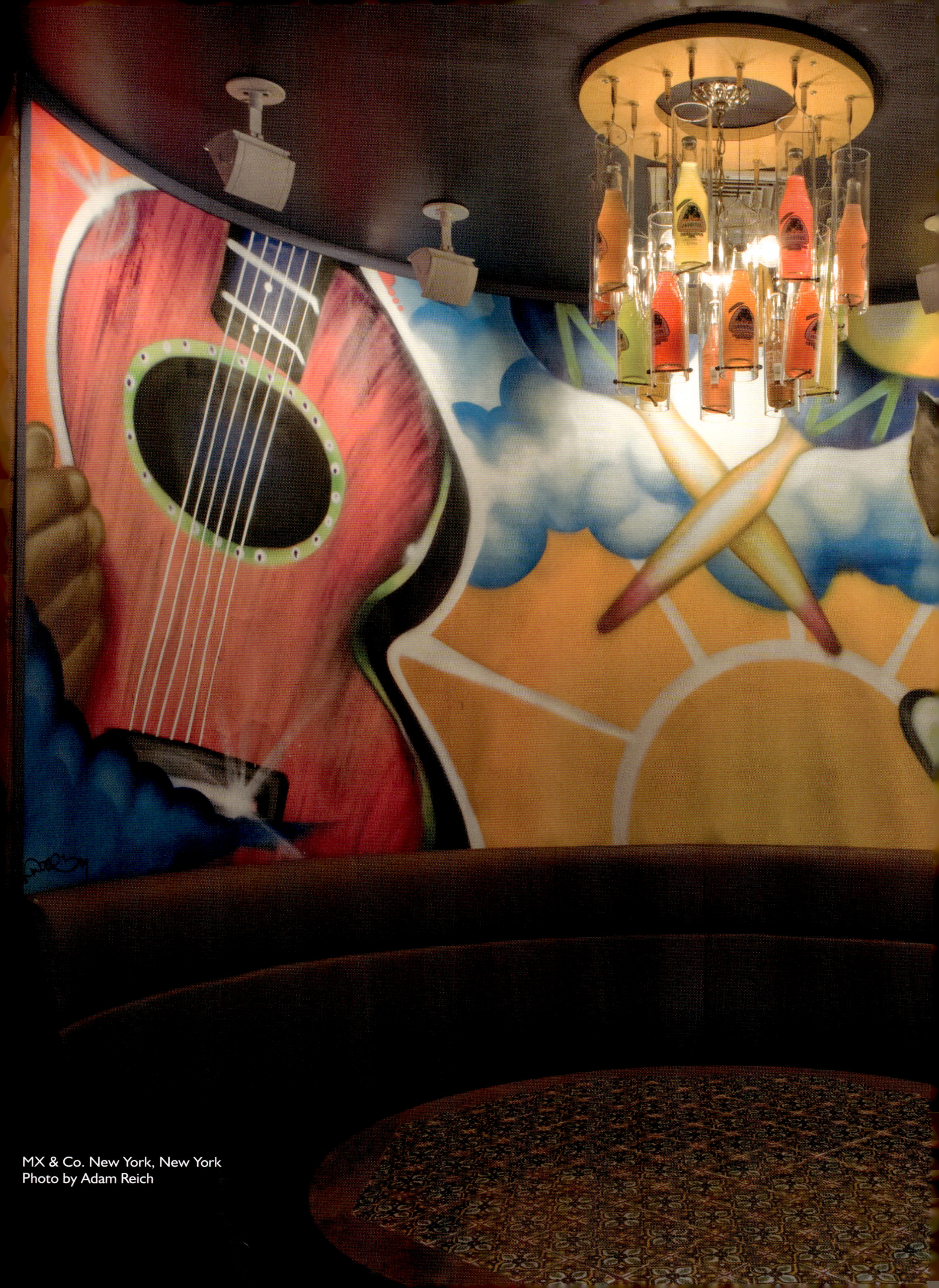

MX & Co. New York, New York
Photo by Adam Reich

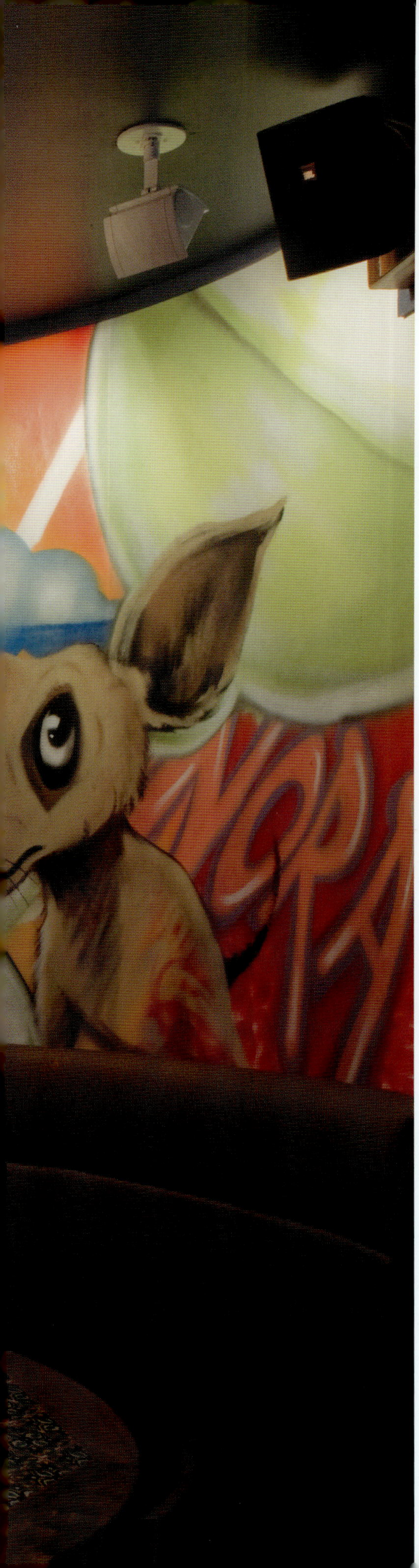

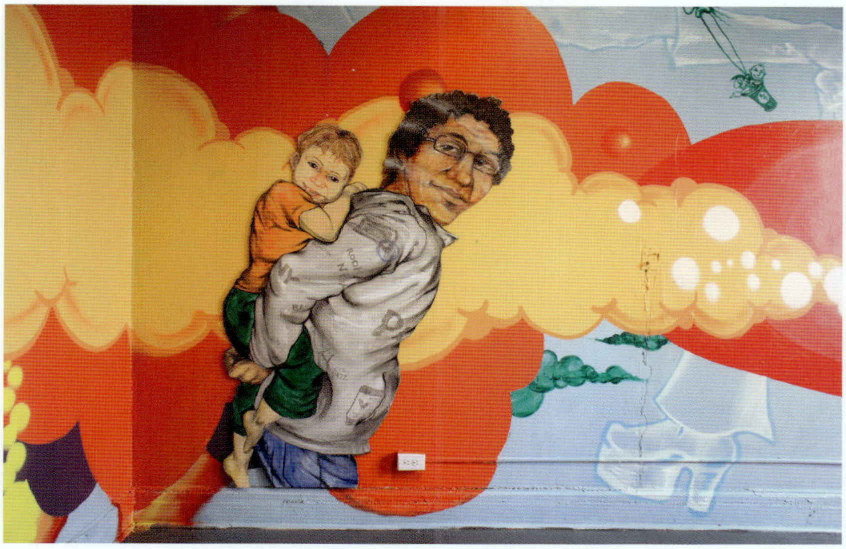

Installation at Andrew Freeman home, 2012

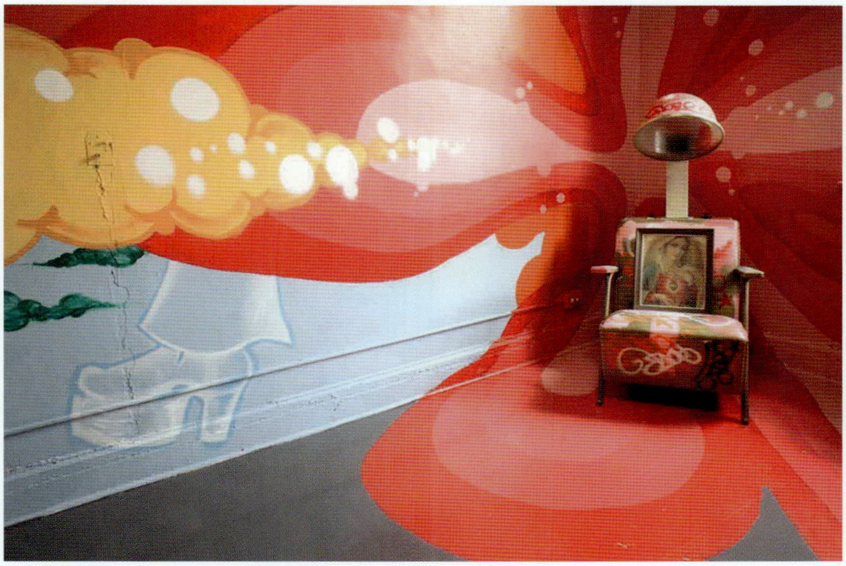

Installation at Andrew Freeman home
This Side of Paradise exhibition curated by No Longer Empty, 2012

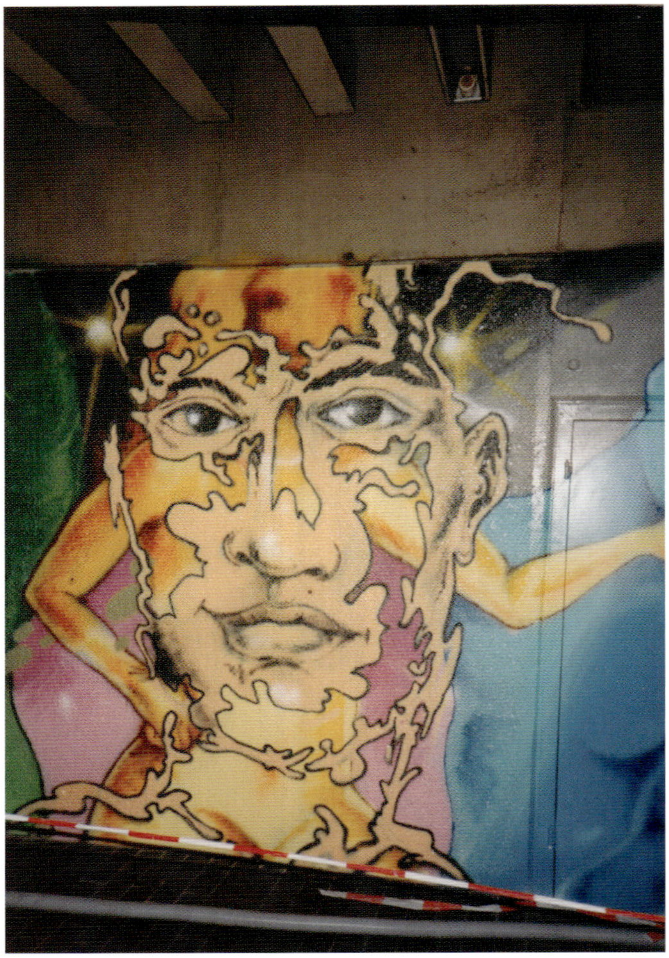

Station platform painting.
Hannover, New York Express project with
Crash and Lee, 1995
Hannover, Germany

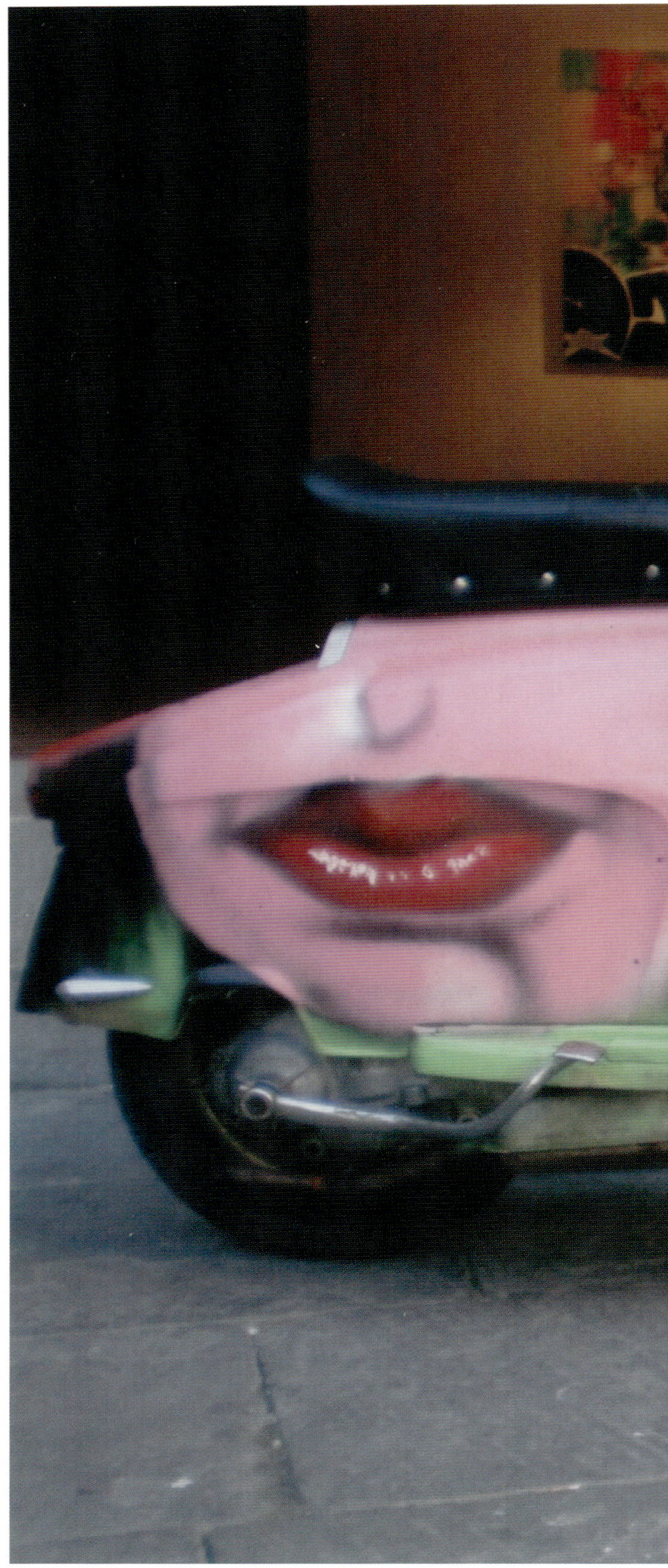

Vespas, Cortona, Italy 2010

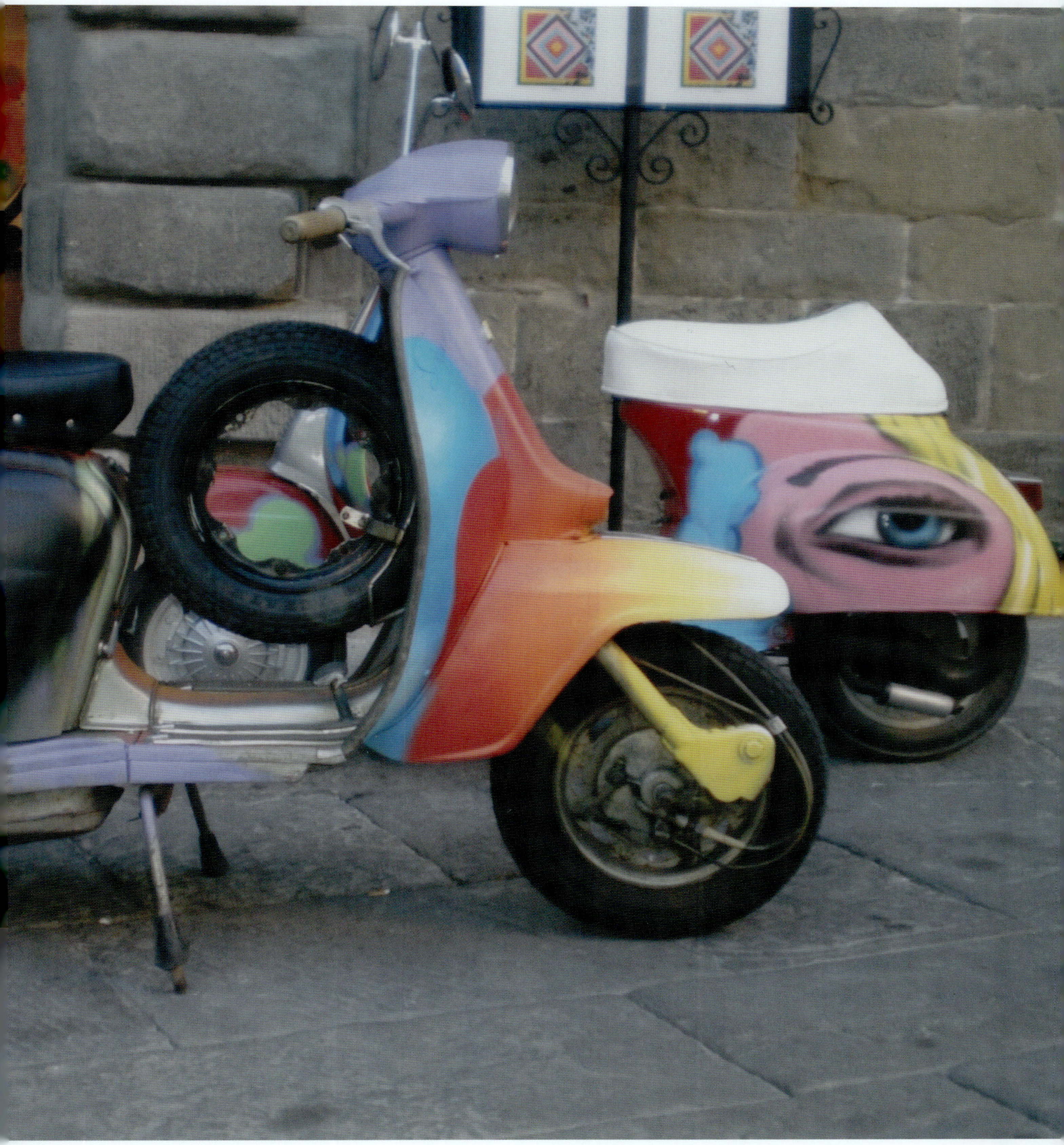

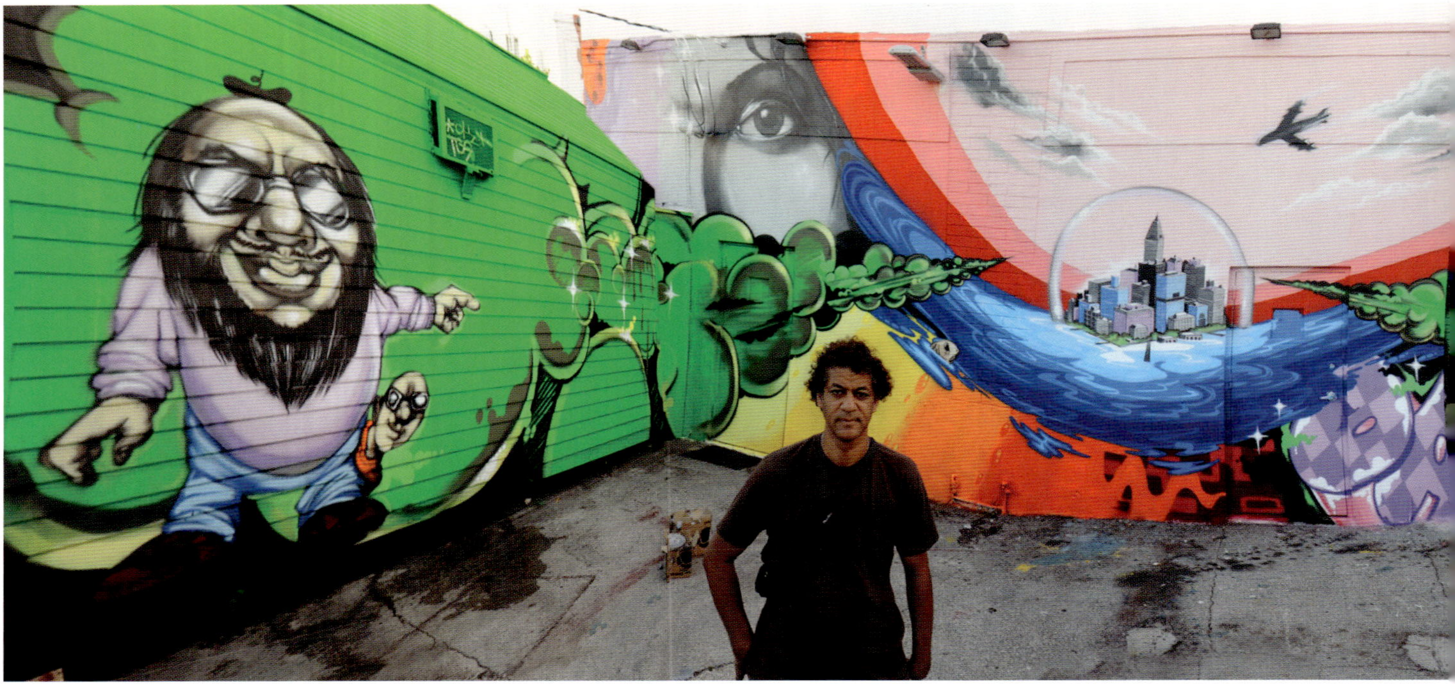

Wynwood Walls mural 2012
Wynwood, Miami, Florida
Photo © Martha Cooper

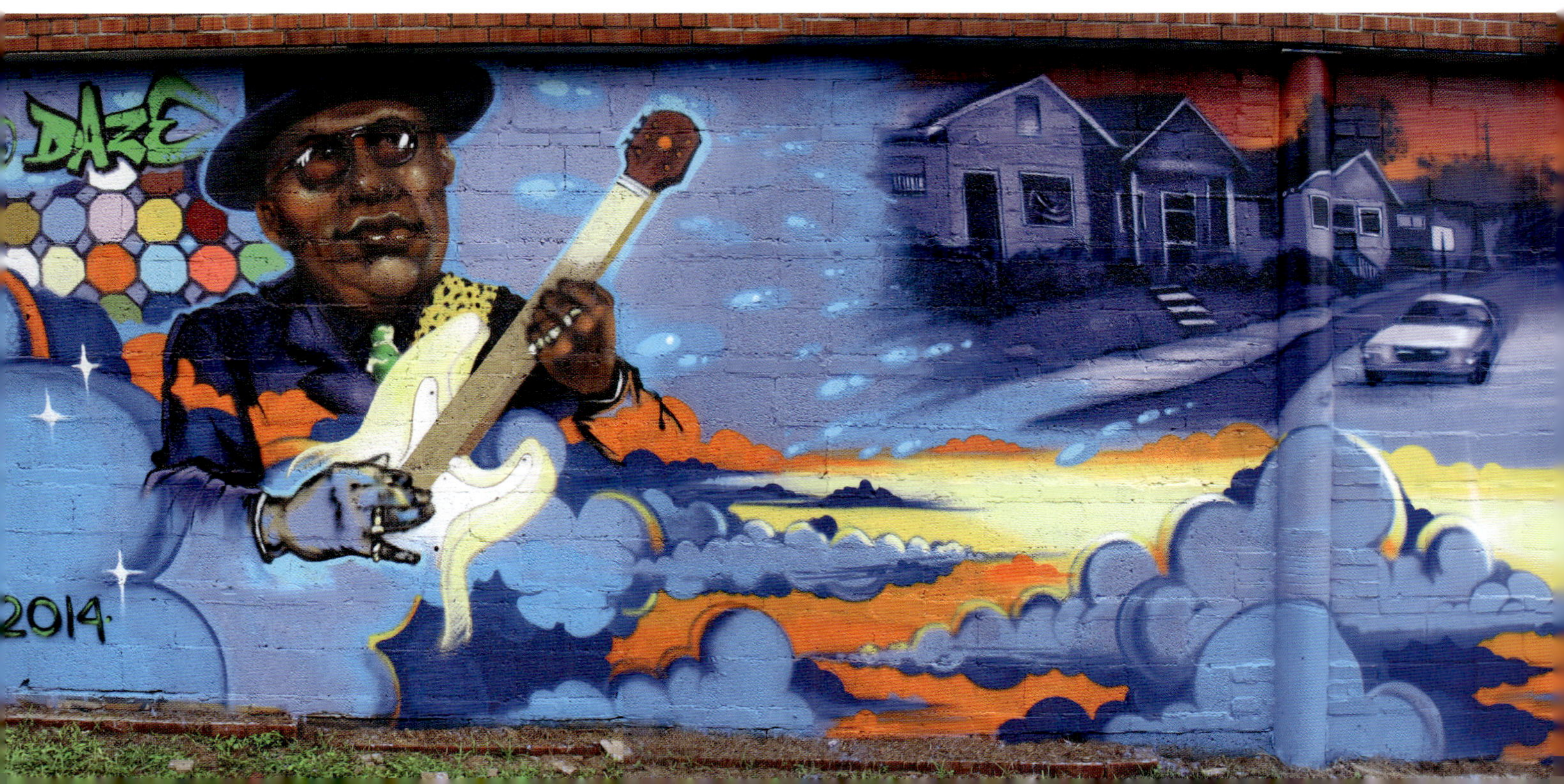

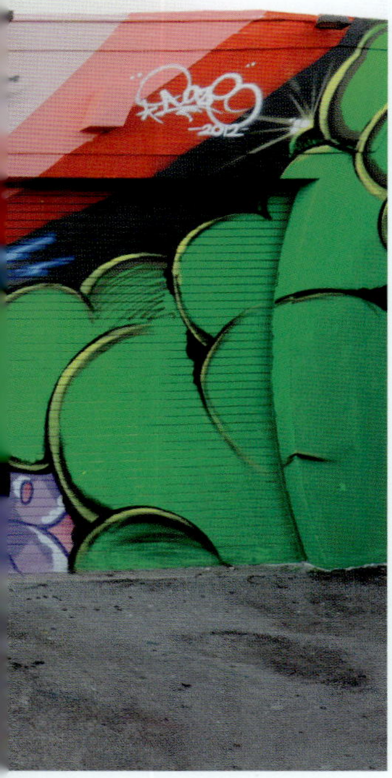

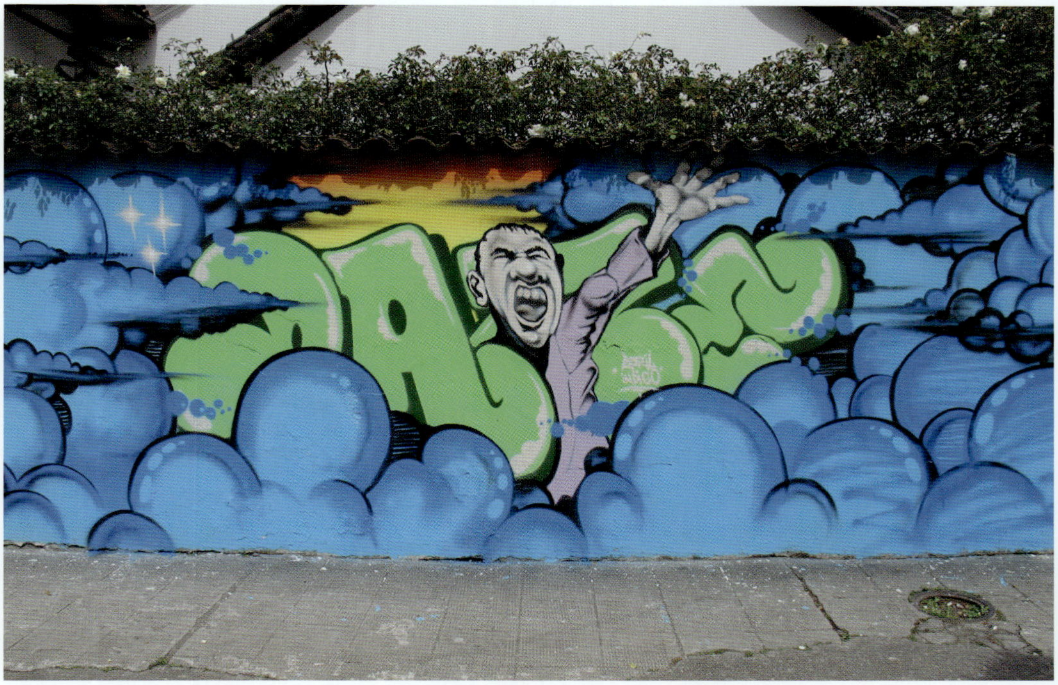

Quito, Ecuador, 2012

Baton Rouge, Louisiana
The Museum of Public Art, 2014

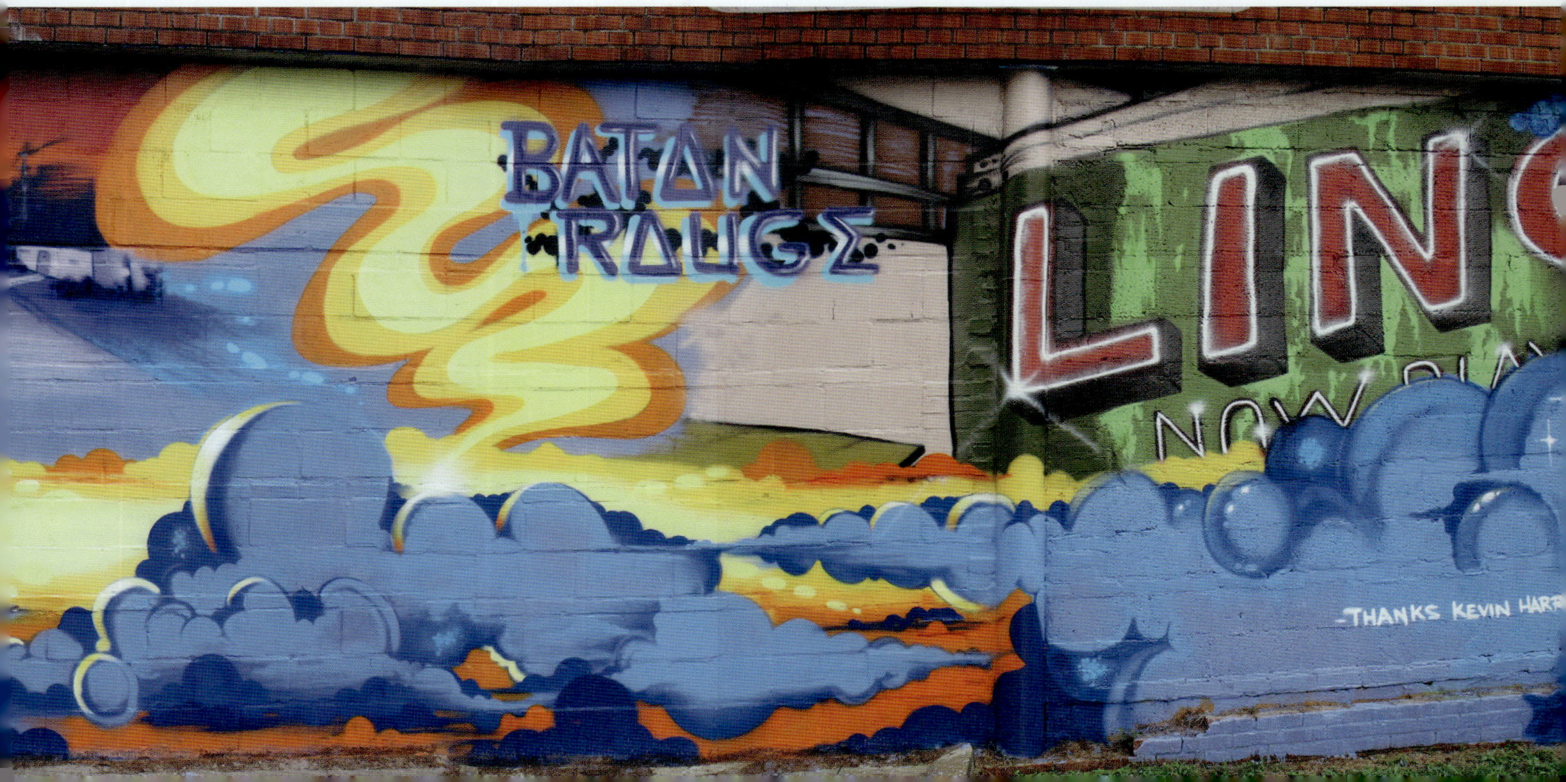

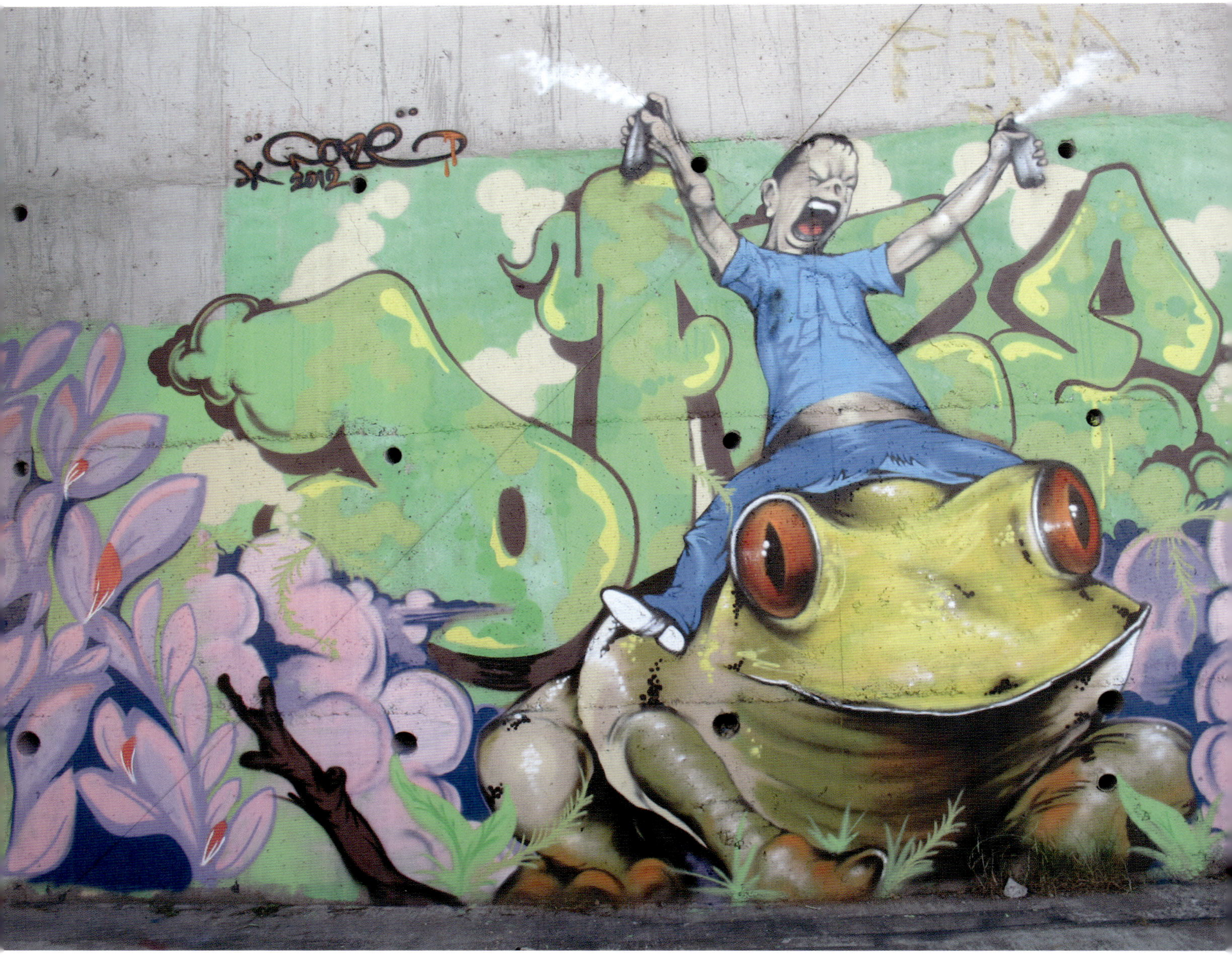

Quito, Ecuador, 2012

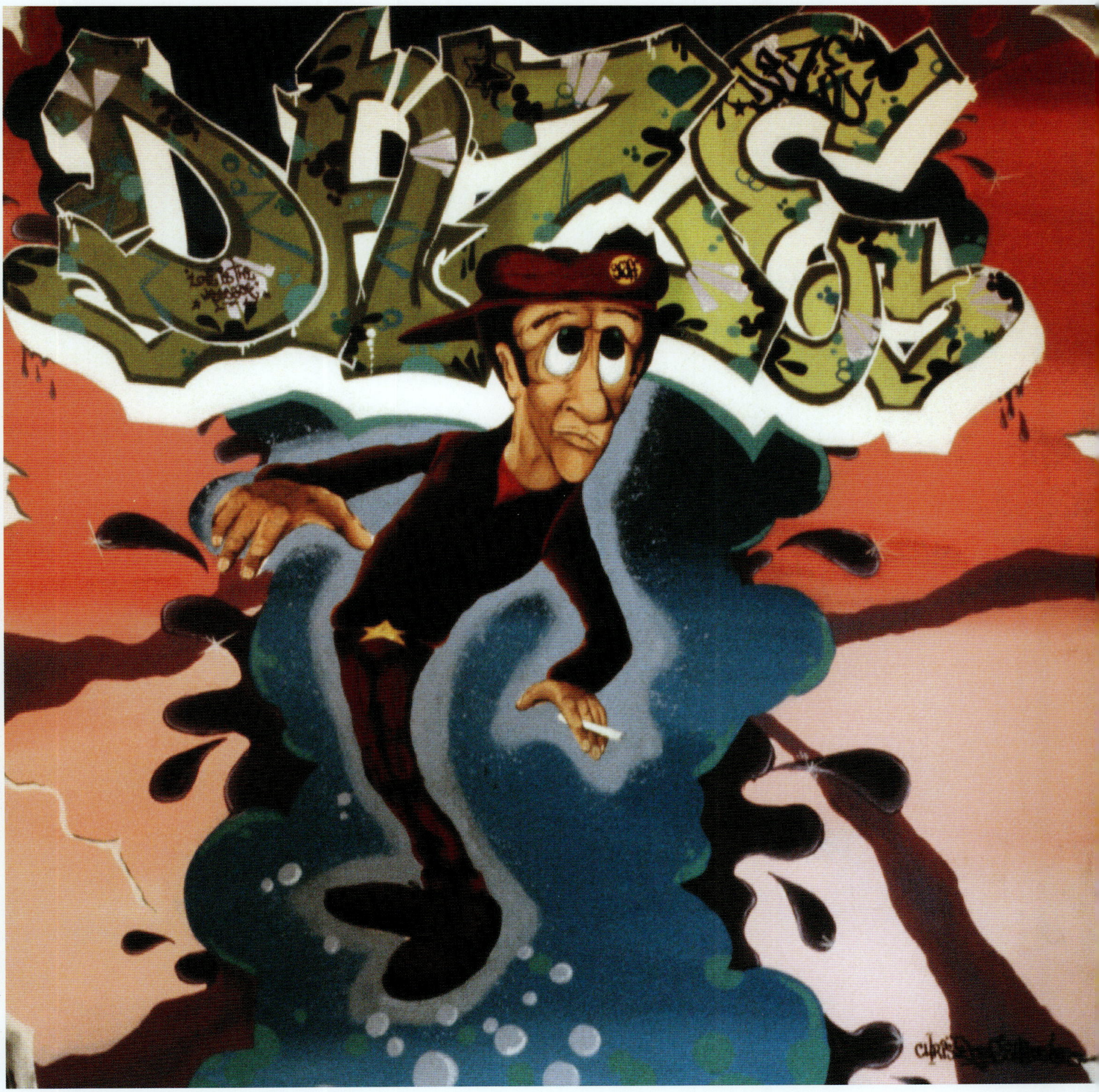

Electric Boogie, 1982
Acrylic on canvas, 60" × 60"
Collection of Willem and Johanna Speerstra

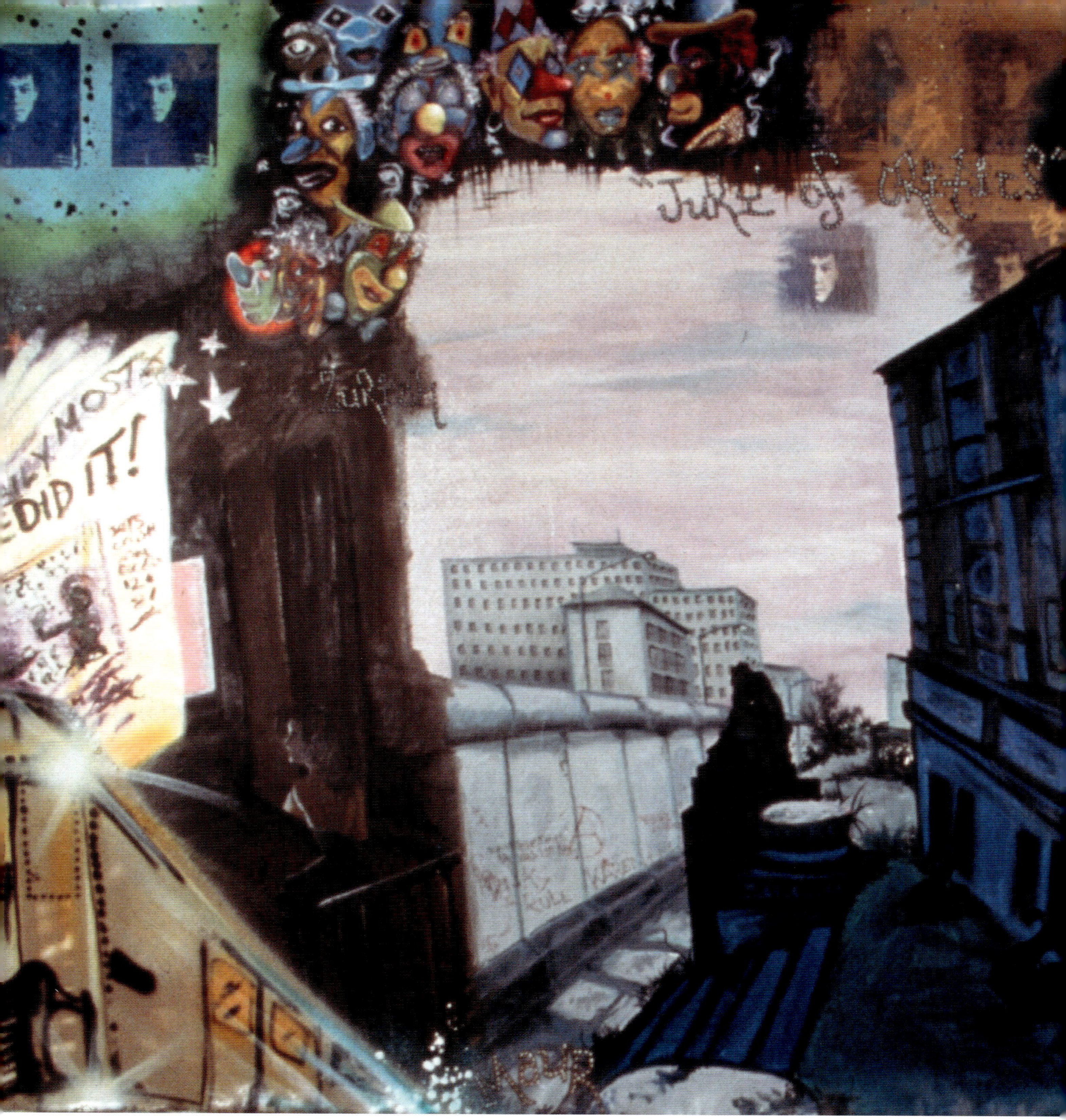

Exile, 1986
Oil, spray paint, silkscreen on canvas, 114" × 190"
Collection of Willem and Johanna Speerstra

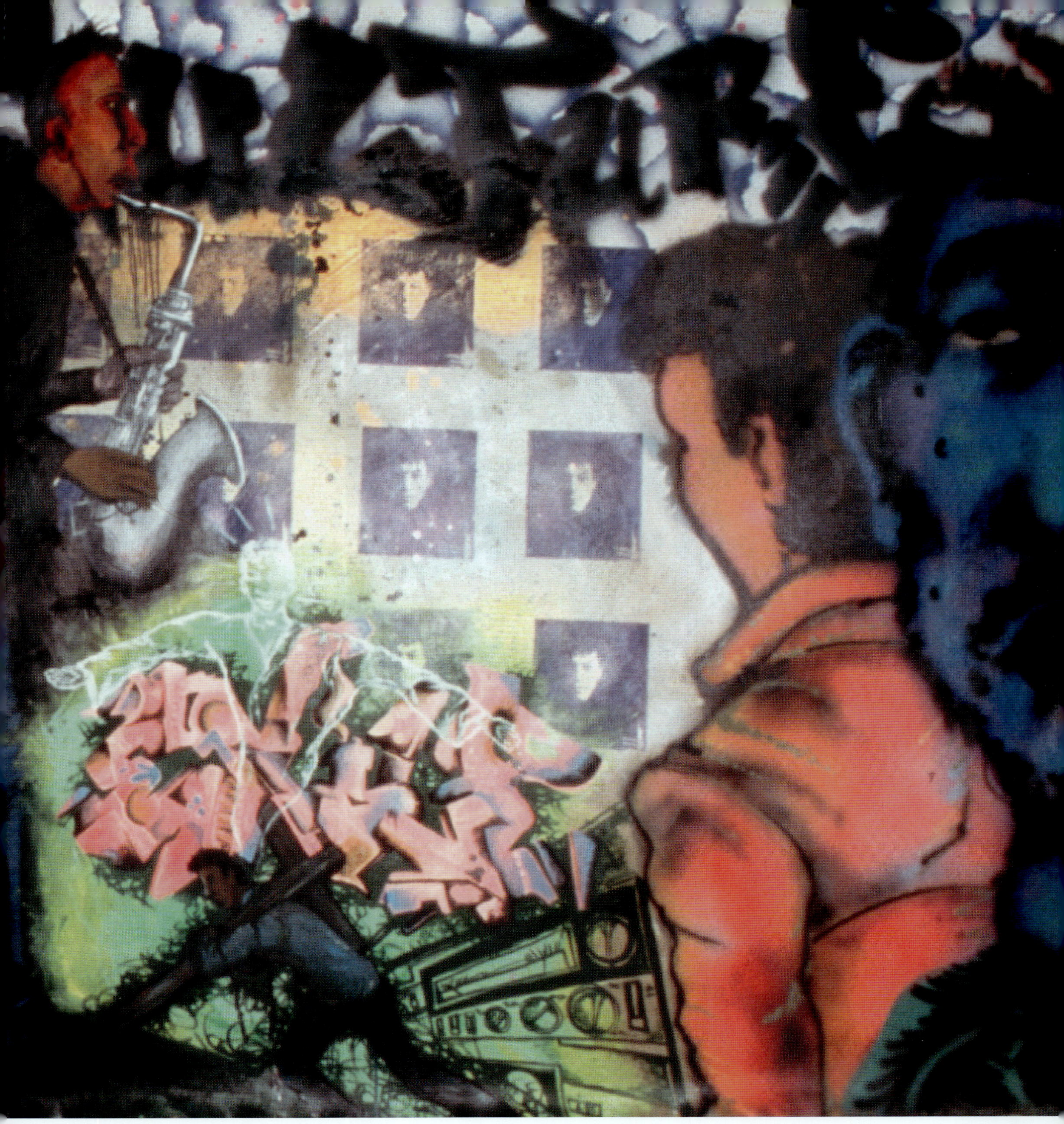

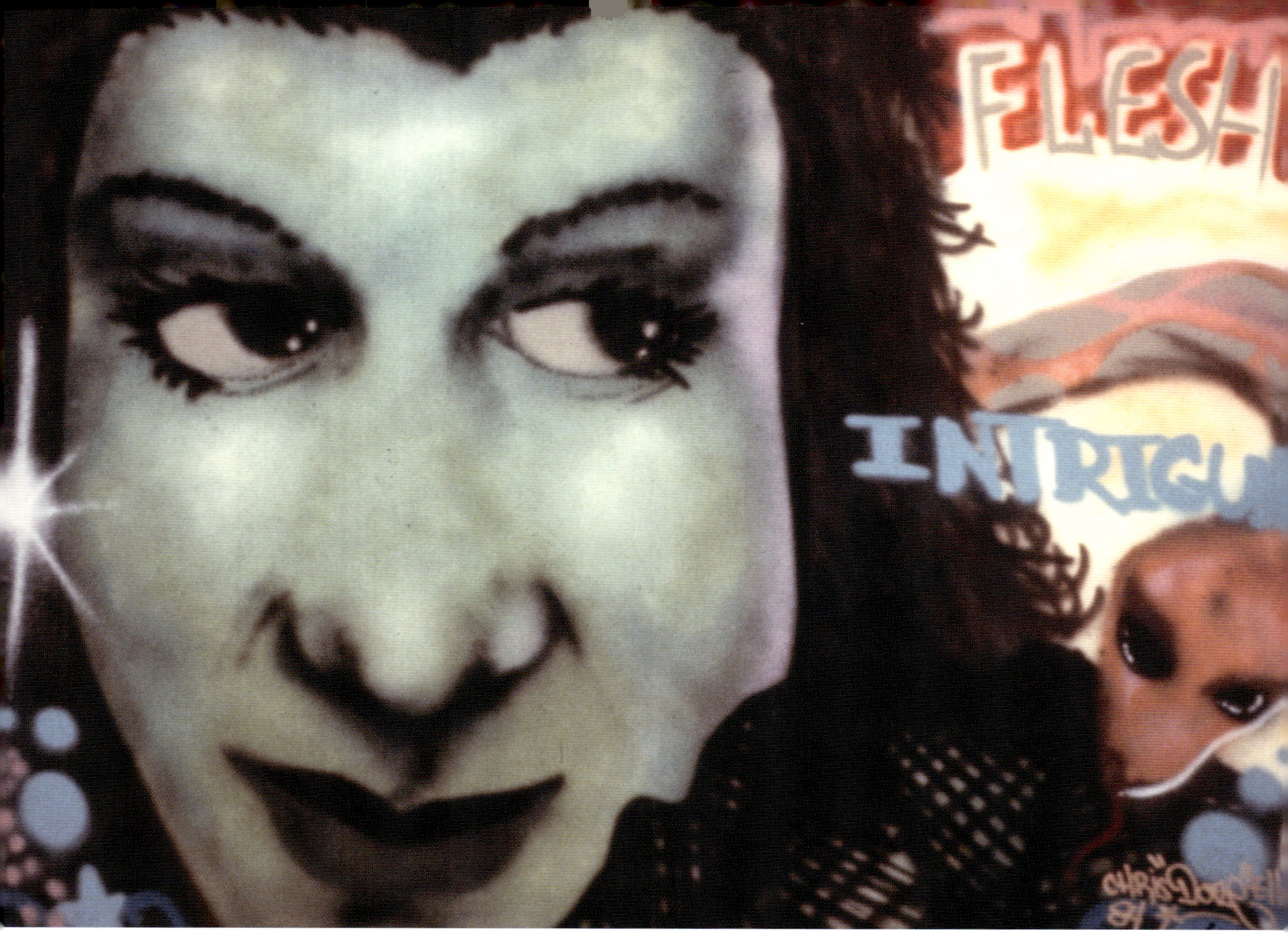

Flesh and Intrigue, 1984
Spray paint on canvas, 97" × 72"
Collection of The Brooklyn Museum, Brooklyn, New York

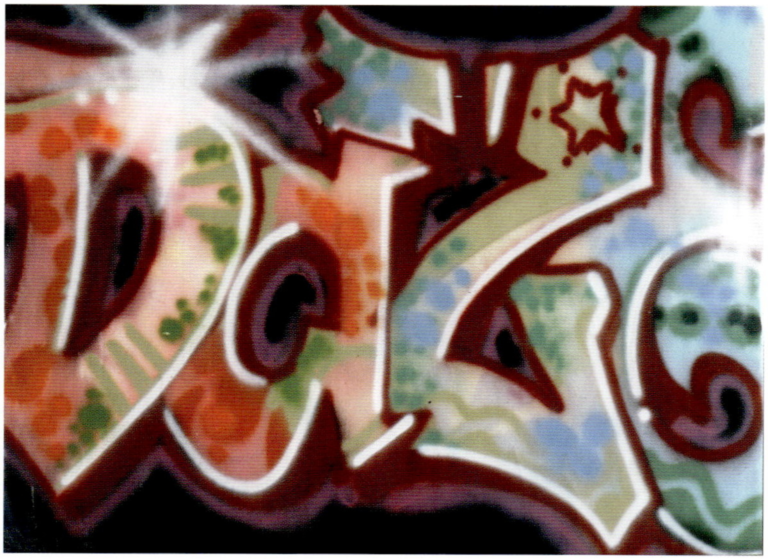

Signature Daze, 1981
Spray paint on canvas, 40" × 50"
Collection of John Axelrod

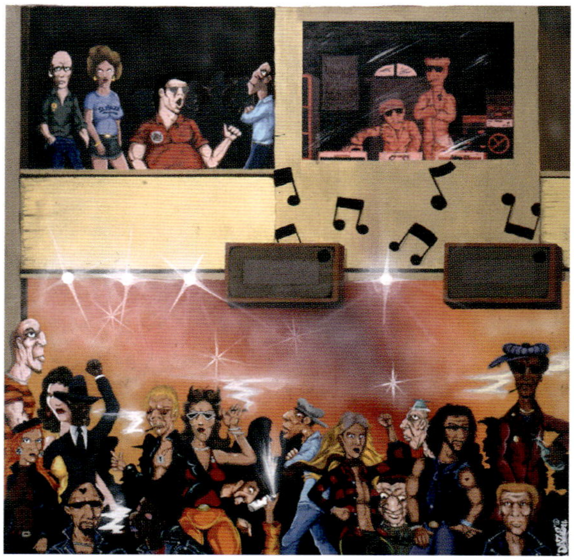

The Club Sleaze, 1981
Acrylic, spray paint on canvas, 30" × 30"
Private collection

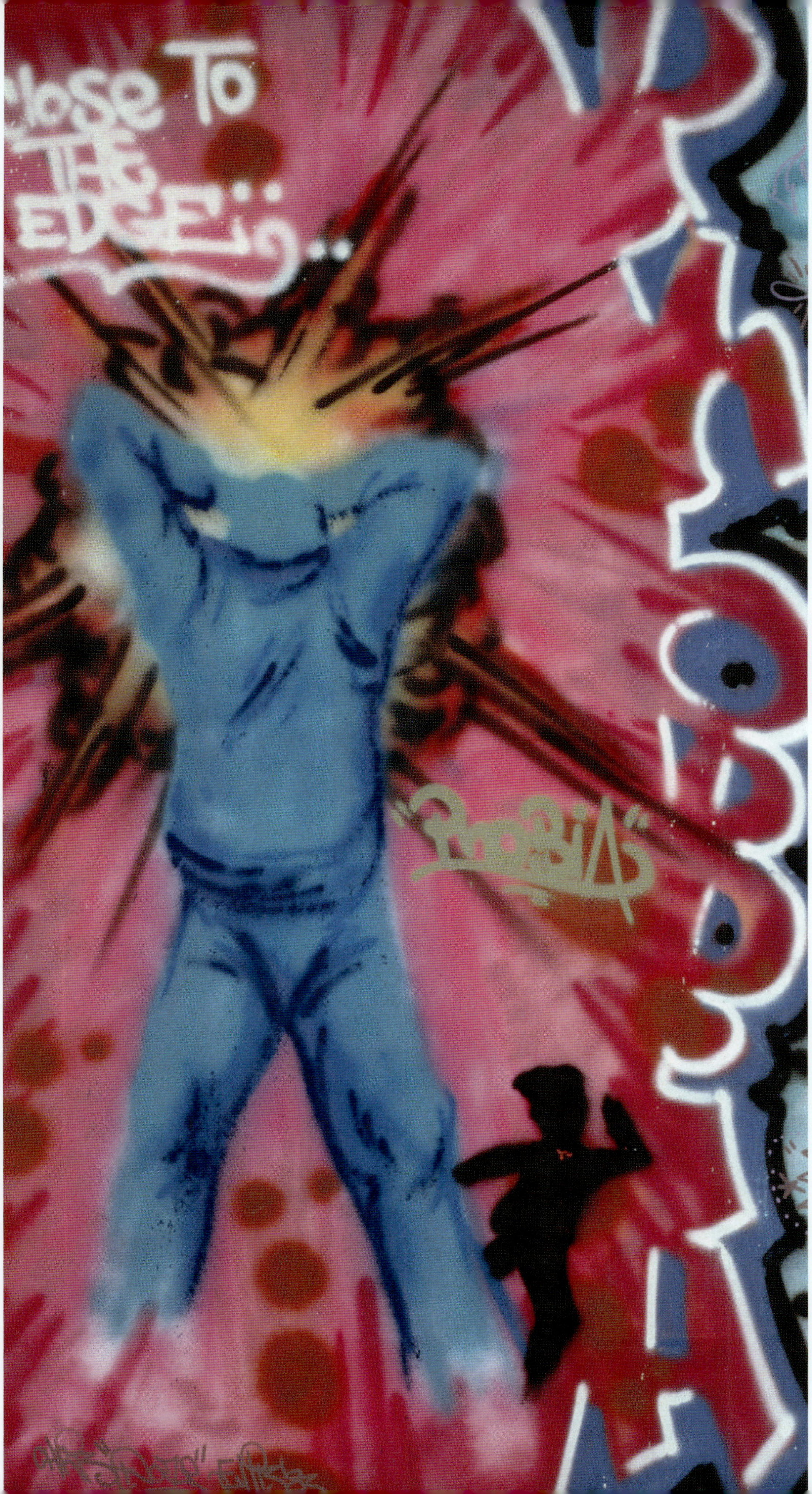

Phobia, 1983
Spray paint on canvas, 68" × 52"
Collection of The Museum of the City of New York, The Martin Wong Collection

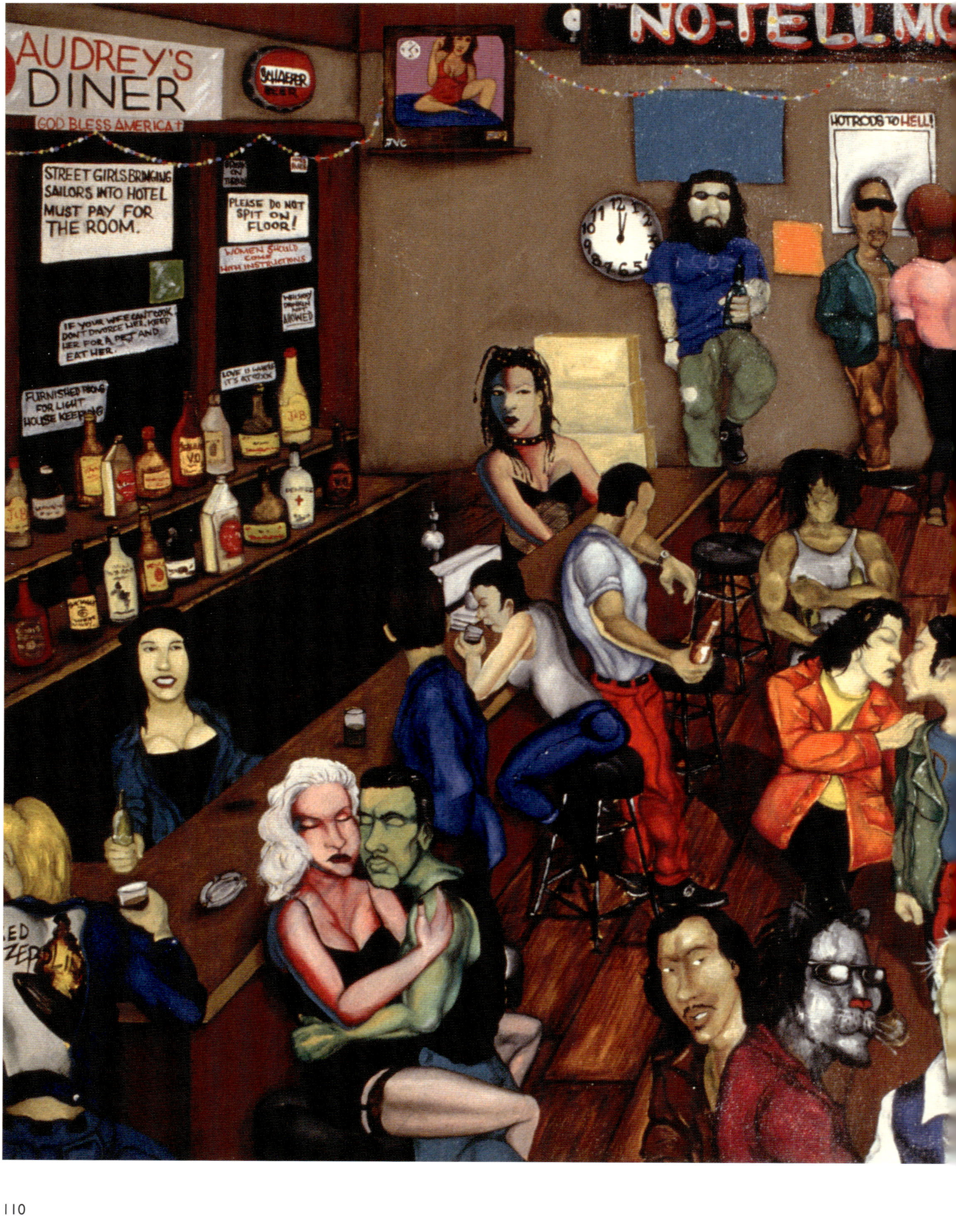
AUDREY'S DINER
GOD BLESS AMERICA
STREET GIRLS BRINGING SAILORS INTO HOTEL MUST PAY FOR THE ROOM.
PLEASE DO NOT SPIT ON FLOOR!
WOMEN SHOULD COME WITH INSTRUCTIONS
HOTRODS TO HELL!
JVC

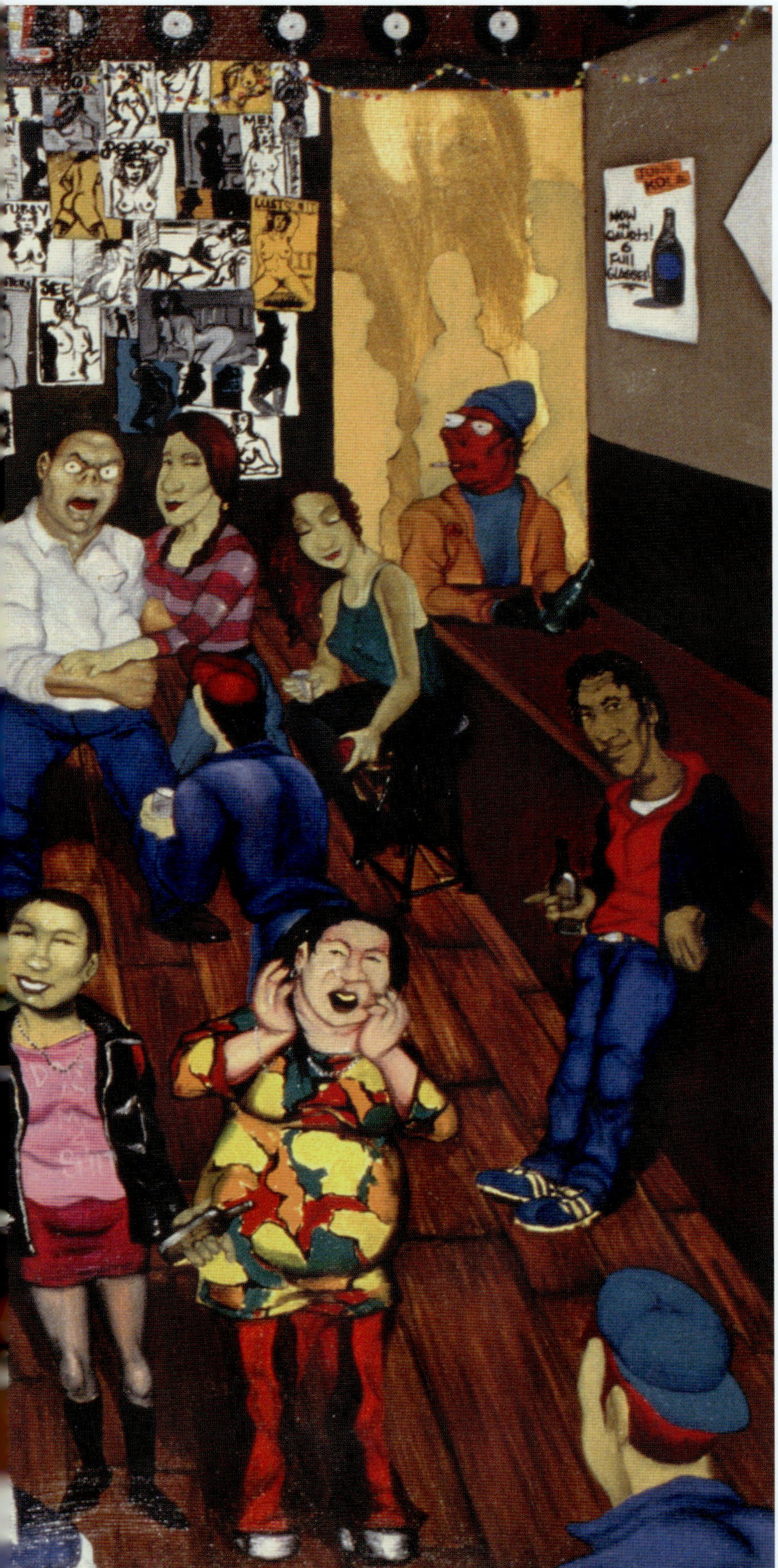

No Tell Motel, 1994
Oil on canvas, 54" × 72"
Collection of Miguel Linares

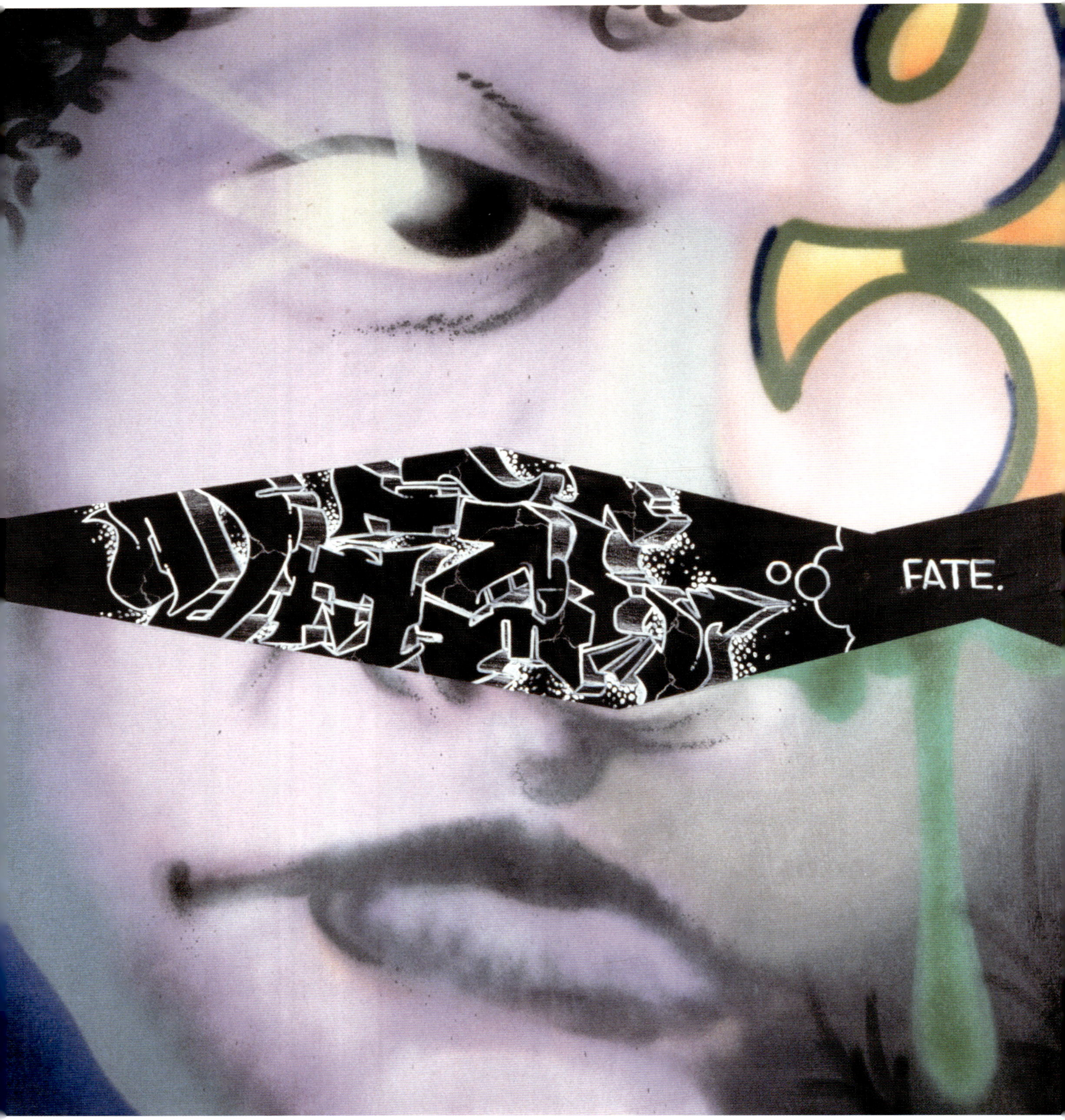

Black Owned, 1996
Spray paint, acrylic on canvas, 60" × 60"
Private collection

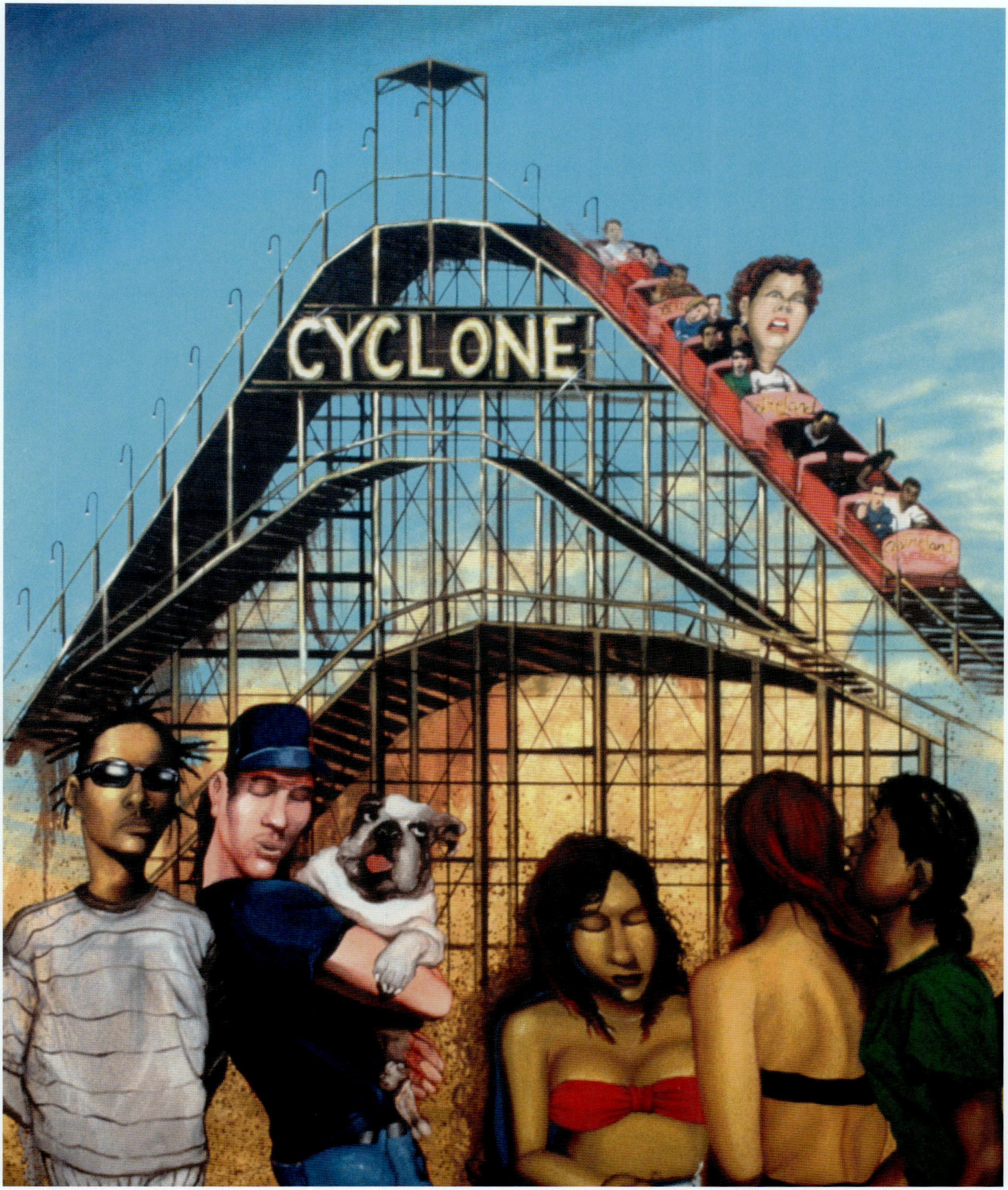

The Cyclone, 1996
Oil, spray paint on canvas, 60" × 80"
Photo by Sue Kwon
Private collection

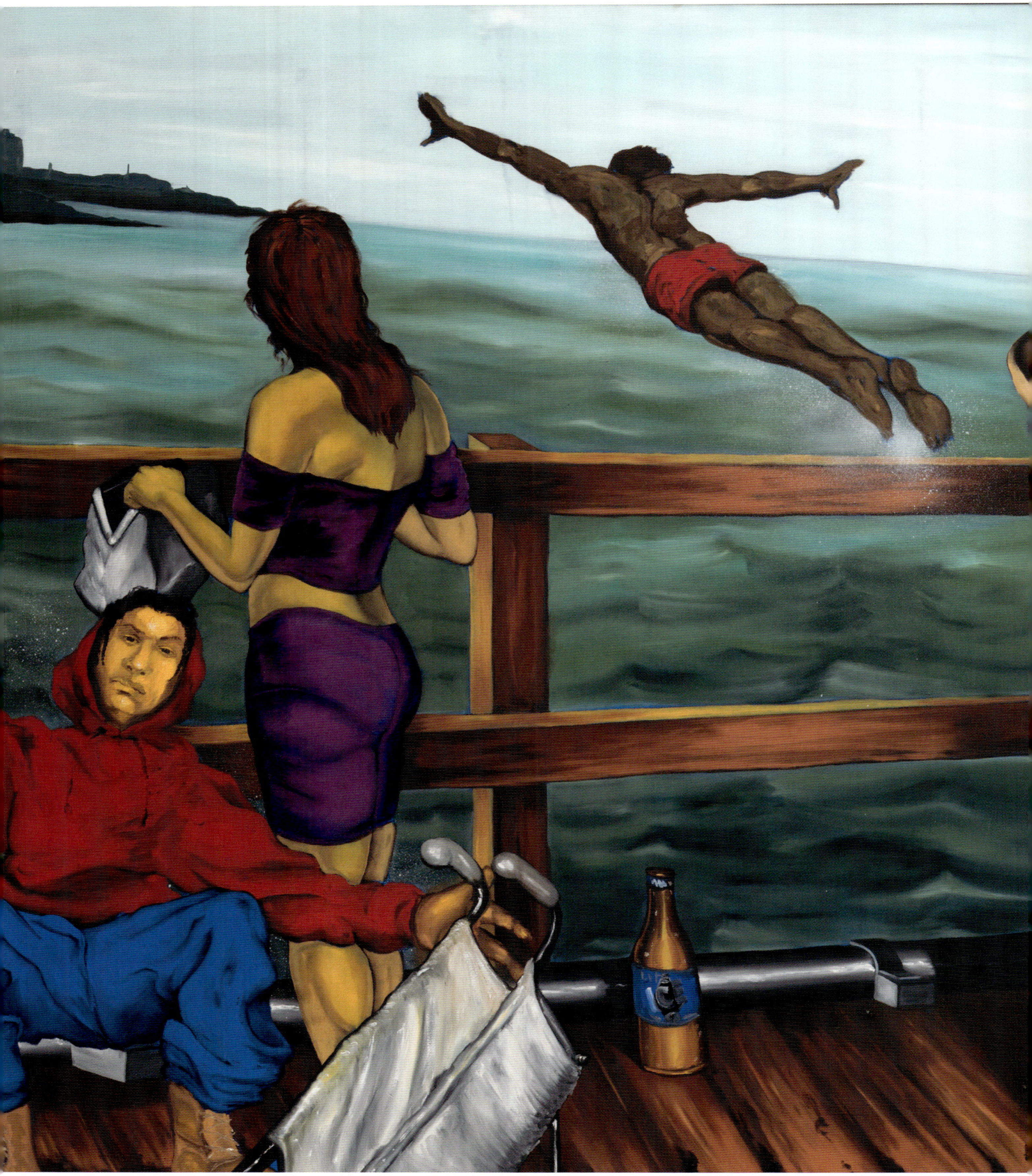

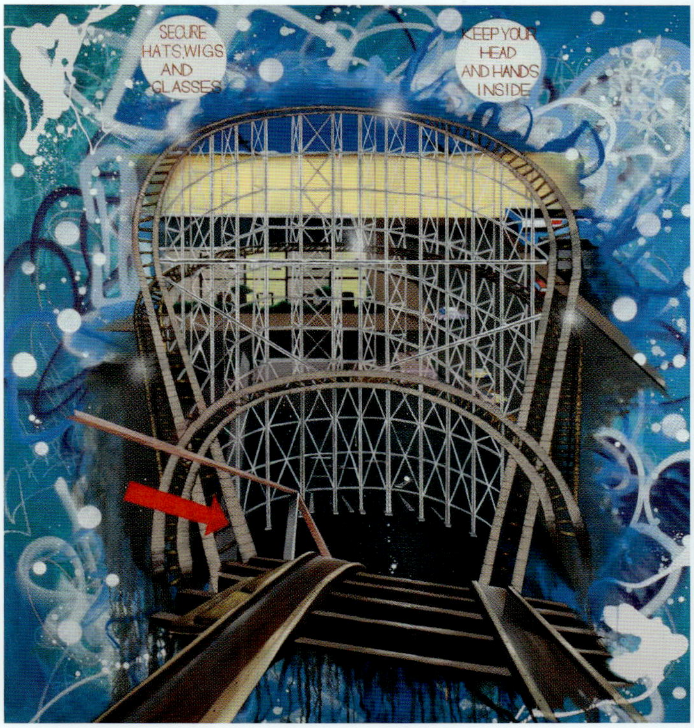

The Cyclone Drop, 2011
Oil, spray paint on canvas, 60" × 56"
Photo by Adam Reich

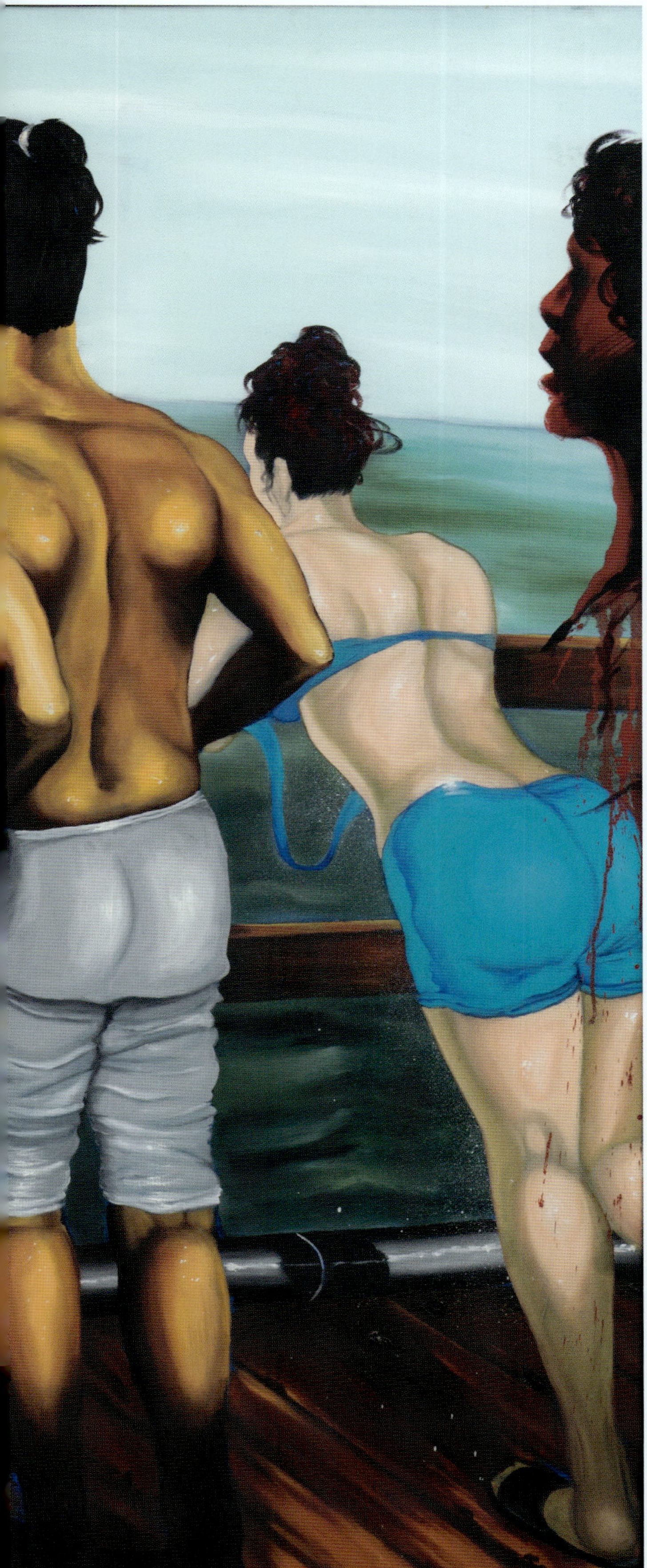

The Pier, 1995
Oil on canvas, 60" × 80"
Collection of the artist
Photo by Adam Reich

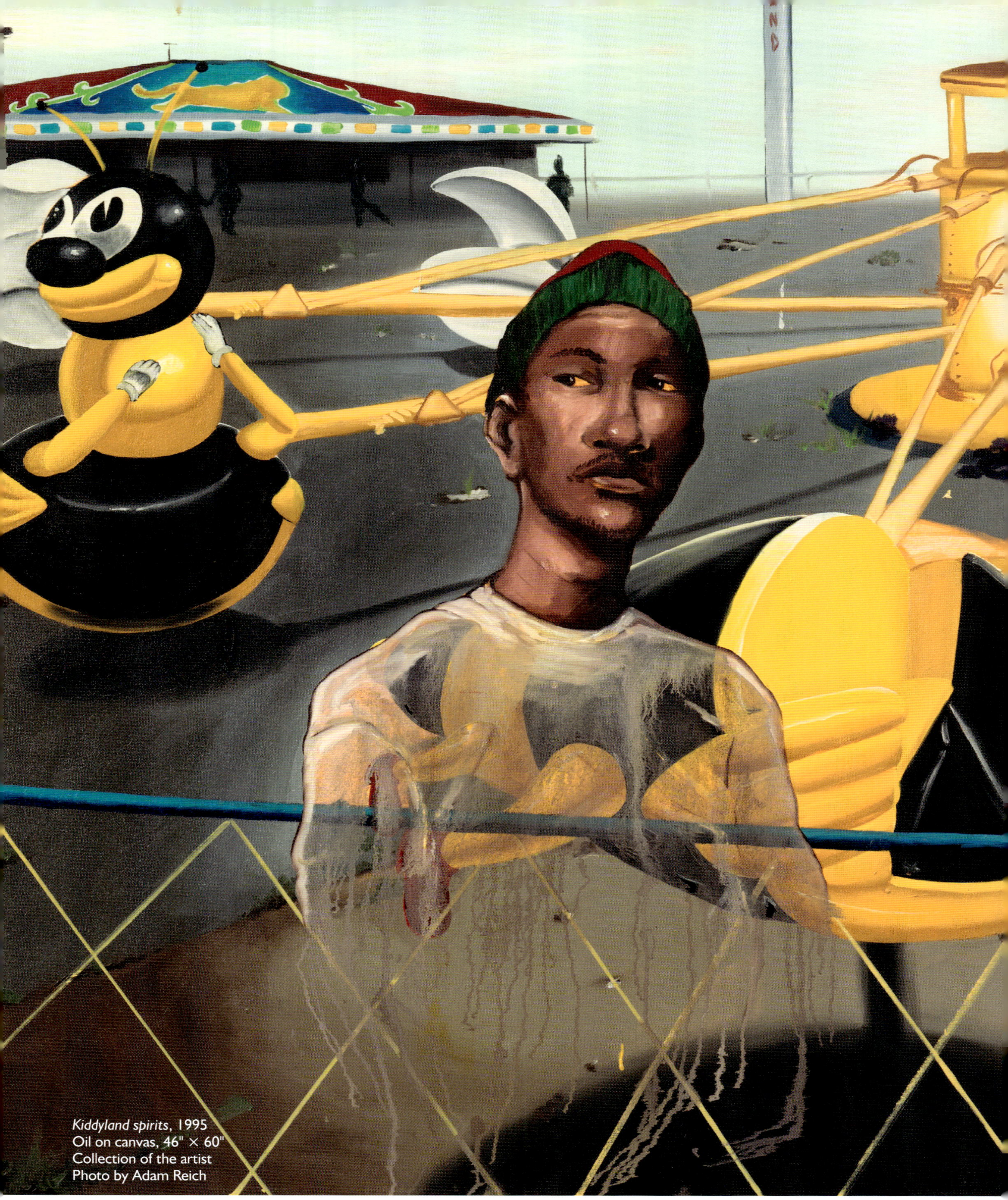

Kiddyland spirits, 1995
Oil on canvas, 46" × 60"
Collection of the artist
Photo by Adam Reich

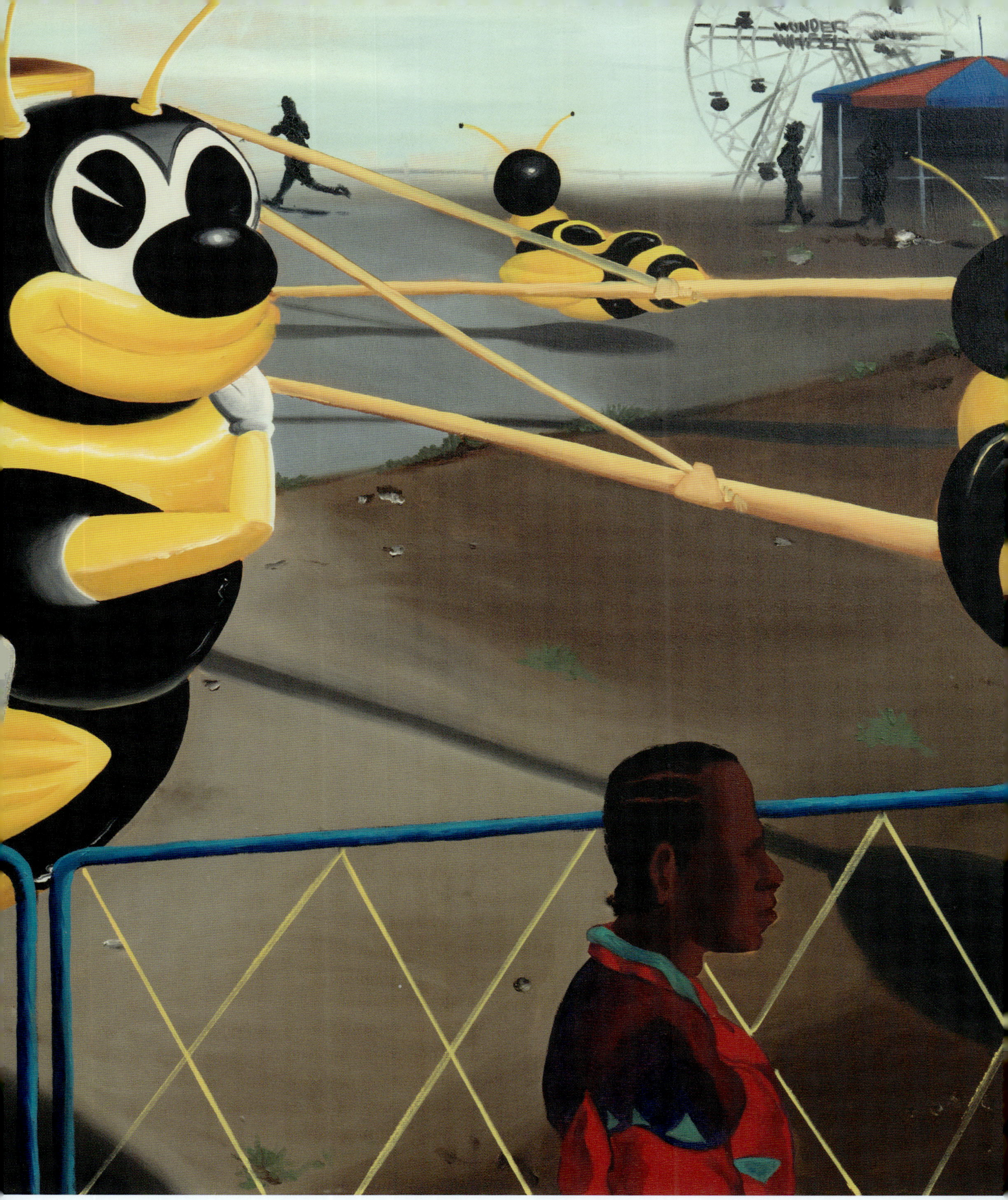
WONDER

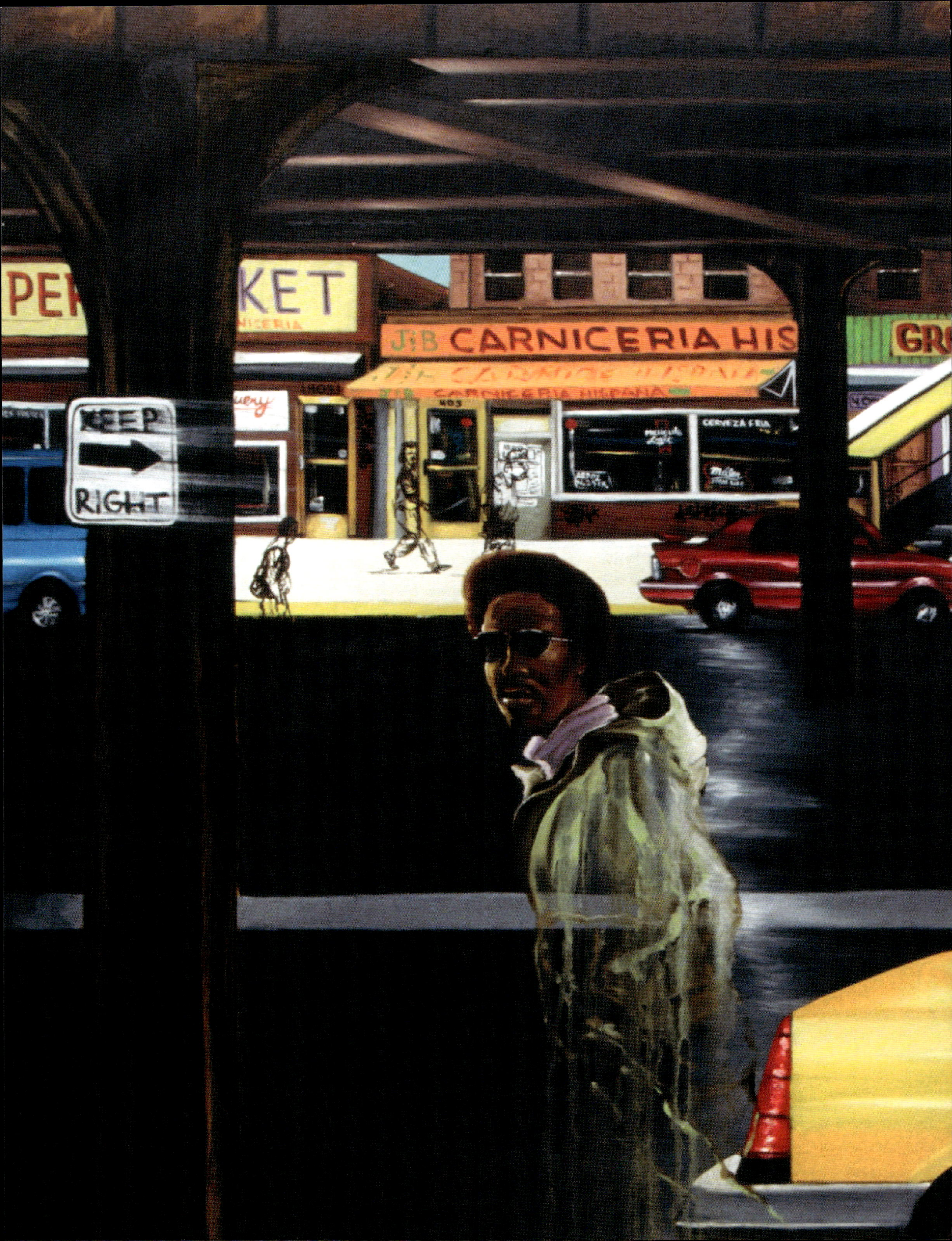
PER
KET
CARNICERIA HIS
CARNICERIA HISPANA
KEEP
RIGHT
CERVEZA FRIA

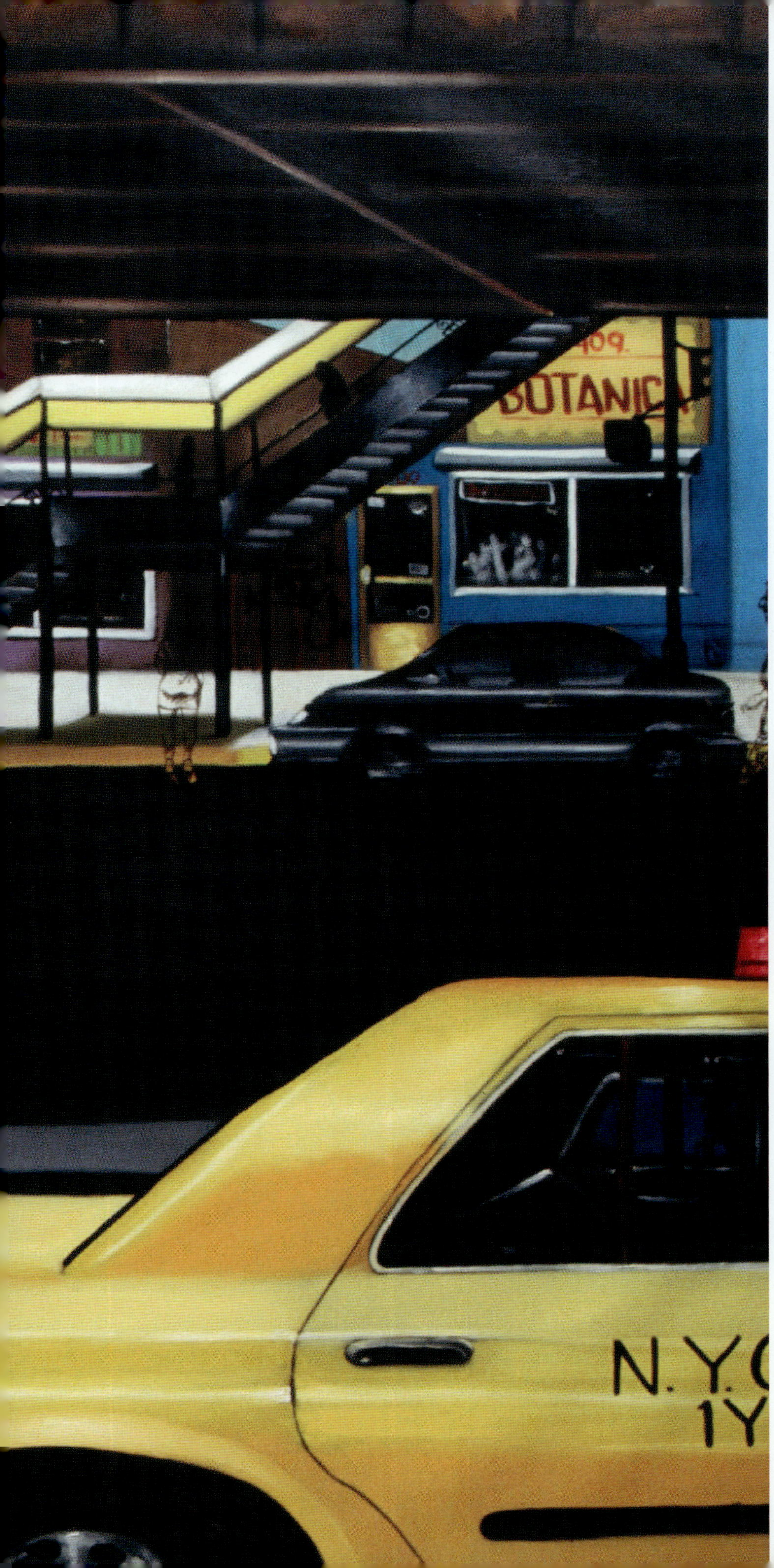

Simpson Street, 2000
Oil on canvas, 70" × 56"
Private collection
Photo by Sue Kwon

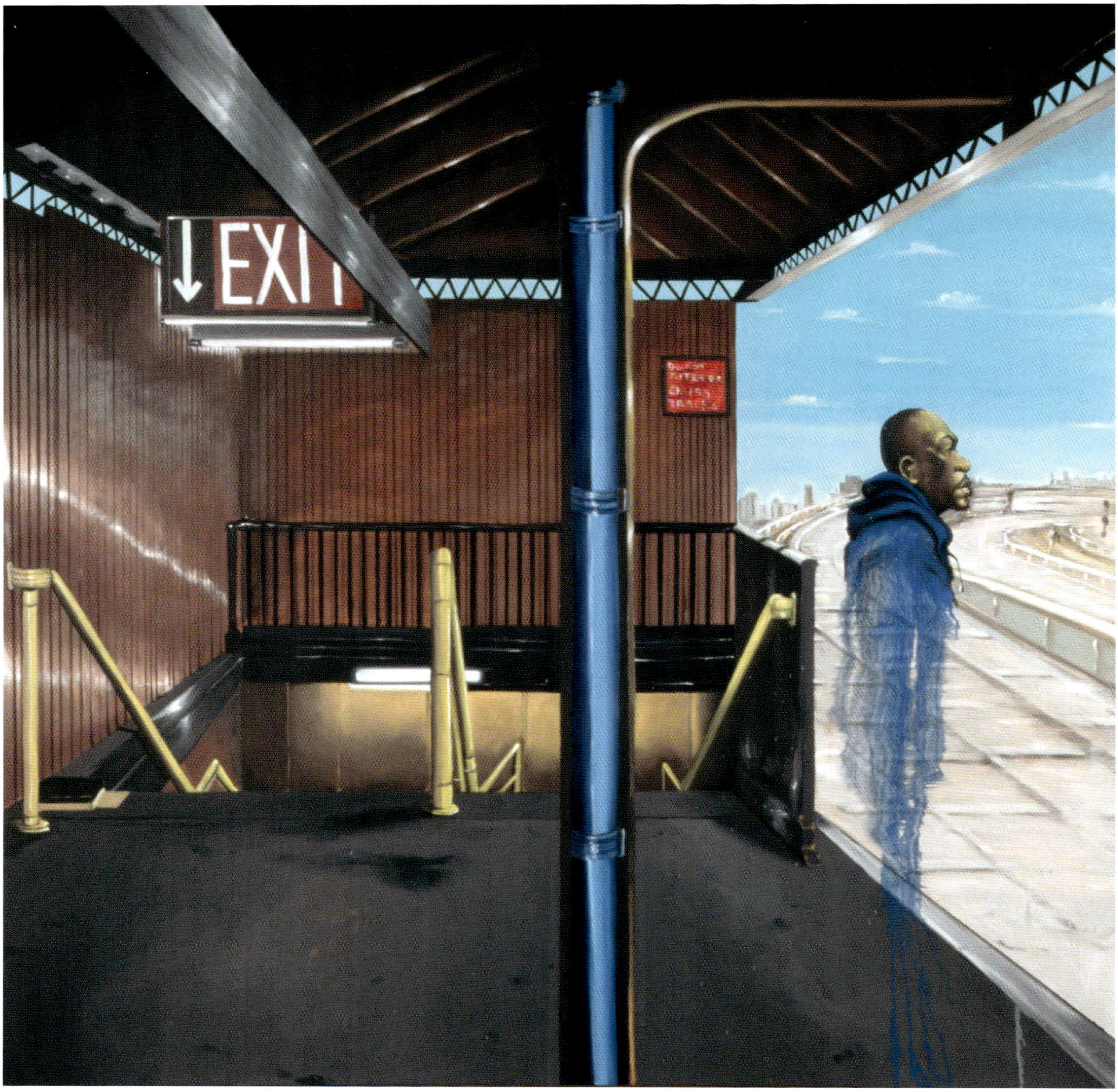

Whitlock Avenue, 2000
Oil on canvas
Private collection
Photo by Sue Kwon

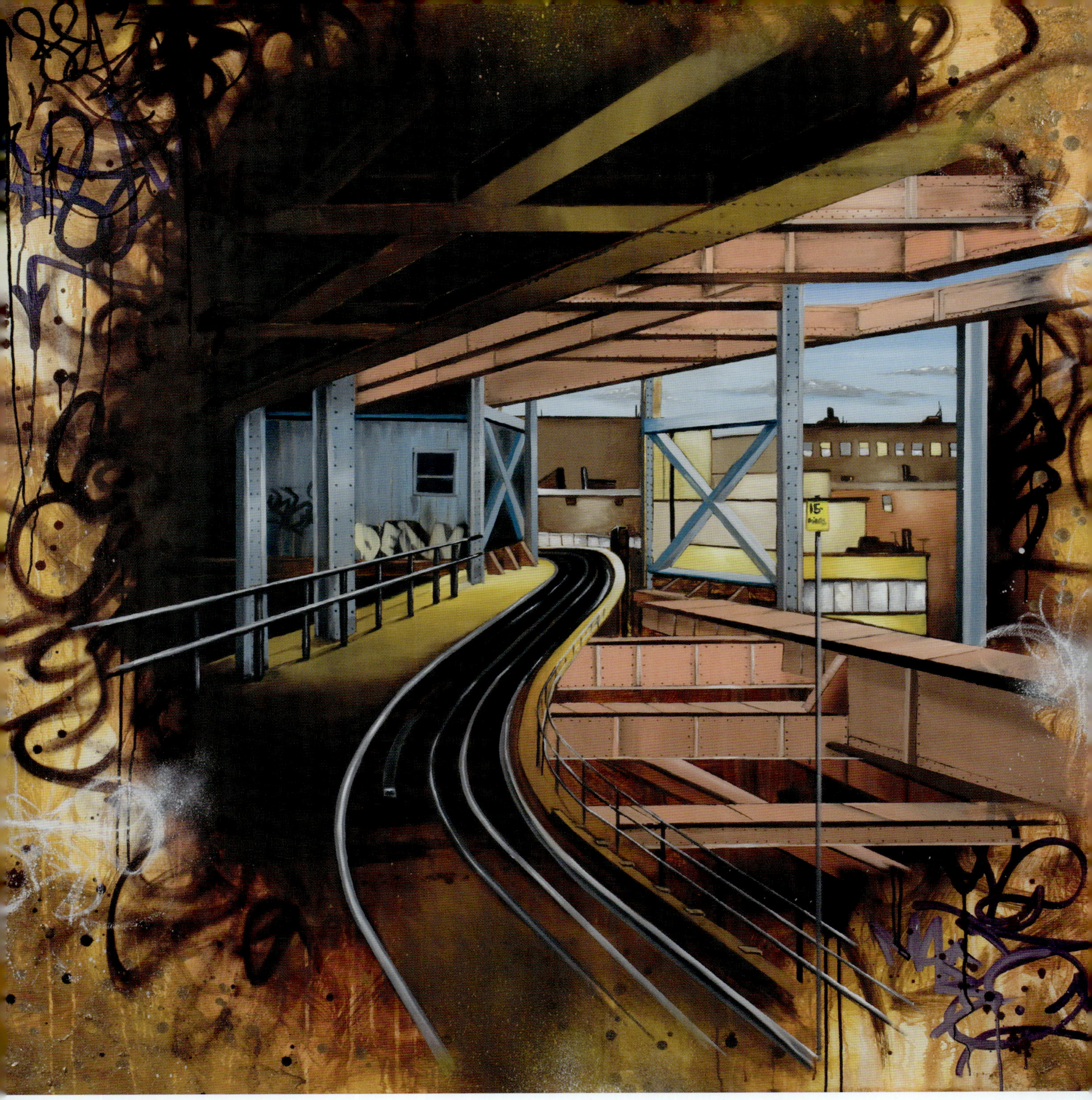

Queensboro Plaza, 2010
Oil, acrylic, spray paint on canvas, 60" × 60"
Photo by Adam Reich

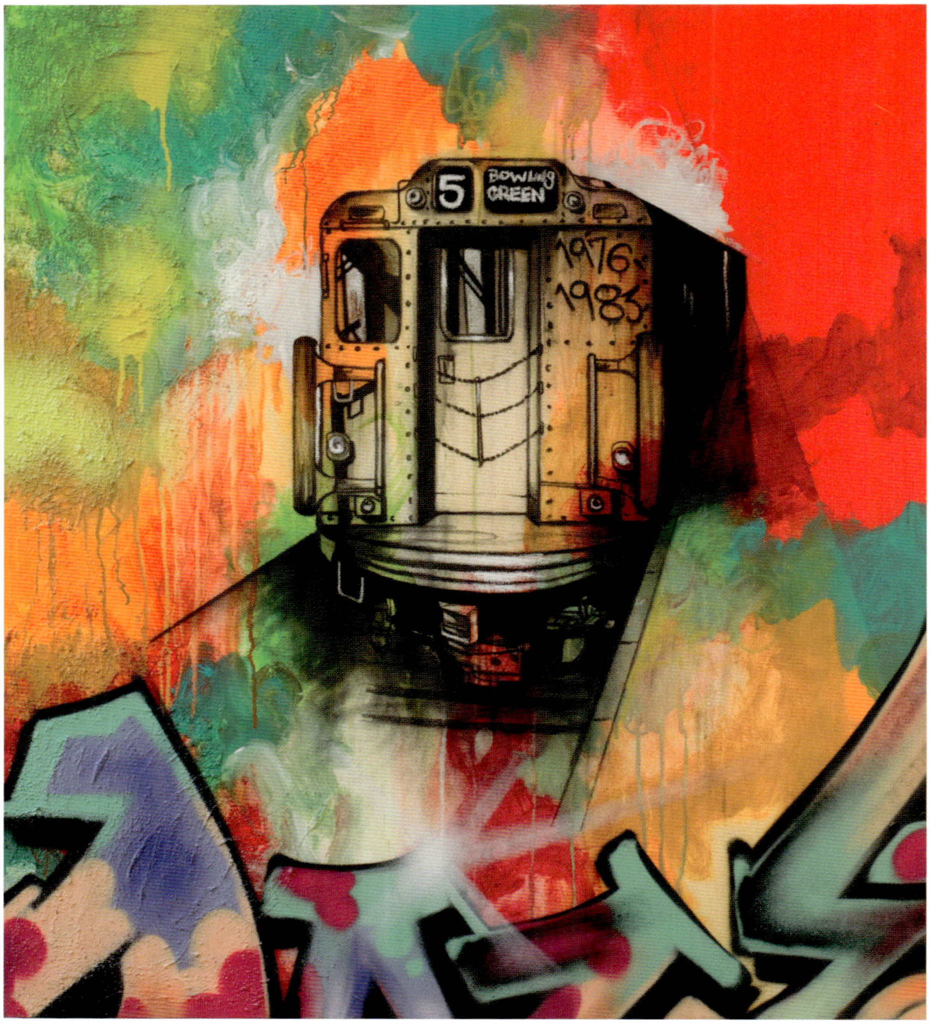

The Golden Years, 2009
Spray paint, charcoal, acrylic on canvas, 46" × 40"
Collection of the artist
Photo by Adam Reich

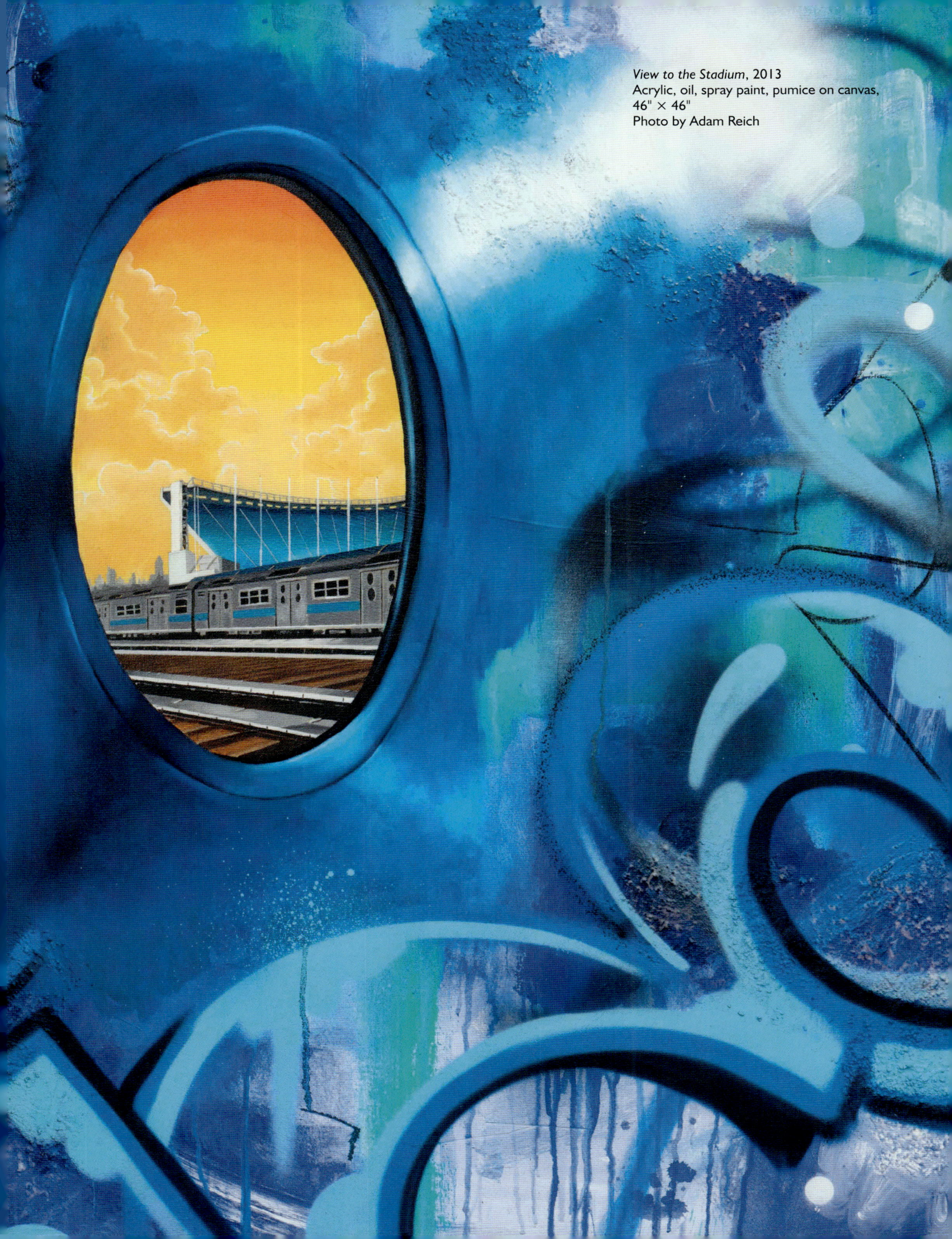

View to the Stadium, 2013
Acrylic, oil, spray paint, pumice on canvas,
46" × 46"
Photo by Adam Reich

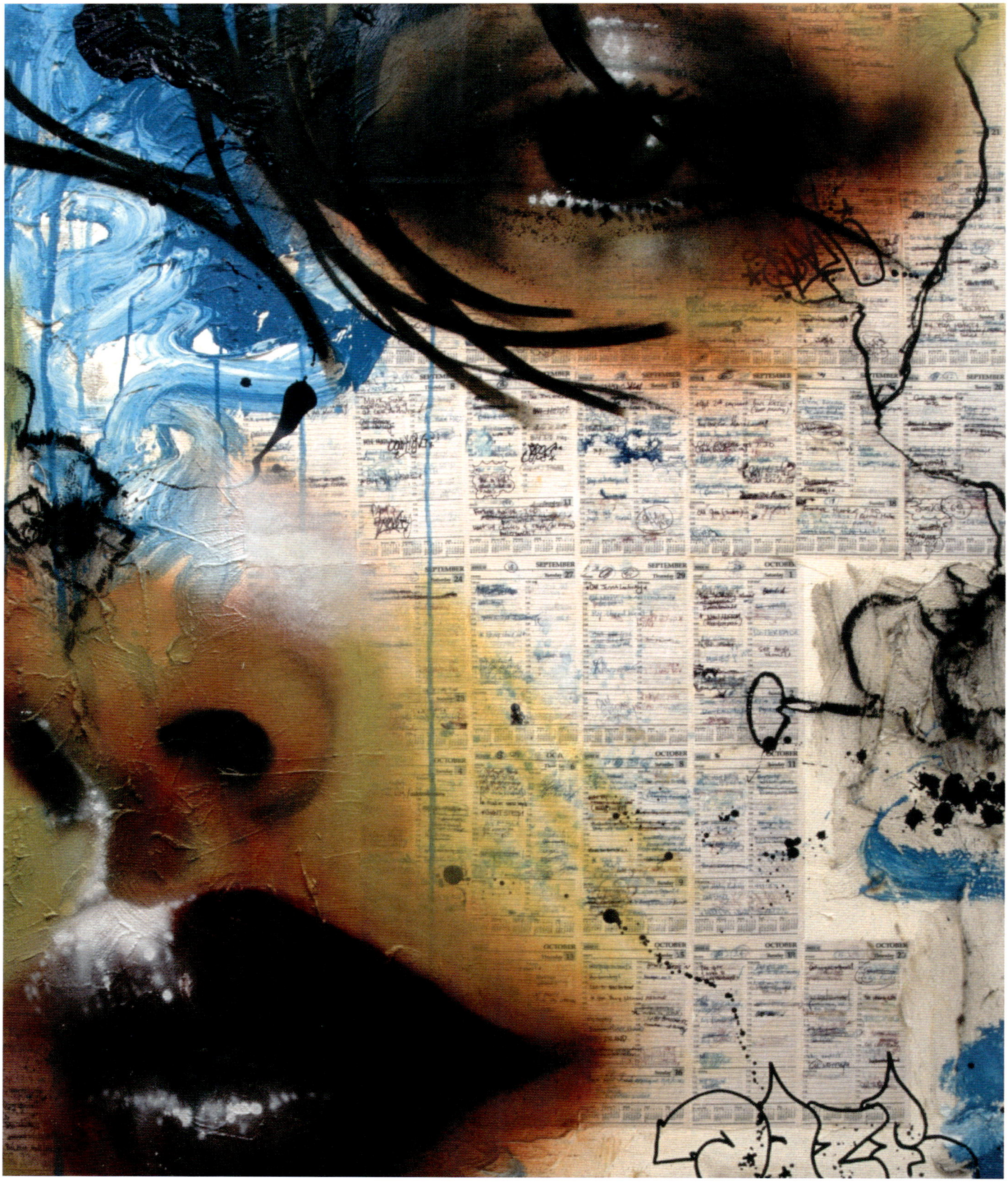

Agenda Painting 17, 2002
Mixed media on canvas, 36" × 48"
Private collection

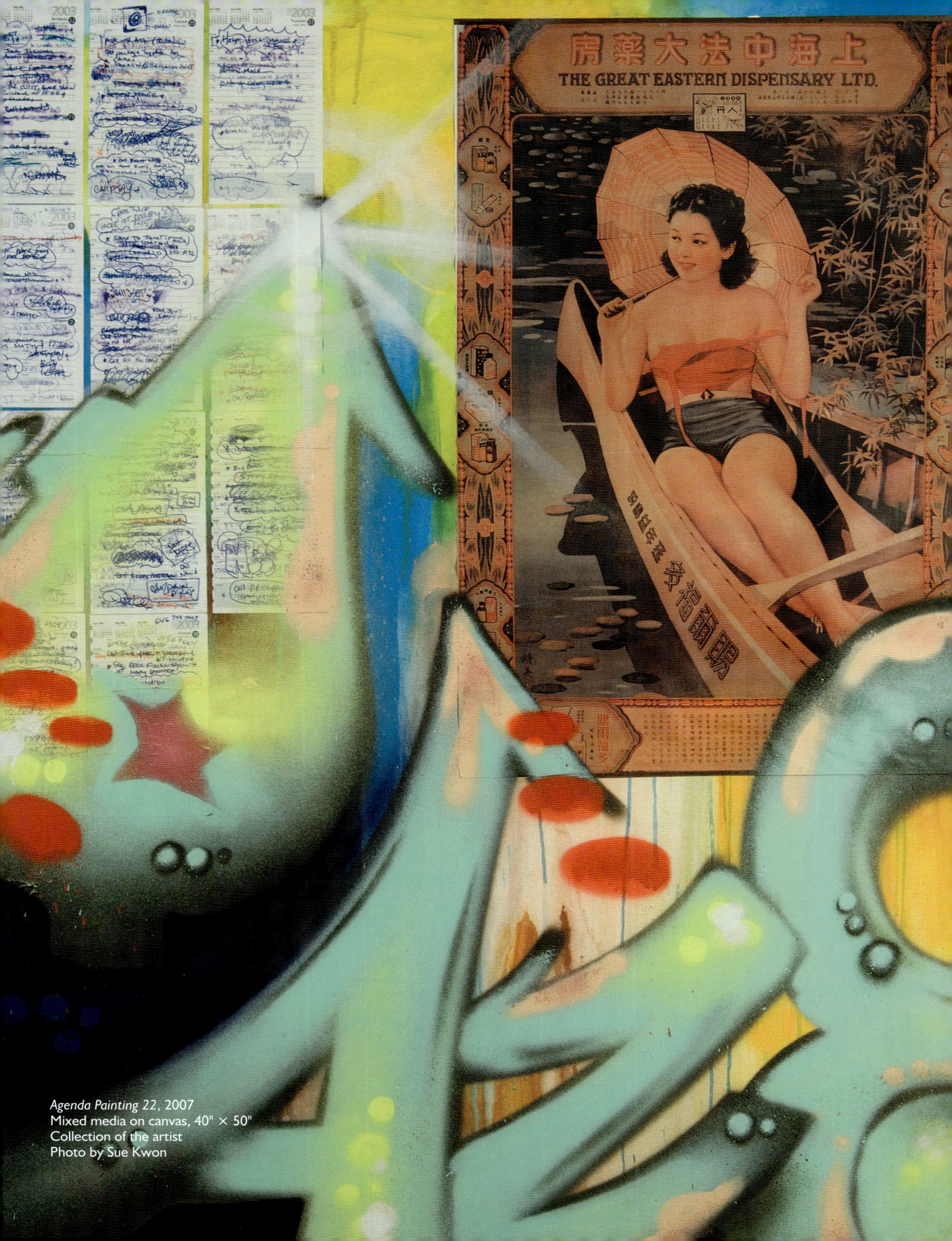

Agenda Painting 22, 2007
Mixed media on canvas, 40" × 50"
Collection of the artist
Photo by Sue Kwon

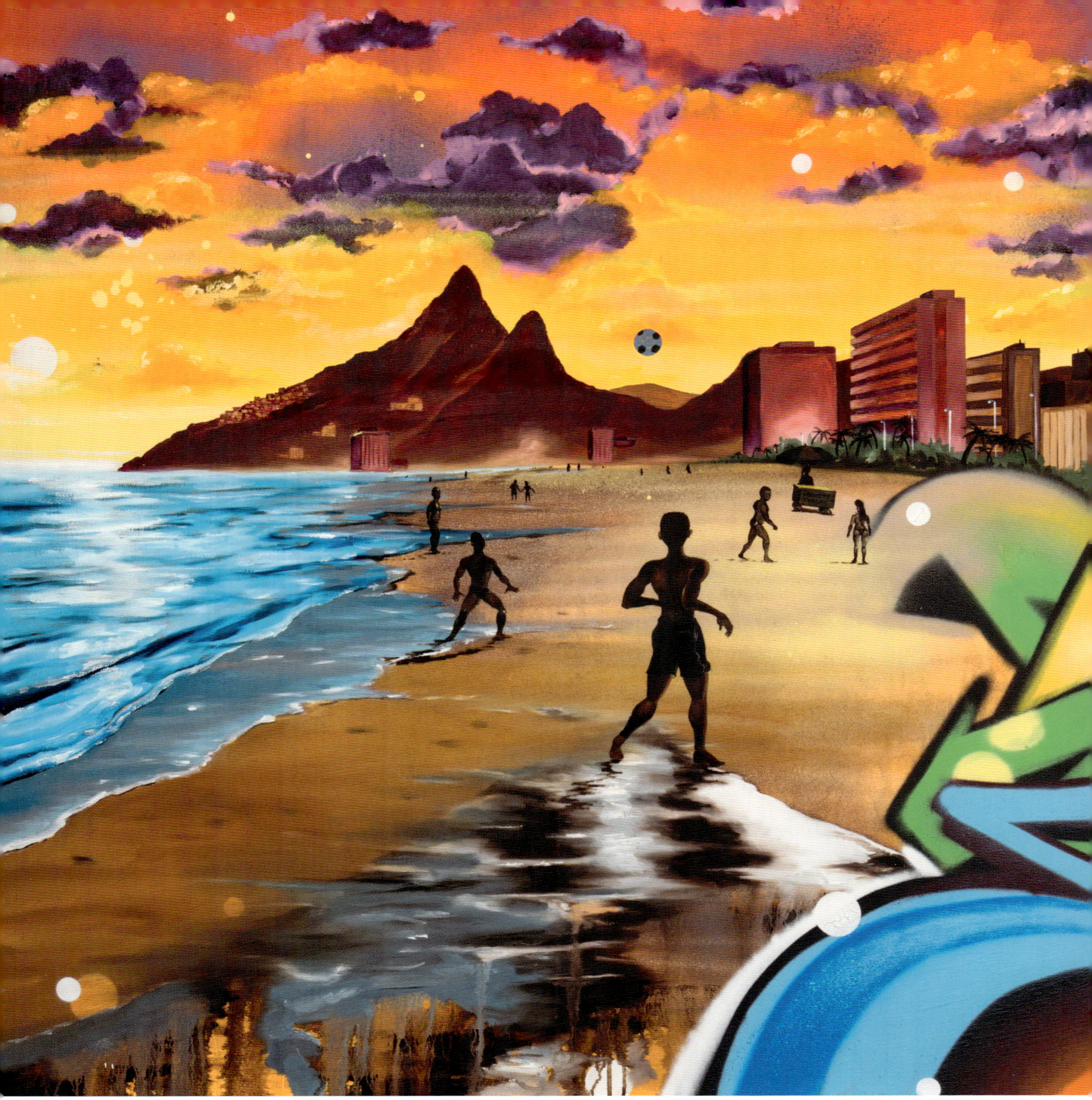

Leblon, 2013
Oil, spray paint on canvas, 46" × 46"
Photo by Adam Reich

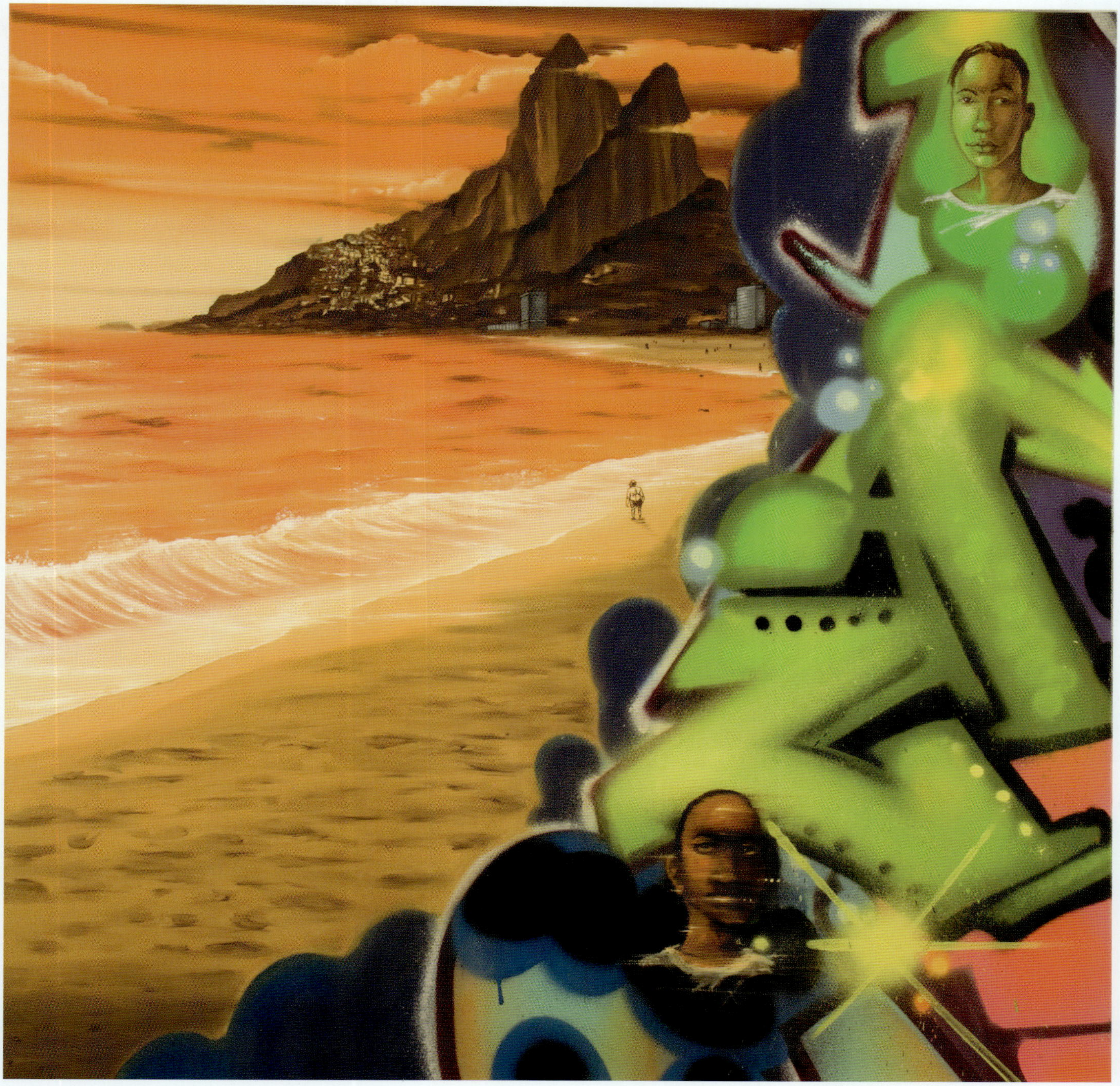

The Other Life, 2008
Oil, spray paint on canvas, 36" × 36"

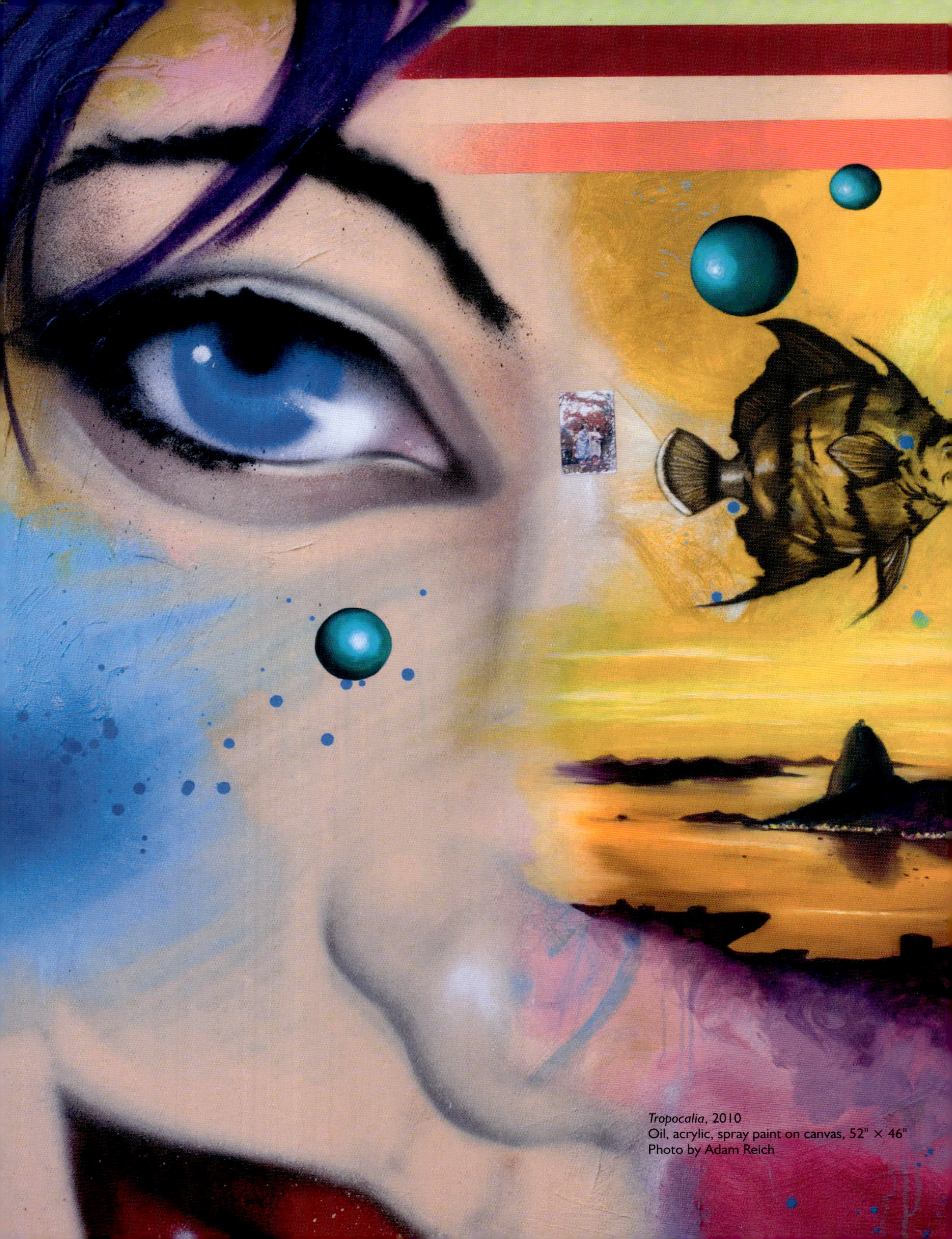

Tropocalia, 2010
Oil, acrylic, spray paint on canvas, 52" × 46"
Photo by Adam Reich

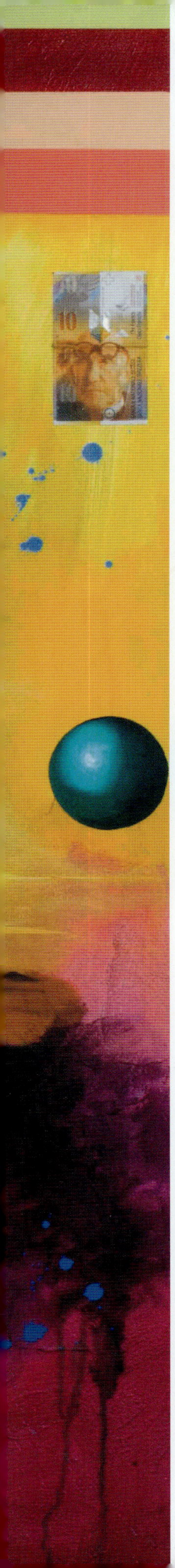

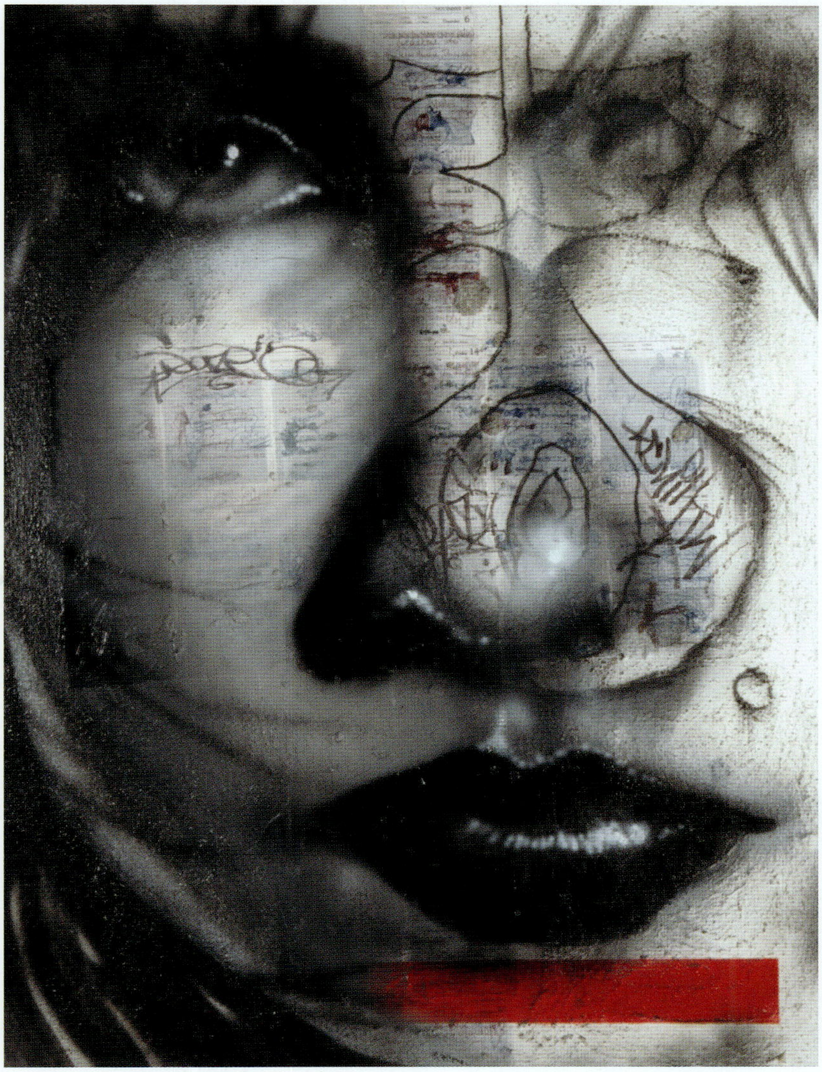

Agenda Painting 8, 2000
Mixed media on canvas, 36" × 48"
Collection of Martin and Janet Blinder
Photo by Sue Kwon

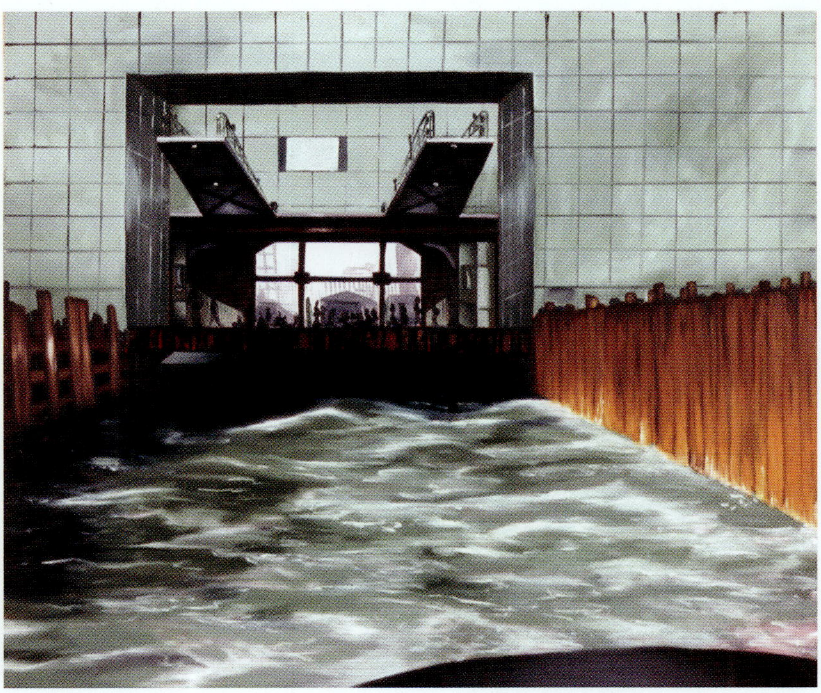

Staten Island Ferry Approaching, 2003
Oil on canvas,
48" × 40"

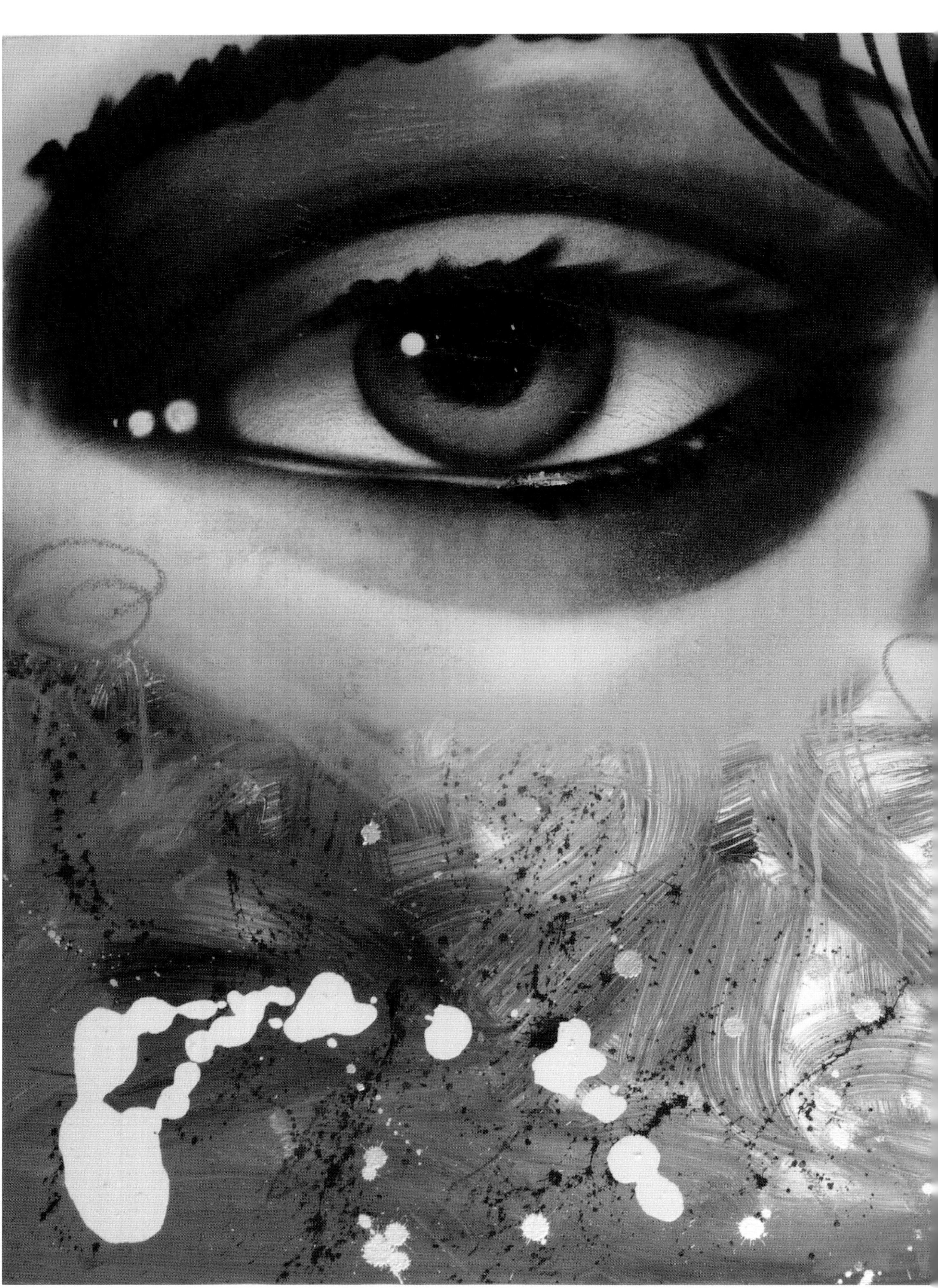

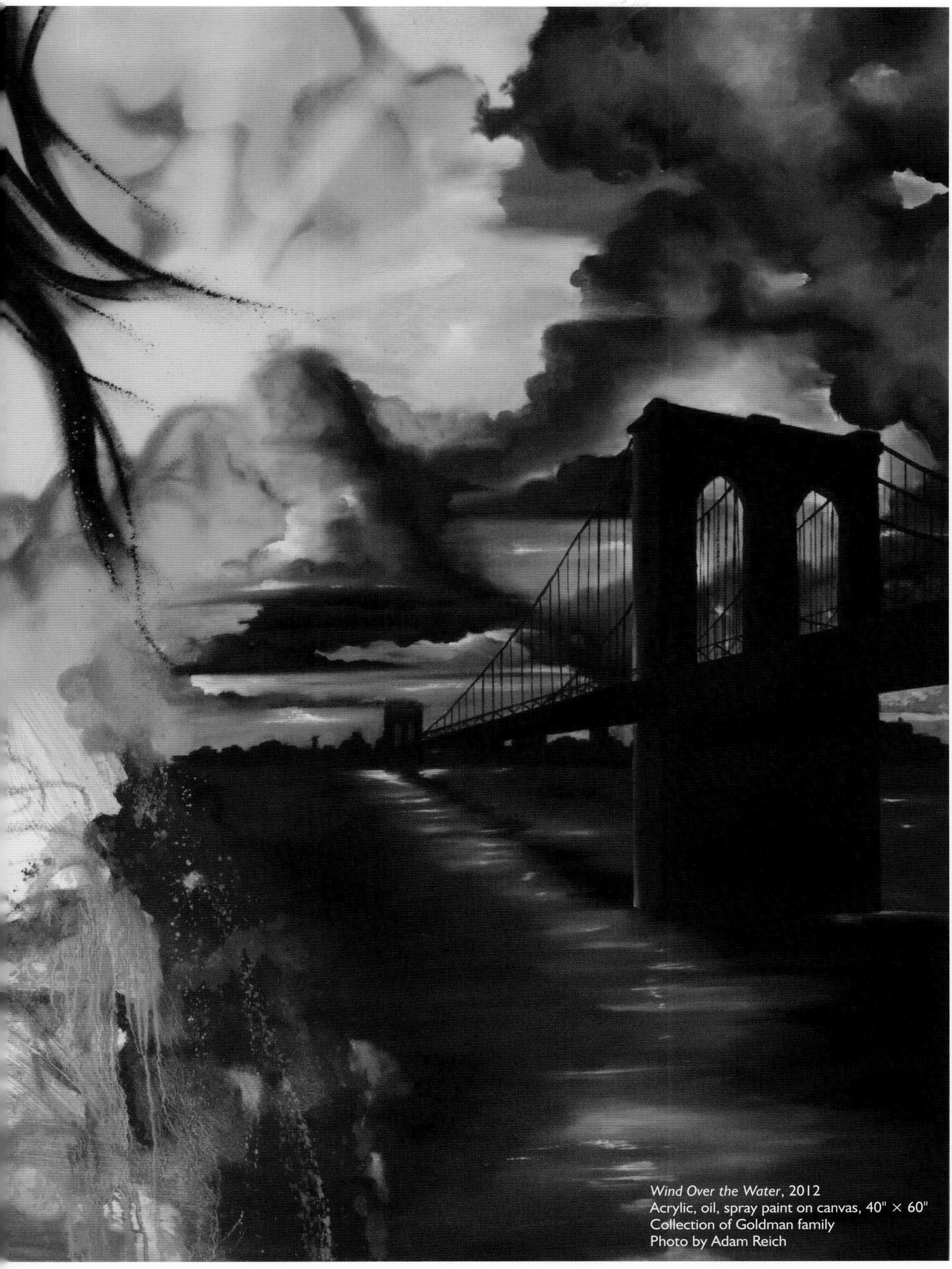

Wind Over the Water, 2012
Acrylic, oil, spray paint on canvas, 40" × 60"
Collection of Goldman family
Photo by Adam Reich

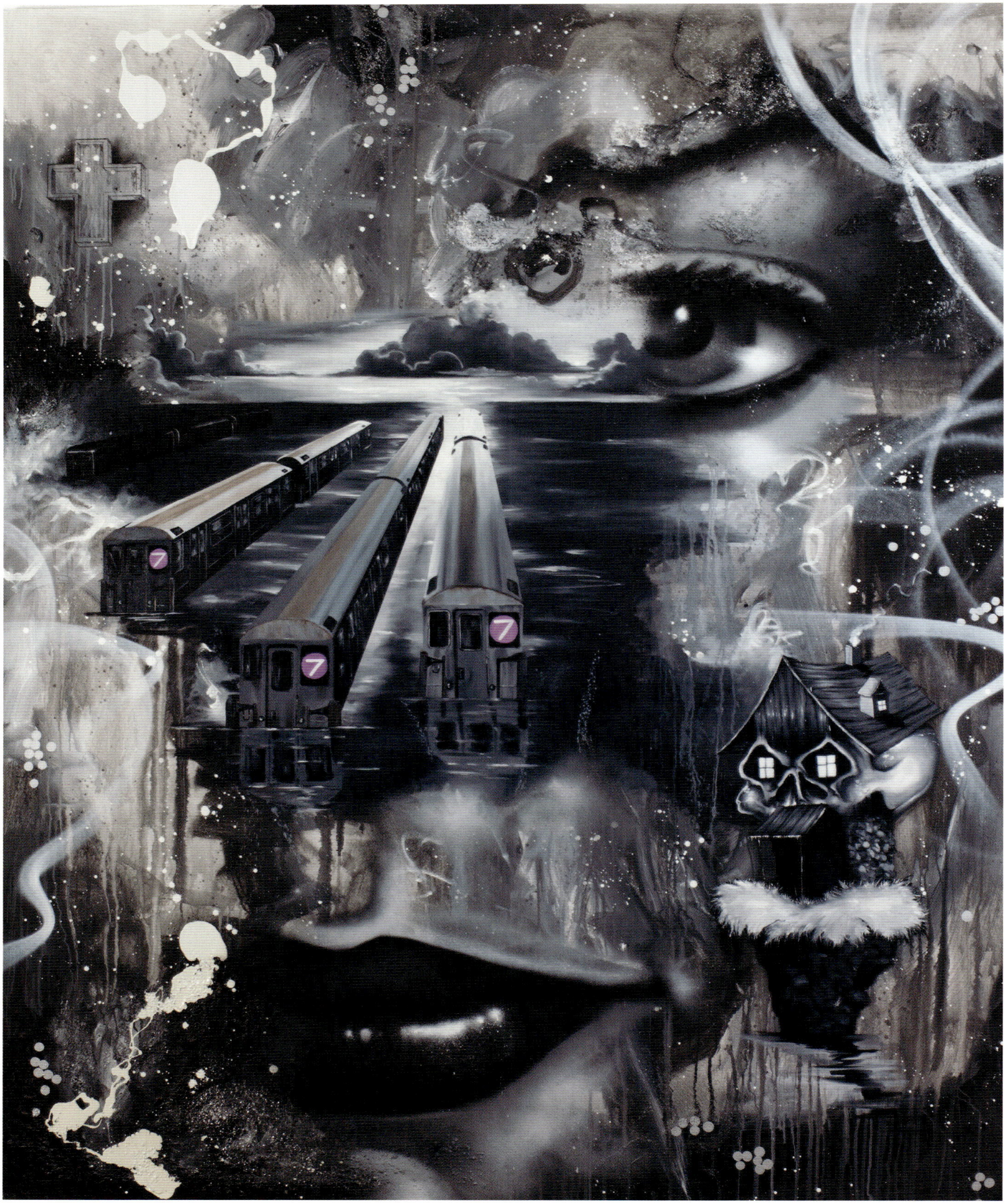

Watery Grave, 2012
Acrylic, spray paint, oil on canvas, 82" × 66"
Photo by Adam Reich

Dekalb Avenue Tunnel, 2011
Oil, spray paint, acrylic, pumice on canvas
Collection of John Axelrod
Photo by Adam Reich

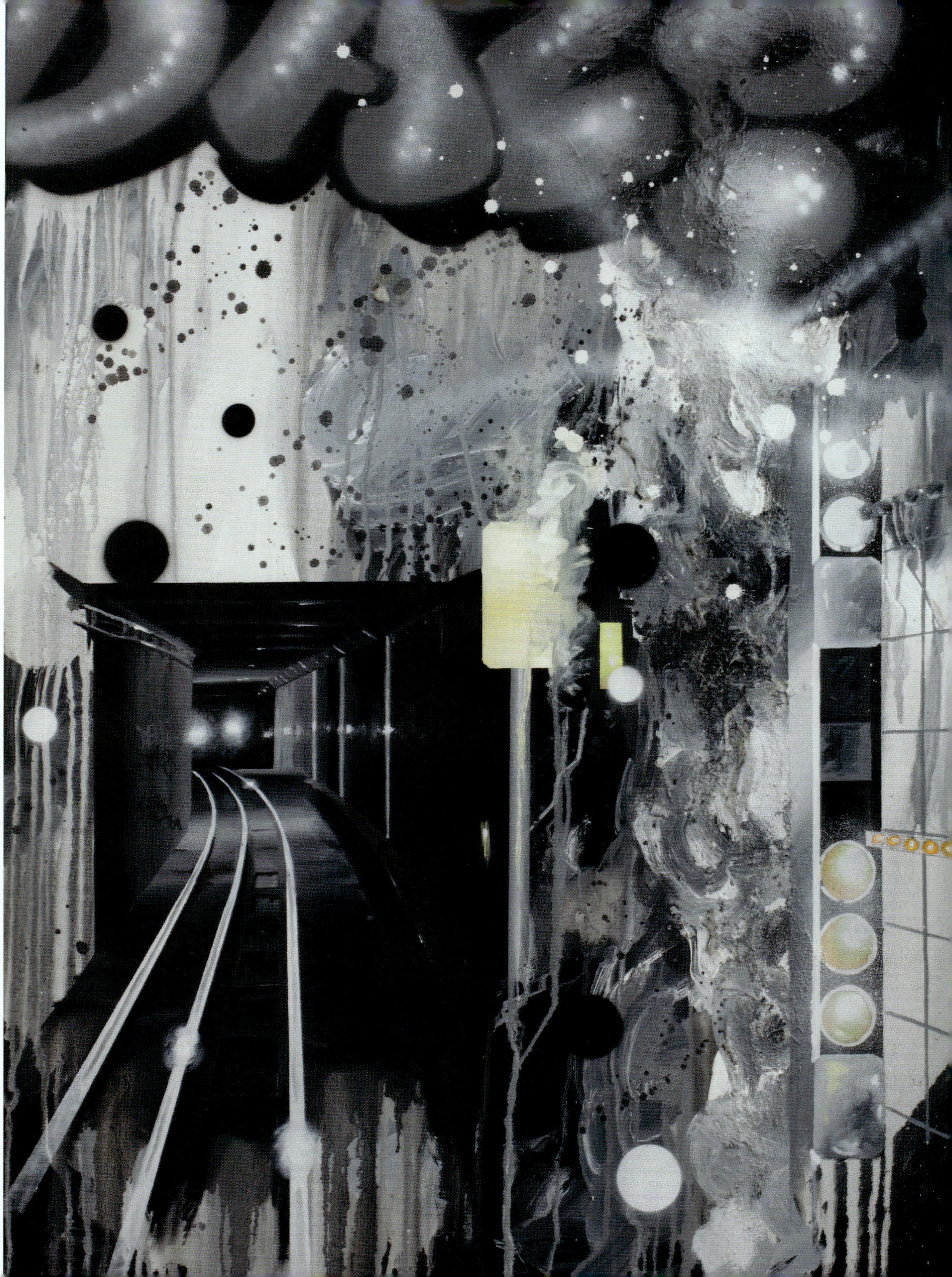

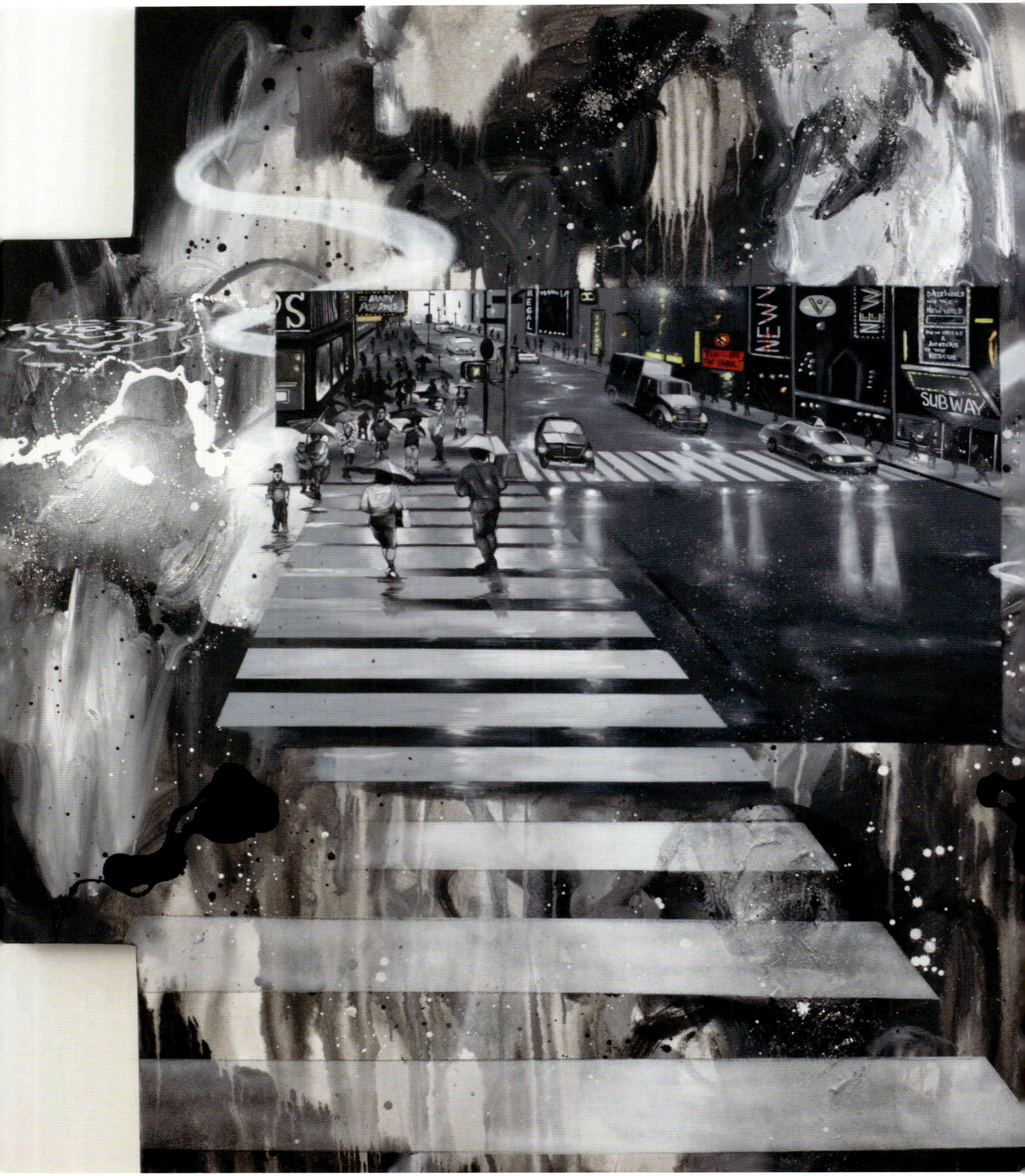
MARY POPPINS
REGAL
NEW
NEW
SUBWAY

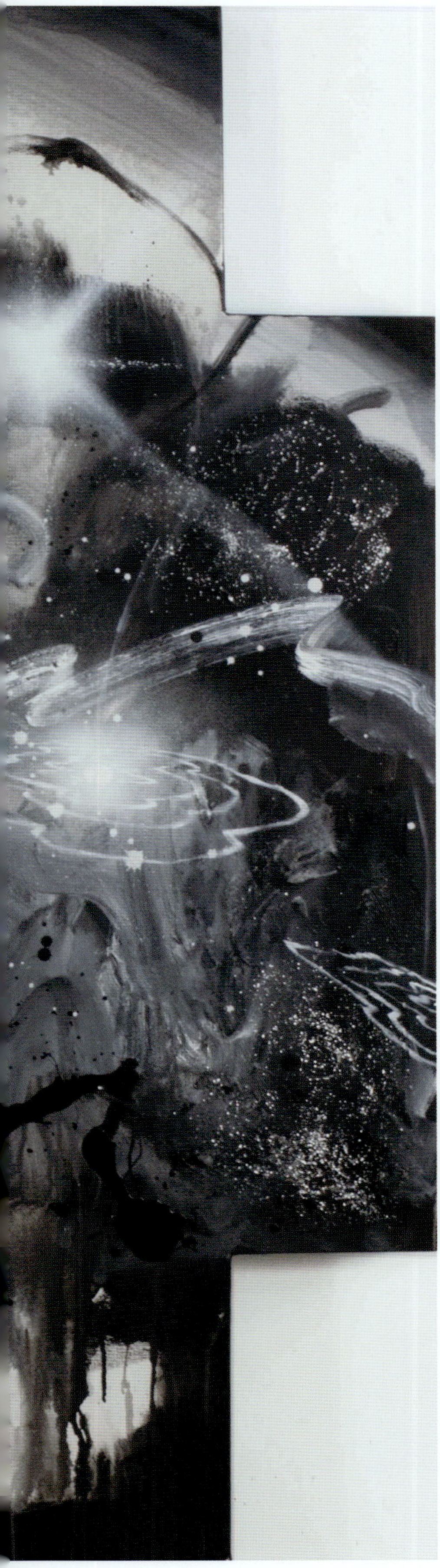

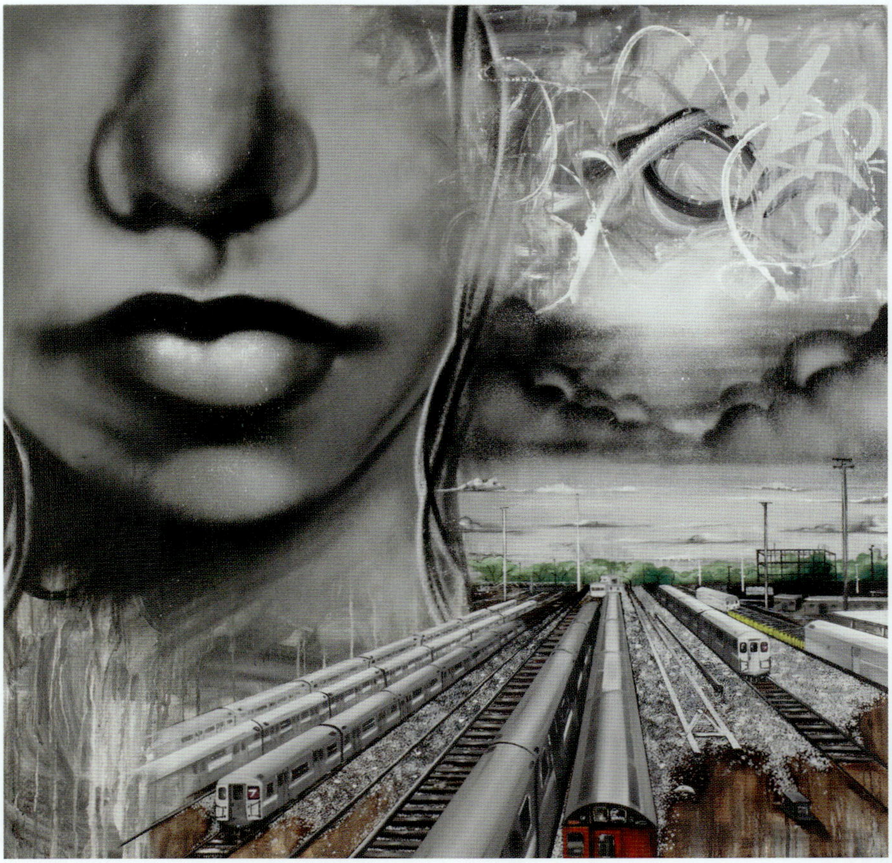

The 7 Yard, 2011
Oil, spray paint, acrylic on canvas, 46" × 46"
Photo by Adam Reich

Crossroads, 2012
Spray paint, oil, acrylic on canvas, 60" × 72"
Collection of The Yale University Art Gallery, New Haven, Connecticut
Photo by Adam Reich

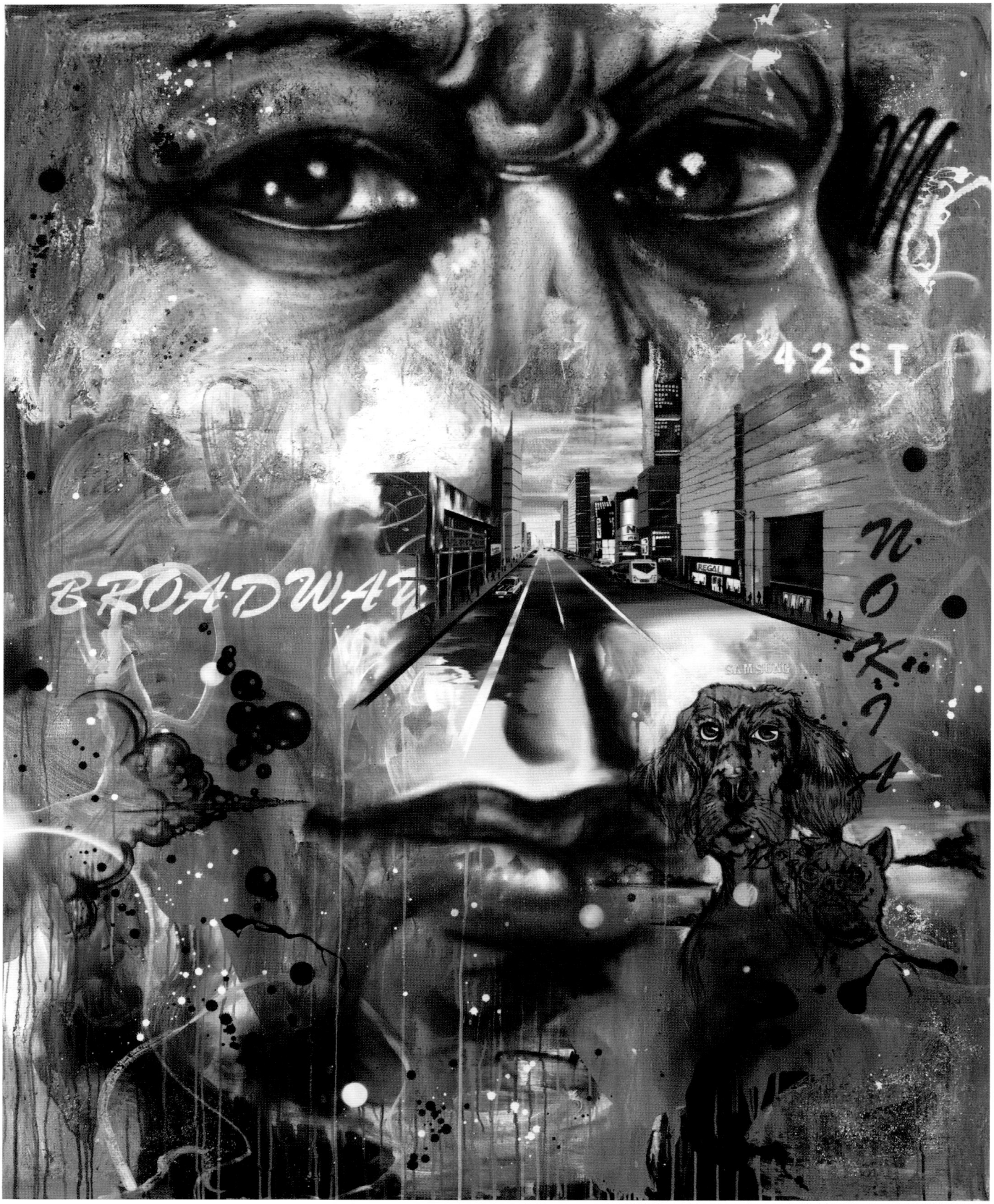

Strays on the Deuce, 2012
Spray paint, oil, acrylic, pumice on canvas, 82" × 66"
Photo by Adam Reich

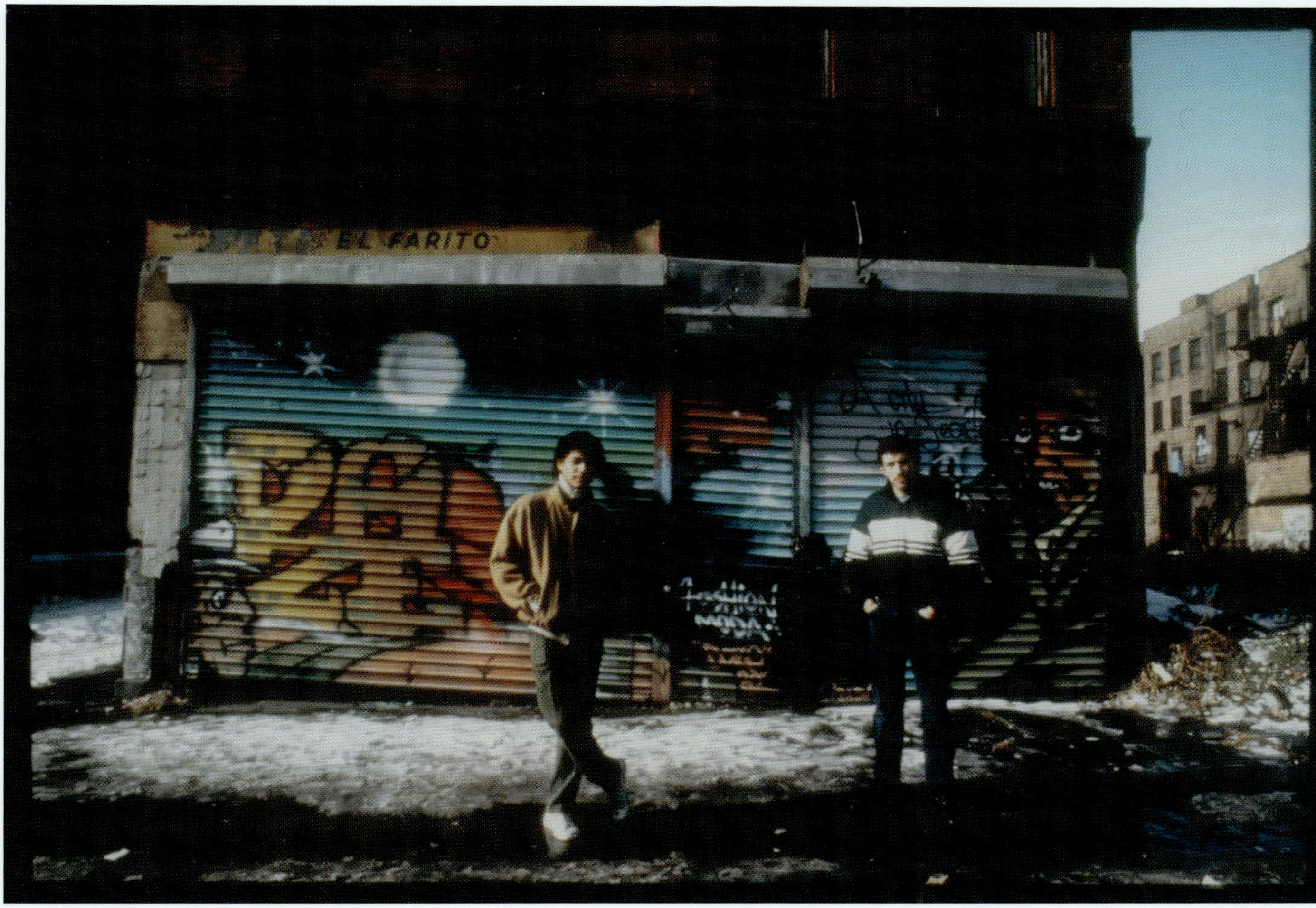

Daze and Crash, Brooke Avenue, 1982
Photo © Lisa Kahane

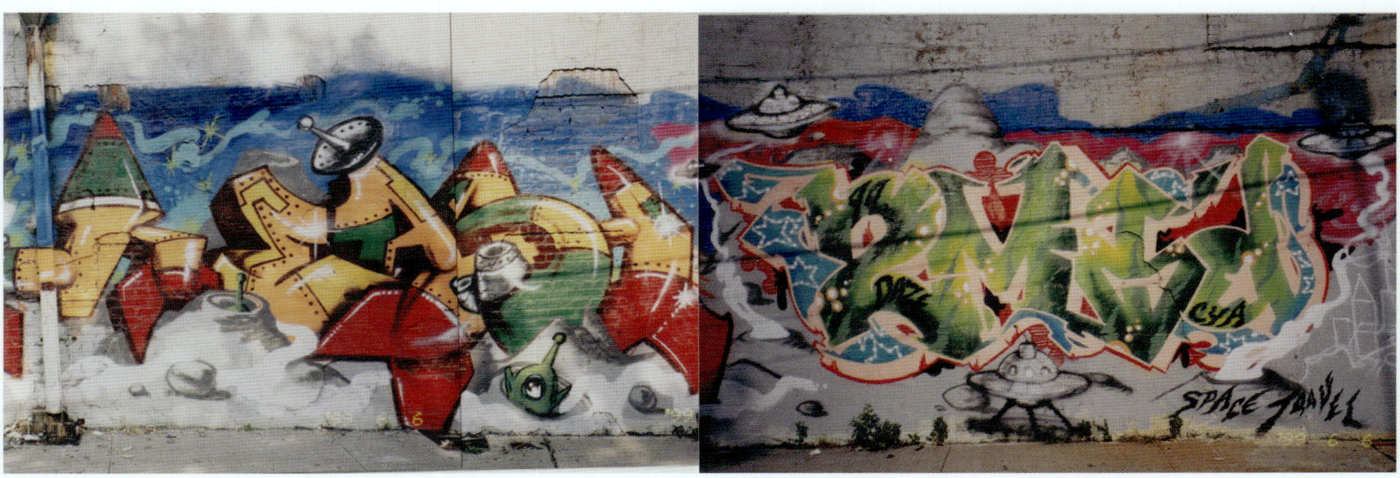

Reas, 2Mad (Daze)
Brooklyn, New York, 1999

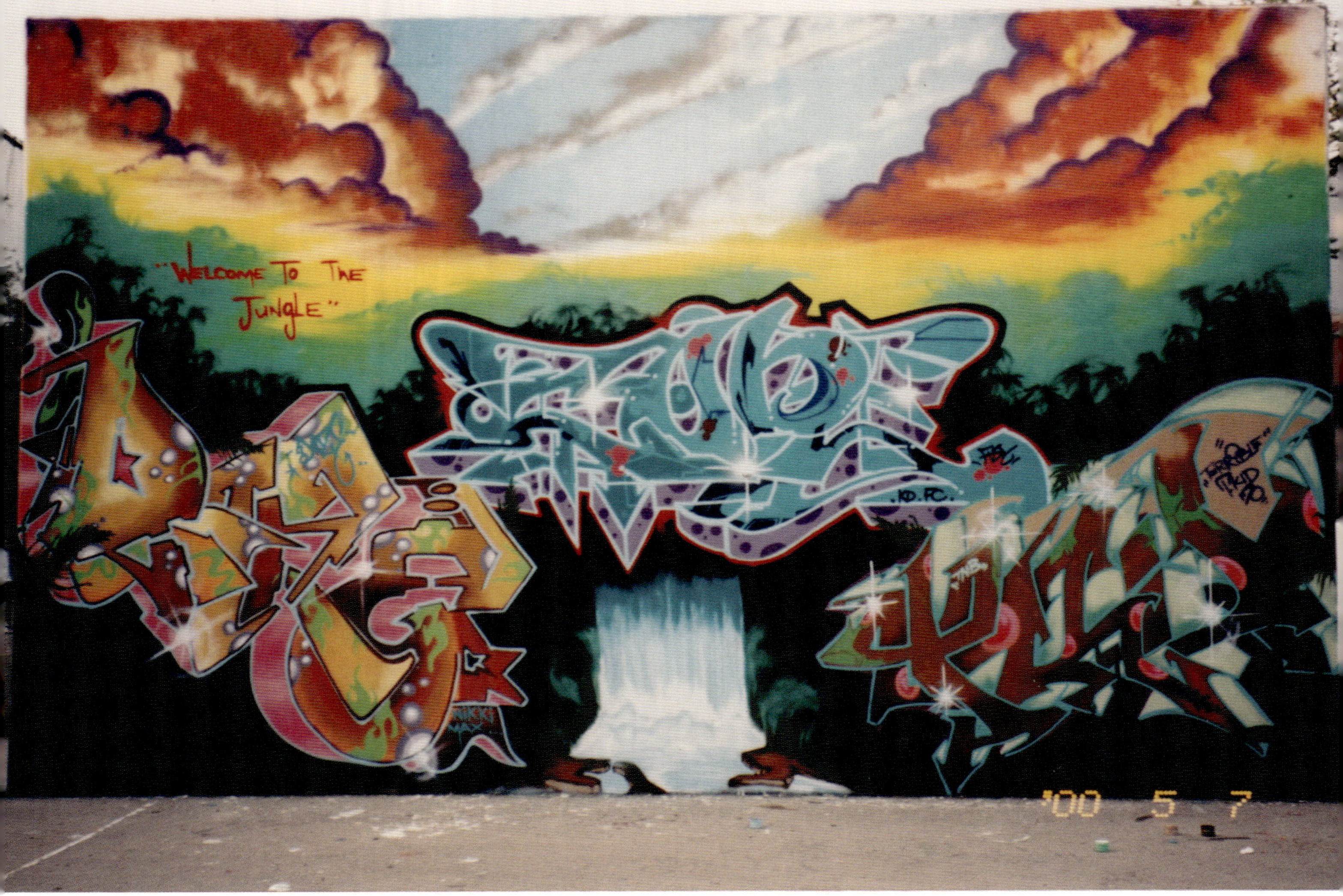

Daze, Cope2, Tkid
Bronx, New York, 2000

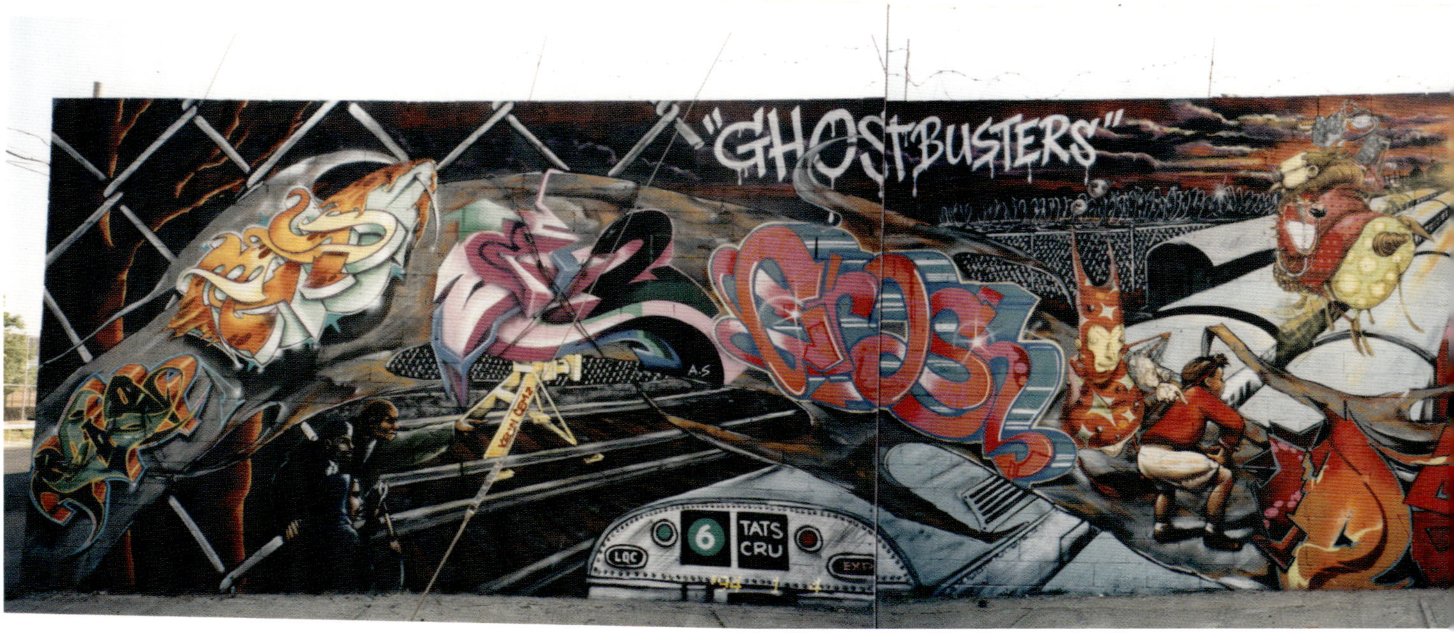

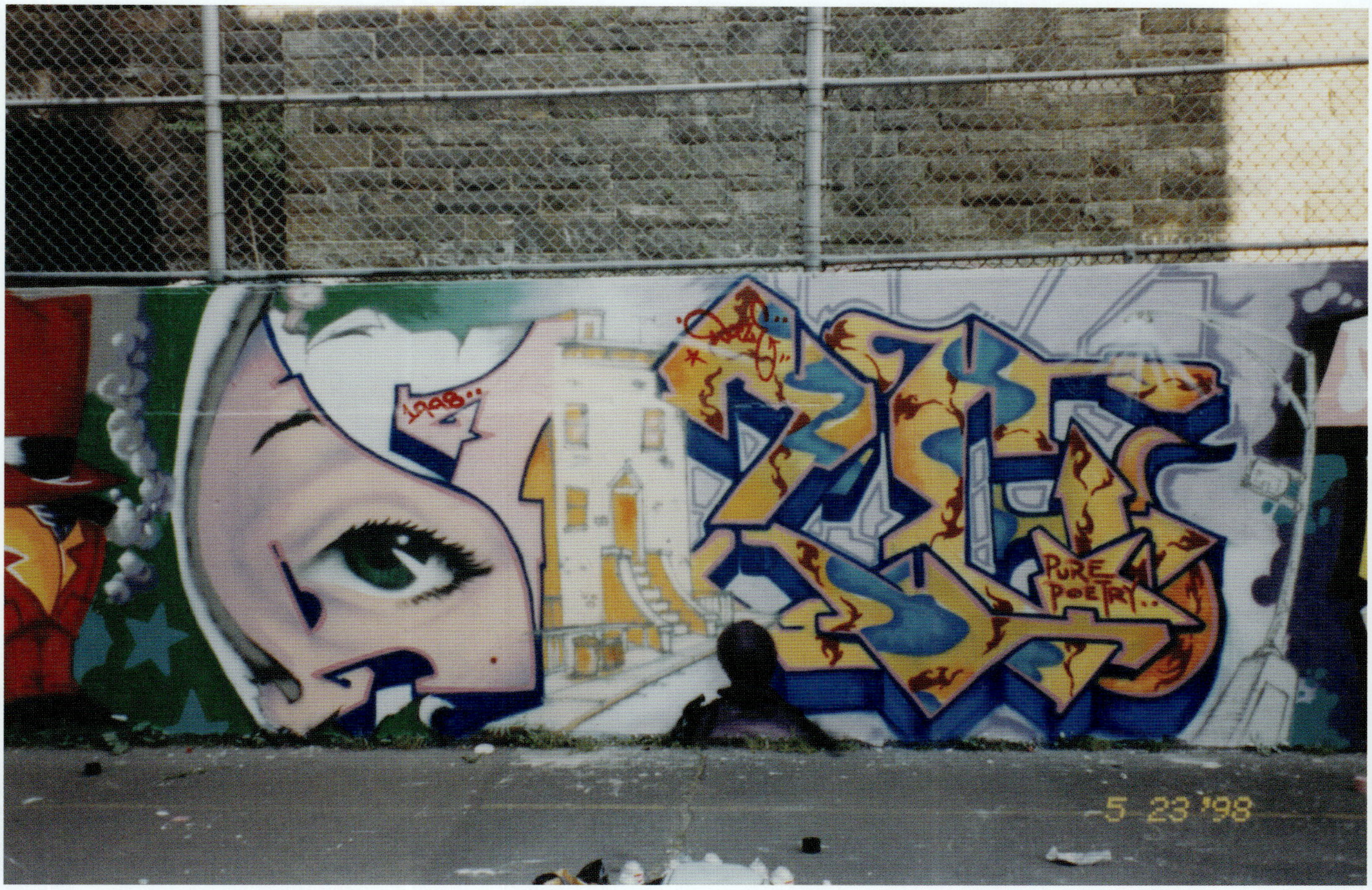

Daze,
Graffiti Hall of Fame, 1998

Bio, BG183, Sen2, Crash, Daze,
Nicer, How, Nosm, Os Gemeos

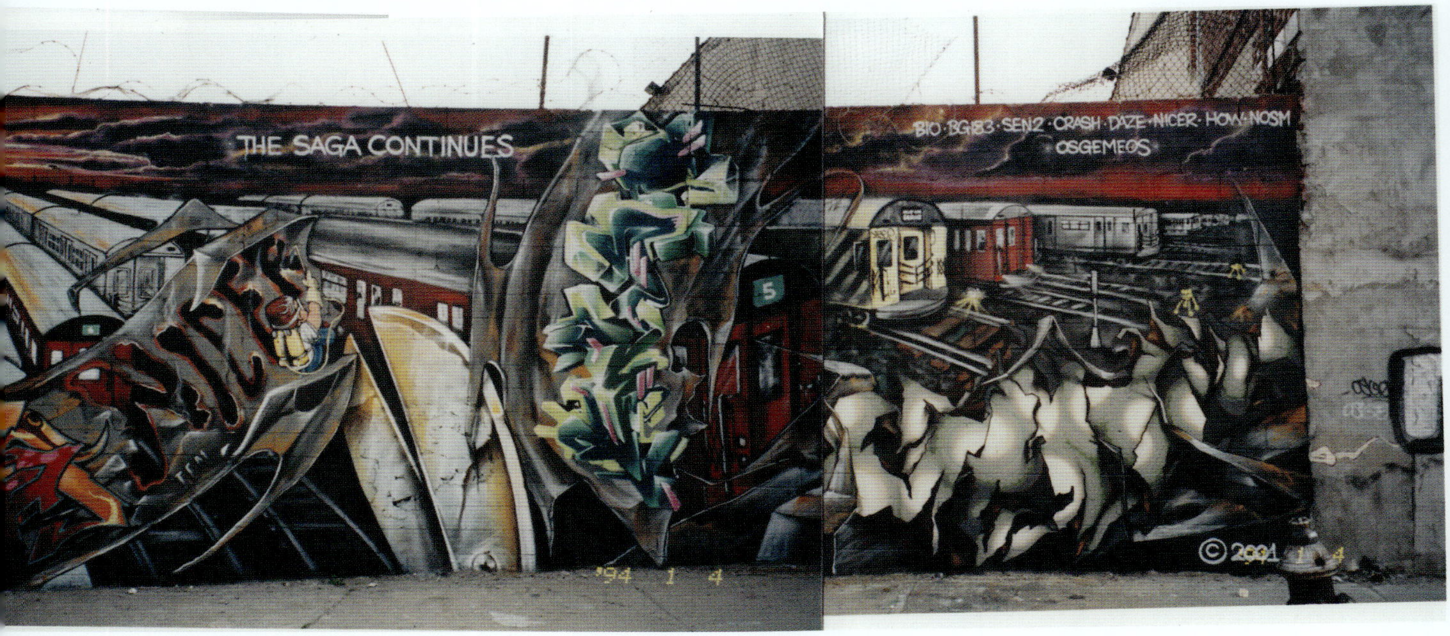

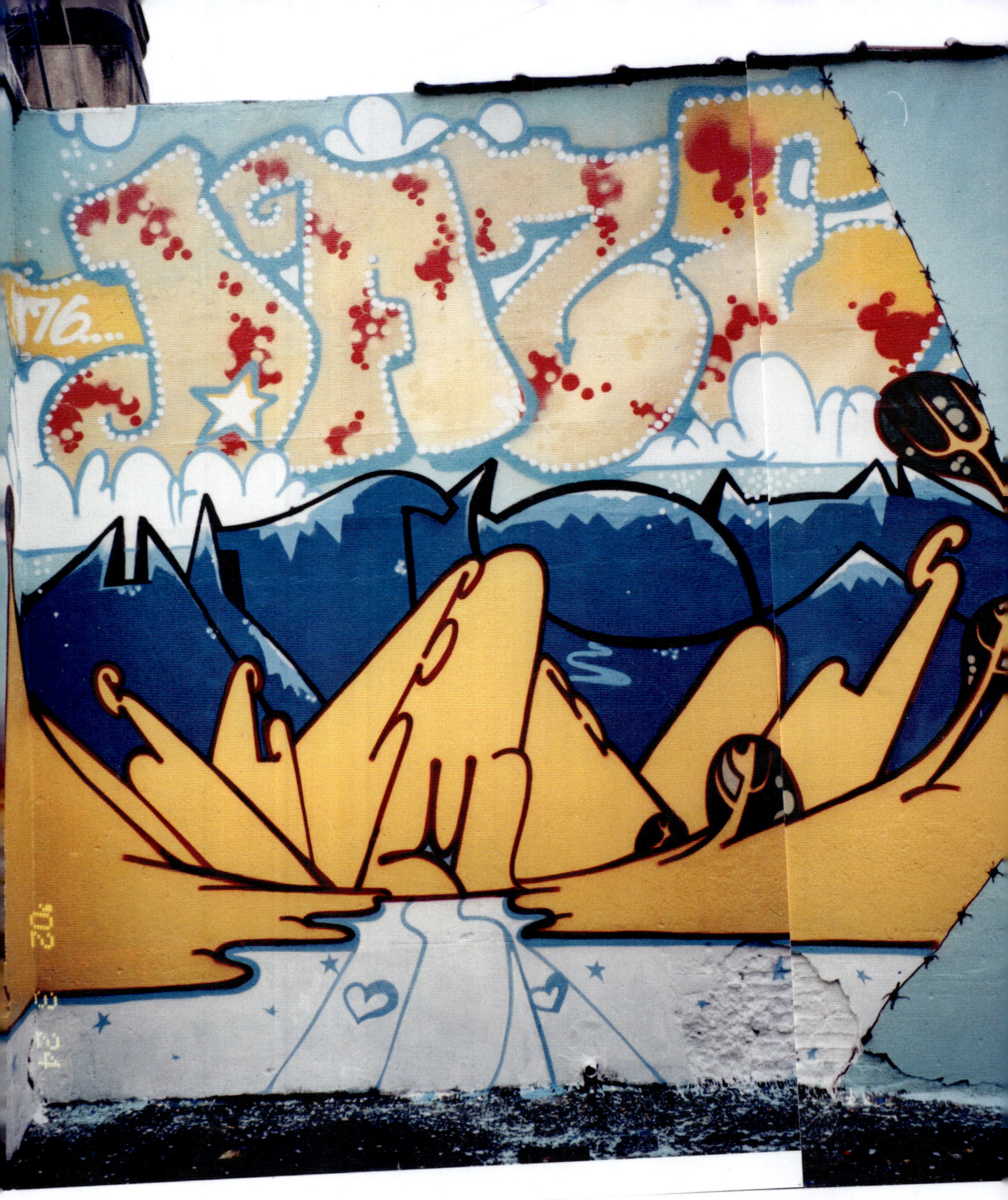

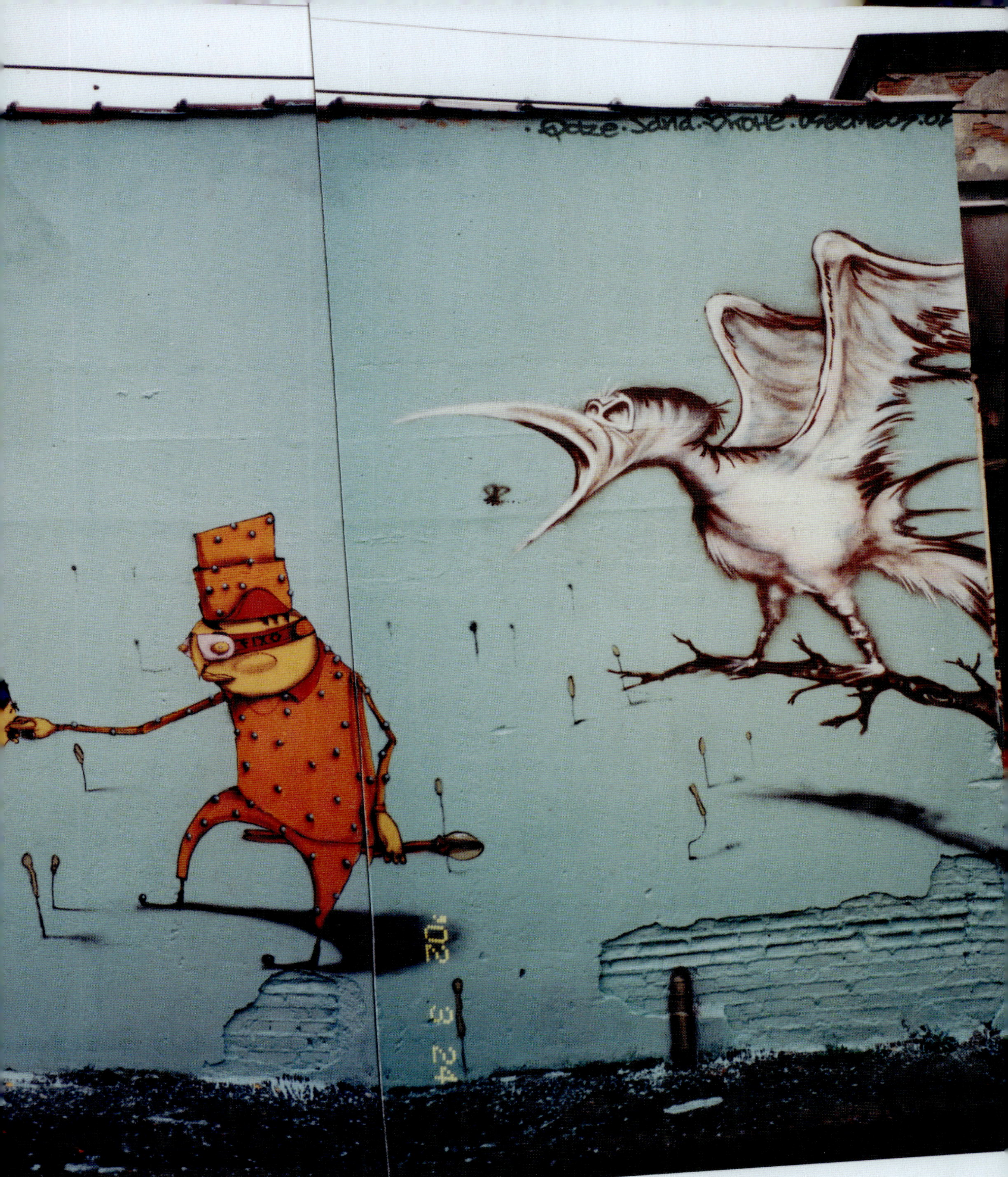

Daze, Os Gemeos, Vitche, Jana
Sao Paulo, Brazil, 2002

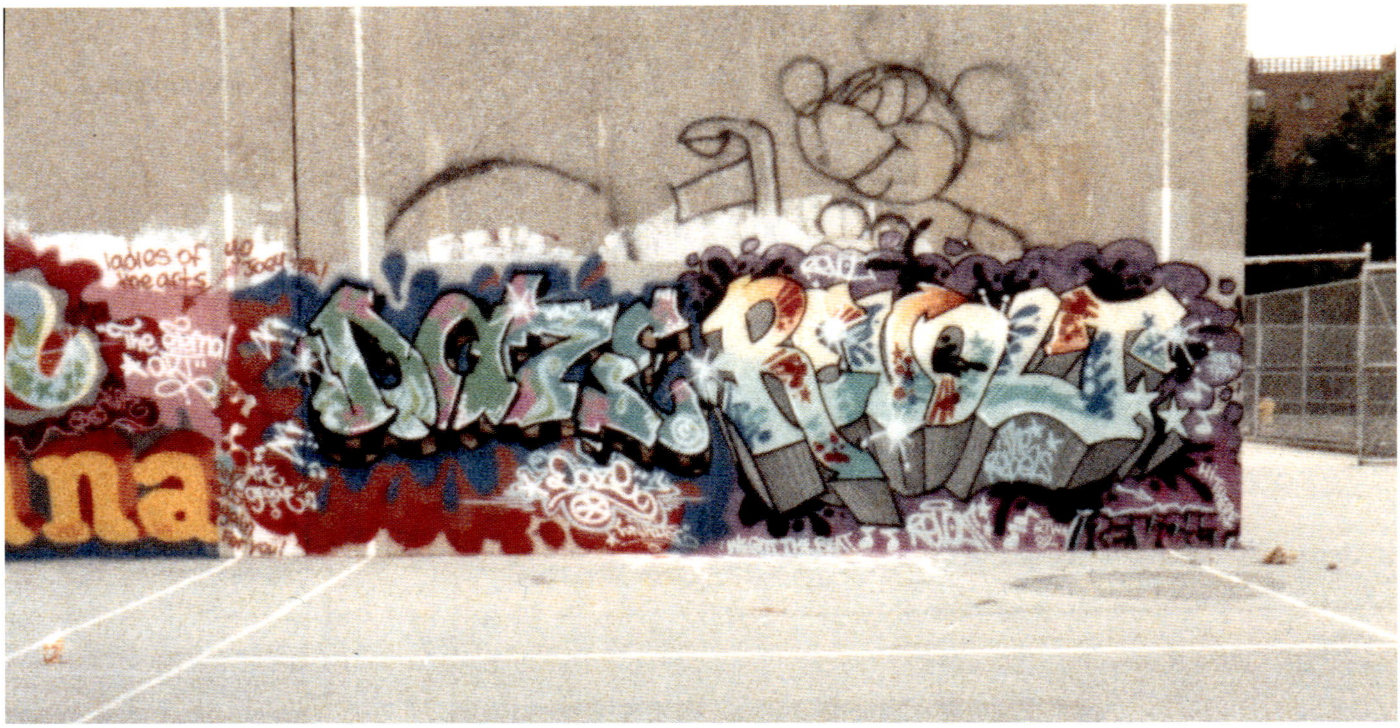

Daze and Revolt, Queens,
New York, 1982

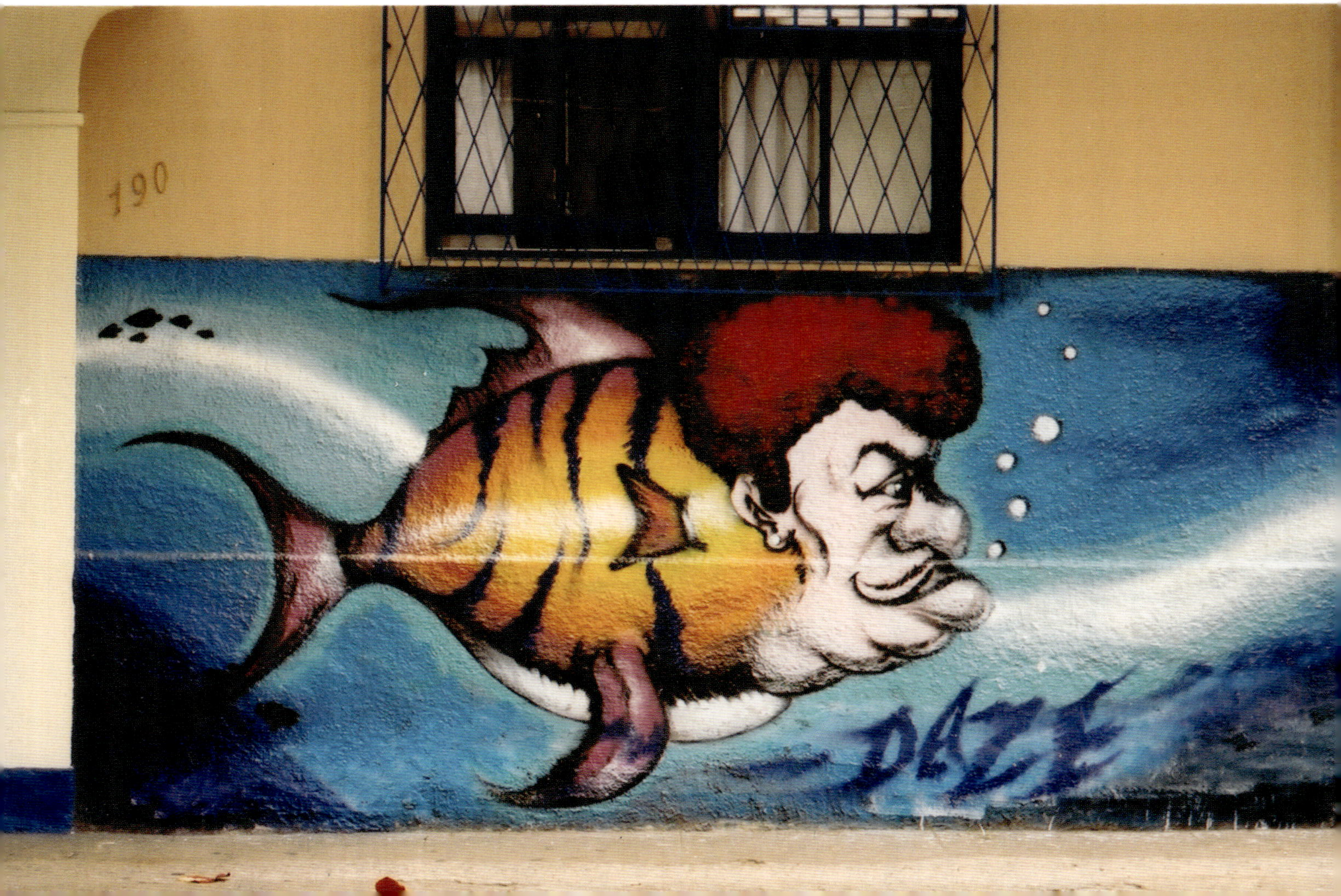

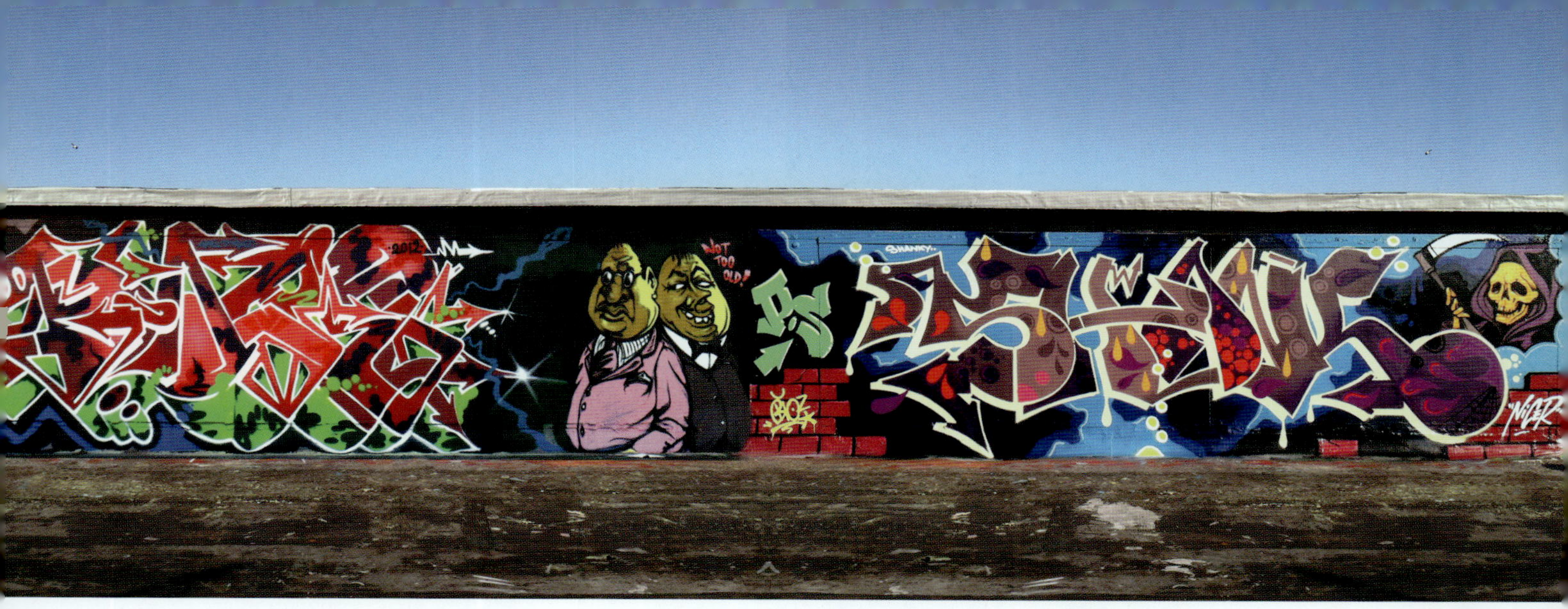

Daze, Shank (Dmote)

Daze, Sonik
Rio de Janiero, Brazil, 2004

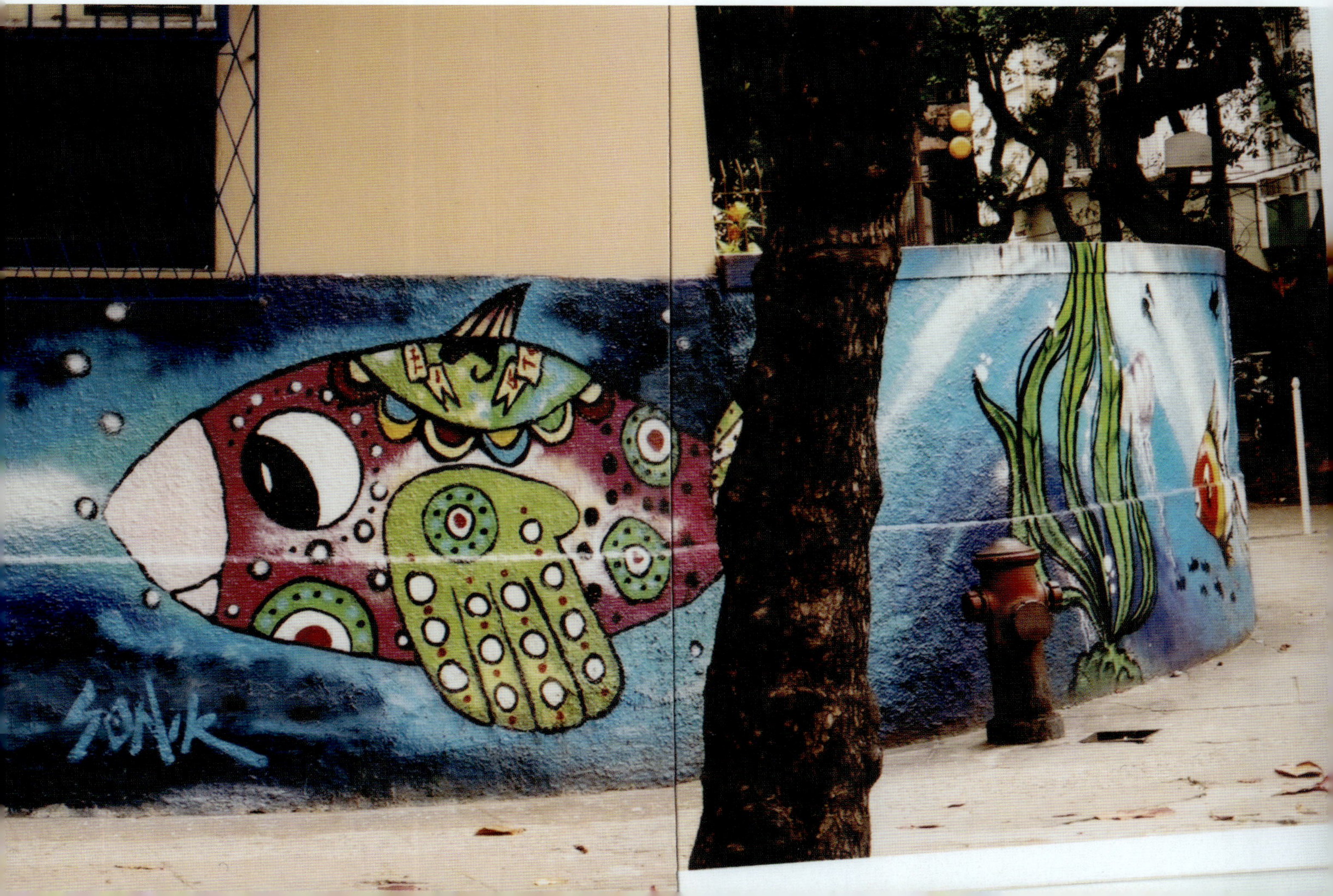

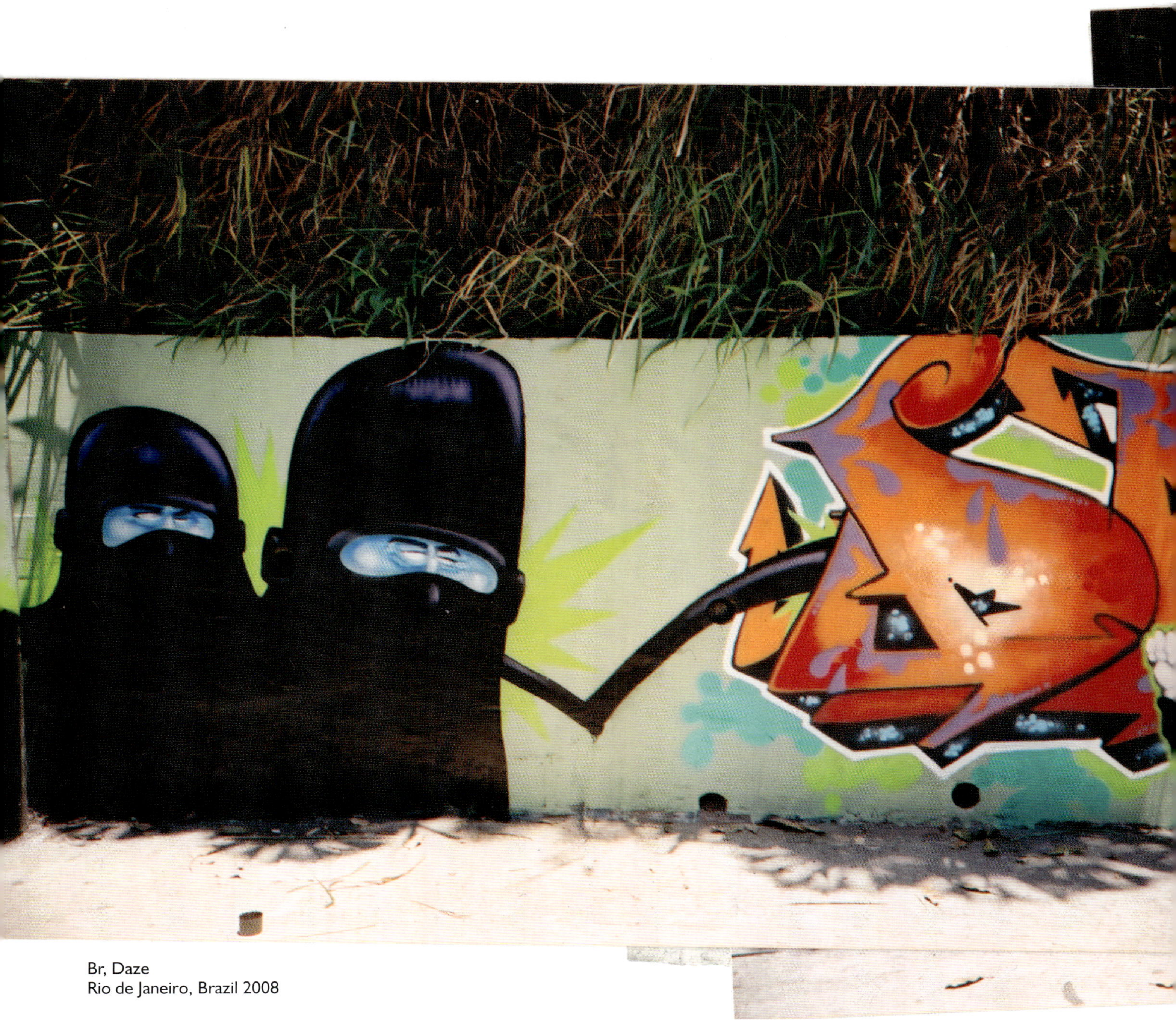

Br, Daze
Rio de Janeiro, Brazil 2008

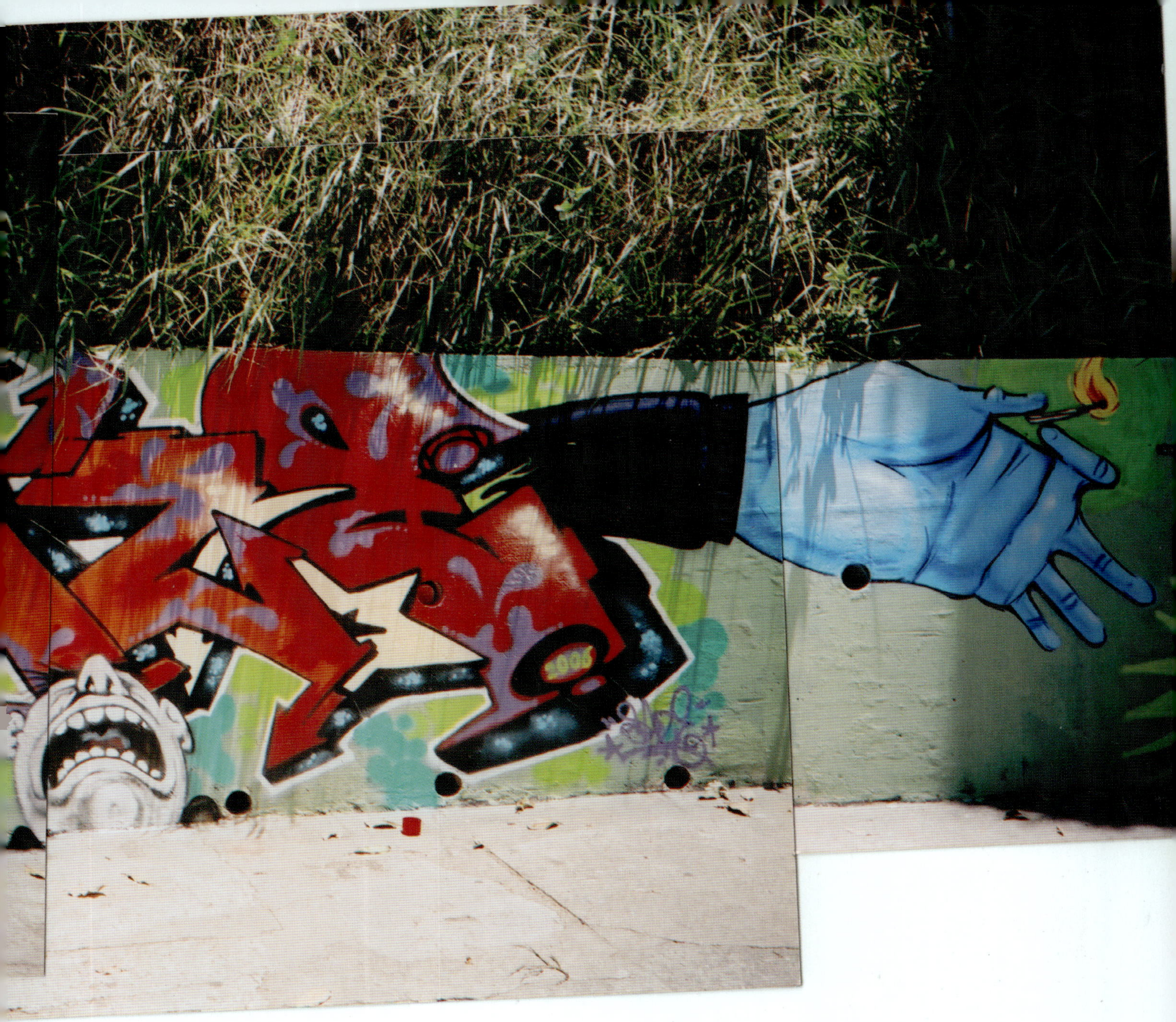

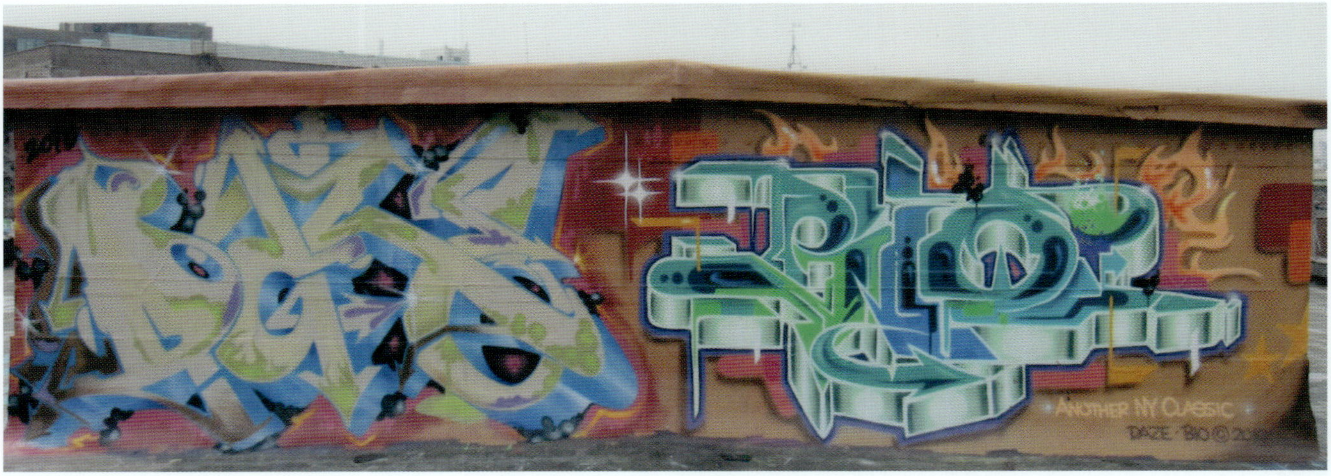

Daze, Bio
Bronx, New York, 2010

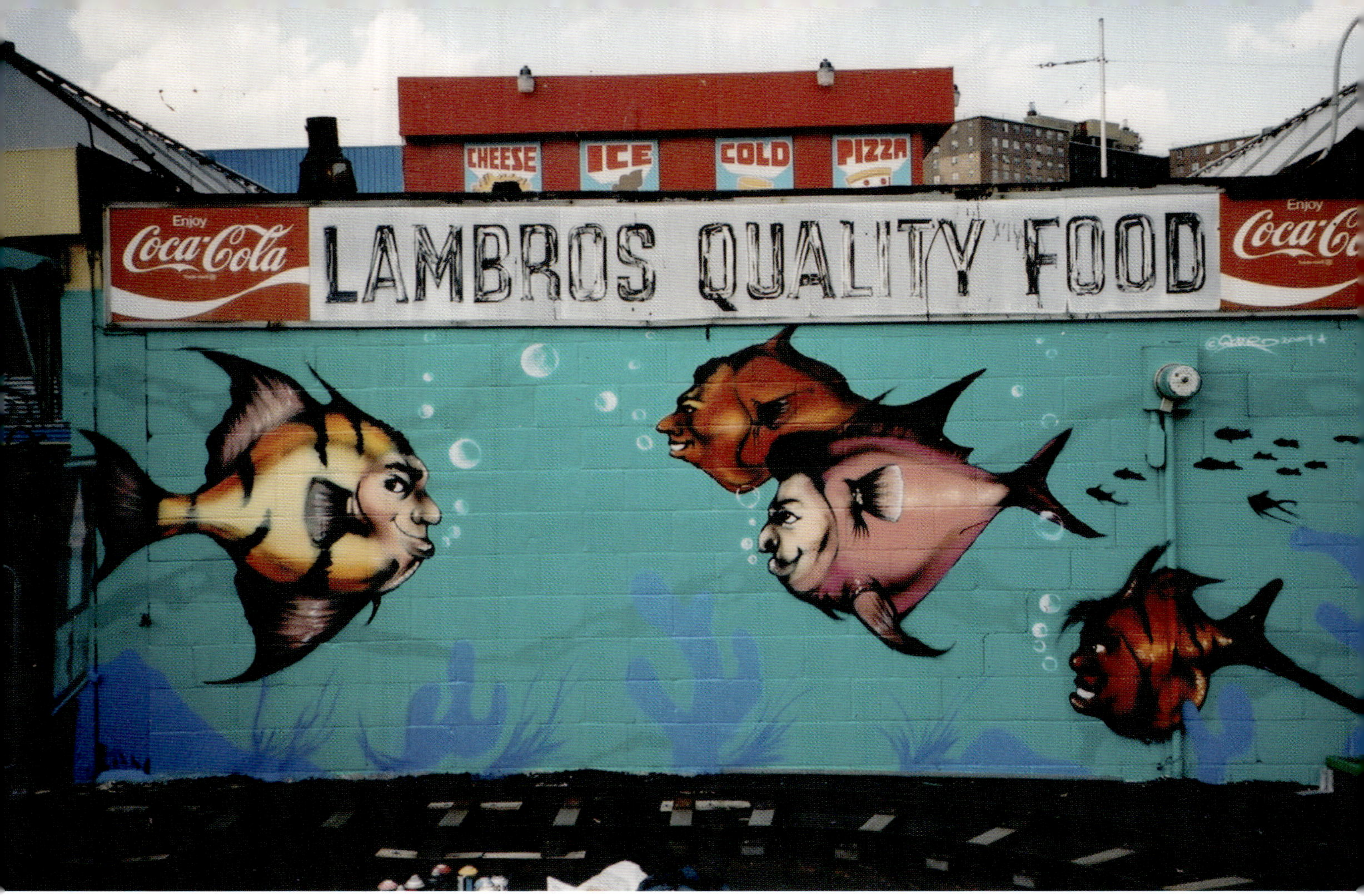

Coney Island, New York, 2005

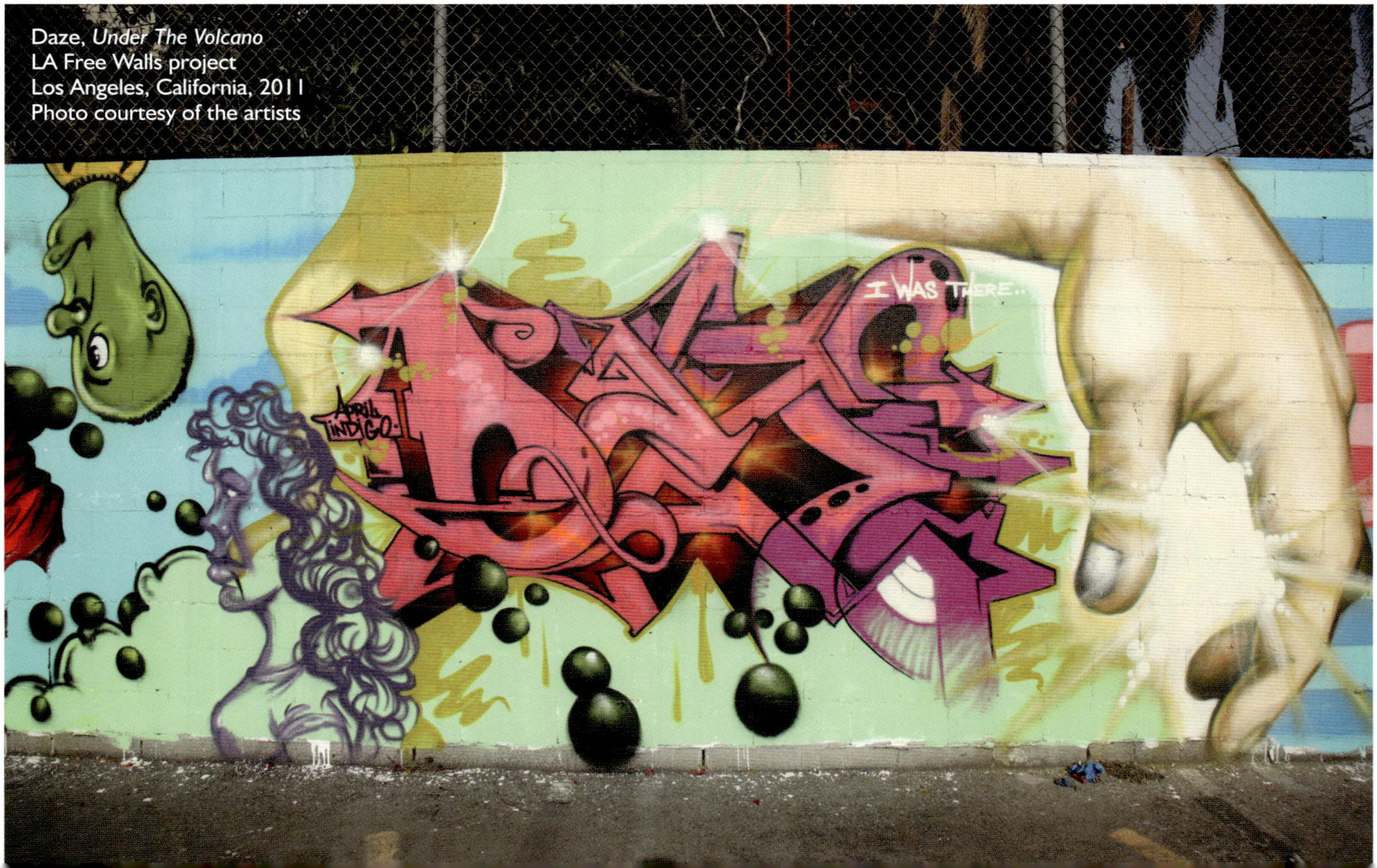

Daze, *Under The Volcano*
LA Free Walls project
Los Angeles, California, 2011
Photo courtesy of the artists

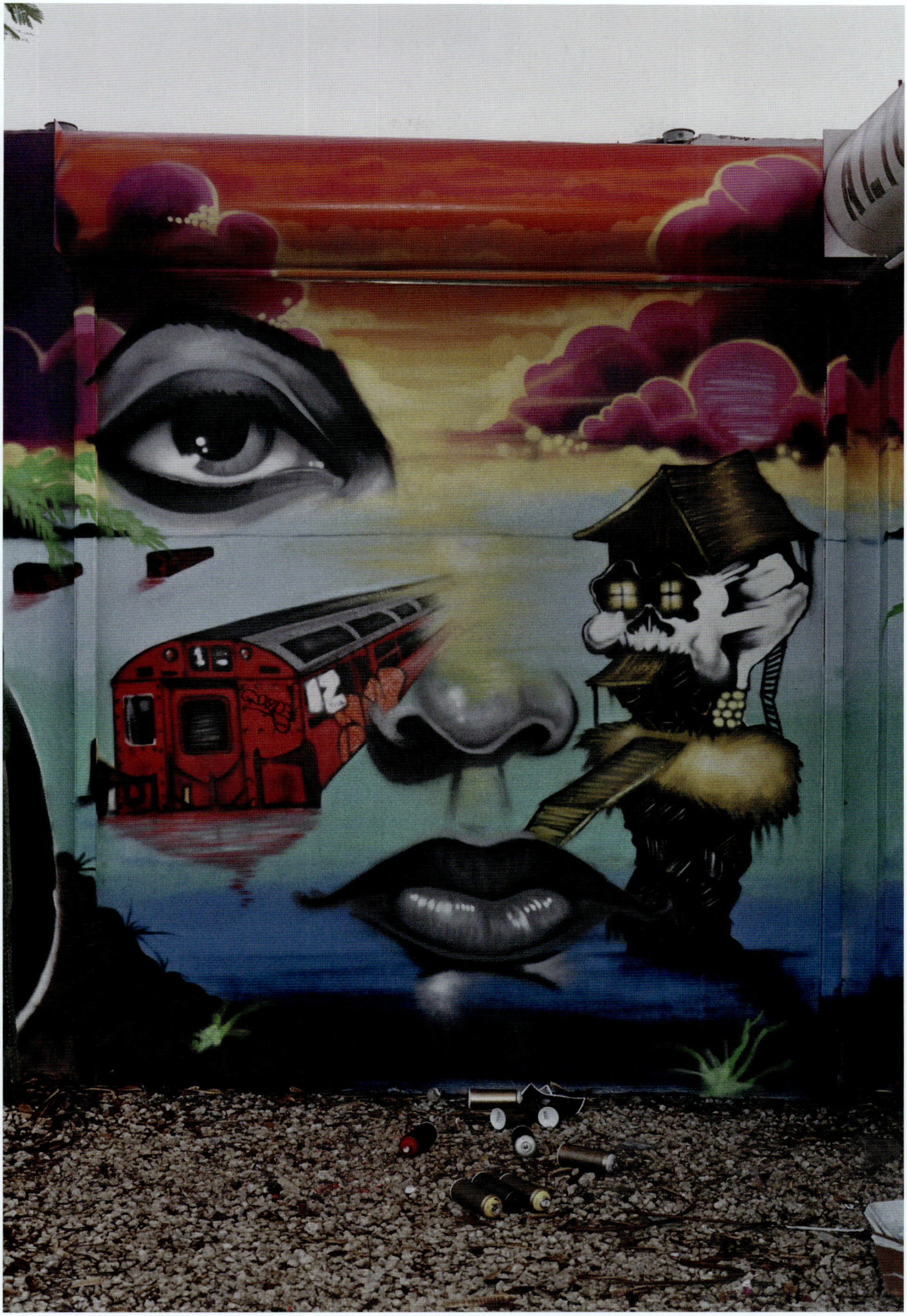

Wynwood Walls,
Miami, Florida,
2012

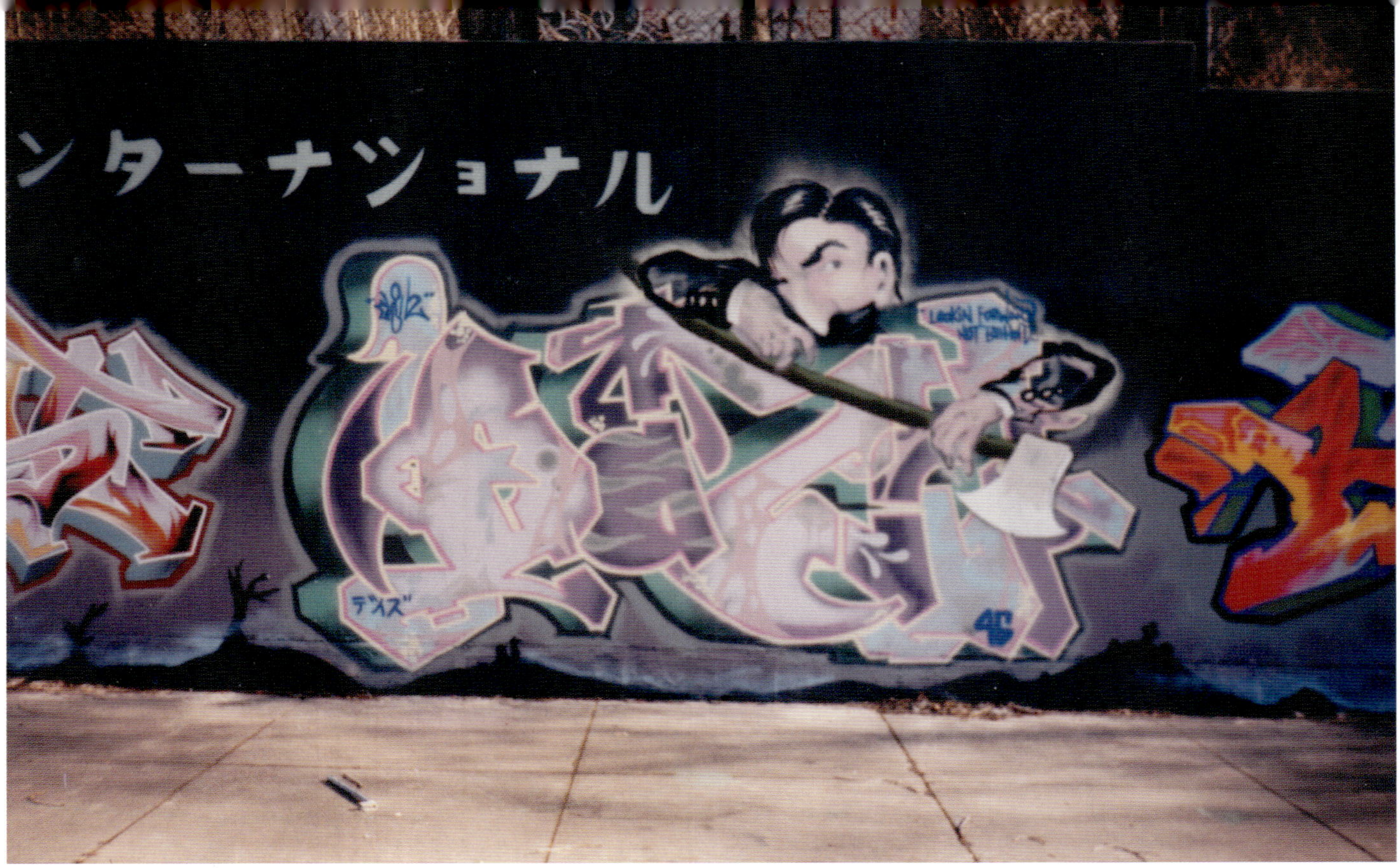

Daze
Bronx, New York, 1996

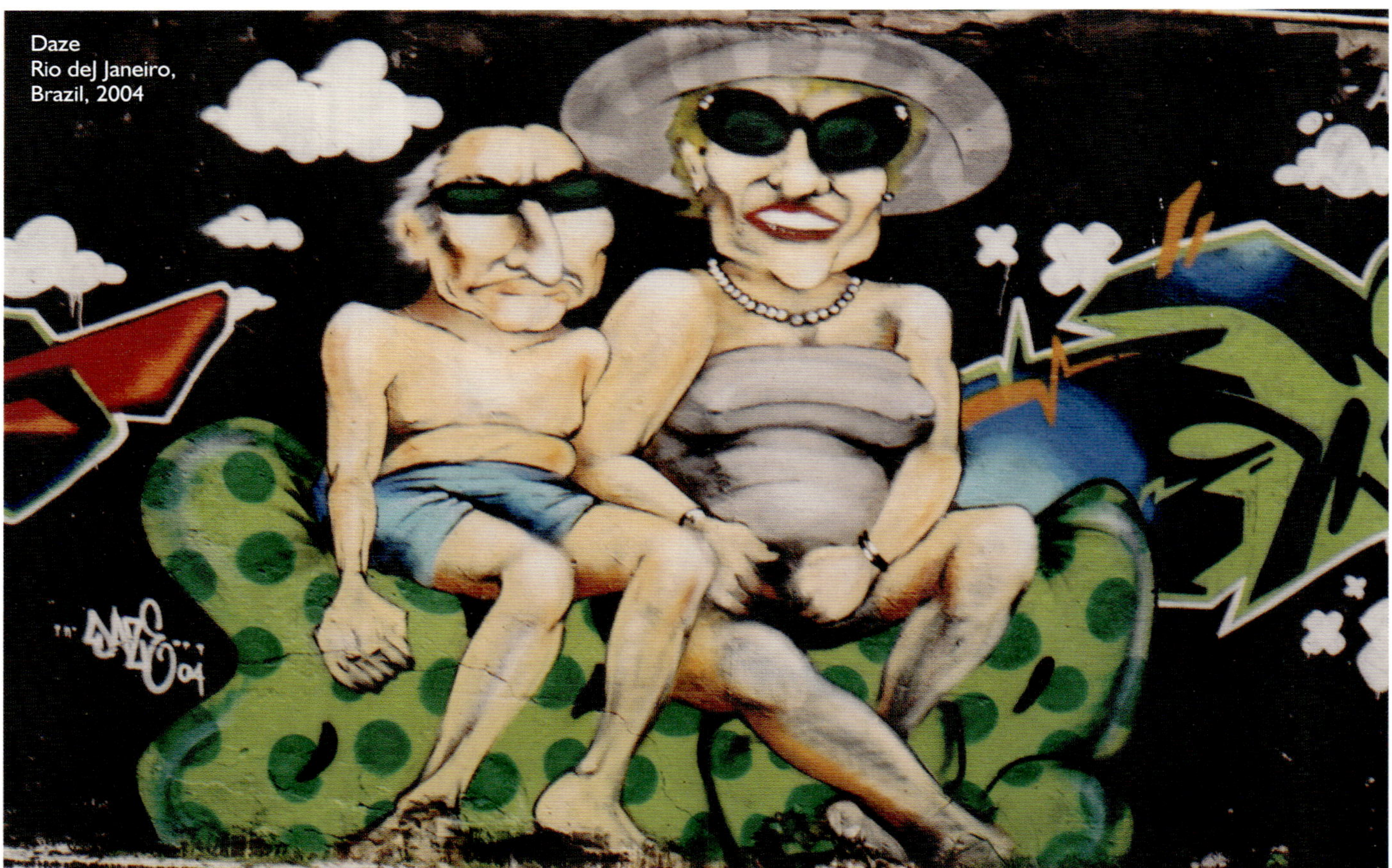

Daze
Rio deJ Janeiro,
Brazil, 2004

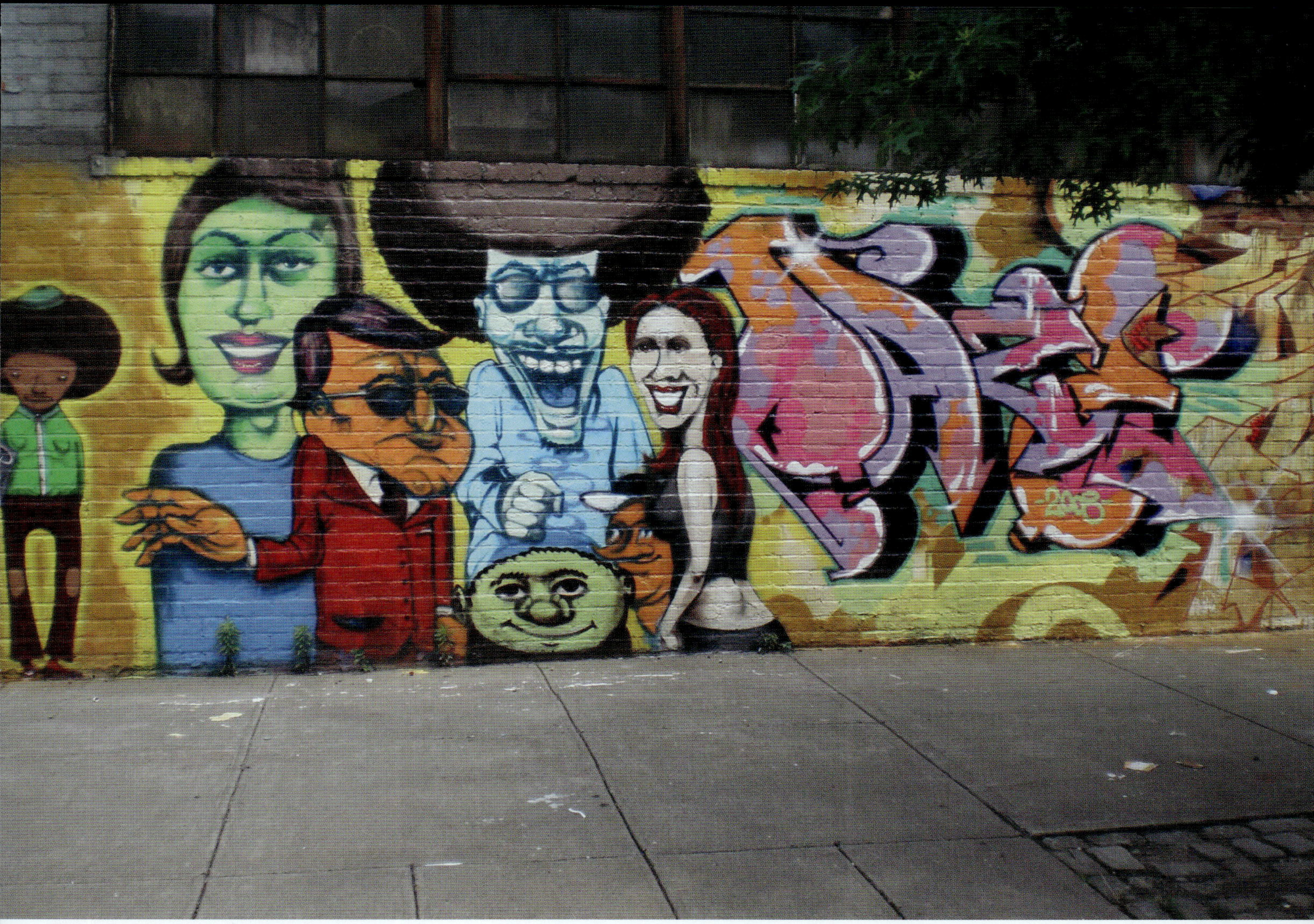

Daze, character on left by Os Gemeos
Brooklyn, New York, 2008

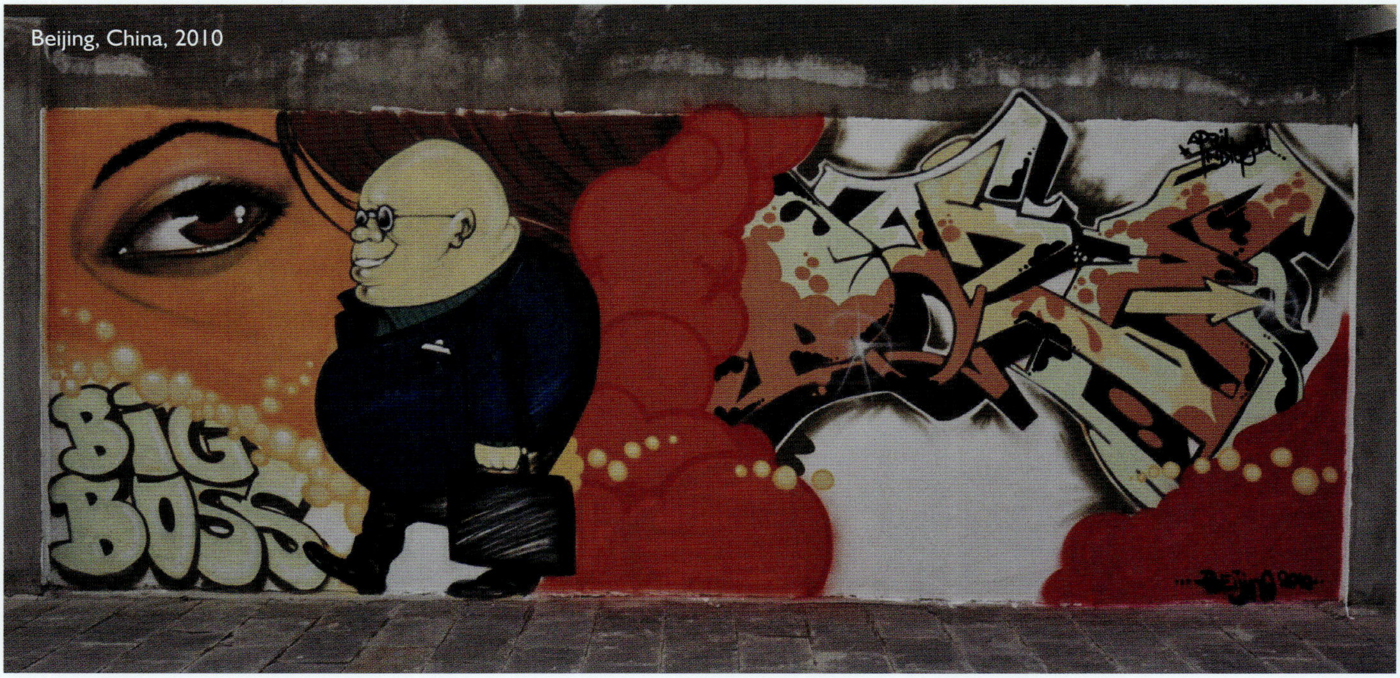

Beijing, China, 2010

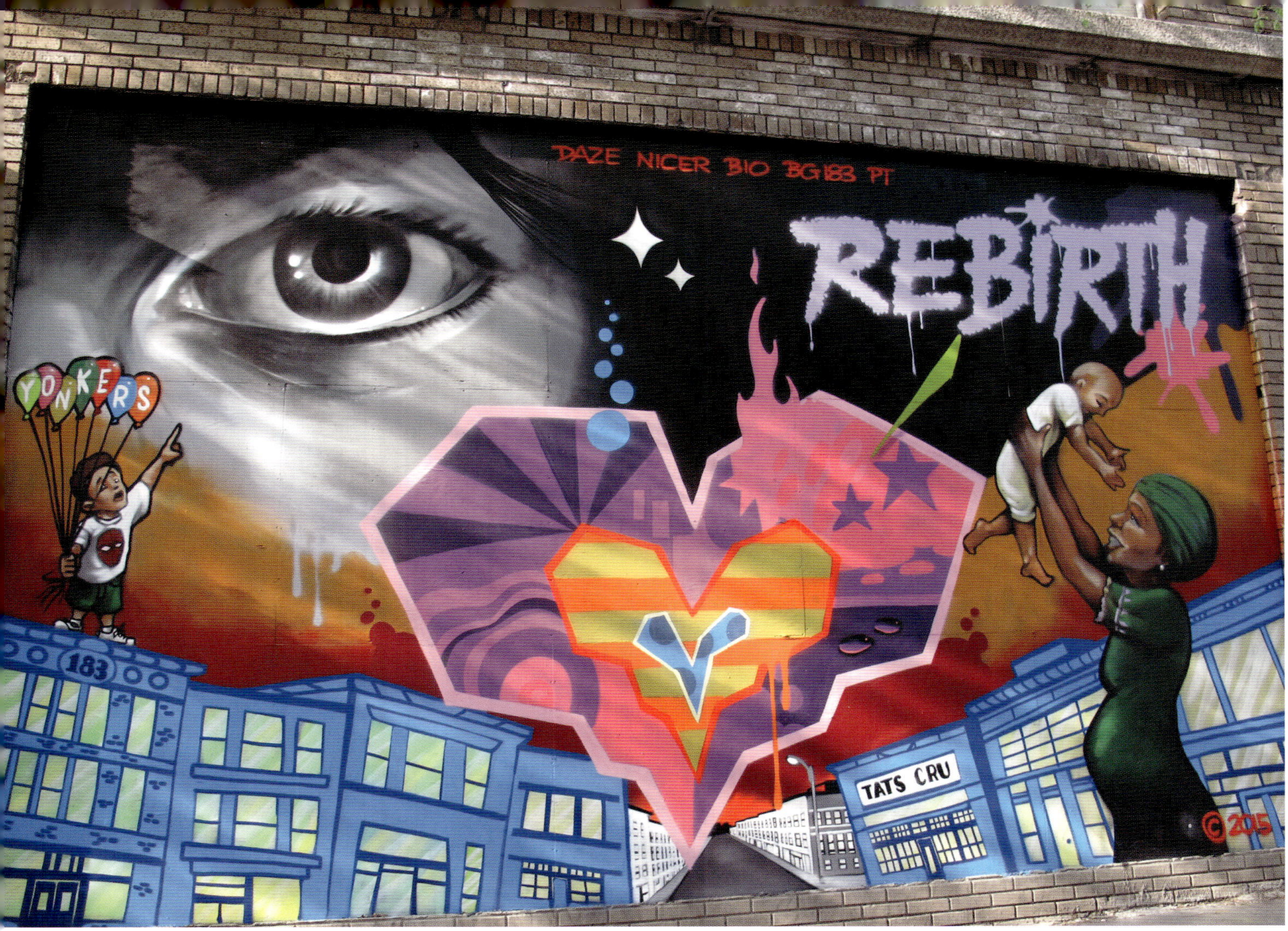

Rebirth by BG183,Daze, Bio,Nicer
Yonkers, New York, 2015

Portrait of April
Wall Therapy
Rochester, New York, 2015

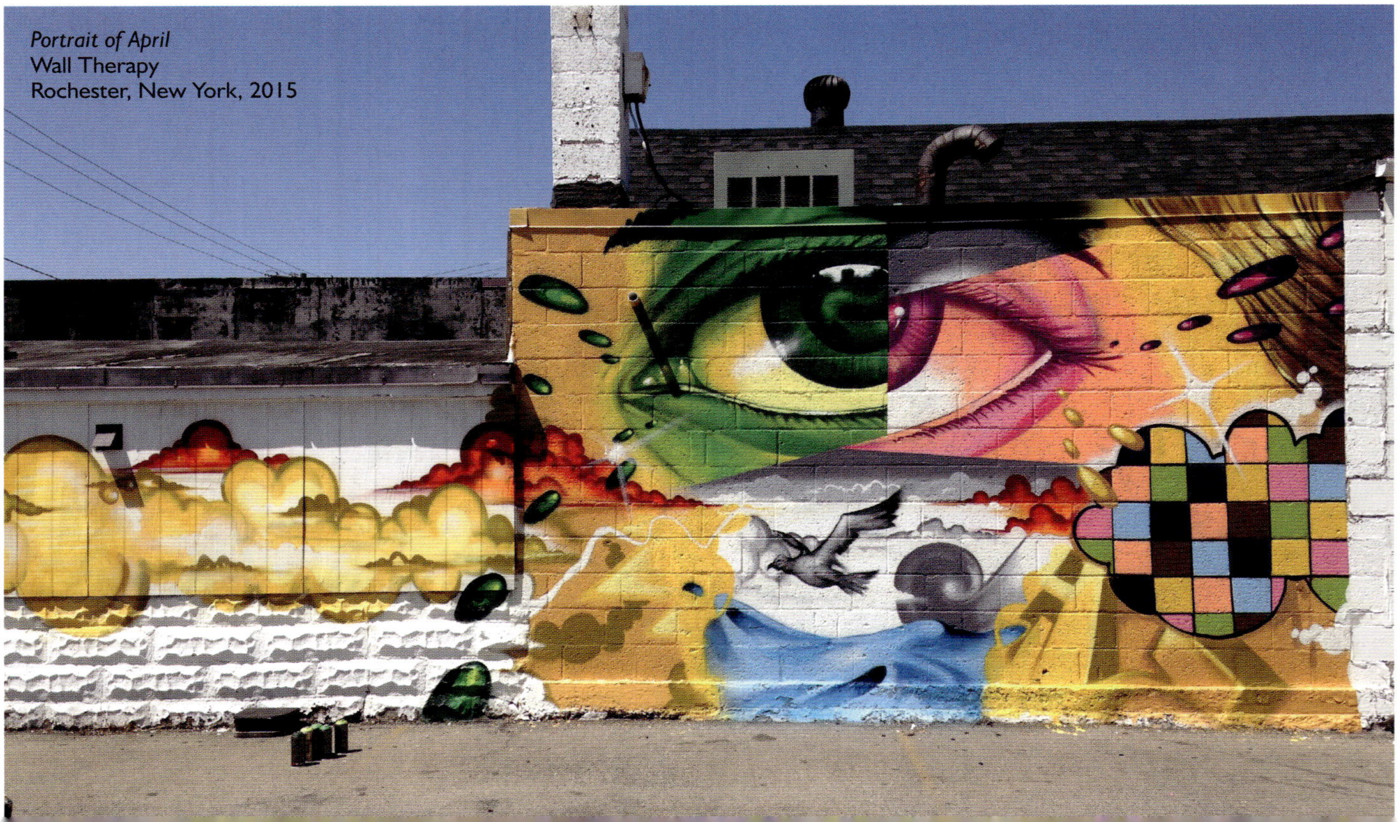

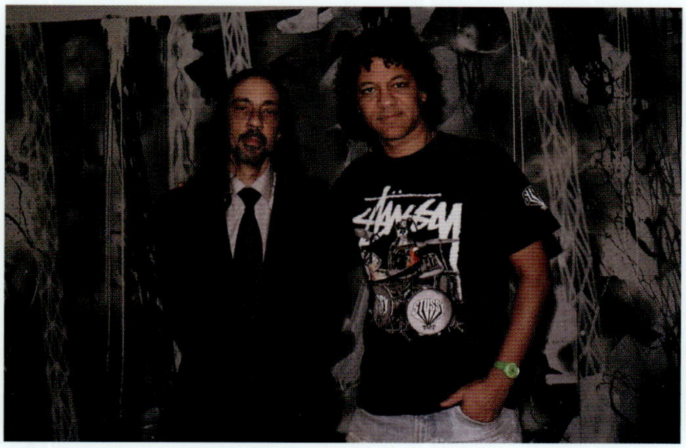

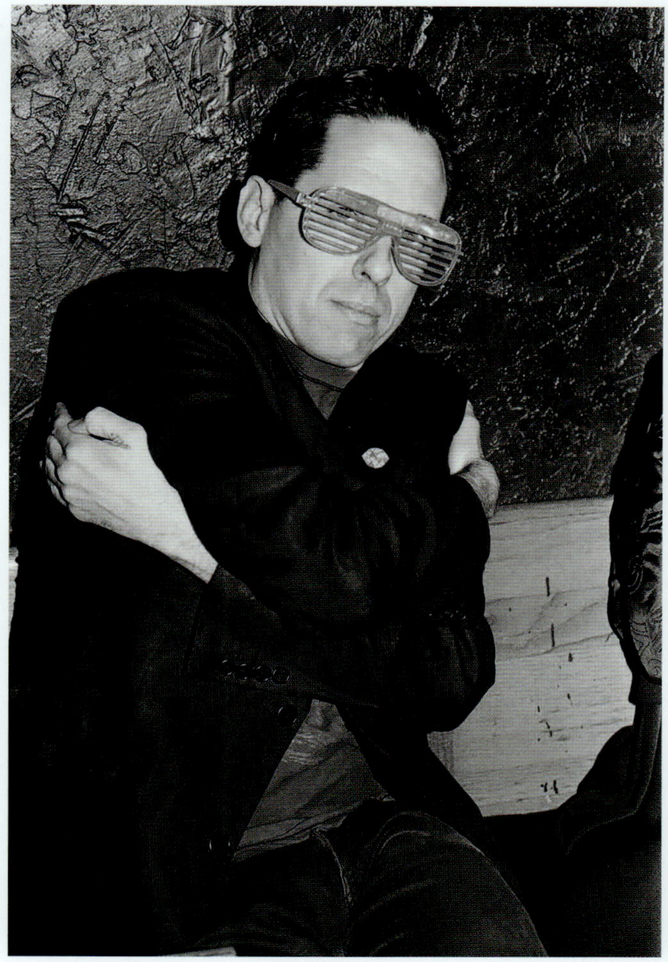

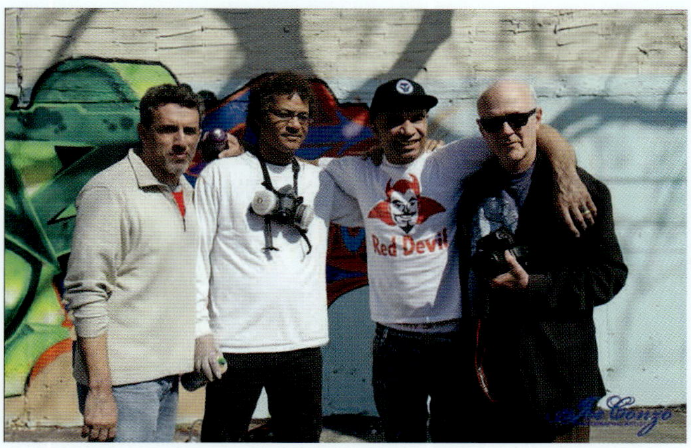
Red Devil

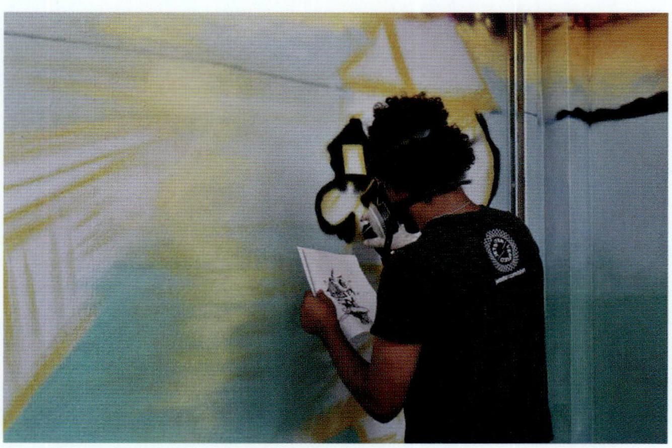

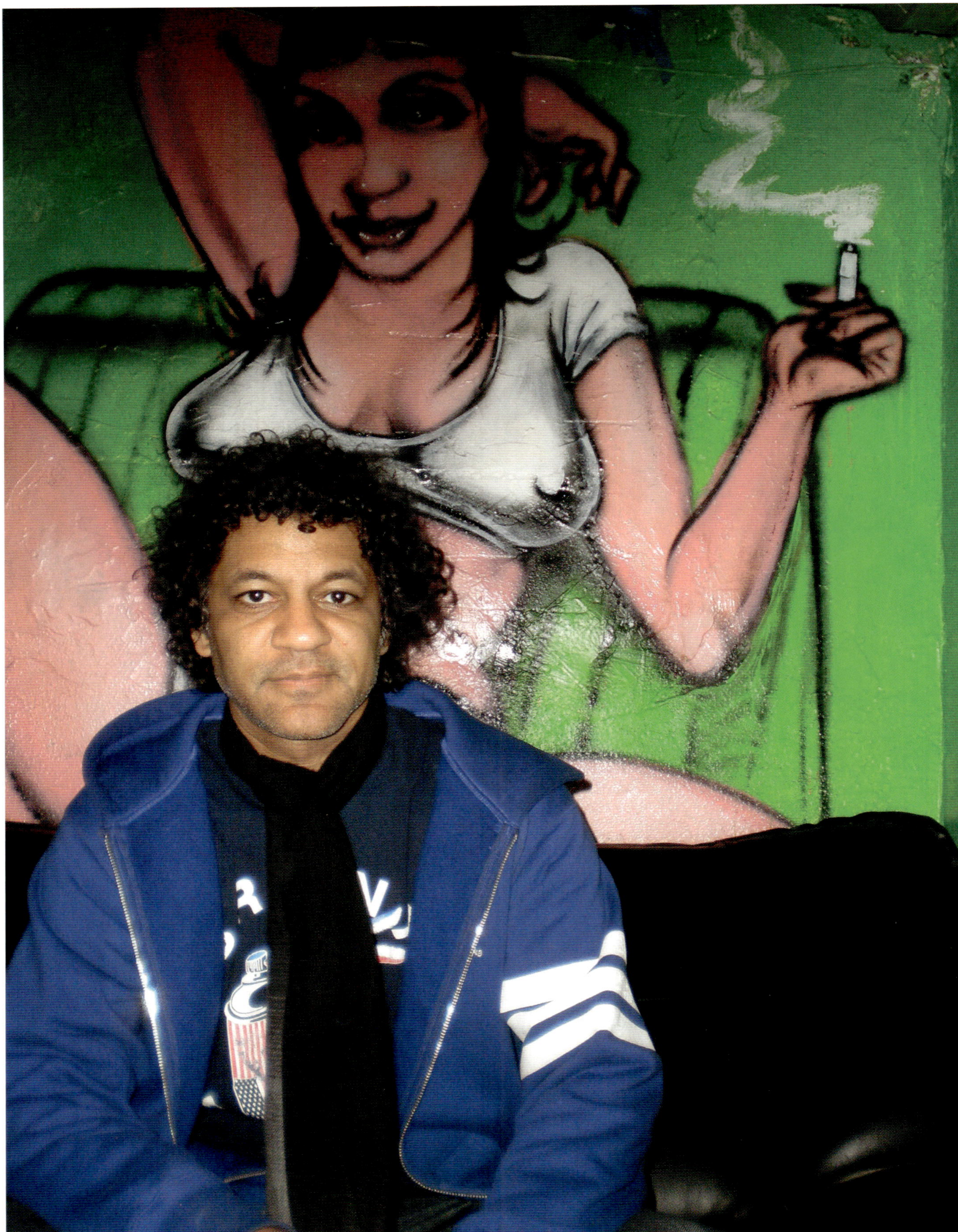

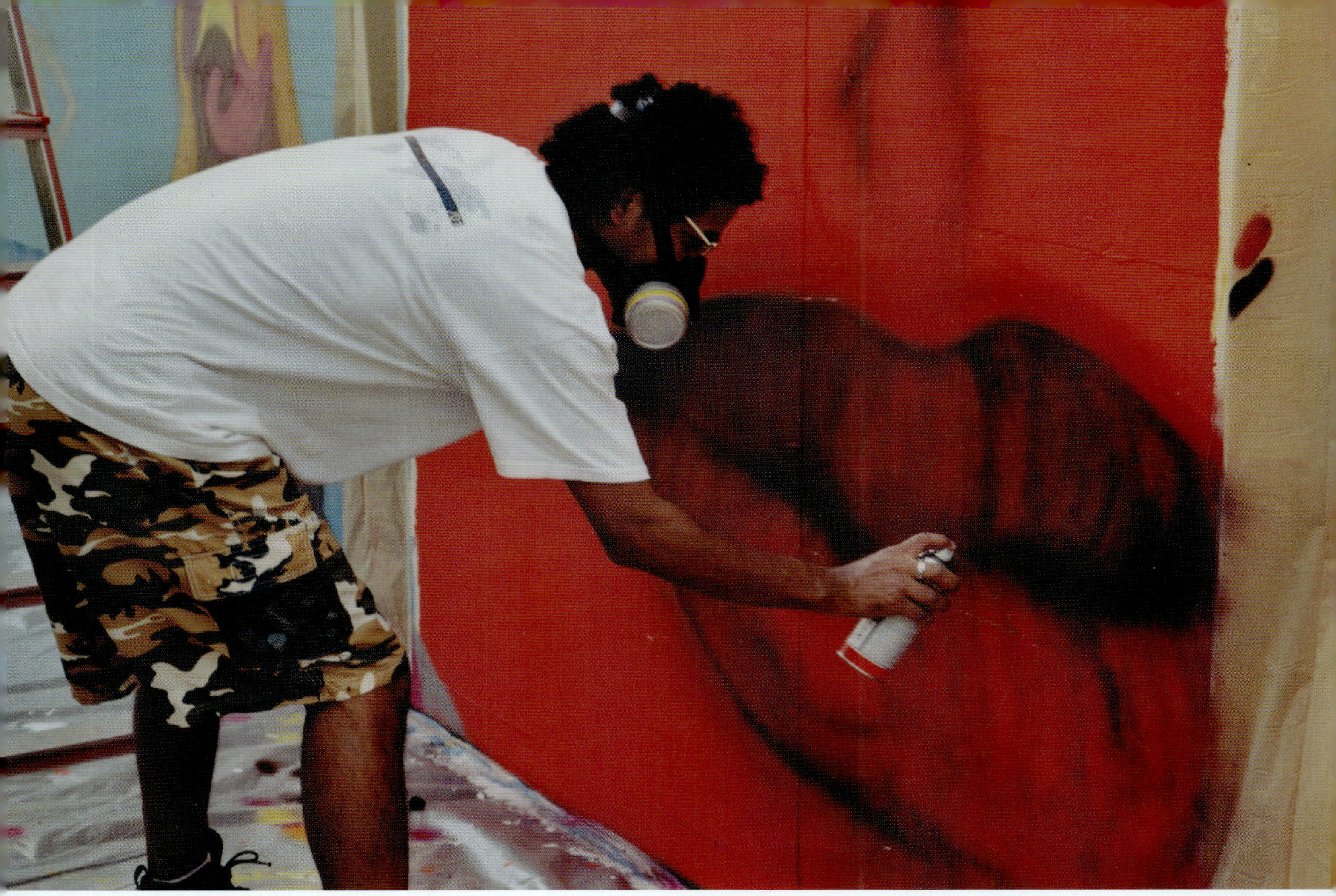

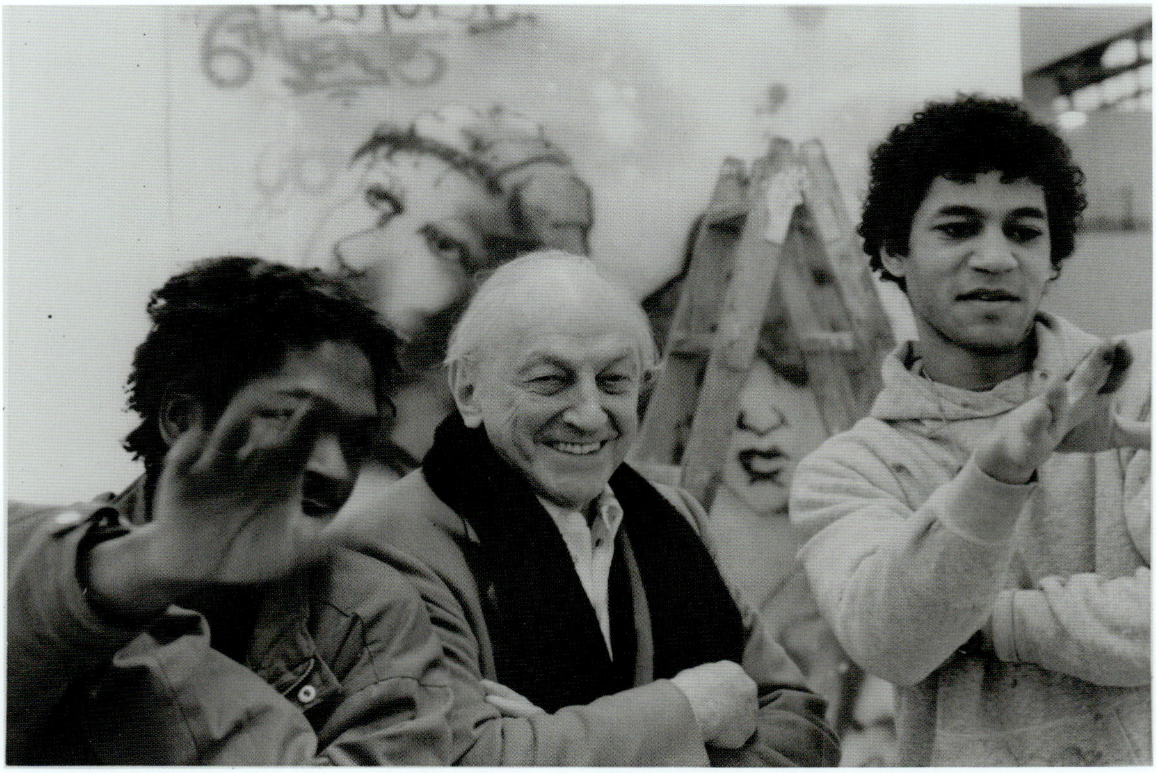

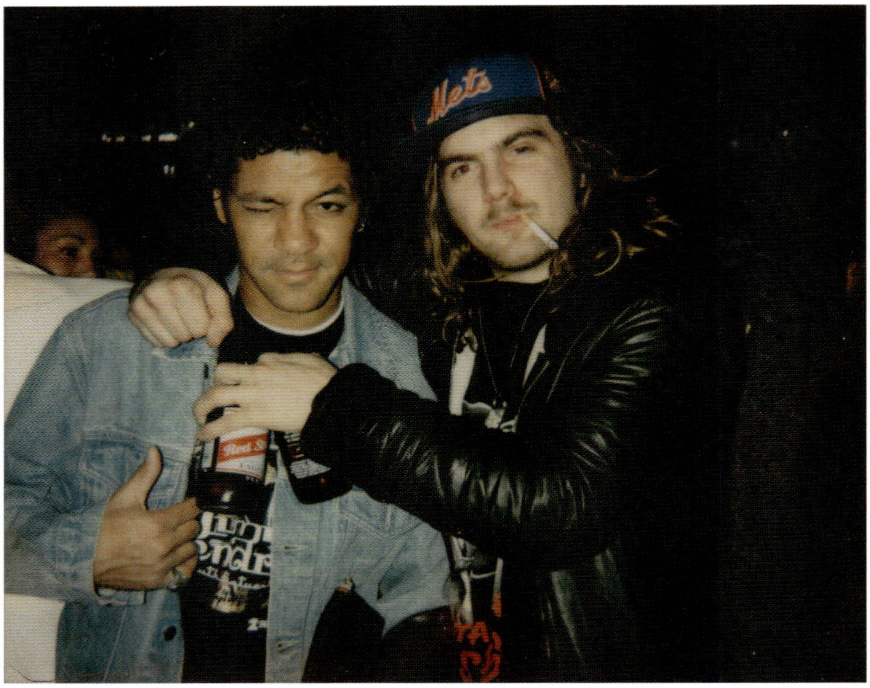
Mets

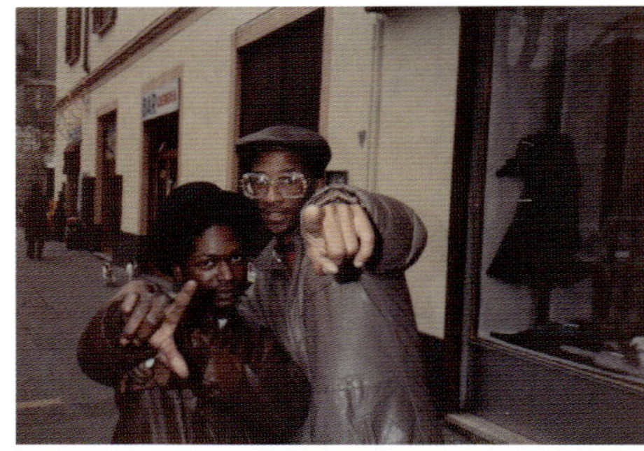

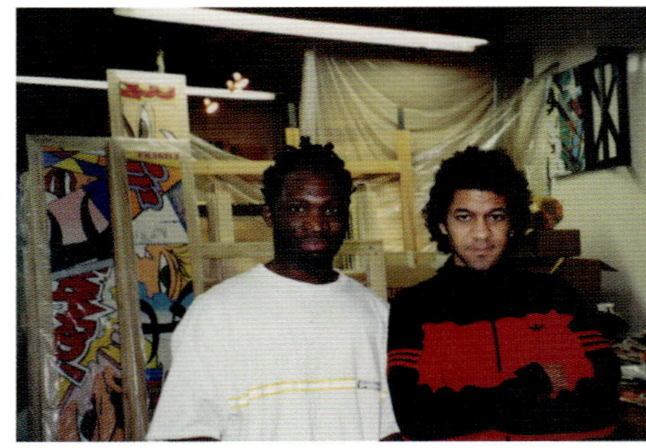

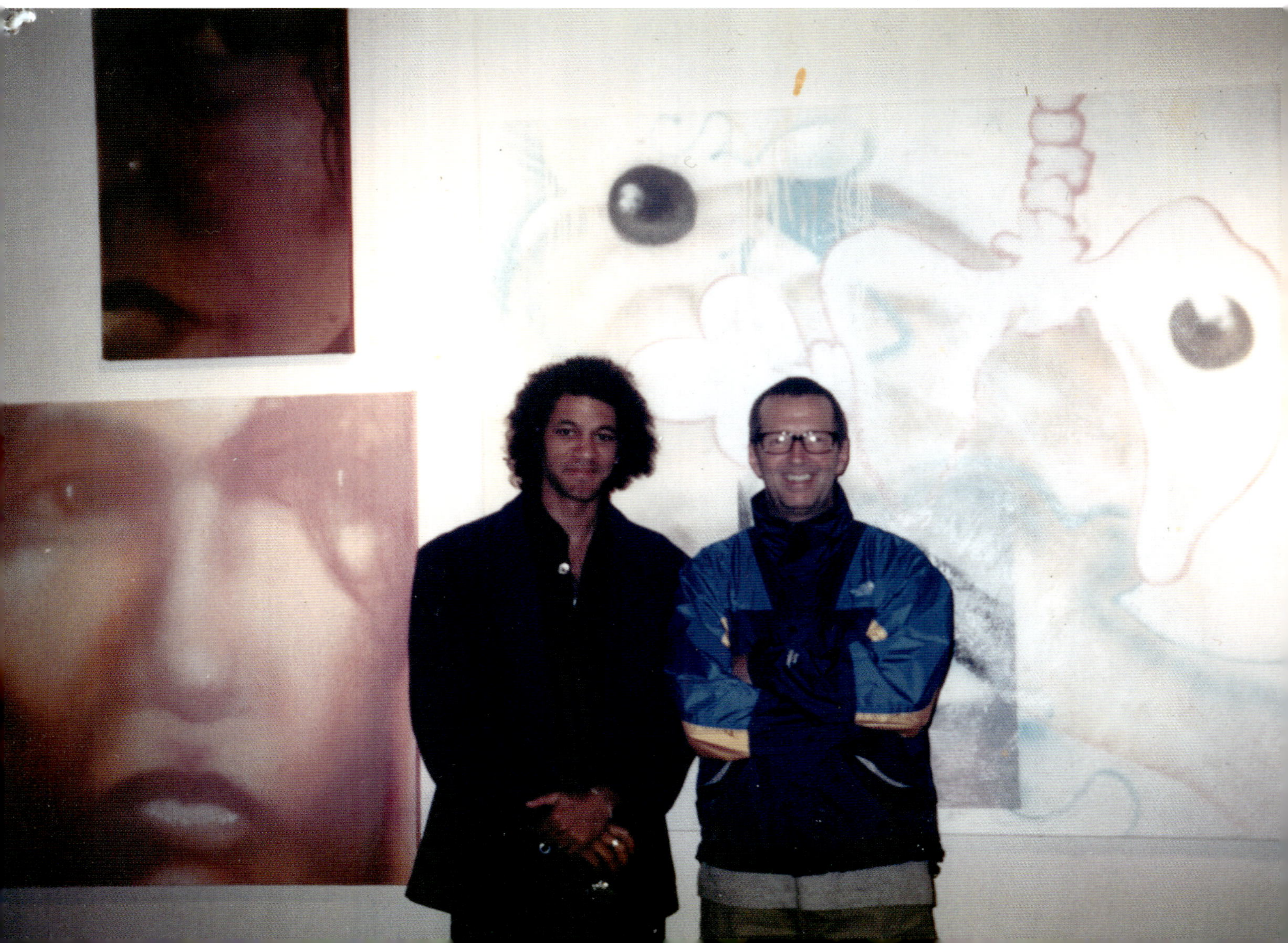

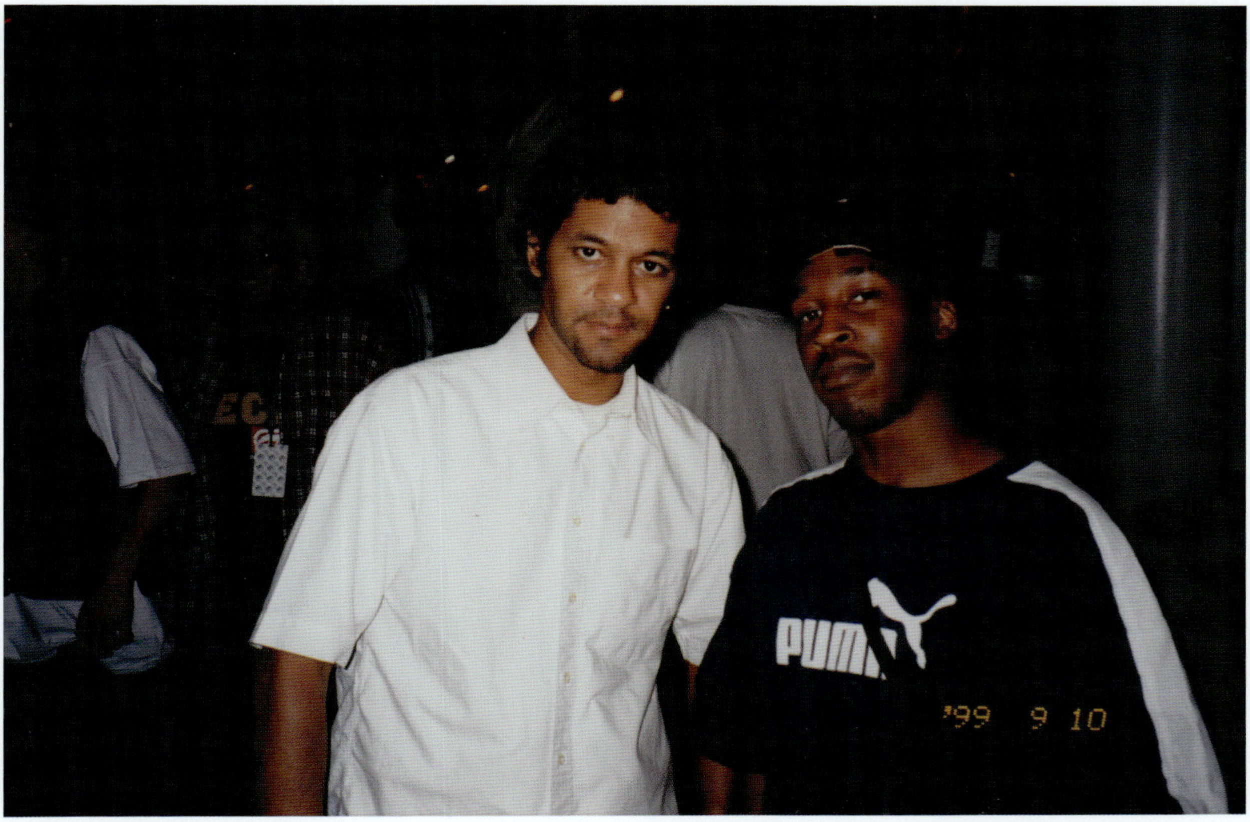
'99 9 10

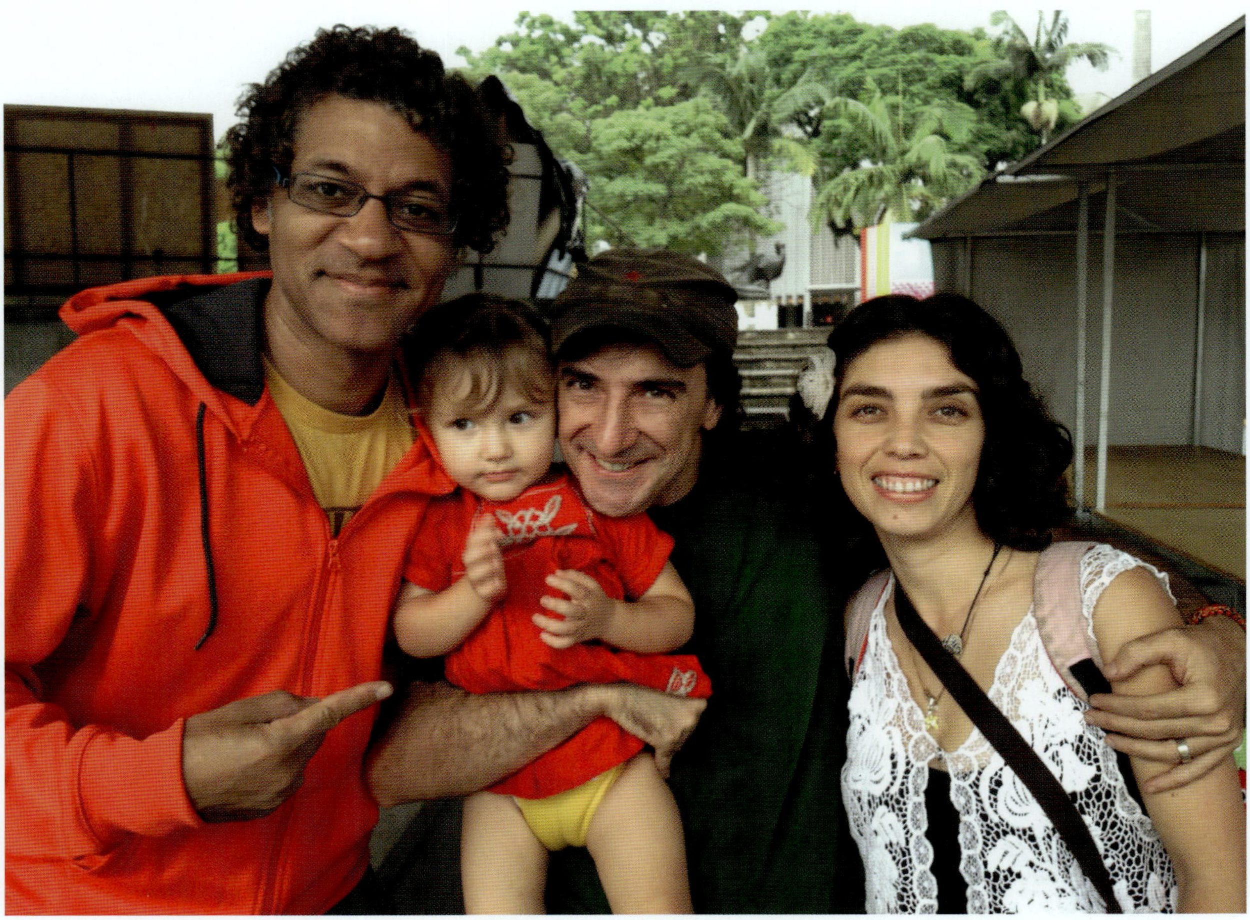

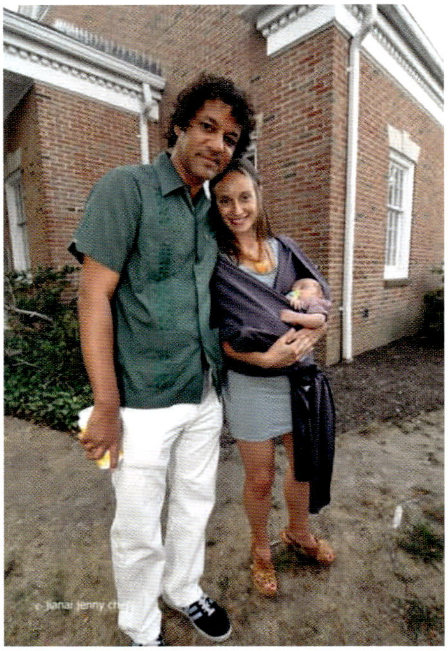

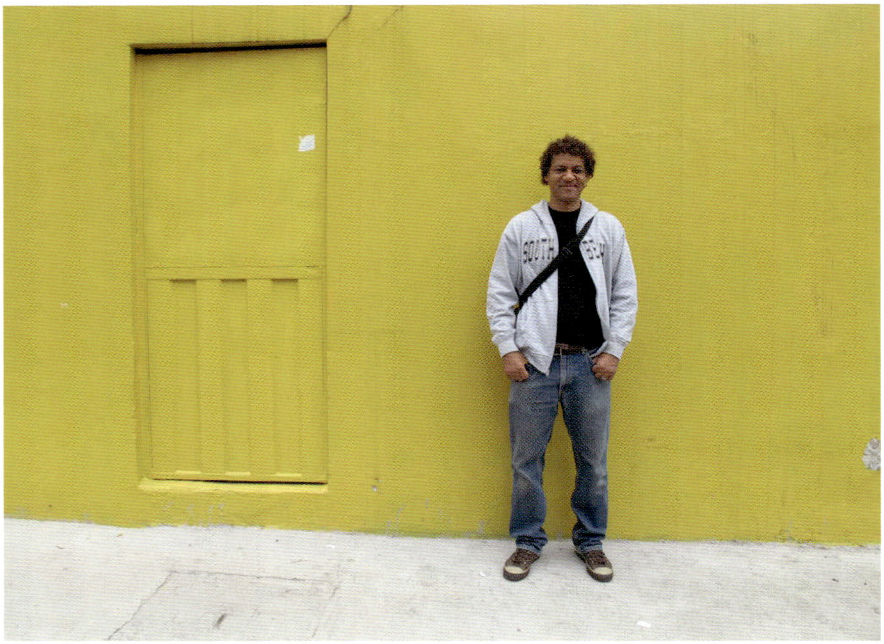

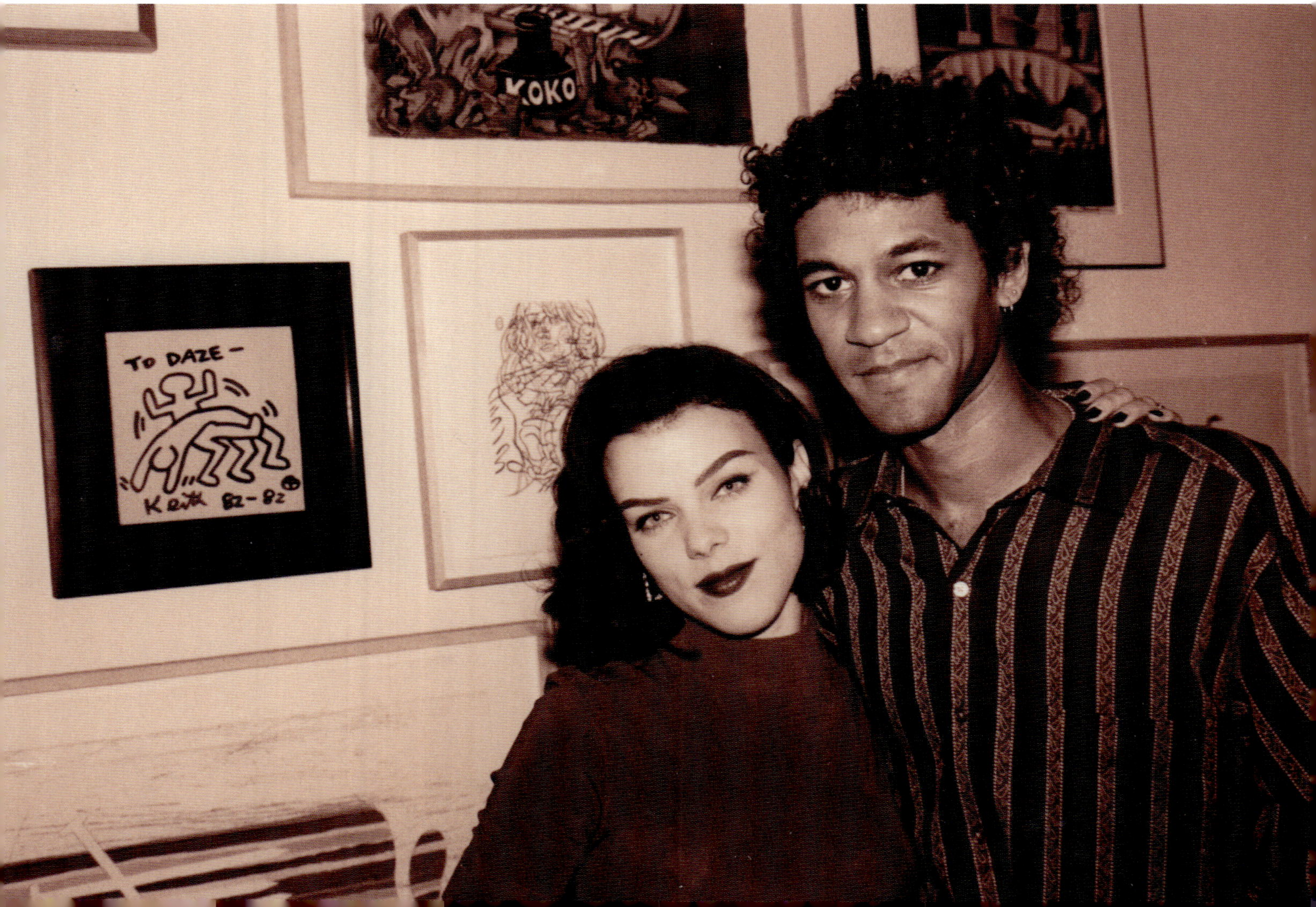
KOKO
TO DAZE –

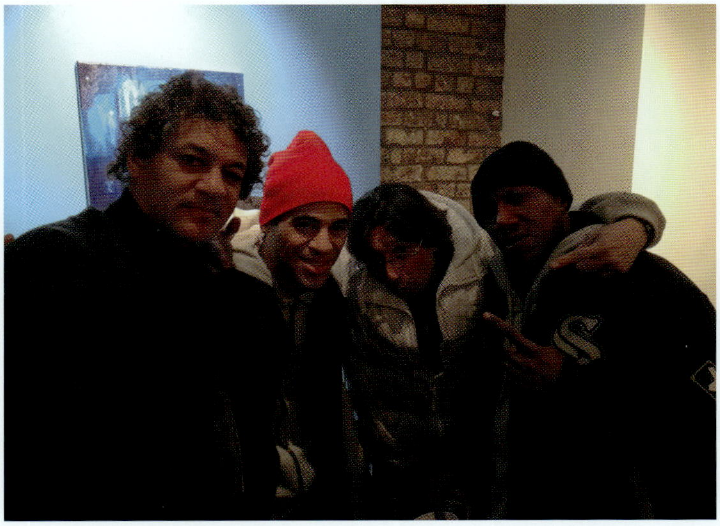

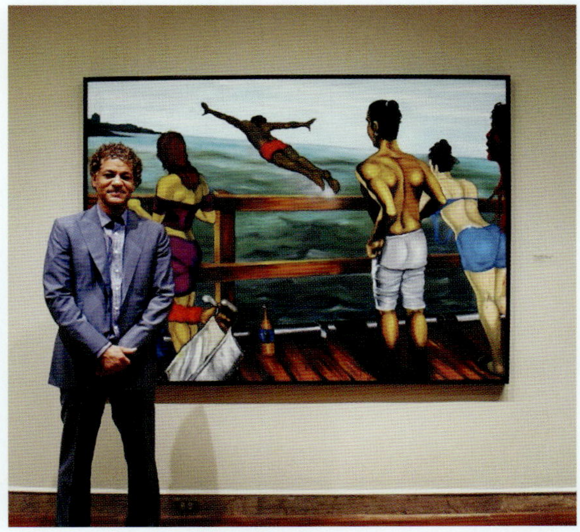

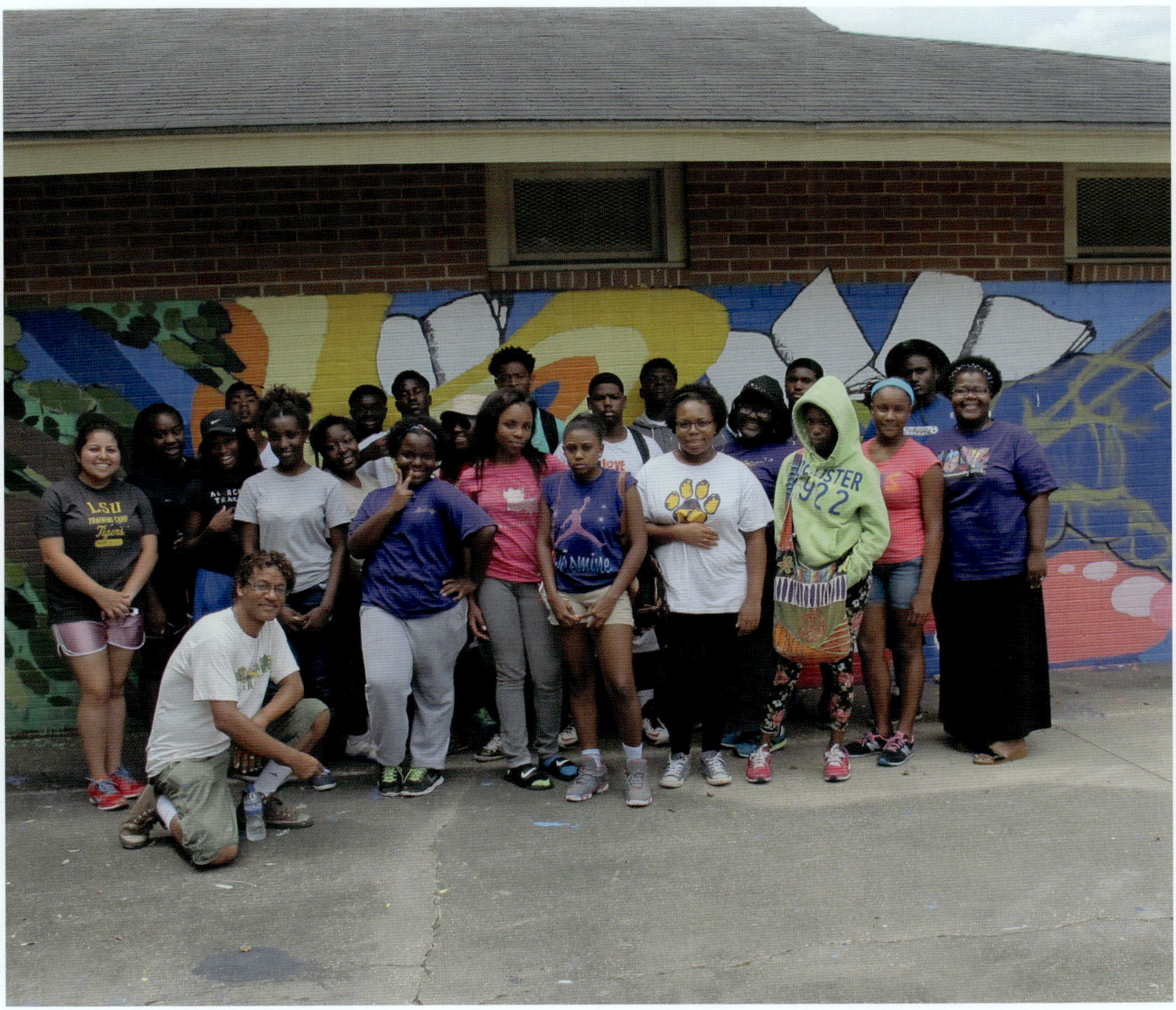
LSU
TRAINING CAMP
Tigers

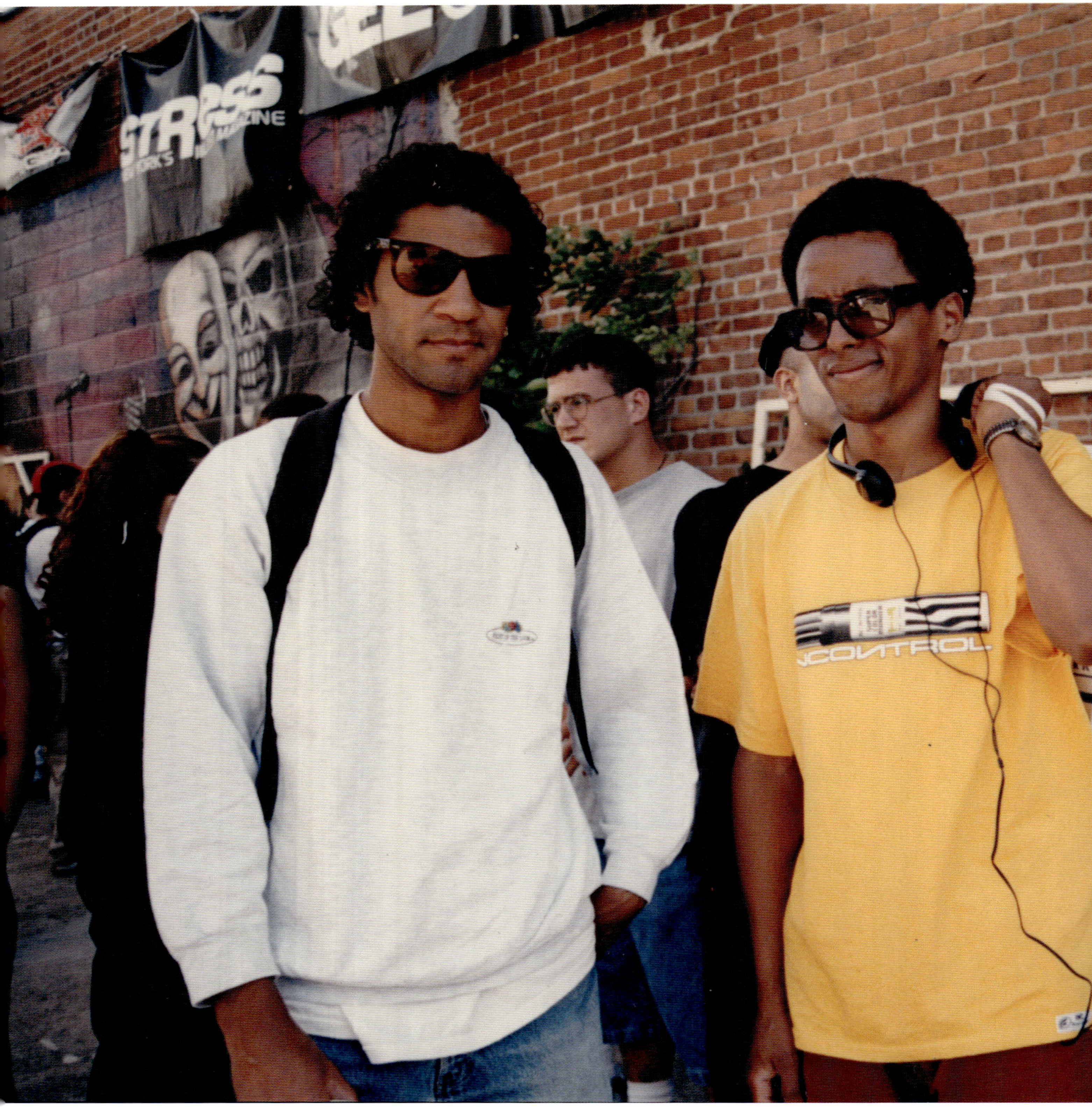
NCONTROL

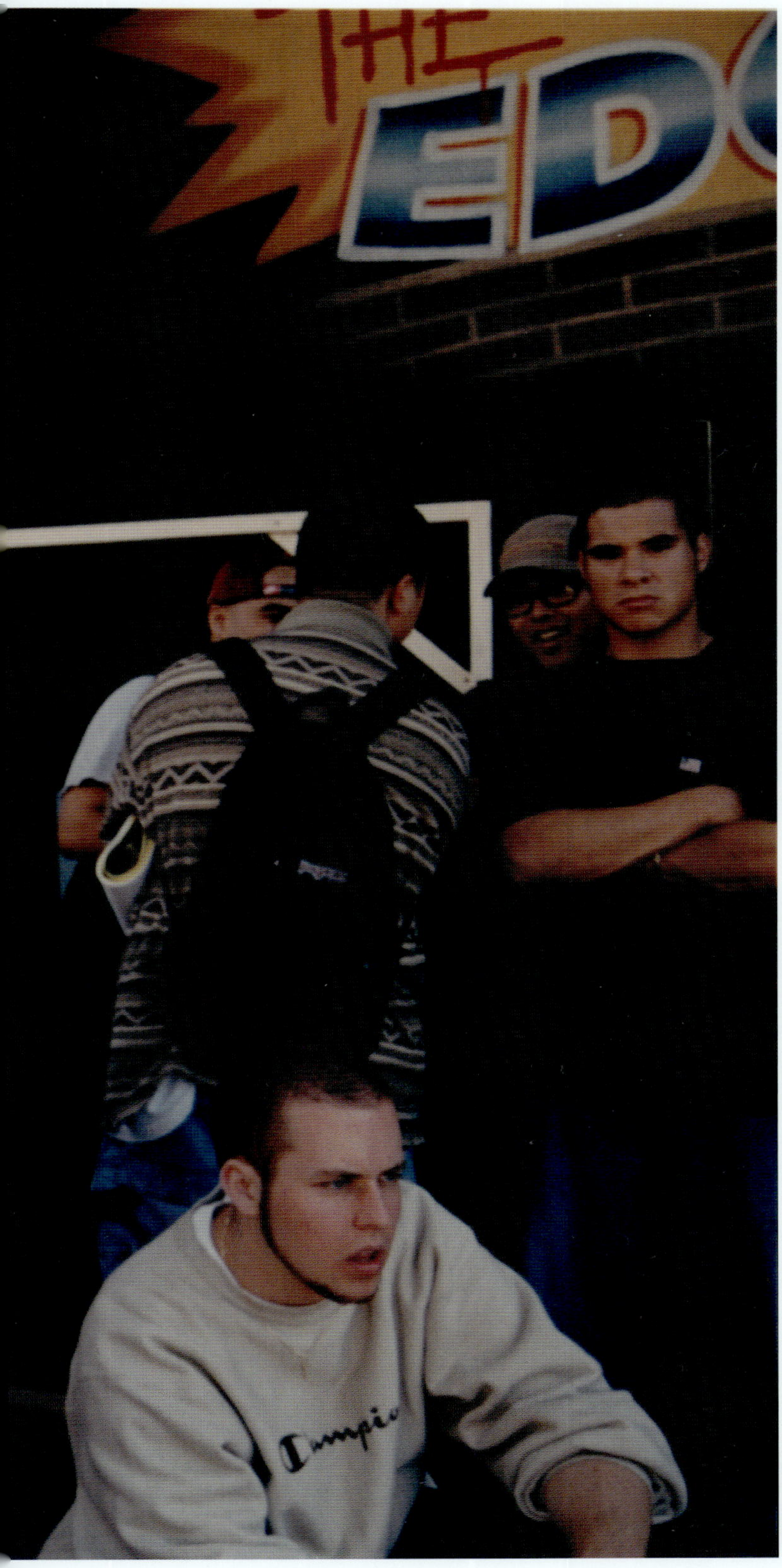

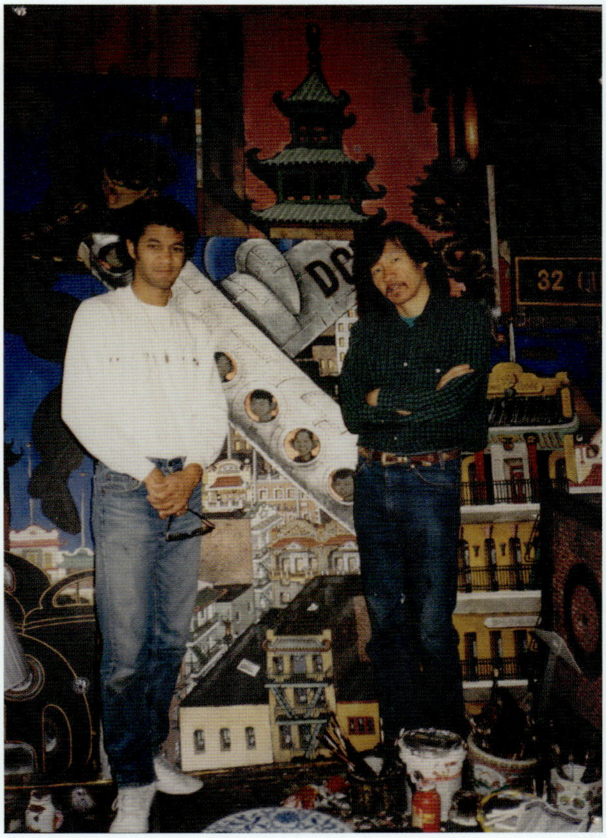

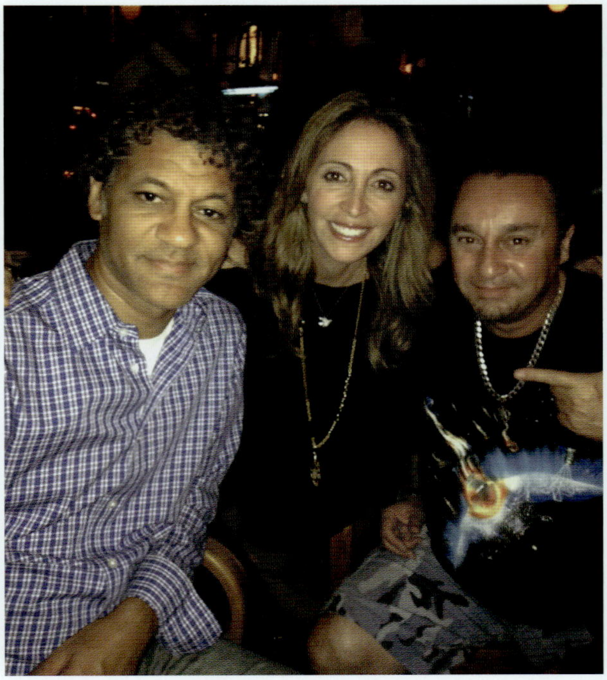

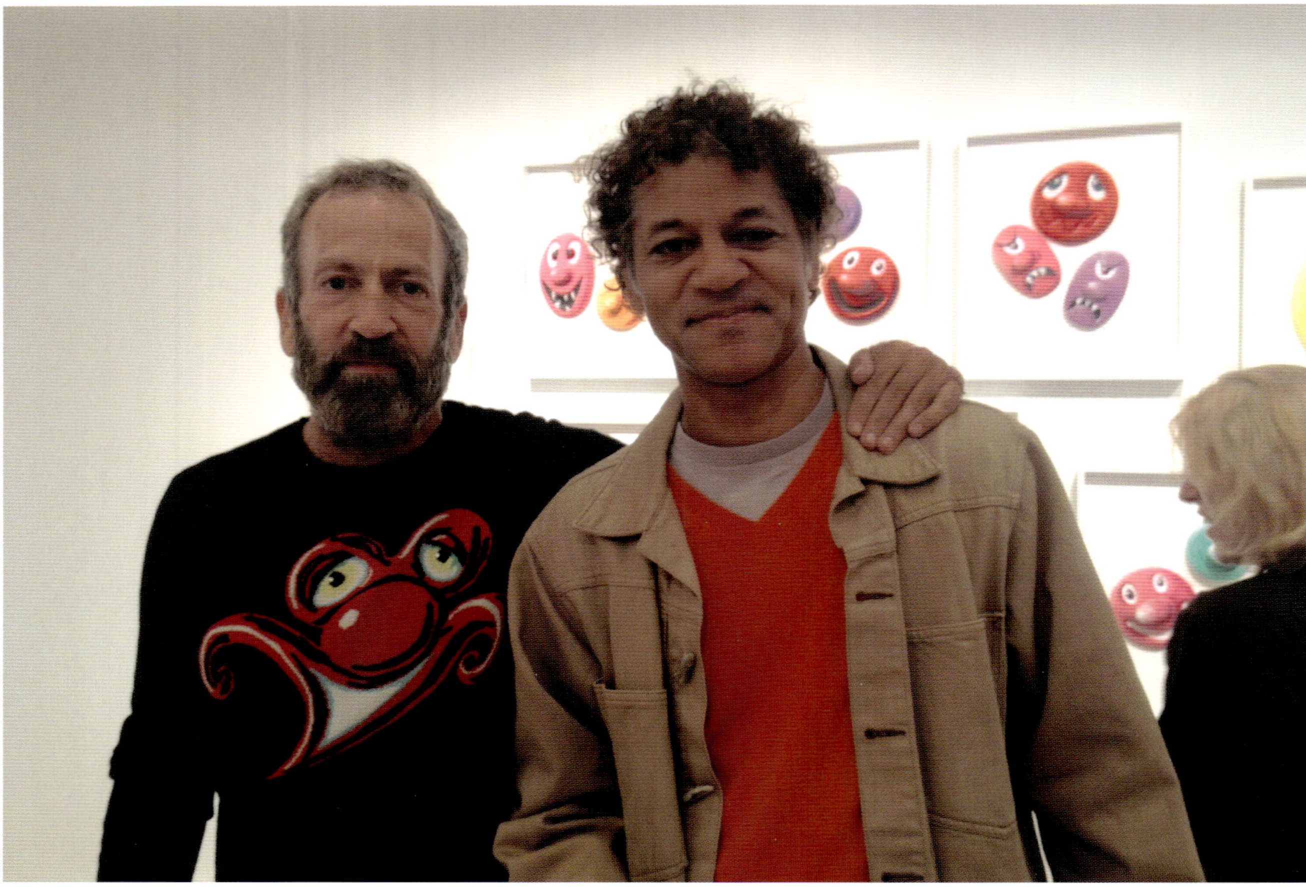

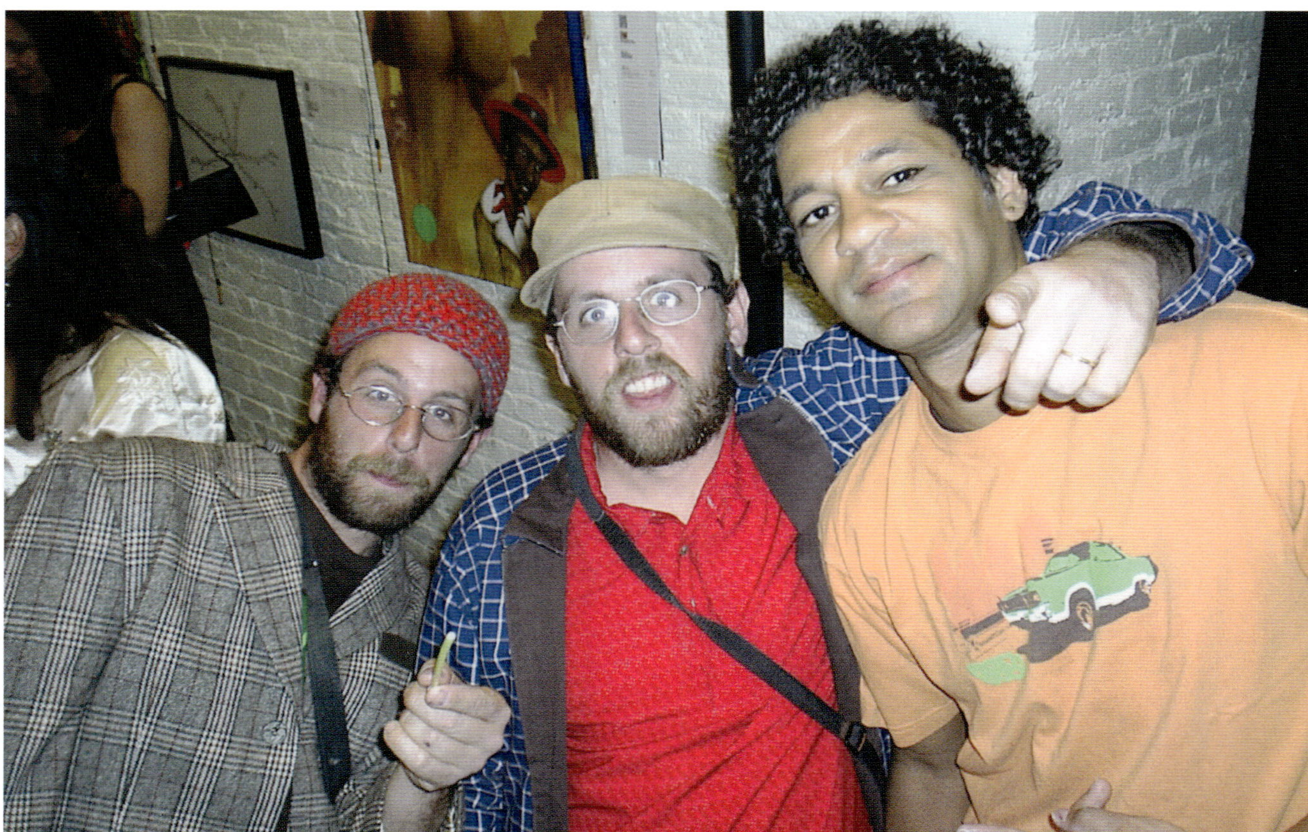

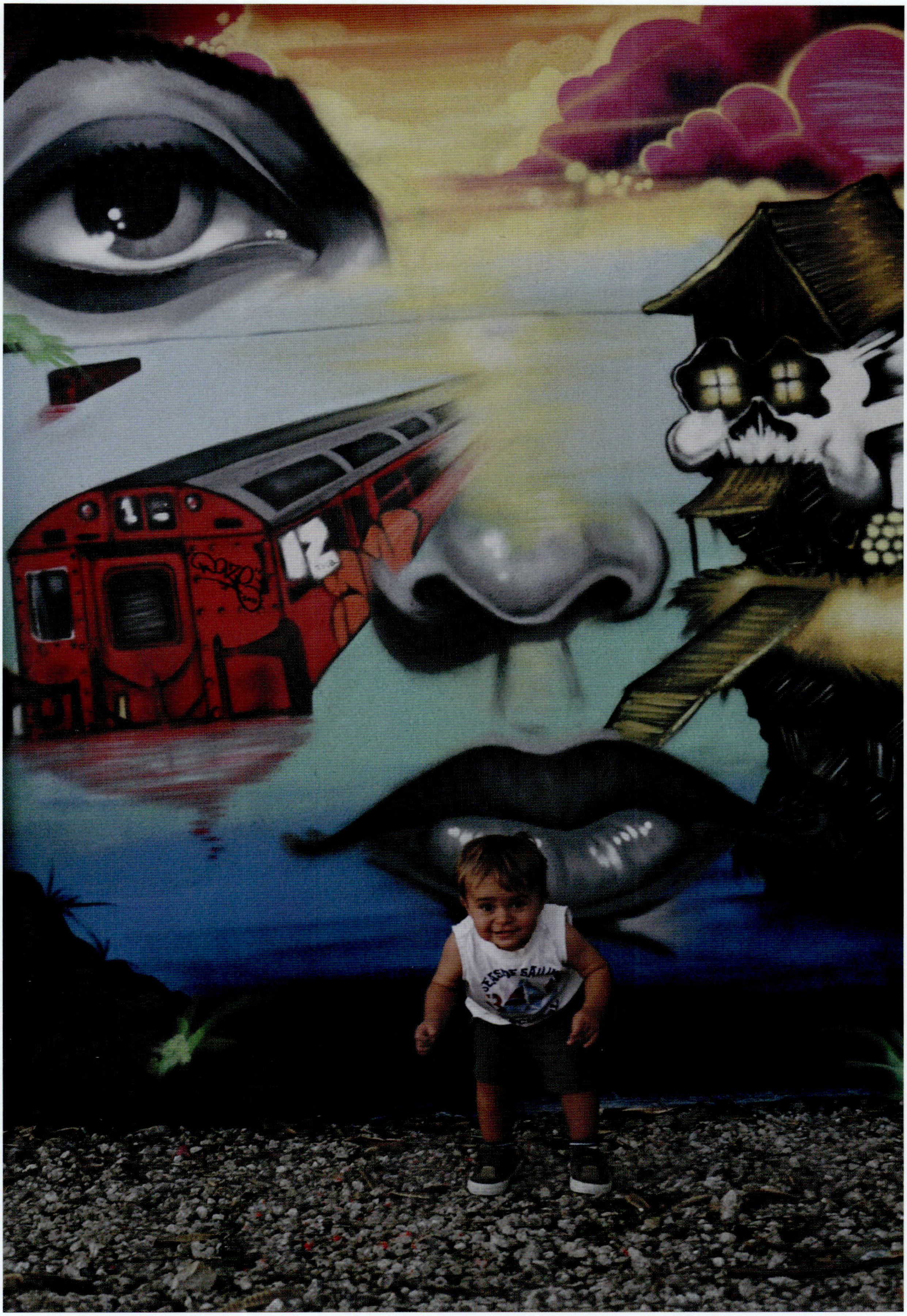

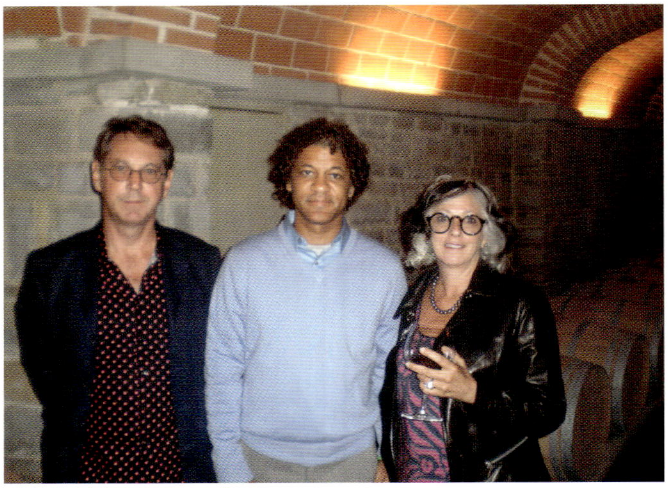

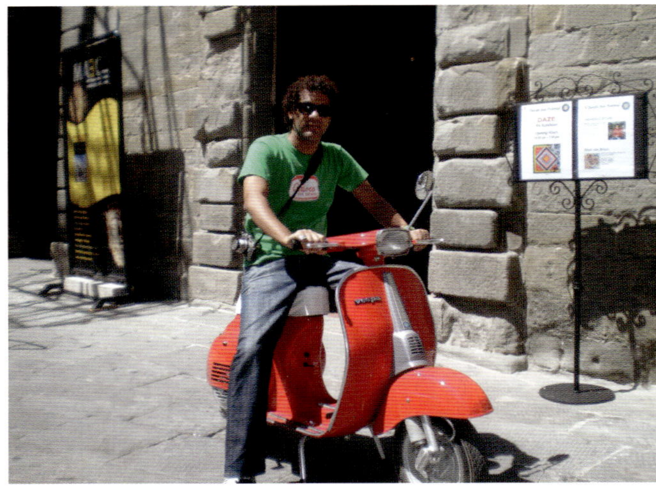

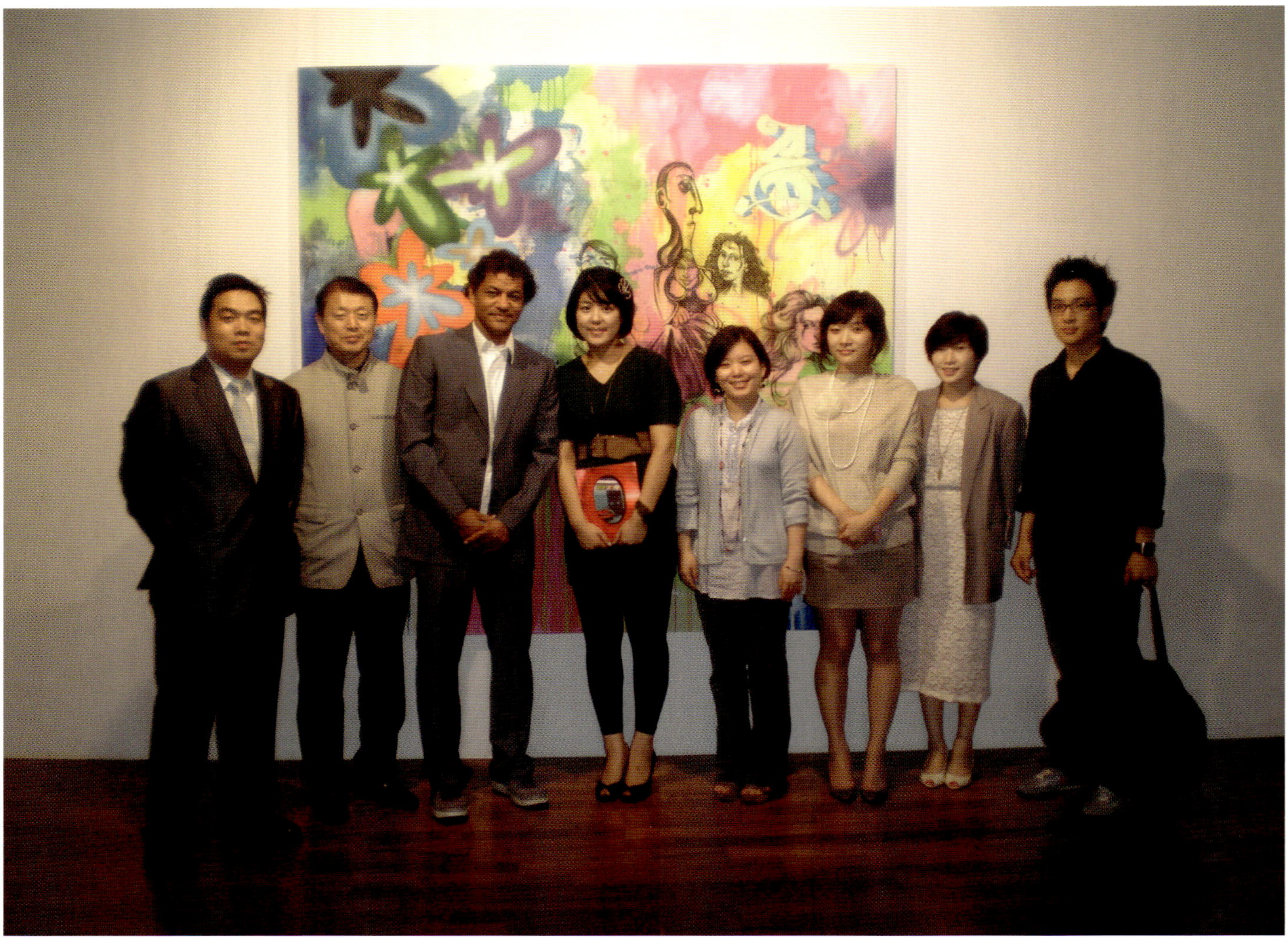

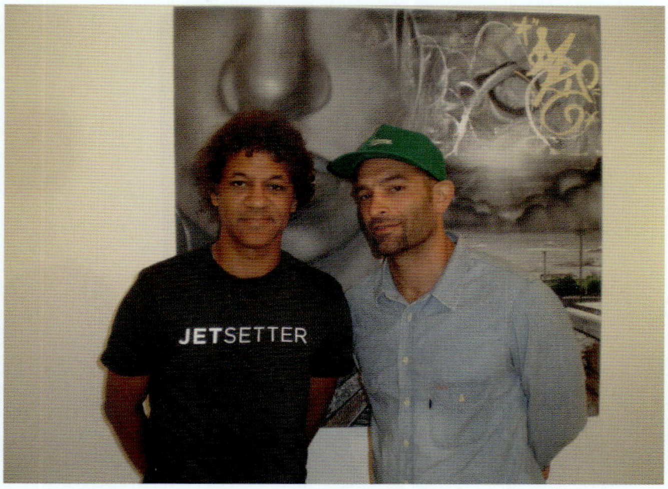

JETSETTER

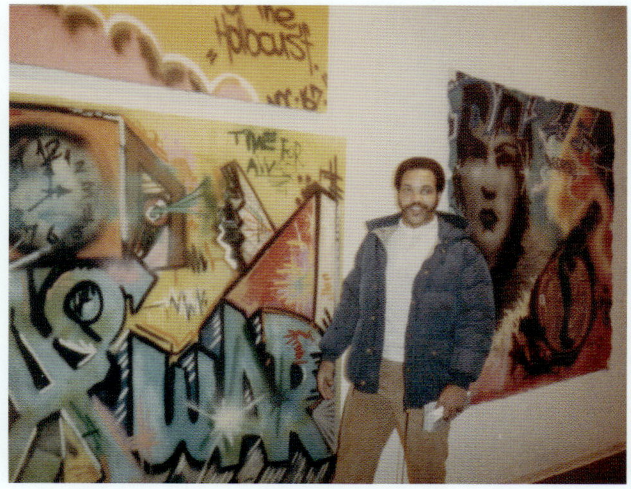

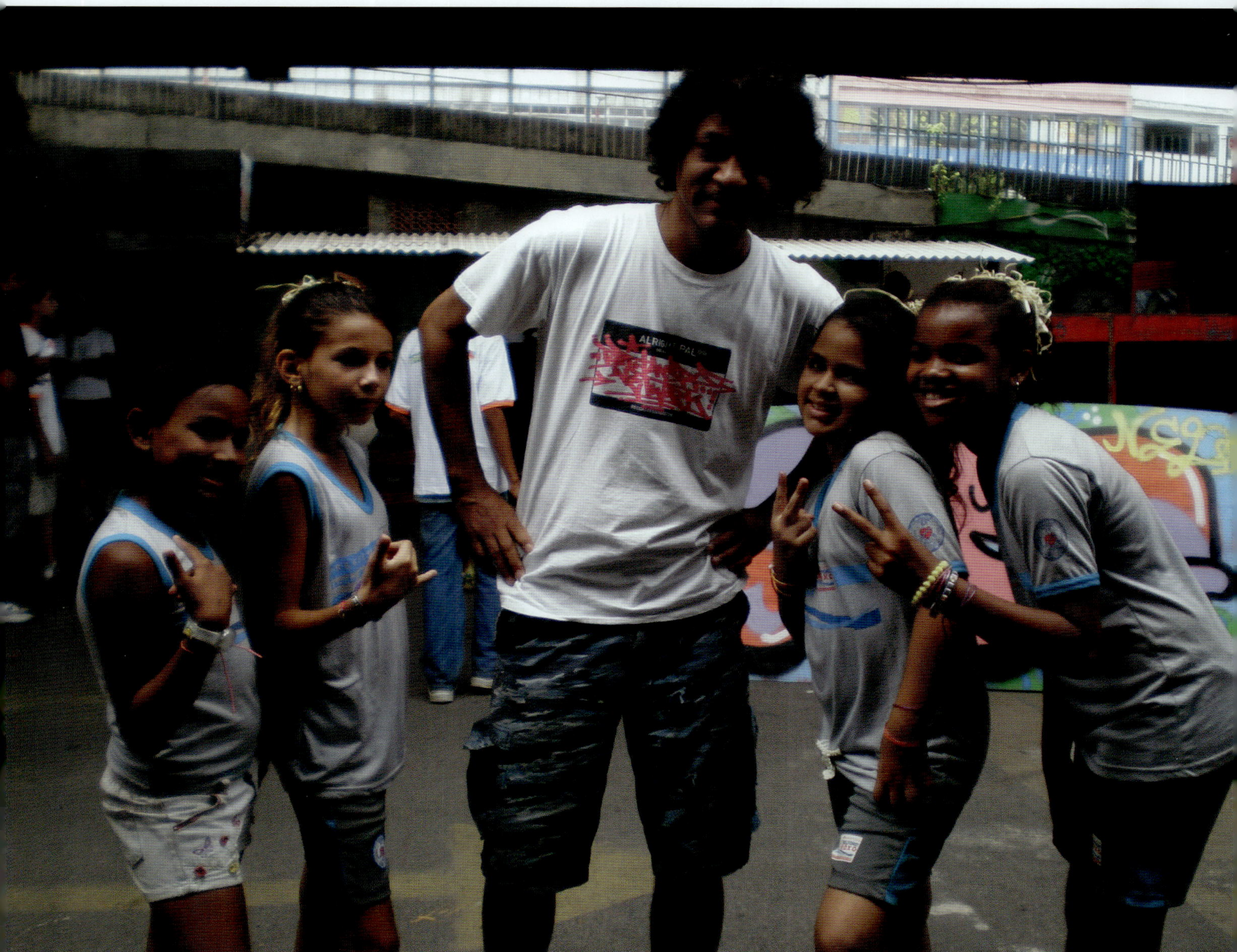

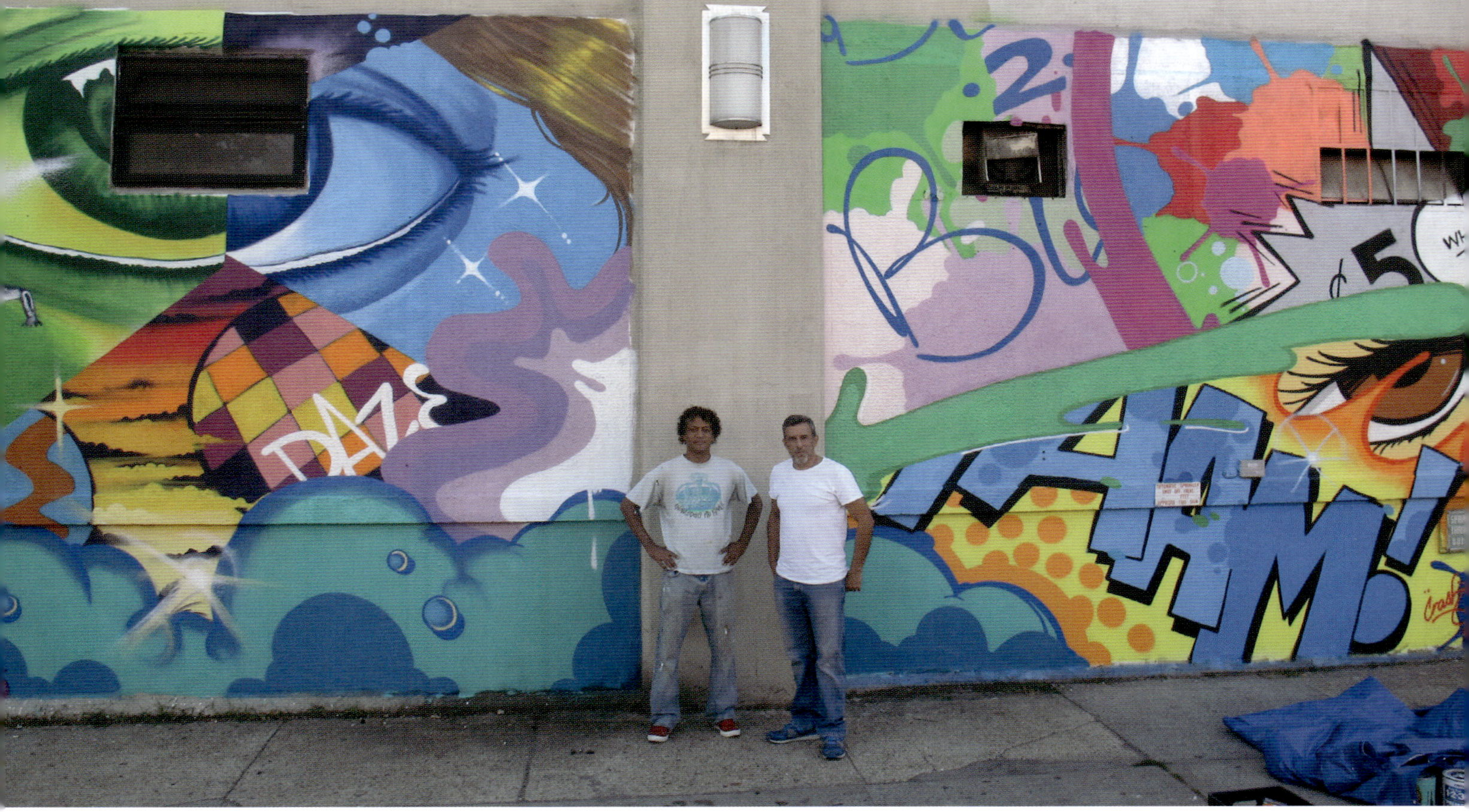
DAZE

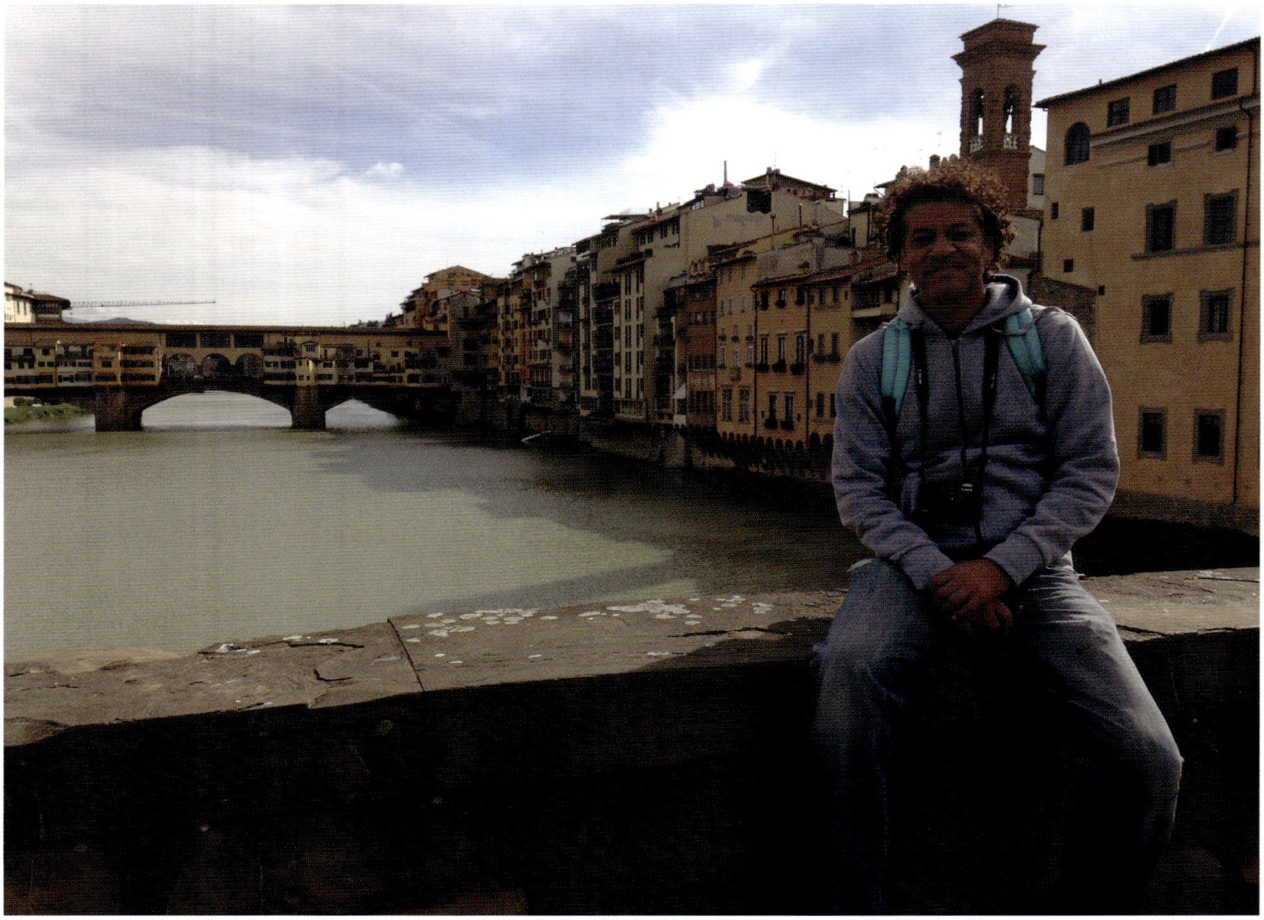

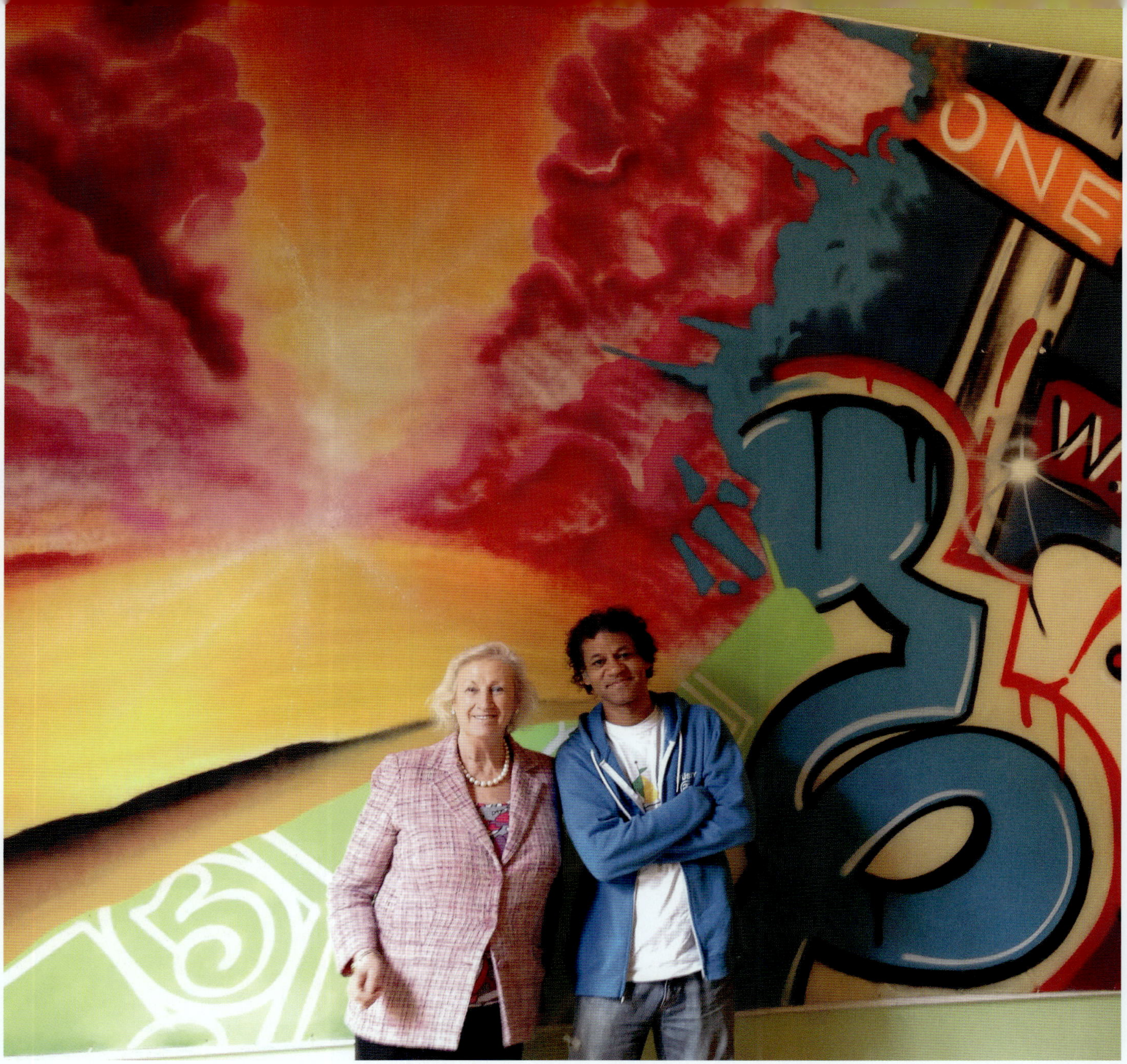
ONE

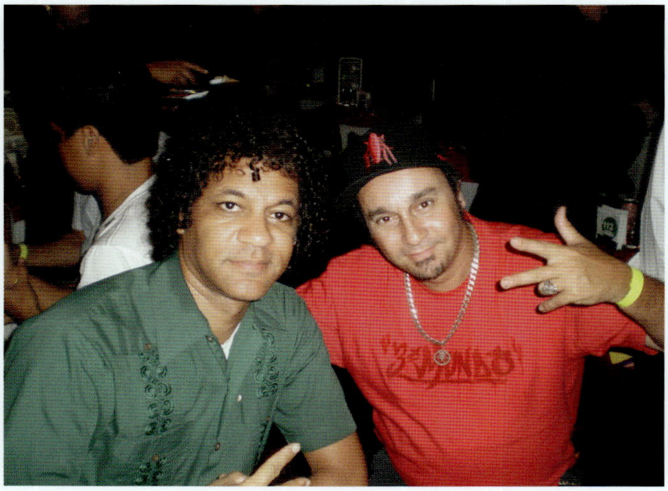

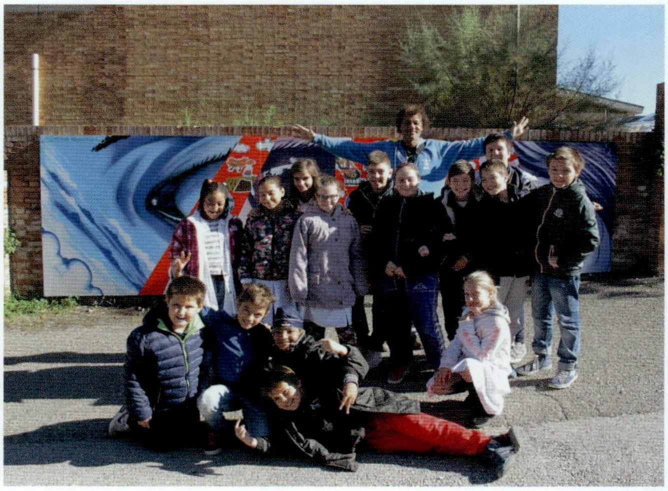

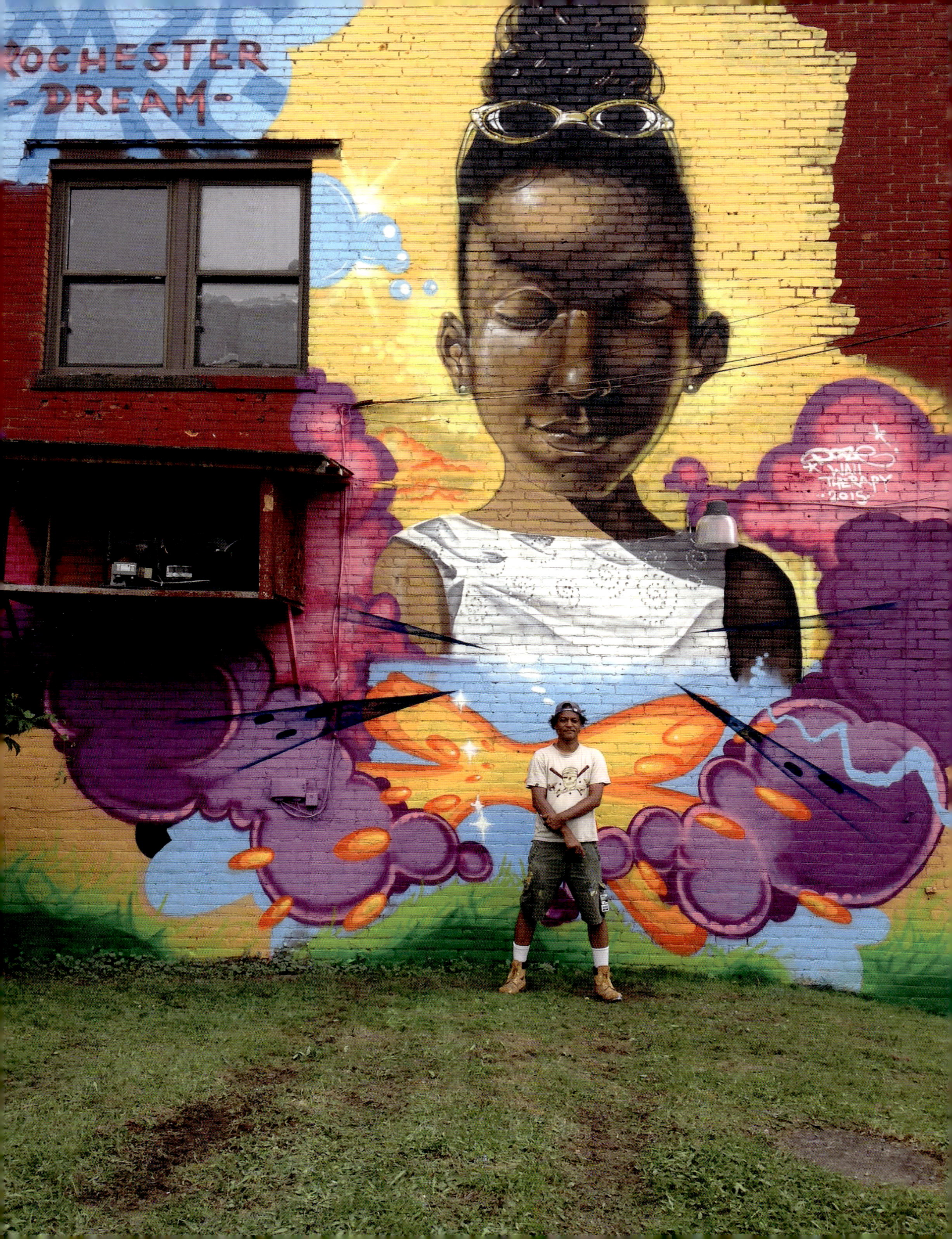
ROCHESTER
-DREAM-
WALL THERAPY
2015

ACKNOWLEDGMENTS

A very special thanks begins with my immediate family—April (babe!), Indigo, and Hudson. Thanks for being my inspiration and my life. My Mom, Lisa, Kim and Gina, Grandma Jeanne, and Grandma Nancy—thanks a million! J.SON, Claire Schwartz, and Sacha Jenkins for providing the incredible texts to this never-ending story. Stephan Snyder and the Web GalleryNYC, John Axelrod, Henry Chalfant, Martha Cooper, Adam Reich, Mark Sink, Lisa Kahane, Beth Baptiste, Sue Kwon, Tom Warren, Michael Transue, Peter Bellamy, Tony, Janet and Jessica Goldman, Kathryn and Dan Miksell, Jock Reynolds, The Addison Museum of American Art, Yale University, Delores Nueman, The Fun Gallery, Graphiti Productions, Fashion Moda, Galerie Thomas, Aone, Bear167, Rammellzee, Keith Haring, Dondi, Dash Snow, Martin Wong, and so many others that are no longer with us—I miss you guys. Danceteria, The Roxy, Area, The Palladium, The Mudd Club—there will never be clubs like that again in this lifetime. Crash, Lady Pink, Lee Quinones, Mode2, Futura2000, Blade, Nac143, Bio, Bg183, Nicer, 2Mad, Binho, Os Gemeos, The Fleshbeck Crew, Mr.Beam, Vitche and Jana, Ise, Tinho, Presto, TitiFreak, Nunca, Onesto, Nina, Acme, SWK, Reas, Freedom, Cern, Dmote, Jon156, Skeme, Dez, Ket, Pose2, Don1, Noc167. Thank you Won for renewing my interest in finishing this book. Alan Bortman, Carlo McCormick, Erik Foss, Nenid, Charlie Ahearn and Jane Dickson, Richard Kern, John Ahearn, Juanita and Carlos, Elis Regina, Tom Jobim, Miles Davis, Jimi Hendrix—for providing the soundtrack to my story. Louie KR for your great advice and direction. Natalie Imbruglia, Kate Cebrano, Nadine, Merda, and Tricky—Down Under crew! Lit Bar, Max Fish—for being kind to starving artists. Speerstra Galerie, Christian Schneeberger, The Galleria del Palazzo, The Coveri family, Cinzia and family, Polo and family. Enrico Pedrini—rest in peace. Wall Therapy, Mary Dinaburg and Howard Rutowski, Sean and Maren, Thomas Shang, Tsgumi Wada, Yvette Armstrong and Ricardo Morales family, Stacy Richman, Matt E. Silver, Andrew Kaufman, Jaime and Steve from Brooklyn street art, 120z.Prophet, Whatyouwrite.com, the saga continues . . .

ABOUT THE AUTHOR

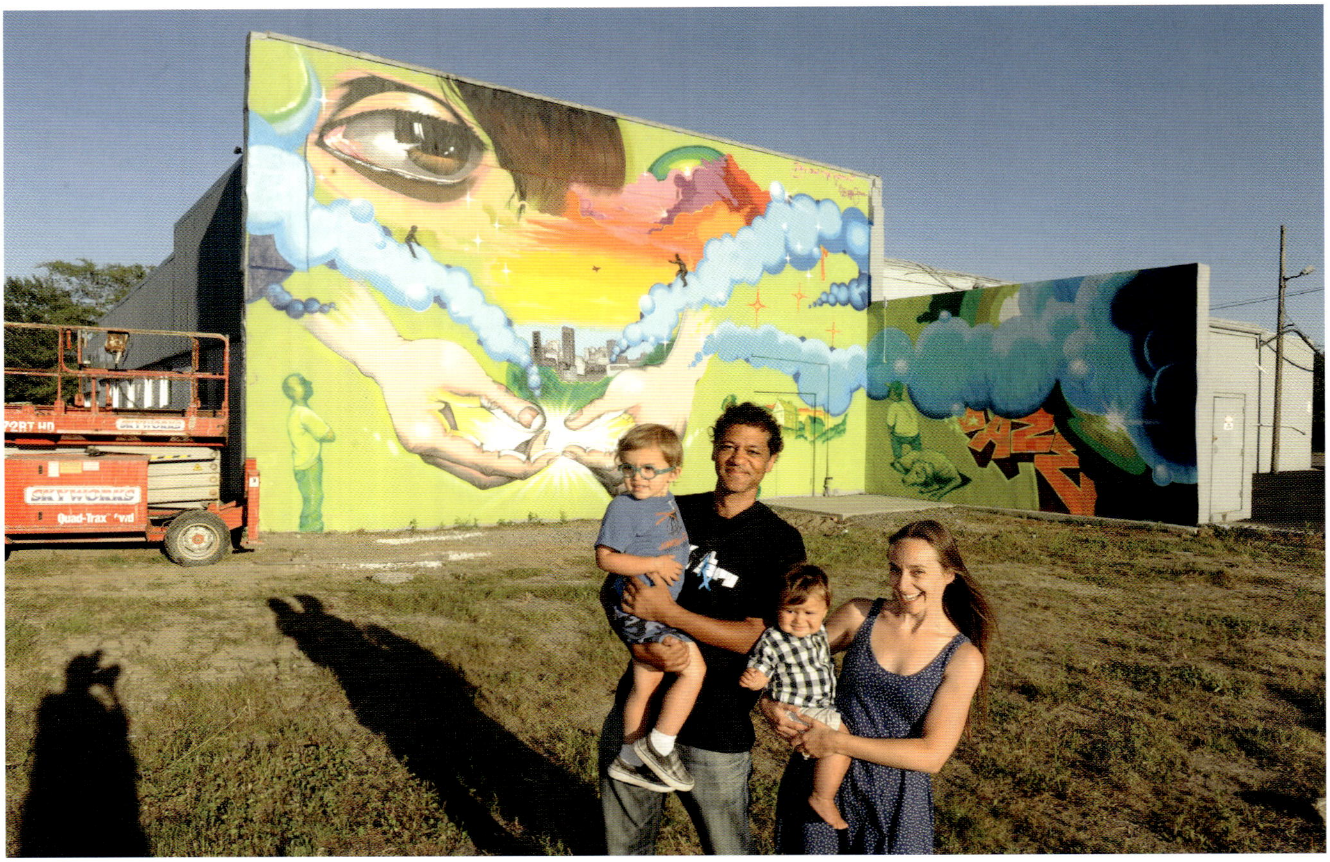

April, Indigo, and Hudson, xoxo
Wall Therapy, Rochester, New York, 2013
Photo © Martha Cooper

Chris Daze Ellis began his prolific career painting gritty New York subways in the mid-1970s while attending the High School of Art & Design. He is one of the few artists from that period to make the successful transition from the subways to the studio. His first group show was the *Beyond Words* exhibition at New York City's Mudd Club in 1981. His first solo show, a year later, was at Fashion Moda, a gallery in the South Bronx. Since then he has had countless solo exhibitions in cities such as Monte Carlo, Paris, Hong Kong, Singapore, Tokyo, Beijing, New York, Chicago, Milan, and Florence. His work has continued to be included in numerous group shows and museum surveys internationally. Alongside these museum and gallery exhibitions Daze has completed many public art projects, including murals for the Star Ferry terminal in Hong Kong, the Vivo City shopping mall in Singapore, and an entire train station in Hannover, Germany—in collaboration with fellow artists Lee Quinones and Crash—and has conducted youth workshops in Brazil, Ecuador, Switzerland, and New York. Daze's paintings are in the private collections of Eric Clapton, Madonna, and Natalie Imbruglia, among others. His work can also be found in the permanent collections of the Brooklyn Museum, New York; the Museum of the City of New York; the Addison Gallery of American Art, Andover, Mass.; the Yale University Art Gallery, New Haven, Conn.; the Ludwig Museum, Aachen, Germany; and the Groninger Museum, Groningen, the Netherlands. Daze continues to live and work in New York City.

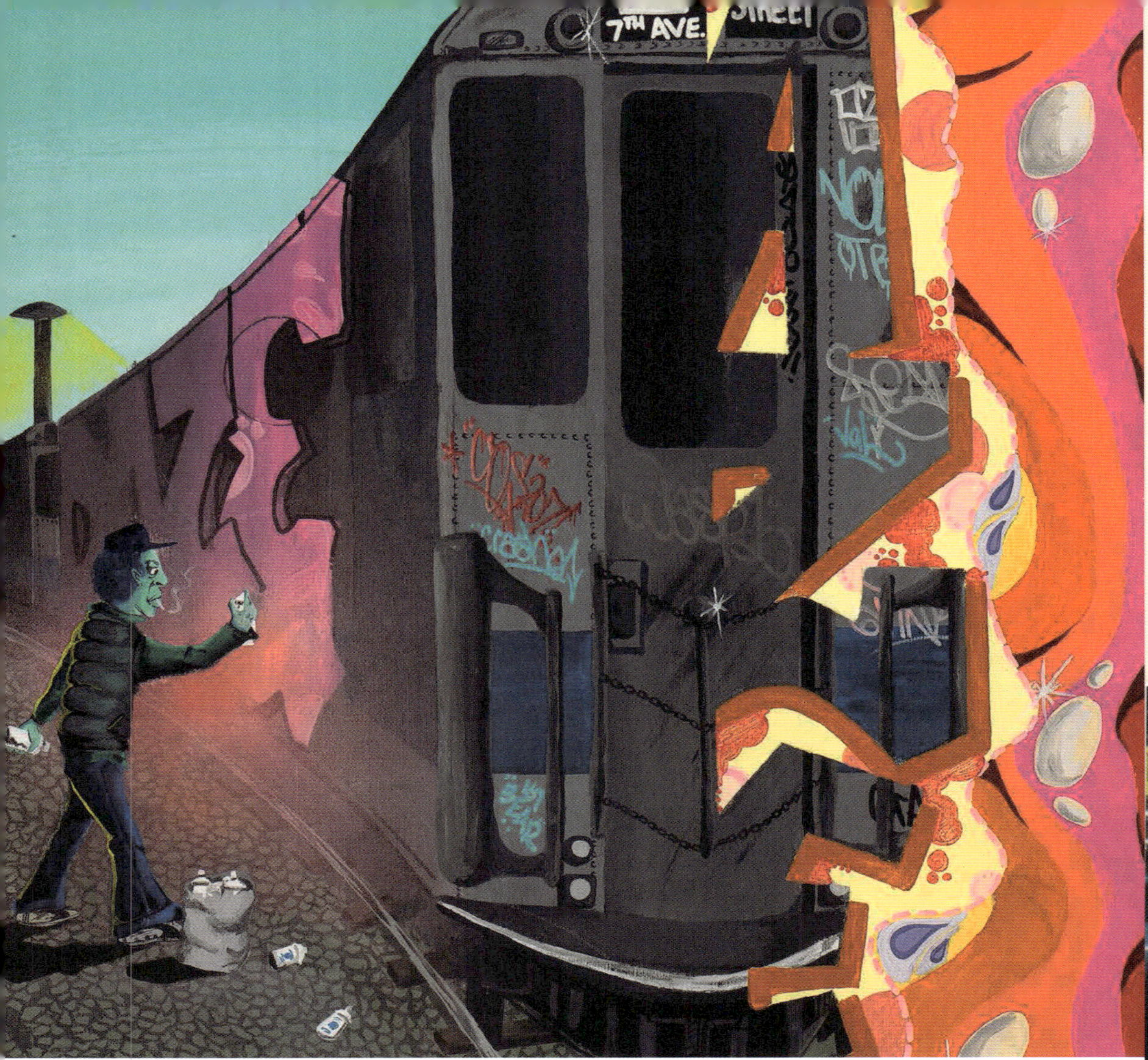

Daze, *Transition*, 1982, Acrylic on canvas, 48 × 29". The Martin Wong Collection

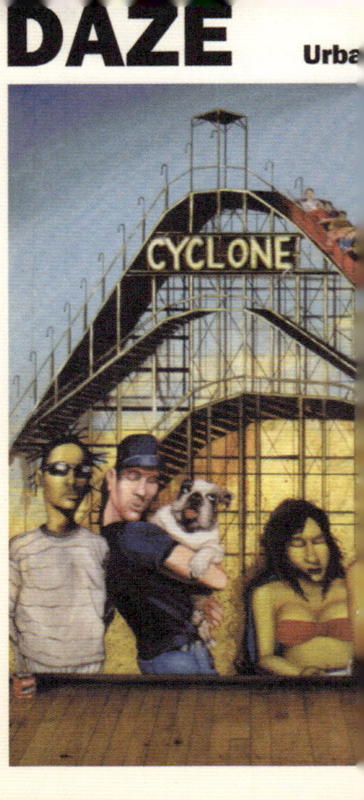

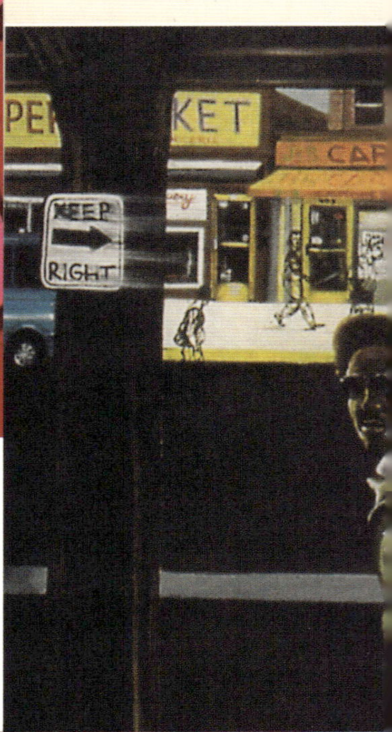

CITY AS CANVAS

MUSEUM OF THE CITY OF NEW YORK

NEW YORK CITY GRAFFITI/THE MARTIN WONG COLLECTION

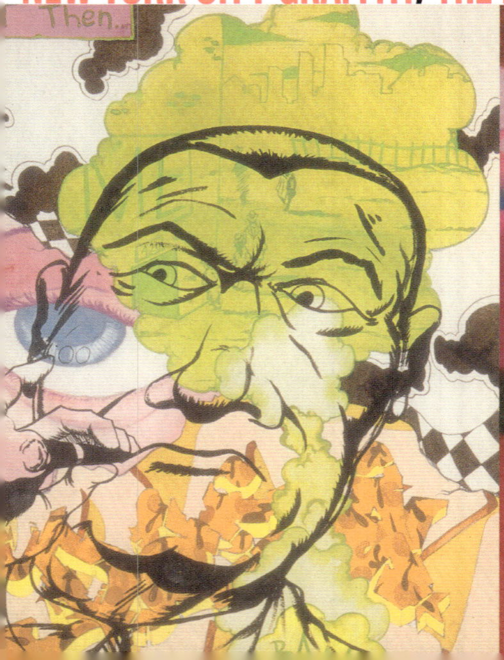

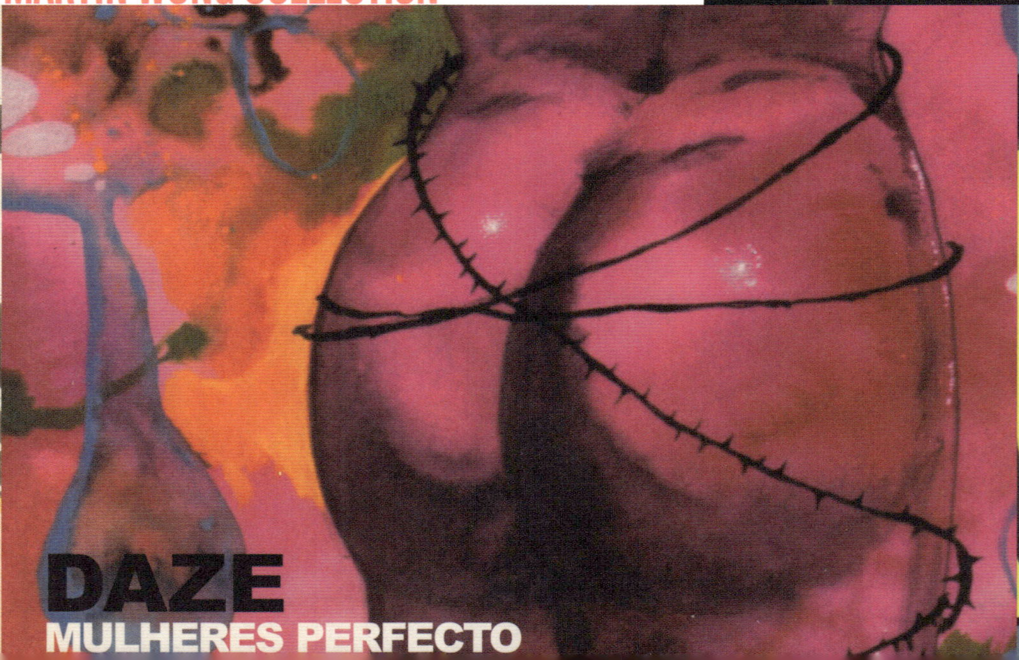